This book comes with access to more content online.

Take practice tests and study
with flashcards!

Register your book or ebook at
www.dummies.com/go/getaccess.

Select your product, and then follow the prompts
to validate your purchase.

You'll receive an email with your PIN and instructions.

GRE® Prep 2024

for dummies®

A Wiley Brand

GRE® Prep 2024

with Online Practice

by Ron Woldoff, MBA

A Wiley Brand

GRE® Prep 2024 For Dummies® with Online Practice

Published by: **John Wiley & Sons, Inc.,** 111 River Street, Hoboken, NJ 07030-5774, www.wiley.com

Copyright © 2023 by John Wiley & Sons, Inc., Hoboken, New Jersey

Published simultaneously in Canada

For general information on our other products and services, please contact our Customer Care Department within the U.S. at 877-762-2974, outside the U.S. at 317-572-3993, or fax 317-572-4002. For technical support, please visit https://hub.wiley.com/community/support/dummies.

Wiley publishes in a variety of print and electronic formats and by print-on-demand. Some material included with standard print versions of this book may not be included in e-books or in print-on-demand. If this book refers to media such as a CD or DVD that is not included in the version you purchased, you may download this material at http://booksupport.wiley.com. For more information about Wiley products, visit www.wiley.com.

Library of Congress Control Number: 2023935172

ISBN 978-1-394-18337-1 (pbk); ISBN 978-1-394-18341-8 (ebk); ISBN 978-1-394-18339-5 (ebk)

SKY10045848_041723

Contents at a Glance

Table of Contents

Introduction

Years ago, during an early gig as a consultant, I sat at a desk that had a *For Dummies* book on the shelf. The book was something office-related, like *SQL For Dummies*. I took a sticky note and wrote the word *Ron* with a black marker, then placed the sticky note over the word *Dummies* on the side of the book, so it read, *SQL For Ron*. It fit nicely.

Since starting my test-prep company, I've had students who would be my boss in the business world, and many have gone on to have amazingly successful careers. You, too, are in this group of future success stories. How do I know? Because you're on your way to an advanced degree, which will open lots of doors, and you're oh-so-close to getting started. You just need to get past this one hurdle called the GRE.

The GRE challenges your ability to conjure up everything you've forgotten since high school — things you haven't thought about in years. Really, all you need is a refresher, some strategies, and practice. This book has all that and more: It goes beyond rehashing what you've learned (and forgotten) by providing exam-specific strategies and tips for answering questions quickly and getting through the exam. There are examples, practice questions, and practice exams to help you hone your skills, identify areas you need to work on, and build your confidence for test day.

I've never met someone who couldn't do well on this exam. I *have* met people who haven't been coached properly, or who haven't practiced enough. With this take, I aim for 100 percent with each student. You're a little rusty here, haven't seen that there, could use a few tips, but you'll pick it up and do just fine. Succeeding on the GRE is like any other skill: If you know what to do, you have some coaching, and you practice, you'll be fine. I get you started with some review and guidance, and you take it from there.

About This Book

In *GRE Prep 2024 For Dummies*, I pretend you forgot everything. You start at the very beginning, covering all the basic math and verbal concepts, and then try some challenging GRE-level questions. You also discover how to approach these questions, avoid common mistakes, and practice the intuitive tricks that help you knock it out of the park.

There are three parts to achieving a top GRE score:

1. **Knowing what's on the exam.**

   Read through this whole book. No matter how well you know a topic, you can discover strategies and common traps specific to the GRE, which has a way of asking a question that's different from what you're used to — or what you learned in the classroom.

2. **Strengthening your weak subject areas.**

   While you're working through the book, mark any sections (and fold the corner of the page, if you have the physical book) that have unfamiliar or unclear topics so you can revisit them during your review. This book is organized to make it easy to find strategies and practice for specific question types that you have trouble with.

3. **Preparing for the test-taking experience.**

Answering the exam questions is one thing, but taking the exam is another. Start with the online practice exams to prep for the experience. ETS offers two excellent online practice exams, free of charge, but you'll need more than two. Packaged with this book, also free (after you buy the book), are *six* online practice exams: three in the book itself and all six online. When your exam is just around the corner, take one or two practice exams in real-life, dress-rehearsal settings. Flip to Part 6, "The Part of Tens," for ten ways to get the most benefit from the online practice exams.

Basically, this book does it all: It prepares you for the exam by taking your skills from the basic level to the GRE level and fixing any gaps. What else is there?

There's vocab.

To help you with vocab, as you work through this book, you'll notice that some words have a style all their own. Each GRE vocabulary word in this text appears in *this font*, followed directly by its *connotation* (meaning). Besides that, when you encounter a GRE vocab word in a question, look up its meaning and write it down. This is an effective complement to studying from a list or flash cards.

Icons Used in This Book

Look for these icons to spot highlights throughout this book:

This indicates a key strategy or point to remember. There are lots of these, which is good, because they're essential to your success on the exam.

This indicates overall knowledge about the exam that's useful for planning your approach, such as managing your time or knowing what to expect.

This marks a GRE trap or common student mistake so you can spot it and dodge it on test day.

This indicates a practice question for you to try.

Beyond the Book

Besides this book, there are more online resources, including these:

>> **Cheat Sheet:** Go to www.dummies.com and type "GRE Prep 2024 For Dummies Cheat Sheet" in the Search box for this book's Cheat Sheet, which gives you last-minute details, including a rundown of what to expect when you take the GRE, a list of what to bring versus what to leave at home, tips for taking the computer-based exam, and more pointers for answering exam questions.

>> **Over 400 GRE vocabulary flash cards:** Stock your mental word bank and boost your verbal score by accessing the meanings of over 400 words that frequently appear on the GRE.

>> **Six full-length practice exams:** You can take the three practice exams in this book along with three more online to help you build your competence and confidence. You can select the level of difficulty and answer the questions through untimed and timed quizzes, so you can practice at your own speed and then try it out under pressure.

To get access to the online flash cards and practice exams, all you have to do is register. Just follow these simple steps:

1. Register your book or ebook at Dummies.com to get your PIN. Go to www.dummies.com/go/getaccess.

2. Select your product from the drop-down list on that page.

3. Follow the prompts to validate your product, and then check your email for a confirmation message that includes your PIN and instructions for logging in.

If you do not receive this email within two hours, please check your spam folder before contacting us through our Technical Support website at http://support.wiley.com or by phone at 877-762-2974.

Now you're ready to go! You can come back to the practice material as often as you want — simply log on with the username and password you created during your initial login. No need to enter the access code a second time.

Your registration is good for one year from the day you activate your PIN.

Where to Go from Here

You can approach this book in three ways:

>> **Work through it from beginning to end.** This approach is best for most test-takers. Although prepping to take the GRE isn't a linear process, I present topics from easy to challenging, so they build on each other as you progress through the chapters. I provide a feel for the test-taking experience along with guidance for each section of the exam — verbal, math, and essays — followed by practice exams, and I wrap things up with some Part of Tens chapters that provide some good, sound strategies to help you get through the exam.

>> **Skip around.** Each chapter is a stand-alone lesson on a specific GRE topic. If your study time is limited, skip around to focus on areas where you need the most guidance. For example, you can skip to Chapter 7 to hone your skills at answering Argument Analysis questions, or visit Chapter 12 to brush up on geometry. Another strategy is to take one of the sample tests to evaluate your skills and identify areas of weakness, and then use that information to develop your plan of attack. (More on this approach in Chapter 2.)

>> **Use it as a reference book.** Whenever you need information and advice on a specific GRE topic or skill, simply flip to the chapter or section that contains the information and guidance you need. *GRE Prep 2024 For Dummies* offers a refresher on the topics and skills you need to get the score you need on the GRE.

As you go through the book, write up some flash cards to note key concepts and strategies. These cards will serve as a handy reference while you review your notes.

I've been helping GRE students beat the test for years, so I know not only students' common questions and mistakes, but also how to make the math and verbal questions easier to answer. This book distills my tricks and secrets, which I'm pleased to share with you. Your success, after all, is why we're both here.

1
Getting Started with the GRE

Chapter **1**

Knowing the GRE

The GRE isn't an IQ test, nor is it a measure of your worth as a human being or a predictor of your ultimate success in life. The GRE is designed to assess your ability to excel in grad school by sizing you up in three areas.

» **Work ethic:** How hard you're willing and able to work to achieve an elusive academic goal — in this case, performing well on the GRE — reflects your work ethic. Graduate schools consider this to be a measure of how hard you'll work in their programs.

» **Study skills:** How well you can master some basic study skills and be able to process and retain new information.

» **Test-taking ability:** How well you can perform on a test, under pressure, which is a separate ability from being able to answer the questions. Exams are *ubiquitous* (appearing everywhere) to grad school, so you need to prove that you can take one without folding under pressure.

This book can guide you in the first area, but it's mostly up to you. As a study guide, however, this book shows you how to achieve the second and third areas, enabling you to study more effectively and efficiently and improve your overall test-taking skills. By knowing the material and taking the practice tests, you establish a foundation for doing well on the GRE. And usually, if you know what to do and how to do it, you might find yourself working a little bit harder. In this way, this book helps you further in that first area.

In this chapter, I discuss the GRE's structure and scoring system so you can build your strategies around them. With this guidance, you're better equipped to avoid surprises that may throw you off your game.

Knowing the GRE Sections

Standardized tests tend to bring on the chills. Telling someone you have to take the SAT, ACT, or GRE usually gets the same response as saying that you need to have your wisdom teeth pulled. However, with this book, the GRE isn't such a chilling experience, and breaking it down to its component parts makes it more manageable and less threatening.

The paper and computer versions of the GRE are slightly different. For one thing, the paper version has 25 questions per section, with four sections, while the computer version has 20 questions per section with five sections — either way, 100 questions.

You are almost certainly taking the computer-based version, but some materials provided by ETS, including the book-based practice tests and downloadable PDFs, are in the paper-based format. The guidance in this book refers to the computer-based version of the GRE, but it's good to know the paper-based differences that you may encounter in the ETS practice materials, so it's clear on why they're different.

Table 1-1 provides a quick overview of what's on the exam. The essays are always first, but the multiple-choice sections may be in any order.

TABLE 1-1   GRE Breakdown by Section (Computer-Based)

Section	Number of Questions	Time Allotted
Analyze an Issue	1 essay	30 minutes
Analyze an Argument	1 essay	30 minutes
Verbal Section	20 questions	30 minutes
Math (Quantitative) Section	20 questions	35 minutes
Verbal Section	20 questions	30 minutes
Math (Quantitative) Section	20 questions	35 minutes
Discreetly Unscored Math or Verbal Section (may be earlier in the exam)	20 questions	30 or 35 minutes

REMEMBER

At close to four hours, the GRE challenges your stamina as much as your ability to answer the questions. No matter how solid your math and verbal skills are, you have to maintain your focus for the whole stretch, which isn't easy on a challenging task such as this. Build your test-taking stamina by practicing in four-hour sessions and taking timed practice tests.

The computer-based GRE includes one unscored Math or Verbal section in addition to the scored sections. You will have three Math *or* three Verbal sections, with one of those sections unscored, meaning it neither helps nor hurts your score. The GRE may indicate that the section is unscored, but it usually doesn't, so be sure to work all the sections to the best of your ability.

TIP

The GRE allows you to skip questions and return to them later, within that section. When you reach the end of a section, the GRE displays a review screen that indicates any unanswered questions. If you have time remaining in the section, return to these questions and answer them as well as you can. This feature is nice because you can knock out the easy questions first before spending time on the hard ones. (See Chapter 2 for more on planning your time.)

So what types of questions are there and how many of these can you expect on the GRE? Here's Table 1-2 with the details.

Note that the question types are mixed throughout their sections, so you may encounter them in any order. Sometimes the software groups similar questions at the beginning or the end. For example, if you're halfway through a Verbal section and haven't seen a Text Completion question, you will.

TABLE 1-2 **GRE Breakdown by Question Type**

Type of Question	Approximate Number of Questions
Per 20-question Math section:	
Multiple-choice with exactly one correct answer	6
Multiple-choice with one or more correct answers	2
Fill-in-the-blank with the correct answer	2
Data Interpretation (based on graphs)	3
Quantitative Comparisons	7
Per 20-question Verbal section:	
Text Completion	6
Sentence Equivalence	4
Argument Analysis	2
Reading Comprehension	8

Knowing the GRE Scores

With the GRE, you receive three separate scores: Verbal, Math, and Analytical Writing. You drive home knowing your unofficial Verbal and Math scores (as explained in the following section), but you get your Analytical Writing score about two weeks later.

On the GRE, you can score a maximum of 340 points on the multiple-choice and 6 points on the essays. Here's the scoring range for each of the three sections.

>> **Verbal:** The Verbal score ranges from 130 to 170 in 1-point increments. You get 130 points if you answer just one question, but that won't help you much: You need to score as well as or better than most of the other test-takers to improve your chances of being admitted to your target school. The chapters in Part 2 give you the lowdown on the Verbal sections.

>> **Math:** The Math score also ranges from 130 to 170 in 1-point increments. The chapters in Part 3 have more on the Math sections.

>> **Analytical Writing:** The Analytical Writing score ranges from 0 to 6, in half-point increments, with 6 being the highest. Each essay is graded separately, and your final score is the average of the two. There is more on the essays in the Part 4 chapters.

REMEMBER

If a multiple-choice question requires two or more answers, you have to get all the answers correct: There is no partial credit. However, you don't *lose* points for a wrong answer, so if you're not sure, take a guess and return to the question later. More on this strategy in Chapter 2.

Calculating your score

Within each section, each question counts exactly the same toward your score: The more questions you get right, the higher your score for that section. An easy question is worth the same as a hard question. Because you can move back and forth within each section, one strategy is to skip around and answer all the easy questions first, then go back and work the hard questions. If you like this idea, *try it out on a practice test* before exam day.

On the computer version of the exam, the *second* Math or Verbal section (not counting the unscored section) becomes easier or harder based on your performance. For example, if you do extremely well on the first Math section, the GRE makes the second Math section harder. Even if you don't get as many right answers in the second Math section, your score will be good, and it'll definitely be higher than the score of someone who bombs the first Math section but gets them all right in the second one. GRE scoring accommodates for the difficulty level of the questions in the second section.

WARNING

The strategy of bombing the first Math and Verbal sections in order to answer more questions correctly on the respective second sections is not a good one, and you'll end up with a low score. The exam doesn't score you based solely on the number of correct answers: It scores you based on how smart it thinks you are. So if you do *great* on the first Math section, the exam thinks you're smart and *ups* the difficulty level for the second Math section. If you don't answer all those questions correctly, that's okay: The questions are harder, and the exam has evaluated your skills. Conversely, if you *bomb* the first Math section, the exam thinks you're not good at math, so it *drops* the level for the second Math section. If you answer most of those questions correctly, it doesn't help your score much because those questions are easier.

When you complete a practice test from Part 5, you can easily estimate your Math and Verbal scores. For the Math score, count the math questions you answered correctly and then add 130 to that number. Because the GRE has 40 math questions (two sections with 20 questions each), this method gives you an approximate score from 130 to 170. You can find your Verbal score the exact same way, because the GRE also has 40 Verbal questions. Note this method doesn't account for the changing difficulty of the second Math and Verbal sections, but it's still an excellent way for you to track your progress as you improve.

Checking your score

If you score close to 340, you did great! If you score closer to 260, not so much. But wait — your score is right in between! Did you pass? Did you fail? What does it mean? Well, you can't really tell much about your score out of context. What does 320 mean? It all goes by a percentile ranking. To download the complete percentile table, visit www.ets.org, click GRE Tests, and search for "percentile ranking." As of this writing, here are some highlights:

>> A raw score of 165 is typically a 96th percentile ranking in the Verbal and an 84th percentile ranking in the Math.

>> A raw score of 160 is typically an 85th percentile ranking in the Verbal and a 70th percentile ranking in the Math.

Basically, with a range of only 40 points per section among 500,000 GRE-takers per year, give or take, each point counts for a lot. How well you do is based on how well the other test-takers did. You need to ask your target school's admissions office what score you need to get in to that school — or, even better, what score you need for a scholarship! Once you're in your program (or you've landed your scholarship), your GRE score doesn't matter. Plus, I've had students who were already accepted to their schools but were retaking the exam for the scholarship.

Also, your exam score is only one part of the total application package. If you have a good GPA, a strong résumé, and relevant work experience, you may not need as high of a GRE score. On the other hand, a stellar GRE score can compensate for other weak areas.

Seeing or canceling your scores

Immediately after finishing the GRE, you have the option of either seeing or canceling your Verbal and Math scores. Unfortunately, you don't get to see your scores first. If you *think* you had a bad day, you can cancel, and your scores are neither reported to the schools nor shown to you. However, the schools are notified that you canceled your test. If you choose to see your score, you see it — minus the essay scores — right away, but you can't cancel it after that.

REMEMBER

How much do the schools care about canceled scores? Probably not much, especially if a strong GRE score (from when you retake the test 21 days later) follows the notice of cancellation. If you really want to know the impact of a canceled score, check with the admissions office of your target school. Each school weighs canceled scores differently. See the section "Using Old Scores" for more about what to do after canceling your GRE score.

Taking advantage of the ScoreSelect option

At the end of the test, you have the option of choosing which test scores to send to your target schools, assuming that you've taken the GRE more than once. You can send the most recent scores, scores from the past (within five years), or all your test scores. However, you can't pick and choose sections from different testing dates. For example, if today you did better in Verbal but last time you did better in Math, you can't select only those sections — you have to send the entire test. Select whether to send the scores of today's test, any previous test, or all your tests.

Your GRE score is good for five years after your testing date, so if you use ScoreSelect, you're limited to exams within the past five years.

Bringing the GRE into Your Comfort Zone

No need to panic about taking the GRE. You want to be confident and relaxed, which means bringing the GRE into your comfort zone. Working through this book and taking the practice tests can bring you very close to that goal, but having the right mindset is also useful. The following sections help put the GRE in the proper perspective and serve to remind you of just how prepared you really are.

Getting familiar with what's on the exam

The GRE focuses on a specific range of core concepts and presents questions in a fairly predictable format. Surprises are unlikely, especially if you're prepared and know what to expect. After you've successfully completed this book, you'll have the knowledge and experience needed to get the score you need on the exam. You will gain even more familiarity with the test questions and format by taking the computerized GRE sample tests.

REMEMBER

A little self-affirmation goes a long way. In the days leading up to the test and on test day, remind yourself just how fully prepared you are. The GRE is designed to be challenging, and everyone who takes it is nervous, but you're better prepared than they are. At least you will be.

Understanding the other admissions requirements

Although your performance on the GRE is important for admission, it's not the only thing that admissions departments look at. Your work experience, GPA, extracurricular activities (including volunteer work), and other factors that define you are also important parts of your application. Of course, you should still do your very best on the exam, but this isn't a do-or-die situation. Worst case: Retake the exam. Some of my best success stories are from students who retook the exam after forgetting key points or making mistakes on their first go-round. This also means you should schedule your exam with time to retake it if needed, but more on this in Chapter 2.

Using Old Scores

What if you took the GRE a long time ago when you thought you were going to grad school and then opted to take a job or start a family instead? Well, if it was within the past five years, you're in luck (assuming you scored well). GRE scores are reportable for up to five years. That means that if you're pleased with your old score, you can send it right along to the school of your choice and say *adios* to this book right here and now. However, if you took the test more than five years ago, you have to take it again, so hold on to this book.

THE IMPORTANCE OF TEST PREP

Stories abound about how someone's friend's cousin's roommate took the GRE cold (with no preparation) and aced it. This story may be true on a rare occasion, but you hear only the success stories. Those test-takers who went in cold and bombed don't brag about the outcome. As an instructor, however, I hear those other stories all the time.

The GRE doesn't test your intelligence: It tests how well you've prepared for the test. I'd put my money on a prepared dunce over an unprepared genius every single time. Dramatically raising a test-taker's score, say from the 30th to the 90th percentile ranking, is something I do every day before breakfast, and it's what I do for you in this book. Being prepared means knowing what to expect and how to answer each question, which means that the first time you calculate a fraction of a circle had better not be on the actual GRE. Make your mistakes *here,* in practice where it doesn't count, *not* on the test, where it could cost you a scholarship.

Chapter **2**

Planning Your Time

The best way to build your confidence and improve your performance is to be prepared, which is as true for anything in life as it is for the GRE. Being familiar with the exam and knowing what to expect gives you fewer distractions so that you can focus on what really matters — the test itself. This chapter guides you through getting the most from the time that you have for both preparing for and taking the exam.

Planning Your Prep Time

As soon as you decide to take the GRE, the clock starts ticking. You have only so much time to study and practice, and suddenly the exam is tomorrow morning. The good news: I've taken many a student down this road, with great results, and here I've *curated* (collected) the best success strategies. The following sections show you how to optimize your study and practice time so you can answer the test questions quickly and easily.

Planning your long-term study time

Best case is if you can start preparing 12 weeks before your exam. This test is based on skills, not memorization, and skills take time to develop. It's like throwing a baseball: You need time to learn, practice, rest, and practice more. Six to eight weeks is enough time for some people, but more time is generally better. At 12 weeks, you can do extremely well, but after 12 weeks, most people get burned out or lose interest, and they forget things they learned early on.

» **Take your first practice test, timed:** Although the practice tests included with this book provide excellent targeted practice, the free online practice exams from www.ets.org provide a more accurate simulated testing experience. ETS provides two practice exams, the first of which has a timed and untimed option, whereas the second can be taken only as a timed test.

Whether you take the Dummies or ETS version, take the test timed, under realistic testing conditions (no phone, distractions, or smart speaker), and record your score. This will tell you both where you stand and what the test is like.

Note: If you've taken the GRE before, you can refer to your old score and skip this step.

>> **Work through this book:** Take three to four weeks to work this book from start to finish. It is a *compendium* (complete collection) of GRE topics, and with an early start, you can check your proficiency on familiar topics which may be rusty (like the Pythagorean theorem) along with new topics that you can pick up easily (like selecting a sentence) but need time to do so.

While working through this book, be sure to mark any topics that you want to return to for more practice. If you're using the print version, you can also fold the corner of the page.

TIP

>> **Take your second practice test, untimed:** Whether you use the exam from ETS or from Dummies, take your second practice test. Take your time to work through the topics, practice your strategies, and think about each step that you will take on the real thing.

While working the practice exam, jot down the number of any question that you weren't sure of or that you took too much time — say, over 3 minutes — to answer. Then, when you review your wrong answers, you can review these, too.

TIP

>> **Review your wrong answers:** This is like shining a flashlight on your exam performance, and it's the best way to find and fix your weak areas. The Dummies practice exams included with this book feature simple answer explanations that are in line with the steps taught in these chapters. The ETS answer explanations tend to be lengthier and more academic. Either way, you *distill* (extract the essentials) a set of topics to focus on, which you then go back and review.

>> **Take a break:** About four weeks from the actual exam, after you're reviewed your topics from the practice tests, take seven to ten days and don't touch anything GRE. You'll come back refreshed, with two to three weeks remaining to get back in gear.

>> **Take your third practice test, timed:** This round, take your practice test under actual testing conditions: no phone or distractions, and with water and snacks only on the breaks. Write the essays, too, as this is part of the exam experience. Note your improvement over the last two practice tests, and again mark topics to review.

>> **Close any final gaps:** With two or three weeks until your exam, you have time to work on areas needing focus. You can also practice and review your test-taking strategies and take another practice exam if you're so inclined.

>> **Take another break:** About ten days from the actual exam, after you've closed the final gaps, take a couple of days and rest up again. Then you can brush up again on your vocab and any topics for review.

>> **Take the exam:** By now you're practically a pro. It's normal to be nervous, but at least everything that happens on the exam is something that you're expecting and prepared for. Refer to the next section, "Planning Your Exam Time," for overall exam strategies along with Chapter 3 for planning for the night before and the day of the exam.

Planning your short-term study time

Don't have 12 weeks to prepare? That's okay. You can fast track this approach and give your score a good boost in about half that time.

» **Brush up on your basics:** Take a week or so to flip through these pages and work any example or practice question marked with the *<play>* icon, so you can brush up on formats and topics of the questions. Each topic in this book has practice questions, so work those questions and mark any topics (and fold the page corners) that you want to revisit.

» **Brush up on your strategies:** While finding and working these practice questions, also read any lines with the *<tip>* icon to pick up on basic, core strategies, which are key to boosting your score. If time allows, also read the lines marked *<remember>* and *<warning>*, but these take a back seat to the *<tip>* topics.

  This is one advantage of the Dummies format, where you can spot the key points that are marked to stand out. It's almost as if the book is highlighted for you.

» **Brush up on your approach:** Take a half-hour and read the Part of Tens in Chapters 24–26. These provide a high-level overview of the nature of the exam along with key dos and don'ts *gleaned* (learned over time) from working with students and observing their successes and mistakes. You get a big-picture perspective that helps with your approach. The information collected in the Part of Tens chapters is another advantage of the Dummies format.

» **Take your first practice test, untimed:** When the exam is still three weeks away, take a practice test. Take your time, work through the questions, mark topics to brush up on, and practice your strategies. Also, look up and note any unfamiliar vocab words, so you can dual-purpose this step and learn the vocab.

» **Review your wrong answers:** Read the answer explanation for any question that you missed or marked for review, and find the sections in this book where I cover those topics. You can use this book's table of contents along with the index to find these topics. Keep a list of these topics for later review.

» **Take a second practice test, timed:** When the exam is two weeks away, take a timed practice test under realistic testing conditions, meaning no phone or distractions. On this round, write the essays, don't look up the vocab, and keep your water and snacks out of reach for access only during the breaks. This way, you become familiar with the testing experience.

» **Review your second set of wrong answers:** As before, read the answer explanations for questions missed or marked for review, and find the sections in this book where I cover those topics. Add these new topics to the list from your first practice exam.

» **Revisit your list of topics for review:** With the exam about ten days away, revisit practice questions from your list of review topics along with the *<play>* questions in this book that you marked to revisit. Make sure you're comfortable answering these questions, even if you've seen them before. Also, check the vocab that you listed from the first exam.

» **Take a break:** After you've finished that last step, and ideally with the exam about a week away, get some rest and rebuild your strength. The preceding steps are more important than this one, so finish those first. If your break is only a couple days before the exam, that's fine. Then you can brush up again on your vocab and any topics for review.

>> **Take the exam:** By now you know what to expect and have practiced most of the topics that you'll see. You've prepped for the bulk of the material in record time, and you should do just fine on the exam. Refer to the next section, "Planning Your Exam Time," for overall exam strategies along with Chapter 3 for more on planning for the night before and the day of the exam.

Planning your last-minute study time

Hey, it happens. There are plans and there's life, and these don't always sync up. If your exam is less than two weeks away, you can still put in some focused effort and increase your score.

>> **Take an untimed practice test:** Whether you take the Dummies or ETS version, take the practice test untimed so you can think about your approach and what works best. Review your wrong answers and collect a list of topics that need focus, then find those topics in the table of contents at the beginning of this book or the index at the end, and read the chapter sections for how to approach those questions.

>> **Brush up on your basics:** Next, flip through these pages and work any example or practice question marked with the *<play>* icon for more practice with the formats and topics of the questions. Be sure to mark any questions (and fold the page corners) that you want to revisit.

>> **Brush up on your strategies and approach:** If you still have time, read any lines with the *<tip>* icon to pick up on basic, core strategies key to boosting your score, and read the Part of Tens, Chapters 24–26, for your overall approach. Then, go back and review the practice questions you marked from the previous step.

>> **Take the exam:** You now know what to expect and have practiced many of the topics that you'll see. Most of the exam will be on topics that you've seen before, and you'll score much higher than you would have without this preparation. Refer to the next section, "Planning Your Exam Time," for overall exam strategies along with Chapter 3 for more on planning for the night before and the day of the exam.

Regardless of the time that you have to prepare, this book provides broad coverage of everything you're likely to encounter on the test. However, if you find major weaknesses in certain areas, you may need to consult additional resources to improve your understanding and skills.

REMEMBER

Prioritize your study time and schedule regular, daily review sessions. Otherwise, other activities and responsibilities are likely to clutter your day and push study time off your to-do list.

Planning your practice time

Just because you know a subject doesn't mean you can ace it on the GRE. Set aside time to take the practice tests, which require a completely separate skill set. The practice tests help you hone your skills, learn from your mistakes, and strengthen your weak areas. I once had a group of financial advisors struggle with all the math. When I asked about this, they told me that they use Excel for everything!

WARNING

Your proficiency with the test itself is as important as your math, verbal, and writing skills. As you take the practice tests, check your testing performance. Many major mistakes begin halfway through the exam, two hours in and two hours to go. Do you still try as hard as you did in the beginning? Do you begin to misread questions, make simple math mistakes, or fall for traps?

Planning Your Exam Time

Taking the GRE is a little like playing *Beat the Clock*. The computer provides you with an on-screen timer for each section. Your goal is to answer as many questions correctly, as quickly as possible, before the clock reaches 0:00. You have the option of hiding this timer, but I don't recommend that. Instead, make the timer familiar and comfortable (or rather, less *un*comfortable) by using a stopwatch while doing homework and practice tests. This is part of preparing for the test-taking experience.

Planning your question time

Don't obsess over giving each question a specific number of seconds, but do know when to give up and come back to a question later. A good rule of thumb is about a minute per question. As long as you haven't exited the section, you can return to any question in that section. Simply call up the Review Screen by clicking Review, click the question you want to return to, and then click Go to Question. You can mark a question for review so it's flagged on the Review Screen, or you can write the question number down on your scratch paper. Just keep in mind that while you're on the Review Screen, the clock still ticks.

Throwing a mental dart

A wrong answer and no answer count exactly the same towards your score, so you may as well pick an answer. If you're not sure how to answer a question, *don't get stuck on it.* Instead, throw a mental dart and take a guess:

>> Rule out as many obviously incorrect choices as possible, and guess from the remaining choices.

>> Write down the question number or mark it for review, so you can return to it before time runs out on that section.

>> Finish the section, even if it means throwing more mental darts (in other words, taking more guesses) near the end. Because a wrong answer counts the same as no answer, you may as well guess and take the chance of getting it right.

Note that this is not really your main strategy. You should be prepared and able to answer most, if not all, of the questions correctly. But as the second Math and Verbal sections increase in difficulty (because you did so well on the *first* Math and Verbal sections — see Chapter 1 for how that works), you may see a question or two that you're not sure how to answer. If that happens, this is what you do.

Planning your intermission time

The GRE provides an optional ten-minute break after the third section of the exam. However, if you're in the testing center, don't expect to have this entire time to yourself: Part of that time is for checking in and out while the proctors go through their security procedures to ensure that you're not bringing in any new materials.

Whether in the testing center or at home, the ten-minute intermission is timed by the computer, which resumes the test whether you're seated or not. You probably have five minutes to do your business, which leaves little time to grab a bite if you're hungry. Plan accordingly by preparing snacks and water to leave in your locker or ready to go at home, so during your actual five minutes, you can refresh yourself without having to scramble.

REMEMBER

Make sure your packed snacks are light and nutritious. Sugar brings you up for a few minutes and then takes you way down. Something heavy, like beef jerky, makes you drowsy. You don't want to crash in the middle of a quadratic equation. Bring a small bag of almonds, some trail mix, or something light that keeps you focused and steady for the rest of the exam.

Between other sections of the test, you get a one-minute break — just enough time to clear your mind. You don't have time to leave your seat and come back before the test resumes. If you absolutely, positively must use the restroom, just remember that the test clock keeps ticking.

Planning your computer time

Sure you know computers, but do you know this particular app — the GRE? Probably not, but it's easy to learn. Just make sure that you learn the ins and outs *before* the actual exam. Don't risk making a mistake that kills your score, such as getting stuck on a question because you forgot that you can skip it and go back.

To gain experience with the computerized GRE, take it for a test drive using the free practice exams from ETS. At the time of this writing, the practice exam package is web-based and features two actual GRE computer-based practice exams for you to become accustomed to the format of the real thing. Access the POWERPREP Online at www.ets.org/gre/revised_general/prepare/powerprep/.

The ETS practice exams look and feel exactly like the real thing, except that they don't hold your life in the balance. Most buttons are self-explanatory, but the following ones deserve special attention.

TIP

>> **Mark:** Mark enables you to flag the question for review, and when you click it, a small checkmark appears on the button. Click it again to remove the checkmark. That's all it does.

   When you mark a question for review, if you haven't answered the question, be sure to guess an answer! That way, if you run out of time, you at least have a shot at guessing it correctly. (See the section "Throwing a mental dart" for more on this.)

>> **Review:** Review takes you to the Review Screen, which shows a list of questions in the section, along with which have been answered and which are flagged for review using the Mark button. Select any question from the list, click the Go To button (which is only on that screen), and you're back at that question. You can then review the question and change your answer if desired.

WARNING

   A common trap is marking every question that you have the slightest doubt on, intending to go back to it later. Problem is, when you've reached the end of the section, you have 16 questions marked and only four minutes to work on them! Be sure to prioritize what you truly want to go back to.

>> **Exit Section:** This button ends the section and saves your essay or answers so you can proceed to the next section. After you click this button, you can't go back to change answers or return to unanswered questions in the section.

>> **Quit Test:** This button ends the exam and cancels your scores. Don't use this one.

Take the computerized practice test from ets.org not only to get a feel for the content and format of the questions but also to become accustomed to selecting answers and using the buttons to navigate.

For additional practice, go to www.dummies.com and register your book for access to computer-based practice exams, albeit in a slightly different format. Instructions for registering are in this book's Introduction. And for even more practice, check out *1,001 GRE Practice Questions For Dummies* (Wiley).

Planning Your Mental and Physical Time

Taking an intense four-hour exam is challenging both mentally and physically. Most people aren't used to concentrating at this level for such a long time. To meet the challenge, your brain needs a good supply of oxygen and nutrients, and it gets these from an active, healthy, and alert body primed with nutritious foods and beverages. The following sections provide guidance on whipping your body into shape for test day.

Staying active

You can't just be a bookworm for the months leading up to the exam: You need to stay active. Exercise helps all parts of the body and leads to clearer thinking by increasing oxygen to the brain, so get moving! You don't need to train for a marathon. Walking, swimming, jogging, yoga, Pilates, basketball, or doing anything active, especially outdoors, gets your body in motion and increases your overall health and circulation.

Eating well

Certain foods and beverages affect your cognitive ability, so avoid highly processed foods and foods high in sugar, starch, or fat. These foods tend to make you feel sluggish or result in bursts of energy followed by prolonged crashes. Lean more toward veggies — especially green, leafy veggies — and foods that are high in protein. When it comes to carbohydrates, go for complex over simple. Complex carbohydrates are typically found in fresh fruits, veggies, and whole-grain products. Avoid simple carbohydrates found in candy, soda, anything made from white flour, and most junk foods, including chips. And forget those energy drinks that combine huge amounts of caffeine and sugar to get you to a state of heightened tension.

TIP

If you plan on taking an energy drink or anything unusual on the day of the test, *try it out first on a practice test*. If the drink gives you the jitters or upsets your stomach, you won't want to discover this on the *day of the exam*.

Relaxing

Relaxation comes in different forms for different people. Some folks are relaxed with friends; some read books and play music; and others practice yoga, meditation, or painting. The only requirement when choosing how to relax is making sure your brain isn't running 100 miles an hour. The whole purpose of relaxing is to give your brain a rest. So find an activity you enjoy, thank your brain by telling it to take some time off, and recharge.

REMEMBER

Relaxation isn't a luxury — it's a requirement for success on the GRE (and a well-balanced life). You're a multifaceted human, not a work-and-study automaton.

WARNING

I've seen students who are so overextended and overachieving that they exhaust themselves before the test. They feel fine, but their performance drops like a rock. One sure sign of this is overanalyzing easy questions. Another is making simple math mistakes, such as $2 + 1 = 5$. This is real, and it happens to *everyone*. If you notice this happening, even if you feel fine, it's time to take a break. Don't touch the exam for a few days, and your performance will come right back.

Scheduling Your Exam

In most parts of the world, the GRE is a computer-based test, which makes it easier to administer to individual test-takers. Sign up early so you can choose the day, time, and place that work best for you. The time-slot availability varies per testing center, so if one testing center doesn't have a time slot that works for you, you may be able to try another nearby testing center, or you can schedule the test for home.

To sign up for the GRE, see the current *GRE Information and Registration Bulletin* (available through most college admissions offices), register online at www.ets.org, or register via phone by calling 800-473-2255. You can also check the GRE testing center locations and available time slots at www.ets.org.

TIP

To get into the right mindset, take at least one practice test at the same time of day that you plan to take the real thing. (Check out the practice tests in Part 5 of this book and in the online access.) If you're used to eating or relaxing at a certain time each day, make sure these tendencies don't sneak up on you during the exam. A recurring theme of this book is to make the exam and testing experience as familiar as possible, so that you're used to it and it's almost no big deal. (See Chapter 3 for more on gearing up for exam day.)

Scheduling for the testing center

Because the computerized GRE is administered to individual test-takers, testing centers tend to have few seats, and those seats fill up quickly during peak admission deadline months (April and November). If you're planning to take the GRE in a testing center (as opposed to at home) around these months to get your test scores in on time, schedule your test early and secure your ideal time slot. You can always reschedule, but the last thing you need is an inconvenient time or location. Before at-home testing was available, I had a student wait until the last minute to schedule his exam, and he had to drive from Phoenix to Tucson (about 120 miles) to take his GRE and get his scores in on time. He called me during his drive, and we reviewed math formulas, but this wasn't an ideal way to ramp up for the test.

Scheduling for home

The at-home GRE test is another option. You will have to submit proof that you're not set up to cheat. ETS provides detailed requirements when you sign up, but anti-cheat measures include taking a video of your room and using software that ensures no other app is open on your computer. This may be invasive, but ETS has to make sure you're not stealing an advantage with your at-home setup. You also have to use a small whiteboard or laminated sheet for your scratch work, along with a dry-erase marker for your scratch notes, instead of the traditional pencil and paper that you get at the testing center.

Some students prefer the testing center so there are no home-based distractions (such as family, dog, or phone notifications). On the other hand, at-home testing ensures you can grab a time that works best for you, rather than selecting from the remaining open time slots at the testing center. Give it some thought and go with what works best for you.

HANDLING UNIQUE CIRCUMSTANCES

If you have a special circumstance or need, the folks at ets.org are usually accommodating as long as you give them a heads-up. Following is a brief list of special circumstances and how to obtain assistance for each.

- **Learning disabilities:** These disabilities refer to attention deficit hyperactivity disorder (ADHD), dyslexia, and other related or similar conditions. To find out whether you qualify for accommodations or a disabilities waiver of any sort, contact ETS Disability Services, Educational Testing Service, P.O. Box 6054, Princeton, NJ 08541-6054; phone 866-387-8602 (toll free) or 609-771-7780 (Monday to Friday, 8:30 a.m. to 5:00 p.m. Eastern Time), fax 609-771-7165; website www.ets.org/gre, or email stassd@ets.org. Qualifying for accommodations is an involved process that takes time, and gathering the required documentation may require significant effort on your part. If you have a qualifying disability, act sooner rather than later to find out what's required and when you need to submit your request and documentation.

- **Physical disabilities:** ETS tries to accommodate everyone. Folks who need special arrangements can get Braille or large-print exams, have test-readers or recorders, work with interpreters, and so on. You can get the scoop about what ETS considers to be disabilities and how the disabilities can change the way you take the GRE in the *Supplement for Test Takers with Disabilities.* This publication contains information, registration procedures, and other useful forms for individuals with physical disabilities. To get this publication, send a request to ETS Disability Services, P.O. Box 6054, Princeton, NJ 08541-6054. Or better yet, head to www.ets.org/gre and click the Test Takers with Disabilities or Health-Related Needs link for all the info you need to know, along with contact information if you have questions or concerns.

- **Financial difficulties:** Until you ace the GRE, get into a top-notch graduate school, and come out ready to make your first million, you may have a rough time paying for the exam. However, fee waivers are available. Note that the waiver applies only to the actual GRE fee, not to miscellaneous fees such as the test-disclosure service, hand-grading service, and so on. Your college counselor can help you obtain and fill out the appropriate request forms. (If you're not currently in college, a counselor or financial aid specialist at a nearby college or university may still be able to help you. Just call for an appointment.)

Chapter **3**

Planning for Exam Day: Everything Outside the Exam

On the morning of the exam, there's no such thing as a pleasant surprise. The goal of this chapter is to help you avoid these surprises so you know exactly what to expect on exam day. This way, you can focus on the GRE in a more relaxed and confident frame of mind. Confidence comes from being prepared, and the last thing you want is to show up rushed and stressed *before* starting the exam.

Planning the Night Before

If you're taking the GRE at a testing center rather than at home, give yourself one less distraction on the morning of the exam by getting all your stuff together the night before. Make sure that morning isn't spent frantically looking for things.

Knowing what to bring

Here's what you need to bring, so get these together the night before the exam.

» **Photo ID:** Your identification needs three key elements.

- A recognizable photo
- The name you used to register for the test
- Your signature

Usually, a driver's license, passport, employee ID, or military ID does the trick. A student ID alone isn't enough (although it works as a second form of ID in case something's unclear on your first one). Note that a Social Security card or a credit card isn't acceptable identification.

>> **Water and a snack:** The testing center provides a locker, so bring a bottle of water and a light snack, such as an energy bar or a granola bar. If you're like me, you'll have a to-go cup of coffee. Avoid snacks high in sugar, simple carbohydrates, or fats. Leave your snacks in the locker and have them during your break.

>> **Map or directions:** Know in advance where you're going. Map your directions, and it doesn't hurt to check the satellite view so you can see where to park. You could drive to the testing center a few days before to check out the drive time, parking, fees, and so on. If you're taking public transportation, find out where and when you need to board the bus or train, how long the ride is, how much it costs, and where you get off.

One student had to take the test at a center in the middle of a downtown area. She had checked out the area on a Saturday, when the streets were empty and parking was clear. But her exam was Monday morning, when the streets were jammed and the parking was taken. Naturally, she wasn't expecting this, and it was an extra stressor that morning.

TIP

Another option is Uber or Lyft. When Google Mapping the route to plan your trip, be sure to set the ride time to *the morning of the exam* so the trip time reflects the traffic. It doesn't hurt to plan on being there 30 minutes early, so if your driver or friend is late or doesn't know the roads, you have a time cushion.

>> **Comfortable clothes:** Dress in layers. Testing centers can be warm, or more typically, cold. Sitting there for hours shivering won't help your performance. Dress in layers so you can be comfortable regardless of how they run the A/C.

>> **Authorization voucher from Educational Testing Service (ETS):** If you pay with a method other than a credit/debit card or have a disability or require certain testing accommodations, ETS provides an *authorization voucher.* Not everyone gets this voucher, but if you do, be sure to bring it with you on the day of the test.

These are things you should bring, but there are also things that you should not bring.

Knowing what not to bring

Just as important as knowing what to bring to the testing center is knowing what not to bring. Leave these things at home, in your car, or with the Uber.

>> **Books and notes:** Forget about last-minute studying. You aren't allowed to take books or notes into the testing center. Besides, if you don't know the material by that time, cramming won't help.

One of my students was almost booted from his exam because during the break, he picked up his test-prep book that was in his testing center locker. Fortunately, he didn't *open* the book, so he was allowed to finish the exam, but you can bet that frazzled him and affected his performance.

>> **Calculator:** You aren't allowed to use your own calculator, but an on-screen calculator is available during the math sections of the exam. One nice thing about the on-screen calculator is that it features a button that transfers the number from the calculator field to the answer space. Your handheld calculator won't do that.

>> **Friends for support:** Meet them after the exam. However, having a friend drop you off and pick you up isn't a bad idea, especially if parking is likely to be a problem, such as at a downtown testing center.

>> **Phones, tablets, or other electronics:** Any electronic device, including your phone or iPad, is strictly prohibited. You can bring these to the testing center, but they stay in a locker while you're taking the GRE.

>> **Scratch paper (at the testing center):** You aren't allowed to bring in your own scratch paper; the testing center provides it for you. If you run low during the test, request more from the proctor during the one-minute breaks between sections. Although you have plenty of room to do calculations and scribbling, your scratch paper stays at the testing center when you're done.

>> **Scratch paper (at home):** Note that if you take the GRE at home, you're not allowed to use paper of any kind, or pens or pencils for that matter. Plan ahead and pick up an ETS-approved small whiteboard or laminated sheet to write on, along with an erasable marker and eraser. At the end of the exam, you'll hold the erased whiteboard or sheet up to the camera to show the proctor that all your notes have been erased.

The testing center provides a locker for you to store your belongings, so if you bring a purse or backpack, you'll have a secure place to keep it.

Planning for Contingency

Upon completing the exam, you have the option of accepting and seeing your scores immediately or canceling the results if you think you did poorly. If you cancel the results, you can always retake the test. Most schools consider only your highest exam score, or you can choose to send only that highest score (see the ScoreSelect discussion in Chapter 1), so only cancel if you *really* think something went wrong on the test that isn't normal for you.

If you cancel a score and later have second thoughts about that cancellation, you can reinstate the canceled score up to 60 days after the test date. As of this writing, the service costs $50, and reinstatement takes up to two weeks.

If you proceed with your exam score and it isn't so hot, don't fret: Most test-takers who repeat the exam tend to do *much* better the second time. It's as if the best way to prepare is by taking the actual GRE. Of course, you want to avoid having to do this, but if the first round doesn't go so well, it's okay, and it happens.

TIP

Be sure to schedule your GRE a month before your school needs the scores. That way, if you do have to retake the exam, you'll still meet the application deadline. Also, just knowing you have a second chance helps ease your nerves in the first round.

If you think you underperformed on the GRE, consider the following when deciding whether to retake it and when preparing to retake the exam:

>> **Was it something in your control?** If you made mistakes because of a lack of familiarity with either the test format (you didn't understand what to do on a Quantitative Comparison question) or substance (you didn't know the vocabulary or the geometry), these are things you can control, and you're a good candidate for doing better the second time.

The practice tests are designed to help you address these issues ahead of time: If you know what you did wrong, you can address it and improve your score.

After taking the actual GRE, you don't get to review the correct and incorrect answer choices. However, you can get a good sense of the types of mistakes that you're likely to make by going through the practice tests in this book and reviewing your wrong answers afterward.

>> **Was it something out of your control?** Maybe your nerves were acting up on the first exam, you were feeling ill, or you didn't get enough sleep the night before. In that case, by all means repeat the exam. You're bound to feel better the next time. If the test was administered poorly or in a

room full of distractions, you really should consider filing a complaint and retaking the exam. (See the next section, "It's Them, Not You: Testing under Adverse Conditions," for details.)

>> **Did I choke?** This happens all the time, especially on the essays at the beginning. Or you could have panicked on a thorny math question, spending several minutes and frazzling yourself for the rest of the test. Fortunately, choking doesn't usually happen on the retake. Almost every test-taker I've seen choke does phenomenally better on the next try.

>> **Did I run out of steam?** Stamina is a key factor of success on the four-hour GRE. If you don't practice writing the essays when taking the practice tests, you won't be prepared for the extra hour of intense work before the Math and Verbal sections. Also, because you're amped on test day, you're likely to crash faster than usual. Knowing what to expect and preparing for it could boost your score on a retest.

>> **Am I eligible to retake the GRE?** As of this writing, you have to wait 21 days before retaking the exam, and you can't take it more than five times in a 12-month period. If you try to take the test more often than that, you won't be stopped from registering or taking the test, but your scores won't be reported.

Can repeating the exam hurt you? Typically, no. Most schools consider only your highest score, and you can choose which scores to send anyway. Find out from the individual schools you're interested in whether that's their policy; it isn't the same for every school. If you're on the borderline, or if several students are vying for one spot, sometimes having taken the exam repeatedly can hurt you (especially if recent scores stayed flat or took a nosedive). On the other hand, an admissions counselor who sees several exams with ascending scores may be impressed that you stuck to it and kept trying. In general, if you're willing to invest the study time and effort and take the repeat exam seriously, go for it.

All your test scores for the past five years are part of your record, but you can choose which scores to send using the ScoreSelect option, as covered in Chapter 1. For example, if you did great in June but not so well in November, you can request that just the June scores are sent to the schools.

It's Them, Not You: Testing under Adverse Conditions

Your test isn't actually administered by ETS. It's administered by a company licensed by ETS, and that company is required to adhere to certain standards. If something odd happens during the test that you believe negatively affected your score, such as construction noises, nonworking air-conditioning, or anything else that shouldn't be the case, register a complaint with ETS at GRE-Info@ets.org for a chance to have those scores canceled and for you to retake the exam, at no charge. You have seven days to register a complaint, so don't delay.

WARNING

Complaining to the testing center staff does no good — it actually says that on the ETS website! You must communicate directly with ETS.

One of my students was seated and ready to begin her GRE, only to have the start time delayed an hour! On top of that, a lot of noise was coming from the next room — definitely an unwarranted distraction. If something like this happens to you, you can petition to have your score withheld and for the opportunity to take the GRE again at no charge.

REMEMBER

Testing centers tend to freeze the heck out of the exam rooms, so being chilly isn't grounds for registering a complaint. It does mean that you should prepare by wearing layers that you can remove if needed. Note that you are typically not allowed to wear a jacket, but a sweater is okay.

2

Tackling the Verbal Section One Word at a Time

Chapter 4

Upping Your Best GRE Verbal Score

I t's time to brush up on your English. That's a *lot* to cover — you can get a college degree in English. But, for the purposes of this test, where do you start? How far do you go?

Fortunately, GRE Verbal is based on a specific set of skills that, with this book, you can identify and build. You don't need outside knowledge of any particular topic except for vocabulary, and even that can be augmented through skills and learning rather than rote memorization.

Building Your Core Skills

Most GRE Verbal questions are based on your comprehension and critical thinking skills from reading at a college level. If you can read — and truly understand — a scientific or business journal piece, along with its vocabulary, then you're well on your way to achieving a good Verbal score, and you'll only need to practice the strategies and vocabulary in the next four chapters.

If you don't regularly read college-level pieces — and who does? — then you should start now. For business, read a few pieces from *The Economist* or *The Financial Times*; for science, visit the List of Scientific Journals in Wikipedia and find some topics that you're interested in, or, better yet, are in your field of study for your upcoming master's program. The harder to read, the better.

Why would you do this? GRE Verbal isn't specific to any topic, and any detail that you need is included with the question. It's because most of GRE Verbal consists of *esoteric* (not understood by most) writing of concepts and passages that the exam expects you to handle with ease, and most people can't *access* (understand) without practice. This is why few test-takers score well on GRE Verbal, and why this section is so challenging on the GRE.

As you read these college-level journal pieces, make sure that you understand each paragraph. Don't just gloss over something that's not clear. You'll have a master's or PhD at this level soon enough, so this piece should be something that you can read and understand. Then — and here's why this is relevant — when you take the GRE, the Verbal section isn't such a challenge.

This approach even builds up your vocabulary. As you read these pieces, look up any word that you don't know. Eventually, you'll see these words repeated, and you'll also see them in GRE Verbal. (Just to be sure, there's also Chapter 8: Expanding Your Vocabulary to Boost Your Score.) You don't need a dictionary or web browser. Just tap on your phone or say, "Hey, Alexa (or Google or Siri), what is *loquacious*?" (It means talkative.)

We review 20 vocab words at the start of each GRE class. One time, a student brought in a *New York Times* article that had three of the words from the last class! She said that she never even noticed those words before we had reviewed them. The takeaway for you: Don't let a *single* word go by without looking up and understanding its meaning.

Managing Your Time

GRE Verbal questions are an odd lot. At 30 minutes for 20 questions, you'd think that one and a half minutes per question is the answer. Not so. Assuming you've brushed up on your reading and learned the vocab, the reading comp questions can each take longer than two minutes, while the argument analysis questions take one minute, and some Text Completion and most Sentence Equivalence questions can each take less than 30 seconds.

If you know what you're doing and don't get stuck, then time isn't an issue. You can pace yourself and answer all the questions in the time allotted without rushing. The problem is that it takes a while to get there, so also try this approach *on a practice test* and see what you think. If it works, great, and you can vary up the strategy so that it fits you even better. Try out these strategies as you practice a verbal section, and see how it works for you:

» **Bounce around the section, but keep track of questions to return to.** Answer the fast questions first, then go back to the slow ones. Simple enough, but you need to make sure you return to *all* of them. Either use the Review Screen to see which ones remain unanswered, write numbers of skipped questions down on your scratch paper, or use a hybrid of these techniques. Either way, *practice this on an online practice exam,* so your process is smooth on test day.

» **Start with the Text Completion and Sentence Equivalence questions.** The 1- and 2-blank Text Completion and Sentence Equivalence questions should take less than a minute each, so knock these out first. The 3-blank Text Completion questions, however, take longer and should be saved for last. More on this in Chapter 5.

» **Work the shorter reading questions next.** Most shorter reading questions are either simpler Reading Comprehension (covered in Chapter 6) or Argument Analysis (Chapter 7) questions. These aren't such time drainers, and you can knock them out fast enough.

» **Work the longer reading and 3-blank Text Completion questions last.** The longer reading comp passages tend to be more complicated, so work those next. The 3-blank Text Completion question is the most challenging question in the GRE Verbal (for most test-takers), and that one question with its three blanks carries the same point value as any other question, so save it for the very end. Fortunately, there's typically only one or two per GRE Verbal section.

One thing you could do is select reading passage topics that are easier to follow, so that you're less likely to get stuck. Topics are split among natural sciences, social sciences, and humanities (per Chapter 6), so you could start with the genre that you're more comfortable with and go back to the others.

» **Regardless, don't get stuck.** Even the 1-2 blank Text Completion and Sentence Equivalence questions can have a curve ball mixed in, so if you find that more than a minute has gone by on one, you know what to do: Take a guess, mark it for review, and come back to it later.

Be sure this strategy works for you, or try a variation that suits you better. Like any strategy, some are lifesavers and others aren't your cup of tea. Everyone responds differently, so this is a taste test: Try it and see what you think. Also, this approach begs a lot of skipping around, so be sure you've practiced navigating via the Review Screen and/or jotting question numbers on scratch paper. Navigating the skipped questions is easy to master, but learn it — vary it up — and make your mistakes — here, now, *before* test day.

Chapter **5**

What Are They Saying: Text Completion and Sentence Equivalence

Text Completion and Sentence Equivalence questions hold all the clues you need to answer them correctly. By using key strategies and avoiding common mistakes, you can rack up points quickly. If you find the vocabulary is slowing you down, turn to Chapter 8 to brush up on words that you're likely to encounter.

Clinching Text Completion and Sentence Equivalence Questions

Text Completion and Sentence Equivalence questions are similar but have some distinct differences:

» **Text Completion:** A Text Completion question consists of a sentence or paragraph with one, two, or three missing words or phrases, along with a short list of word or phrase choices to complete the text. If the text has one word missing, the list has five choices, while if the text has two or three words missing, each blank has a list of three choices.

Each choice gives the text a different meaning. Your job is to choose the word or words that best support the meaning of the sentence. If the text is missing more than one word, you don't get partial credit for choosing only one correct word.

REMEMBER

Text Completion questions tend to have slightly easier vocabulary but are more challenging to interpret.

» **Sentence Equivalence:** A Sentence Equivalence question consists of a single sentence with exactly one word missing and a list of six choices to complete it. Your job is to select the two words that fit the sentence *and* mean the same thing, and, as with the Text Completion questions, you don't get partial credit for choosing only one correct word.

TIP

Sentence Completion questions tend to be easier to interpret but have more challenging vocabulary. The correct answers are *almost always* synonyms. If you find a word that works well but doesn't have a match, then you've likely found a *trap answer*.

» **Both question types:** The answer choices always fit perfectly and have perfect grammar: Make your choice based on the *meaning* of the words. Each word you place gives the sentence a different meaning, so find the meaning of the text *without* the answer choices, and then eliminate the wrong answer choices.

Keeping it straight

Don't worry about memorizing how many answers to click. On the exam it's clear, and just to be sure, at the top of the screen is always an instruction that reads something like "Pick one answer for each missing word (in Text Completion)" or "Pick two answer choices that create sentences most alike in meaning (in Sentence Equivalence)."

Also, the one-answer questions allow you to select only one answer, and the two-answer questions allow you to select more than one. Go through it once and you'll be fine: I've never had a student mix this up.

Trying it out

The following example of a Text Completion question shows how all answer choices appear to fit perfectly but only two specific words actually make logical sense.

Directions: For each blank, select one entry from the corresponding column of choices. Fill all blanks in the way that best completes the text.

PLAY

Frustrated that she missed the simple trick to answering the GRE question, Faye (i) _____ her Dummies book out the window with such (ii) _____ that it soared high into the sky, prompting three of her neighbors to grab their phones and post videos on TikTok.

Blank (i)	Blank (ii)
Ⓐ tossed	Ⓓ ferocity
Ⓑ hurled	Ⓔ glee
Ⓒ pitched	Ⓕ gentleness

The key word in this example is *frustrated,* which conveys a strong negative emotion. Choices (B) and (D), **hurled** and *ferocity,* are the only choices that support such a negative emotion. Note that this is a single, two-part question. You may select any of the three answer choices for each blank, but you must choose *both* correct answers to earn credit for the question.

The following example of a Sentence Equivalence question shows how all six answer choices appear to fit within the sentence structure, but only two answers actually support the meaning of the sentence.

Directions: Select the two answer choices that, when used to complete the sentence, fit the meaning of the sentence as a whole and produce two completed sentences that are alike in meaning.

Well-prepared and ready, Billy _____ the GRE and made everyone proud.

A aced

B missed

C dominated

D held

E took

F knew

The sentence suggests that Billy did well on the GRE. The best words to convey GRE success are *aced* and *dominated,* making Choices (A) and (C) the correct answers. Again, you must select both correct answers to earn credit for the question.

Developing Your Skills for Finding the Correct Answers

Text Completion and Sentence Equivalence questions are designed to measure two core proficiencies: interpreting the text and using the vocabulary. These are two distinct skills that you build separately but use together.

Most of the vocab words that you encounter on the GRE are used commonly in most professional industries, including business and journalism. Such words as *ephemeral* (fleeting), *abscond* (sneak away), and *imbroglio* (entanglement) stump exam-takers every day but appear regularly in publications.

This chapter guides you through the basics, and Chapter 8 has the vocab. Interpreting the text can be challenging; otherwise, it has no place on the GRE. The following sections give you an overview along with how you can eliminate incorrect answers.

Interpreting the Text 101

Interpreting the text means discerning its meaning in the absence of key words. Do this prior to looking at the answer choices to understand the text and quickly eliminate choices that don't make sense. Try this simple example:

Directions: Select the two answer choices that, when used to complete the sentence, fit the meaning as a whole and produce two completed sentences that are alike in meaning.

PLAY

The boxes were so heavy that we could _____ lift them.

A easily
B hardly
C fully
D nearly
E barely
F effortlessly

Even without the missing word, you can construe the meaning of the sentence. The phrase *so heavy* tells you that these boxes are difficult or impossible to lift. After realizing this, you can immediately eliminate *easily* and *effortlessly*. The words *fully* and *nearly* are a little tougher to ignore, but they really don't make sense either. The correct answers are Choices (B), *hardly*, and (E), *barely*.

Getting the gist of the text

One way to figure out the meaning of a challenging sentence is to see whether it has a positive or negative connotation. This high-level perspective can help you find words that convey the correct meaning. Try it out on this example. Though not really a tough sentence, it shows you what I mean:

Directions: Select the two answer choices that, when used to complete the sentence, fit the meaning of the sentence as a whole and produce two completed sentences that are alike in meaning.

PLAY

Everyone is so _____ that you did great on the GRE: We knew you could do it!

A ecstatic
B stunned
C thrilled
D shocked
E dumbfounded
F bewildered

All the choices suggest that you did better than expected, but *stunned, shocked, dumbfounded,* and *bewildered* imply that everyone thought you would tank, and what kind of friends are those? However, we knew you would do great, probably because you used *GRE Prep For Dummies 2024.* The second half of the sentence doesn't convey doubt ("We knew you could do it!"), so the correct answers are Choices (A) and (C).

Taking the Best and Only Approach

Whether you're taking on a Text Completion or Sentence Equivalence question, your approach is the same. These steps are the *only* way to knock out these questions so you can beat the exam and get on with your life.

1. **Interpret the text without looking at the answer choices.**

2. **Complete the text with your own words.**

3. **Eliminate wrong answer choices.**

The following sections explain these steps in detail.

Interpret the text without looking at the answer choices

First, figure out what the sentence is saying. If you know this, then you know the meanings of the words that go in the blanks. How else do you know which answer choices work, and more importantly, which ones don't work?

WARNING

While interpreting the text, don't look at the answer choices! Each answer choice not only seems to fit perfectly but also gives the sentence a very different meaning. Then, you have no idea what the sentence is trying to say, and you've turned a relatively workable question into something that's impossible. Whoa, right into the trap. Instead, *first* get the meaning of the sentence and *then* look at the answer choices!

TIP

To avoid involuntarily glancing at the answer choices, cover them up with your scratch paper. Hold that scratch paper right up on the computer screen. (You're not working math now, anyway.) Silly? Yes. Effective? Absolutely. Students tell me it's a lifesaver.

The following example illustrates the different meanings that a sentence can convey using different words in the blanks. If you first try out all the answer choices, it becomes impossible to tell what the sentence is actually saying, so they're not shown here yet.

PLAY

Coerced by his kids into watching *The LEGO Movie*, Andy was (i) _____, although the movie surprisingly turned out to be (ii) _____.

First, interpret what the sentence is trying to say. The word *although* in the middle of the sentence tells you that the two phrases have different meanings — that the words in those blanks should be opposite, or close to it. *Although* is an example of a transition word, which can function as a valuable clue. (See the later section "Use transition words to get the gist of the phrases" for more on this.)

Ask yourself this: Was Andy eager or reluctant? Was *The LEGO Movie* surprisingly lame or good? That he was *coerced* tells you that Andy didn't want to go, so he probably was *reluctant* and expected a lousy movie. Then he was *surprised,* so the movie was probably pretty good. This is how you tell what the sentence is trying to say.

Complete the text with your own words

The next step is finding your own words to complete the text. Your words don't have to be perfect — you're not *writing* the sentence — but they *do* have to support its meaning. This way, you know exactly what to look for and can eliminate answer choices (which is the following step). Right now, you're still covering up the answer choices with your scratch paper.

Try to picture what's happening in the text. Even though you may arrange it differently, your key words will match the missing words in the question.

> Coerced by his kids into watching *The LEGO Movie,* Andy was *reluctant,* although the movie surprisingly turned out to be, *well . . . awesome.*

You already know that Andy wasn't looking forward to the movie, but the movie surprisingly was good.

TIP

Your own words may not fit perfectly or match the answer choices — but they don't have to. Instead, they serve a more important purpose. *They make the wrong answers clearly stand out.* Now you go to the next step: Eliminate wrong answer choices.

Eliminate wrong answer choices

The final step to knocking out these questions is eliminating the wrong answer choices. Now that you know what the sentence is saying, the wrong answers are clear.

Here's the example question again, this time with the answer choices provided.

Directions: For each blank, select one entry from the corresponding column of choices. Fill all blanks in the way that best completes the text.

PLAY

Coerced by his kids into watching *The LEGO Movie,* Andy was (i) _____, although the movie surprisingly turned out to be (ii) _____.

Blank (i)	Blank (ii)
Ⓐ thrilled	Ⓓ lousy
Ⓑ excited	Ⓔ subpar
Ⓒ hesitant	Ⓕ a blast

Compare the answer choices, one at a time, to the words you already came up with on your own (*reluctant* and *awesome*). Cross *thrilled* and *excited* off the first list, because they have nothing to do with *reluctant*. Similarly, *lousy* and *subpar* are far from *awesome*. The correct answers are Choices (C), *hesitant,* and (F), *a blast,* which both match your predictions and make sense when you read the sentence.

TIP

These questions can be challenging, so if you're not sure whether an answer choice should be crossed off, don't spend time on it. Instead, mark it as "maybe" and go on to the next answer choice. Usually, you'll finish reviewing the answer choices with one marked "maybe" and the others eliminated. Go with the "maybe" choice and move on.

Worst case, if you have to guess, you've narrowed down the answers to guess from. Then mark the question for review and return to it later.

REMEMBER

Most of these verbal questions should take you less than a minute each, saving you valuable time for the time-intensive Reading Comprehension. (For more on GRE Reading Comprehension, read over to Chapter 6.)

Interpreting Trickier Sentences

If every Text Completion and Sentence Equivalence question were this easy, everyone would get a perfect 170 on the Verbal section (those who have this book, anyway), and testing would be pointless. However, the actual GRE questions can be more challenging to interpret. When you come across these sentences, start with the three basic strategies mentioned earlier and build on them with these steps:

1. **Use transition words to get the gist of the phrases.**

2. **Start with the second or third missing word.**

The following section goes further into these steps.

Use transition words to get the gist of the phrases

Transition words exist in most Text Completion and Sentence Equivalence questions (and other sentences) and serve as valuable clues to interpreting the meaning of a sentence. (*Transition words* connect two ideas in a sentence or paragraph and tell you whether the two ideas in the sentence agree or contradict one another.) Transition words help you decipher the meaning of a sentence with key words missing.

For example, changing the transition word in the following sentence completely alters its meaning:

> *Although* he ran as fast as he could, Eric ＿＿＿ the bus.

The transition word *although*, indicating contrast, tells you that Eric missed the bus. Here's the same sentence with a different transition word:

> *Because* he ran as fast as he could, Eric ＿＿＿ the bus.

The transition word *because*, indicating cause-and-effect, tells you that Eric caught the bus.

With a little practice, transition words become easy to identify and use to your advantage. They're helpful when breaking the sentence into pieces (which is the next step) and are used frequently in the Analytical Writing portion of the GRE. (See Part 4 for more on the Analytical Writing essays.)

Common transition words include the following:

although	and	because	but
despite	either/or	however	in spite of
moreover	nonetheless	therefore	or

The English language has hundreds of transition words. Fortunately, you don't need to memorize them, but you do need to be able to spot them.

TIP

Most transition words can be divided into two categories: *continuing* and *contrasting*. Continuing transition words — *and, because, moreover,* and *therefore* — indicate that the one part of the sentence will continue the thought of the other part. Contrasting transition words — *although, but, despite, however, in spite of,* and *nonetheless* — indicate that one part of the sentence will contrast the other part.

In the previous example with Eric and the bus, changing the transition from a *continuing* to a *contrasting* word (in this case, *although* to *because*) directly changes the meaning of the sentence. Note that the transition word isn't always in the middle of the sentence. Now to work on the second step.

Start with the second or third missing word

Many Text Completion questions have two or three words missing. Often the first missing word could be anything, and the second (or third) missing word tells you the first one. Look at this example:

PLAY

Although she usually was of a (i) _____ nature, Patty was (ii) _____ when the professor assigned a paper due the day after spring break.

The transition word *although* clues you in to the gist of the first phrase. It tells you that Patty's usual nature is different from the way she felt when receiving her assignment. But this isn't enough — Patty could usually be of any nature: good, bad, *cantankerous* (cranky), *sanguine* (cheerful), *capricious* (fickle). You need the gist of the *second* missing word to find the first one.

> Second missing word: Patty was ____ when the professor assigned a paper due the day after spring break.

From the second missing word, you can infer that she was *annoyed* when the professor assigned a paper. It could be different, but probably not. Most people are usually some form of disappointed when assigned papers, especially over spring break. Anyway, knowing she wasn't happy, the continuing transition word *although* tells you that she's usually the opposite:

> First missing word: Although she usually was of a ____ nature,

The opposite of *annoyed* is *happy*. Patty is usually *happy*, but today she is *annoyed*. Now take on the whole question:

Although she usually was of a (i) _____ nature, Patty was (ii) _____ when the professor assigned a paper due the day after spring break.

Blank (i)	Blank (ii)
Ⓐ frugal	Ⓓ enigmatic
Ⓑ keen	Ⓔ lugubrious
Ⓒ cheerful	Ⓕ ebullient

Eliminate answer choices that don't match the words you used (*happy* and *annoyed*) to complete the text. Start with the second missing word.

Using the word clue *annoyed*, which words from the second column can you eliminate? *Enigmatic* means mysterious or cryptic, which doesn't match *annoyed*. If you don't know what *lugubrious* and *ebullient* mean, you can guess that *lugubrious* is heavy and *ebullient* means upbeat, based on how the words sound. (*Ebullient* means very happy, and *lugubrious* means sad. Flip to Chapter 8 for a lot more vocabulary.) Eliminate *ebullient* for not matching *annoyed*, so *lugubrious* remains and is the second missing word.

Now for the first missing word. Using the word clue *happy*, which words from the first column can you eliminate? *Frugal* doesn't fit based solely on its meaning (economical), and it has no opposite in the second column. *Keen*, which means *intense*, also doesn't fit, so *cheerful* seems to be the remaining choice for the first blank. The correct answers are Choices (C) and (E).

Getting Your Hands Dirty with Some Practice

You're ready to tackle some practice Text Completion and Sentence Equivalence questions for a better grasp of how to solve them using all the tools described in this chapter.

Text Completion questions

PLAY

Directions: For each blank, select one entry from the corresponding column of choices. Fill all blanks in the way that best completes the text.

1. As a public relations specialist, Susan realizes the importance of treating even the most exasperating tourists with kindness and _____.

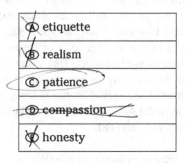

Ⓐ etiquette

Ⓑ realism

Ⓒ patience

Ⓓ compassion

Ⓔ honesty

First, ask yourself, "What's important when dealing with exasperated tourists?" A public relations specialist would need to be polite. The first word choice, *etiquette,* looks good, but you don't treat someone with etiquette. (*Etiquette* is a system of rules for manners.) Cross that word off the list. You don't show exasperating tourists *compassion,* either. Gone. *Honesty* won't help. Gone! *Realism* isn't even close. Gone! Through logic and elimination, or just because it's the only one remaining, the correct answer is Choice (C), *patience.*

2. Enabled by his (i) _____ and unimpeded by any sense of (ii) _____, Henry reached the end of the Ironman Triathlon.

Blank (i)	Blank (ii)
Ⓐ knowhow	Ⓓ weariness
Ⓑ appetite	Ⓔ courage
Ⓒ stamina	Ⓕ power

What's one thing that helps and another that hinders a triathlete? *Strength* and *fatigue* are good choices. In the first column, you can rule out *knowhow.* Either of the remaining words, *appetite* (in the sense of desire) and *stamina,* could fit, but stamina is more closely related to strength. In the second blank, eliminate words that don't match *fatigue,* and *weariness* is left over. Correct answers: Choices (C) and (D).

3. Although dismayed by the pejorative comments made about her inappropriate dress at the diplomatic function, Judy (i) _____ her tears and showed only the most calm and (ii) _____ visage to her critics.

Blank (i)	Blank (ii)
Ⓐ suppressed ✓	Ⓓ incensed
Ⓑ monitored	Ⓔ articulate
Ⓒ succumbed to	Ⓕ placid ✓

If Judy had a calm and (something) *visage* (a form of the word *vision*; a countenance, or facial expression), the (something) must go hand in hand with *calm*. Although the second word doesn't have to be an exact synonym, it can't be an antonym, either. Look for a word that means calm. *Placid* means calm and tranquil, from the root *plac*, meaning peace (as in *placate*). Check the remaining two choices in the second column: *Incensed* means burning mad (think of burning incense); *articulate* means well-spoken. Her visage (or facial expression) would not be well-spoken, although Judy herself may be, so cross off *articulate*. *Placid* is therefore best for the second word, so now find something suitable for the first word. *Monitoring* or *succumbing to* (giving in to) her tears is unlikely to make Judy appear calm and placid, but *suppressing* her tears will. The correct answers are Choices (A) and (F).

4. There are employees who pontificate on the (i) _____ work opportunities in this industry. However, many forward-thinking professionals insist that these employees don't speak for most of the workforce who believe in the (ii) _____ of the industry and the (iii) _____ of its future.

Blank (i)	Blank (ii)	Blank (iii)
Ⓐ enhanced	Ⓓ resilience ✓	Ⓖ morbidity
Ⓑ diminished ✓	Ⓔ chaos	Ⓗ security ✓
Ⓒ seasonal	Ⓕ generosity	Ⓘ lampoon

The employees could *pontificate* (comment) on any kind of work opportunities (good, bad, medium) in the industry, so find the other missing words first. The forward-thinking professionals would have a positive perspective, so the workforce believes in something *positive* about both the industry and its future, taking care of the second and third missing words. In the second column, rule out *chaos* (confusion and disorganization), because it's not positive, and *generosity* (charitableness), because though positive, it doesn't necessarily lead to a *positive* future. *Resilience* (the ability to recover) is the remaining choice there. As for the third word, *lampoon* means mockery, and *morbidity* (desperation) conveys a negative tone, so eliminate those choices and choose *security*, which describes a positive future state. Now for the first missing word: The continuing transition *however* tells you that this phrase is the opposite of the other phrases, so it's *negative*. Cross off *enhanced* and *seasonal*, neither of which matches *negative*, for the remaining word *diminished*. The correct answers are Choices (B), (D), and (H).

5. Although often writing of (i) _____ activities, Emily Dickinson possessed the faculty of creating an eclectic group of characters ranging from the *reticent* to the epitome of (ii) _____.

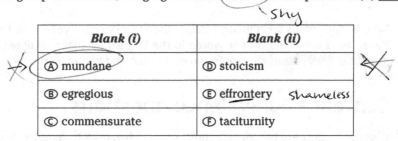

Blank (i)	Blank (ii)
Ⓐ mundane	Ⓓ stoicism
Ⓑ egregious	Ⓔ effrontery *shameless*
Ⓒ commensurate	Ⓕ taciturnity

If you know that *reticent* means shy and holding back, you know from the expression "from . . . to" that the second blank must be the opposite, something bold and forward. *Effrontery* is shameless boldness and audacity. You have *effrontery* when you ask your boss for a raise right after he or she chews you out for bungling a project. *Effrontery* is the only word that fits the second blank. *Taciturnity* is the noun form of the word *taciturn*, meaning quiet, not talkative or forward. *Stoicism* is not showing feelings or pain.

Also, the contrasting transition *although* tells you that the first blank must be the opposite of *eclectic*, which means from multiple sources or, in this case, diverse. *Mundane* means common, which is a good opposite of eclectic. Mundane activities are day-to-day tasks, nothing exciting like winning a lottery or visiting Antarctica. *Egregious* means terrible or flagrant. An egregious mistake is right out there for the world to see, not nearly the opposite of eclectic, so you can eliminate it. *Commensurate* means equivalent to or proportionate (your score on this section is commensurate to your vocabulary); again, this word isn't an opposite of eclectic, so cross it off the list. The correct answers are Choices (A) and (E).

6. Unwilling to be labeled _____, the researcher slowly and meticulously double-checked each fact before expounding upon her theory to her colleagues at the convention.

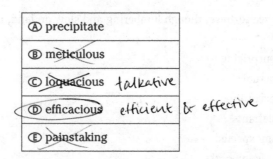

Ⓐ precipitate
Ⓑ meticulous
Ⓒ loquacious   *talkative*
Ⓓ efficacious   *efficient & effective*
Ⓔ painstaking

First, break the sentence into two parts at the comma. Using the word *unwilling* in the first part, you know that the second part is going to be the opposite meaning of the word required to complete the first part. Now work from the second part back. The gist of the second part is that the researcher is being careful, so now all you need to do is eliminate the words that don't mean *careless*.

Loquacious means overly talkative, a label that the researcher may want to avoid, but that has little relevance to preparing her theory. *Meticulous* and *painstaking* mean careful with detail, paying close attention, so they're both the opposite of what you're looking for. *Efficacious* means efficient and effective, which the researcher *does* want to be labeled.

Precipitate means overly quick, leaping before looking, and is the only word you can't readily cross off. Correct answer: Choice (A).

Even if these words seem totally foreign, they're all words I've seen on the GRE quite a few times. Never mind the millions or so words in the English language — the GRE uses the same bunch again and again. Study the words you encounter, and you're on the right track.

Sentence Equivalence questions

Directions: Select the two answer choices that, when used to complete the sentence, fit the meaning as a whole and produce two completed sentences that are alike in meaning.

7. A successful business-process _____ designed to streamline existing operations will, by its nature, also support the company's strategic planning.

   A reaction
   B management
   C innovation ←
   D initiative ←
   E supply chain
   F method ←

   Is this business-process thing a new event or ongoing? That it's designed to affect "existing operations" tells you that it doesn't currently exist and is therefore new. Look for words that suggest an early phase of development. *Reaction* obviously doesn't fit. *Management* and *supply chain* are business-sounding words that don't suggest anything new. *Method* also isn't distinctly new (a method could have been around for a while). The words *innovation* and *initiative* suggest something in the early stages of development. The correct answers are Choices (C) and (D).

8. The sea tortoise, though lumbering and slow on land, moves with _____ speed and agility in water.

   A surprising ←
   B actual
   C according
   D defiant
   E unexpected ←
   F unequivocal

   If the tortoise is lumbering and slow on land, wouldn't you expect it to be slow in water, too? The crocodile, for example, is fast and nimble in either environment (which can be bad news). In this sentence, however, the transition word *though* tells you that the tortoise's speed and agility in water is a surprise. The words *actual, according, defiant,* and **unequivocal** (straightforward) don't suggest any sort of surprise. The correct answers are Choices (A) and (E).

9. The speaker _____ the very point he had stood up to make and hurriedly sat down, hoping no one had caught his solecism.

[A] prognosticated

[B] divulged

[C] refuted

[D] countered

[E] duplicated

[F] ferreted out

A *solecism* is an inconsistency, such as a mistake. From the context of the sentence, you can gather that something negative happened because the speaker hoped no one had noticed it. Sounds like the speaker had contradicted himself. Now review and eliminate wrong answers:

To *prognosticate* is to predict, which is out. *Divulge,* meaning to reveal, is also out. To *ferret out* is to search diligently, and you know what *duplicate* is, both of which don't work, leaving *refute* (disprove) and *counter* (contradict), similar enough to produce sentences alike in meaning. The correct answers are Choices (C) and (D).

10. Dismayed by the _____ evidence available to her, the defense attorney spent her own money to hire a private investigator to acquire additional evidence.

[A] dearth of

[B] scanty

[C] vestigial

[D] immense

[E] concrete

[F] impartial

Predict words to fit in the blanks. If the attorney is dismayed by the evidence and hires an investigator to get *more* evidence, she must not have had much evidence to begin with. *Vestigial* means functionless, *immense* means large, *concrete,* in this context, means irrefutable, and *impartial* means neutral, which has nothing to do with the amount of evidence.

What remain are *scanty,* meaning barely sufficient, and *dearth of,* meaning lack of, both of which match the meaning of the sentence and each other. So the correct answers are Choices (A) and (B).

11. Rather than be decadent, the actor adopted an _____ lifestyle to help him focus on the professional side of his work.

[A] austere

[B] anachronous

[C] ascetic

[D] assiduous

[E] abject

[F] avaricious

The actor could have adopted any kind of lifestyle, but look for a meaning that indicates the opposite of decadent. *Anachronous* describes something out of the proper time, as if Robin Hood had a flashlight. *Avaricious* means greedy, so that's definitely out. *Assiduous* means hardworking, which may also describe the actor, but you need a word that's the opposite of decadent, and has a synonym in the list. *Abject* means miserable or wretched, which may also be true, but it doesn't fit the opposite of decadent.

Austere and *ascetic* both describe one who practices self-denial, so these surviving words match each other and fit the sentence. The correct answers are Choices (A) and (C).

WARNING

Assiduous (hardworking) is a trap answer. It fits both the meaning of the sentence and your assessment of the actor: He certainly is hardworking. But it doesn't go with the *self-denial* words, and it doesn't have a match. If you find a perfect word that doesn't have a match, you've found a trap answer.

TIP

A trap answer may still have a trap match, so don't rely only on the presence of a synonym to tell whether the answer is correct. Instead, when filling the missing word with your own meaning, *stick with the meaning that you picked.*

12. A fearless countenance may only belie a(n) _____ affect. *attitude*

   A. artless *false front*
   B. contentious
   C. craven *true respect*
   D. deferent *insincere*
   E. mealymouthed
   F. pusillanimous

   fearful

REMEMBER

This is an example of Sentence Equivalence questions being simpler to interpret but having challenging vocab, both to choose from and in the sentence. *Countenance* means facial expression, while *belie* means to put up a false front (think *lie* in *belie*). *Affect* as a noun means attitude (not to be confused with *effect* as a noun, which means result). So you're looking for a word that means the opposite of fearless, say, *fearful.*

Artless means honest and natural, which may be the face behind a pretense, but you're looking for fearful. *Contentious* describes someone willing to take a stand, which may be this posturing person, but it, too, doesn't mean fearful. *Deferent* means giving in out of respect for another, and *mealymouthed* means insincere, which may refer to the pretense but wouldn't be behind it.

What's left are *craven* and *pusillanimous*, both synonyms for fearful, so the correct answers are Choices (C) and (F).

13. Inspired by their leader's diatribe, the protestors took it upon themselves to continue the _____. *violent dialogue*

   A. tirade
   B. diffidence
   C. harangue
   D. hyperbole
   E. euphemism
   F. equivocation

A *diatribe* is a poignant verbal attack, so the protestors could only continue with their own diatribes. *Tirade* and *harangue* are synonyms for *diatribe*, making the correct answers Choices (A) and (C).

Diffidence refers to a lack of confidence. *Hyperbole* is an exaggeration, *euphemism* is the use of gentle words in place of intense language, and *equivocation* is the use of intentionally vague language.

14. The welfare system, designed to help the _____, is in dire need of reform.

[A] indigent _–destitute_

[B] mendacious

[C] mendicant _– dishonest_ _destitute_

[D] misanthropic _— antisocial_

[E] morose

[F] quiescent _at rest_

indigent } _poor & destitute_
medicant }

The welfare system was designed to help the poor or destitute. *Indigent* and *mendicant* are synonyms for *destitute*, making the correct answers Choices (A) and (C).

Mendacious means dishonest, *misanthropic* means antisocial, *morose* means sullen, and *quiescent* means at rest.

15. As a rule, the company hires only _____ engineers, believing years of experience tend to jade engineers and blind them to new ideas.

[A] felicitous _→ suitable_

[B] fledgling ←

[C] gregarious

[D] insensible

[E] ingenuous

[F] neophyte

If the company wants only inexperienced engineers, then the engineers would have to be beginners or novices. *Fledgling* and *neophyte* fit this meaning, making the correct answers Choices (B) and (F).

Felicitous means suitable or appropriate, which may be true of the desired engineers but doesn't support the sentence's meaning of hiring novices. *Gregarious* means sociable and outgoing, which is also possibly true of the new hires but again doesn't support the sentence's meaning. *Insensible* means unresponsive. *Ingenuous* means naive and trusting, which is close, but a company wouldn't necessarily look to hire someone who is naive.

16. Many _____ social media hacks continue to aver countless half-truths, despite ample evidence to the contrary.

support

[A] dissonant

[B] doctrinaire _– biased_

[C] dogmatic _–_

[D] ebullient _–_

[E] eclectic _– weird_

[F] erudite _– wise_

Aver means to declare something to be true. If these hacks declare half-truths to be true despite the contrary evidence, then they're ignoring the evidence. *Doctrinaire* and *dogmatic* fit this meaning, making the correct answers Choices (B) and (C).

Dissonant means ill-fitting, which may be true of the hacks but doesn't address their aversion to the evidence. *Ebullient* means buoyant in disposition, which also doesn't fit. *Eclectic* means derived from various sources, and *erudite* means educated.

17. The buffalo, once _____ to this area, has been hunted nearly to extinction.

- (A) endemic
- (B) indigenous
- (C) quintessential
- (D) truculent
- (E) veracious
- (F) viable

The buffalo must have originated and lived in the area. *Endemic* and *indigenous* fit this meaning, making the correct answers Choices (A) and (B).

Quintessential refers to a perfect state, *truculent* means displaying poor behavior, *veracious* means truthful and accurate, and *viable* means practical.

18. The _____ spares no time for a cordial gesture.

- (A) stolid   *blunt*
- (B) wistful
- (C) consummate
- (D) contrite
- (E) coy
- (F) stoic

a nice thing

You know that the sentence is talking about a person, because only a person spares time. *Cordial* refers to an effort to be friendly.

What kind of person would not spare time to be friendly? One who is emotionless, such as a *stolid* or a *stoic*. The correct answers are Choices (A) and (F).

Wistful means regretful and *consummate* means complete and perfect, neither of which is the case here. *Contrite* refers to one who is filled with sorrow for a wrongdoing, and *coy* means shy or modest.

19. A talent for easy conversation can help one build relationships, but too much can make one appear _____ and have the opposite effect.

- (A) abstruse   *not easily understood*
- (B) garrulous   *nerdy; too talkative*
- (C) loquacious
- (D) lachrymose
- (E) gregarious
- (F) recondite — *not easily understood*

If too much conversation can be bad, then find words that mean too talkative. *Garrulous* and *loquacious* refer to one who talks too much, in a bad way, so Choices (B) and (C) are correct.

Abstruse and *recondite* refer to one who isn't easily understood, and they wouldn't necessarily have the ill effect of talking too much. *Lachrymose* means tearful, which is certainly not the case here. *Gregarious* refers to one who is social and outgoing — also talkative, but in a good way.

Gregarious is another type of trap answer, but its giveaway is that it has a *positive* connotation, as a social connector. *Garrulous* and *loquacious* have a *negative* connotation, as in a nuisance.

20. Beneath the _____, the man is something else entirely.

   A disingenuousness
   B divergence
   C exculpation – *not guilty*
   D superciliousness – *arrogant*
   E superfluity
   F veneer

   false front

   false front

If the man is something else, then he puts up a false front, so *disingenuousness* and *veneer* both accurately describe what is in front of this person. The correct answers are Choices (A) and (F).

Divergence refers to straying away from the main point of a discussion. *Exculpation* means no longer considered guilty. *Superciliousness* would refer to someone who is arrogant. *Superfluity* refers to someone or something that's extraneous.

Chapter **6**

Getting the Gist: Reading Comprehension

Reading Comprehension questions on the GRE comprise about half of the Verbal questions and therefore about half of your Verbal score. Each question concerns a single passage that is sort of like a graduate-level journal article on a science, social sciences, or humanities topic that you've probably never considered before and never will again.

Each Verbal section contains about four Reading Comprehension passages, each having one to four questions. The computer screen is split, with the passage on the left and a question on the right. You get the questions one at a time while the passage stays in place.

This chapter introduces the three Reading Comprehension question formats, presents strategies for identifying the correct answers quickly, and provides some sample passages along with questions and answers so you know what to expect on the test.

REMEMBER

All Reading Comprehension questions are based directly on what's in the passage. To answer the questions, you don't need to know anything about the topic beyond what's in the passage. If you're familiar with the topic, use this to help you understand the passage, but don't mix in your own knowledge with what you read.

Recognizing the Three Reading Comprehension Question Formats

Being familiar with the question formats for the Reading Comprehension section helps you field the questions more confidently, because you know what to expect. The GRE presents each question in one of the following three formats:

» **Multiple-choice:** Choose one answer only.

» **Multiple-choice:** Choose one or more answers.

» **Sentence-selection:** Choose a sentence from the passage.

The following sections describe each question format in greater detail and provide an example of each format based on the following short passage from *Food Allergies For Dummies* by Robert A. Wood, MD, with Joe Kraynak (Wiley):

> Anaphylaxis resulting in death is relatively uncommon among children and young adults, because their cardiovascular systems are so resilient. This does not mean, however, that younger people are immune to severe anaphylaxis. Anaphylaxis in younger people typically results in breathing difficulty — a constricted or blocked airway that causes a fatal or near fatal reaction.

Multiple-choice questions: Choose one answer

The following format is the traditional multiple-choice question. You get five answers to choose from, and only one is correct.

PLAY

Based on the passage, how common is anaphylaxis that results in death in children and young adults?

Ⓐ Very common

Ⓑ Relatively uncommon

Ⓒ Practically nonexistent

Ⓓ In theory only

Ⓔ Not stated in the passage

You pick one and only one answer. In this case, the correct answer is Choice (B), because the first sentence directly answers the question.

Multiple-choice questions: Choose one or more answers

The next question format is a spin on the traditional multiple-choice question. Three choices follow the question, and one, two, or all three of them are correct. You must pick *all* of the correct choices and no incorrect choices to receive credit for your answer. You don't receive partial credit for picking only some of the correct answers. The GRE treats a partially answered question as a wrong answer.

PLAY

When anaphylaxis occurs in a child or young adult, what happens? Consider each of the three choices separately and select all that apply.

Ⓐ Breathing difficulty

Ⓑ Blocked airway

Ⓒ Result of a bee sting

You pick all answers that are correct. In this case, Choices (A) and (B) are correct.

TIP

You can quickly tell whether to select only one answer or more than one answer by looking at the instruction that accompanies the question: The GRE always instructs you to choose either *one* or *all answers that apply*. Also, the selection bubbles near the answer choices are ovals to select one answer or squares to select multiple answers.

Sentence-selection questions: Choose a sentence from the passage

In sentence-selection questions, the GRE presents a description or question followed by instructions to click the sentence in the passage that most closely matches the description or answers the question. Clicking any part of the sentence selects the entire sentence.

PLAY

Choose the sentence in the passage that parents of young children are likely to find most reassuring.

In the passage, you click the answer sentence, and it highlights on the screen, like this:

> **Anaphylaxis resulting in death is relatively uncommon among children and young adults, because their cardiovascular systems are so resilient.** This does not mean, however, that younger people are immune to severe anaphylaxis. Anaphylaxis in younger people typically results in breathing difficulty — a constricted or blocked airway that causes a fatal or near fatal reaction. In a fatal reaction, the heart stops only because the body eventually runs out of oxygen.

The other sentences in the passage may not be so reassuring to parents of young children.

Developing Strategies for Success

Reading Comprehension questions can be the most time-consuming questions of the Verbal section. The best way to ace these questions is to master and use strategies for quickly reading the passages, identifying key facts called for in the questions, and drawing inferences based on subtle implications. Ask yourself the purpose of the passage: Why is the author writing this? The following sections explain four useful strategies for effectively and efficiently arriving at the correct answers (and avoiding incorrect answers).

TIP

The best way to master reading comprehension — meaning you can read the passage quickly and understand it on all its levels — is through *practice*. Make these graduate-level paragraphs something you read before breakfast, not something you force yourself through every few weeks. They don't have to be GRE examples, but mobile clips from Facebook and LinkedIn don't bring your reading skills up to par. Instead, practice reading *The Economist, Financial Times, Wall Street Journal, New Yorker,* or any number of intellectual publications on a topic you're interested in, maybe even in your field of study.

Using the context as your road map

Read the passage lightly and get a general idea of where the key information is and what is going on in the passage. This helps you figure out where to find the information as you begin to answer questions. *Remember:* Don't sweat the details (yet). After reading a question, you can quickly revisit the passage to locate the details for answering the question correctly.

TIP

Usually, the first paragraph or sentence and/or the last paragraph or sentence tells you what the passage is about (the main idea). The rest of the passage supports or develops this idea. As you read each body paragraph, pay attention to its purpose and how it supports the main idea. This is a key strategy to understanding the passage, and it becomes almost a habit with practice.

REMEMBER

Sometimes the entire passage is one giant paragraph. Don't let that deter you from using this strategy. Look for where one idea ends and another begins and treat that as where the paragraphs should be separated. This can help you map the details as you would for a passage that is actually in separate paragraphs.

Grasping the gist of the passage

Understanding the main idea of the passage is the key to establishing the context of the paragraphs within. The main idea is typically the basis of one of the questions. If you can briefly sum up *why* the author is writing the passage, then you've not only developed a contextual understanding of the passage, but also answered one of the questions ahead of time.

Avoiding common traps

The folks who write the GRE are a tricky lot. They bait you with wrong but tempting answers, hoping you'll bite. By recognizing these common traps, you have a better chance of avoiding them. Here are a few to watch out for:

>> **Mixing the main idea with details:** Questions asking the main idea or primary purpose of the passage have answer choices that are true but aren't the main idea. These are trap answers. For example, a passage may describe light pollution from cars or streetlights that obscures stars at night. The main idea isn't the car headlights or streetlights: It's the overall effect on nighttime visibility.

TIP

Double-check the first and last sentences. Is the author asking for increased funding or a course of action? Is the passage challenging a common notion? If you know *why* the author is writing this, you'll know the primary purpose of the passage and not be distracted by detail answers.

One strategy is to work main idea or primary purpose questions last, especially with a long Reading Comprehension passage. Because you can go back and forth through the questions, you can work them in any order. As you answer the detail questions, you learn more about the main idea; then you can go back and answer that main idea question. Just don't *forget* it and move forward, leaving that question unanswered.

>> **Mixing cause-and-effect relationships:** Answer choices typically mix up the cause-and-effect relationships of details in the passage. If the tide comes in because of the moon, for example, and this causes all the ships to rise, the question will check your understanding of what caused what to happen.

TIP

Skim the passage for key words relating to the cause-and-effect described in the question. From the preceding example, look for the words *moon, tide,* and *ships.* Find the discussion of these events, and make sure the answer choice reflects the events discussed in the passage.

>> **Mixing in your own knowledge:** You may know something about the topic at hand. If you're like most people, you add detail based on your own knowledge and expertise from other things that you've read. Sometimes, these details tempt you to choose an answer that's true by your understanding but wrong per the passage. Be careful not to mix your own knowledge with what's in the passage.

WARNING

I had a student who was a chemistry major work on a Reading Comp passage on chemistry, and she vehemently disagreed with what was in the passage. She was probably right — but she got all the questions wrong, based on what she *thought* it should be instead of what the passage said.

TIP

If you're familiar with the topic, that's a good thing: You'll understand the passage better than the other test-takers. However, the passage may take a break from reality, so just take what it says with a grain of salt. Note the differences, but don't challenge the passage. Instead, go along with its fantasy story and get all the questions right.

Answering the question yourself

One good way to dodge the answer-choice traps is to answer the question yourself first, before looking at the answer choices. Get a sense of what the right answer *should be*, then eliminate the wrong answer choices.

The right answer won't match your own answer. That's okay, it doesn't have to. What it does is make the *wrong* answers clearly stand out, so that you can take them out of the running and focus on what remains. With a sense of what the right answer *should* be, four answers will stand out as *not a chance* and one will stand out as *maybe*. Go with the *maybe:* You can always return to it later.

WARNING

Don't change your own answer based on the answer choices! Don't think, "maybe it's *that.*" I've had students do this, and it defeats the whole strategy. You're sharp, you get it, you know what the answer choice should look like — so trust yourself! Besides, four of the answer choices are dead wrong, so why would you change your own answer to match one of those?

Acing the Three Commonly Tested Reading Comprehension Passages

Reading Comprehension passages are typically based on either biological and physical sciences, social sciences, or humanities. Each of the following sections explains one passage type; presents a passage of that type along with sample questions, answers, and explanations to get you up to speed; and provides additional guidance and tips for successfully answering each question. Note that some GRE passages have fewer paragraphs than the examples shown here.

The biological and physical science passage

A biological or physical science passage is straightforward, giving you the scoop on something. It may be how stellar dust is affected by gravity, how to build a suspension bridge, or how molecular theory applies. The passage may be difficult to get through (because it goes into depth on an unfamiliar subject), so read it quickly for the gist and go back later for the details.

REMEMBER

When approaching biological and physical science passages, don't get hung up on the scientific terminology. Just accept these terms as part of the story and keep reading. The terms may function as key words to help you locate the answers within the passage even if you don't know what the terms mean.

Here's a science passage for you to practice on. Don't forget to check the introduction paragraph for the overall gist of the passage and to look for the high-level contribution of each paragraph. If you know each paragraph's purpose, you can quickly find the details when you need them.

> Microbiological activity clearly affects the mechanical strength of leaves. Although it cannot be denied that with most species the loss of mechanical strength is the result of both invertebrate feeding and microbiological breakdown, the example of *Fagus sylvatica* illustrates loss without any

sign of invertebrate attack being evident. *Fagus* shows little sign of invertebrate attack even after being exposed for eight months in either a lake or stream environment, but results of the rolling fragmentation experiment show that loss of mechanical strength, even in this apparently resistant species, is considerable.

Most species appear to exhibit a higher rate of degradation in the stream environment than in the lake. This is perhaps most clearly shown in the case of *Alnus.* Examination of the type of destruction suggests that the cause for the greater loss of material in the stream-processed leaves is a combination of both biological and mechanical degradation. The leaves exhibit an angular fragmentation, which is characteristic of mechanical damage, rather than the rounded holes typical of the attack by large particle feeders or the skeletal vein pattern produced by microbial degradation and small particle feeders. As the leaves become less strong, the fluid forces acting on the stream nylon cages cause successively greater fragmentation.

Mechanical fragmentation, like biological breakdown, is to some extent influenced by leaf structure and form. In some leaves with a strong midrib, the lamina breaks up, but the pieces remain attached by means of the midrib. One type of leaf may break cleanly, whereas another tears off and is easily destroyed after the tissues are weakened by microbial attack.

In most species, the mechanical breakdown will take the form of gradual attrition at the margins. If the energy of the environment is sufficiently high, brittle species may be broken across the midrib, something that rarely happens with more pliable leaves. The result of attrition is that where the areas of the whole leaves follow a normal distribution, a bimodal distribution is produced, one peak composed mainly of the fragmented pieces, the other of the larger remains.

To test the theory that a thin leaf has only half the chance of a thick one for entering the fossil record, all other things being equal, Ferguson (1971) cut discs of fresh leaves from 11 species of leaves, each with a different thickness, and rotated them with sand and water in a revolving drum. Each run lasted 100 hours and was repeated three times, but even after this treatment, all species showed little sign of wear. It therefore seems unlikely that leaf thickness alone, without substantial microbial preconditioning, contributes much to the probability that a leaf will enter a depositional environment in a recognizable form. The results of experiments with whole fresh leaves show that they are more resistant to fragmentation than leaves exposed to microbiological attack. Unless the leaf is exceptionally large or small, leaf size and thickness are not likely to be as critical in determining the preservation potential of a leaf type as the rate of microbiological degradation.

PLAY

1. The passage is primarily concerned with

    Ⓐ Why leaves disintegrate

    Ⓑ An analysis of leaf structure and composition

    Ⓒ Comparing lakes and streams

    Ⓓ The purpose of particle feeders

    Ⓔ How leaves' mechanical strength is affected by microbiological activity

The passage reads primarily about leaves, making that its primary concern, so eliminate Choices (C) and (D) right off. Choice (A) is too broad, as other causes of disintegration may exist that the passage doesn't mention. Choice (B) is too specific: The passage mentions leaf structure, but not as its primary focus. Correct answer: Choice (E).

2. Which of the following is mentioned as a reason for leaf degradation in streams? Consider each of the three choices separately and select all that apply.

    Ⓐ Mechanical damage

    Ⓑ Biological degradation

    Ⓒ Large particle feeders

The second paragraph of the passage tells you that "loss of material in stream-processed leaves is a combination of biological and mechanical degradation." Choice (C) is incorrect because the passage specifically states that the pattern of holes is contrary to that of large particle feeders. The correct answers are Choices (A) and (B).

3. The conclusion that the author reached from Ferguson's revolving drum experiment was that

 Ⓐ Leaf thickness is only a contributing factor to leaf fragmentation.

 Ⓑ Leaves submerged in water degrade more rapidly than leaves deposited in mud or silt.

 Ⓒ Leaves with a strong midrib deteriorate less than leaves without such a midrib.

 Ⓓ Microbial attack is made worse by high temperatures.

 Ⓔ Bimodal distribution reduces leaf attrition.

The middle of the last paragraph tells you that leaf thickness *alone* is unlikely to affect the final form of the leaf. You probably need to reread that sentence a few times to get past the jargon, but a detail or fact question is the type of question you should be sure to answer correctly. Choice (B) introduces facts not discussed in the passage; the passage doesn't talk of leaves in mud or silt. Choice (C) is mentioned in the passage but not in Ferguson's experiments.

Nothing about high temperatures appears in the passage, which eliminates Choice (D). Choice (E) sounds pretentious and pompous — and nice and scientific — but has nothing to do with Ferguson. To answer this question correctly, you need to return to the passage to look up Ferguson specifically, not merely rely on your memory of the passage as a whole. Correct answer: Choice (A).

WARNING

Be careful to answer *only* what the question is asking. Answer-choice traps include statements that are true but don't answer the question.

4. The tone of the passage is

 Ⓐ Persuasive

 Ⓑ Biased

 Ⓒ Objective

 Ⓓ Argumentative

 Ⓔ Disparaging

The passage is hardly persuasive; it isn't really trying to change your opinion on an issue. It objectively presents scientific facts and experimental evidence. Because you know the gist of the passage and the context of each paragraph, the answer is obvious. Correct answer: Choice (C).

5. Select the sentence in the fourth paragraph that explains the form of mechanical breakdown of most species of leaves.

Skim for key words to answer this question. The first and only place *mechanical breakdown* is mentioned is in the first sentence of the fourth paragraph. Correct answer: "In most species, the mechanical breakdown will take the form of gradual attrition at the margins."

6. Which would be an example of "energy of the environment" (fourth paragraph, second sentence)?

 Ⓐ Wind and rain

 Ⓑ Sunlight

 Ⓒ Animals that eat leaves

 Ⓓ Lumberjacks

 Ⓔ Fuel that may be harvested

The passage is about the degradation of leaves, which you already know. The fourth paragraph discusses factors that may break a brittle leaf across its center, or midrib. Sunlight may do this, but it wouldn't necessarily target the midrib, so out with Choice (B). Animals would digest the leaves such that the leaves wouldn't degrade, so no more Choice (C). Lumberjacks may leave leaves behind (so to speak), but the passage is all about natural factors, so down with Choice (D). Finally, there's nothing about harvesting fuel, so Choice (E) is out. This leaves Choice (A), wind and rain, which makes sense. The wind and rain physically affect the leaf and both cause degradation and breaking along its weak point, the midrib. Correct answer: Choice (A).

The social sciences passage

The GRE usually includes a social sciences passage about history, psychology, business, or a variety of other topics. If the social sciences passage offers a perspective on a subject that you may already be familiar with, you can use your understanding of the subject as a backdrop to make the passage easier to read and understand.

TIP

Within each section, you can work the passages in any order. If you find that you prefer a social sciences passage over a biological or physical science passage, you can work the passage you prefer first.

Here's a social sciences passage. Though you need to read the passage more carefully, the underlying strategy is the same: Look for the gist of the passage, usually in the first paragraph, and identify the purpose of each paragraph thereafter. You'll still need to revisit these paragraphs to find details, so knowing where the details are located is easier and more useful than memorizing them.

Multinational corporations frequently encounter impediments in their attempts to explain to politicians, human rights groups, and (perhaps most importantly) their consumer base why they do business with, and even seek closer business ties to, countries whose human rights records are considered heinous by United States standards. The CEOs propound that in the business trenches, the issue of human rights must effectively be detached from the wider spectrum of free trade. Discussion of the uneasy alliance between trade and human rights has trickled down from the boardrooms of large multinational corporations to the consumer on the street who, given the wide variety of products available to him, is eager to show support for human rights by boycotting the products of a company he feels does not do enough to help its overseas workers. International human rights organizations also are pressuring the multinationals to push for more humane working conditions in other countries and to, in effect, develop a code of business conduct that must be adhered to if the American company is to continue working with the overseas partner.

The president, in drawing up a plan for what he calls the "economic architecture of our times," wants economists, business leaders, and human rights groups to work together to develop a set of principles that the foreign partners of United States corporations will voluntarily embrace. Human rights activists, incensed at the nebulous plans for implementing such rules, charge that their agenda is being given low priority by the State Department. The president vociferously denies their charges, arguing that each situation is approached on its merits without prejudice, and hopes that all the groups can work together to develop principles based on empirical research rather than political fiat, emphasizing that the businesses with experience in the field must initiate the process of developing such guidelines. Business leaders, while paying lip service to the concept of these principles, fight stealthily against their formal endorsement because they fear such "voluntary" concepts may someday be given the force of law. Few business leaders have forgotten the Sullivan Principles, in which a set of voluntary rules regarding business conduct with South Africa (giving benefits to workers and banning apartheid in the companies that worked with U.S. partners) became legislation.

7. Which of the following best states the central idea of the passage?

Ⓐ Politicians are quixotic in their assessment of the priorities of the State Department.

Ⓑ Multinational corporations have little if any influence on the domestic policies of their overseas partners.

Ⓒ Voluntary principles that are turned into law are unconstitutional.

Ⓓ Disagreement exists between the desires of human rights activists to improve the working conditions of overseas workers and the pragmatic approach taken by the corporations.

Ⓔ It is inappropriate to expect foreign corporations to adhere to American standards.

In Choice (A), the word *quixotic* means idealistic or impractical. The word comes from the fictional character Don Quixote, who tilted at windmills. (*Tilting* refers to a knight on horseback tilting his joust toward a target for the purpose of attack.) Although the president in this passage may not be realistic in his assessment of State Department policies, his belief isn't the main idea of the passage.

Choice (E) is a value judgment. An answer that passes judgment, saying something is right or wrong, better or worse, or more or less appropriate (as in this case), is almost never the correct answer.

The main idea of any passage is usually stated in the first sentence or two. The first sentence of this passage touches on the difficulties that corporations have in explaining their business ties with certain countries to politicians, human rights groups, and consumers. From this statement, you may infer that those groups disagree with the policies of the corporations. Correct answer: Choice (D).

TIP

Just because a statement is true doesn't necessarily mean it's the correct answer to the question, especially a main idea question. All the answer choices are typically true statements, though only one is the main idea.

8. According to the passage, the president wants the voluntary principles to be initiated by businesses rather than by politicians or human rights activists because

Ⓐ Businesses have empirical experience in the field and thus know what the conditions are and how they may/should be remedied.

Ⓑ Businesses make profits from the labor of the workers and thus have a moral obligation to improve their employees' working conditions.

Ⓒ Workers will not accept principles drawn up by politicians whom they distrust but may agree to principles created by the corporations that pay them.

Ⓓ Foreign nations are distrustful of U.S. political intervention and are more likely to accept suggestions from multinational corporations.

Ⓔ Political activist groups have concerns that are too dramatically different from those of the corporations for the groups to be able to work together.

TIP

When a question begins with the words *according to the passage*, you need to go back to the passage and find the answer. *Empirical* is the key word here, buried in the middle of the second paragraph.

Find the word and read the sentence, and you've found the answer: "The president vociferously denies their charges, arguing that each situation is approached on its merits without prejudice, and hopes that all the groups can work together to develop principles based on *empirical research* rather than political fiat, emphasizing that the *businesses with experience in the field must initiate the process* of developing such guidelines." You don't even need to know what *empirical* (derived from observation or experiment) means. The reasoning of Choices (B), (C), (D), and (E) isn't stated in the passage. Correct answer: Choice (A).

9. Select the sentence from the second paragraph that describes the human rights activists' response to the president's plan.

The passage contains only one mention of *human rights activists*, and it appears in the second sentence of the second paragraph. So the correct answer is "Human rights activists, incensed at the nebulous plans for implementing such rules, charge that their agenda is being given low priority by the State Department."

10. Which of the following is a reason the author mentions the boycott of a corporation's products by its customers? Consider each of the three choices separately and select all that apply.

   A To show the difficulties that arise when corporations attempt to become involved in politics

   B To suggest the possibility of failure of any plan that does not account for the customer's perspective

   C To indicate the pressures that are on the multinational corporations

Choice (A) makes a valid point. Difficulties may arise when corporations attempt to become involved in politics. However, the passage doesn't give that as a reason for a boycott, so Choice (A) is wrong. Choice (B) seems logical because a company that ignores its customers will probably fail. The passage mentions corporate communications with customers in the first sentence but not the customer's perspective, so Choice (B) is wrong. Choice (C) is also true, because according to the passage, multinational corporations run the risk of alienating any group and thus inciting a boycott, which is a reason given by the passage. Correct answer: Choice (C).

REMEMBER

Just because you *can* choose more than one answer doesn't mean you *have* to. (Except on Sentence Equivalence, where the instructions specifically indicate *two* answers.) These questions can have one, two, or three correct answers. Never zero, though.

11. Which of the following statements about the Sullivan Principles can best be inferred from the passage?

   Ⓐ They had a detrimental effect on the profits of those corporations doing business with South Africa.

   Ⓑ They represented an improper alliance between political and business groups.

   Ⓒ They placed the needs of the foreign workers over those of the domestic workers whose jobs would therefore be in jeopardy.

   Ⓓ They will be used as a model to create future voluntary business guidelines.

   Ⓔ They will have a chilling effect on future adoption of voluntary guidelines.

Choice (A) is the trap here. Perhaps you assumed that because the companies seem to dislike the Sullivan Principles, they hurt company profits. However, the passage says nothing about profits. Maybe the companies still made good profits but objected to the Sullivan Principles, well, on principle. The companies just may not have wanted governmental intervention, even if profits weren't decreased.

The key words to search for are *Sullivan Principles*; then read around them. The Principles appear in the last sentence, and just before that, the passage states that business leaders "*fear* such 'voluntary' concepts may someday be given the force of law." Because business leaders fear that the adoption of voluntary guidelines will lead to forced legislation, the Sullivan Principles will have a chilling effect on the future adoption of voluntary guidelines. The correct answer is Choice (E).

The humanities passage

A humanities passage may be about art, music, philosophy, drama, or literature. It typically places its subject in a positive light, especially if it's about a person who was a pioneer in his or her field, such as the first African American astronaut or the first female doctor. Use this to your advantage: If someone is worthy of mention historically or in a Reading Comprehension passage, then he or she probably was an amazing person or did something truly noteworthy. Look for this sense of admiration from the author to create the context in which to frame the passage.

REMEMBER

The humanities passages seem to be the most down-to-earth of the lot. They're easy to read, informative, and can even be enjoyable. Too bad they're rare. The approach is the same, though: Look for the gist of the passage in a few words and establish a context for the whole story and each paragraph. You can always go back for the details later.

REMEMBER

Although the passage doesn't require meticulous reading, the questions are another matter. The questions following a humanities passage often require you to get into the mind of the author in order to read between the lines and make inferences. While you're reading a passage about a particular person, for example, try to ascertain not just what the person accomplished but why this person worked toward those goals and what mark was left on the world.

Here's an example of a typical humanities passage, taken from *LSAT For Dummies* by Amy Hackney Blackwell (Wiley), about someone you've probably never heard of before but will still enjoy reading about.

Junzaburou Nishiwaki, a 20th-century Japanese poet, scholar, and translator, spent his career working to introduce Japanese readers to European and American writing and to break his country out of its literary insularity. He was interested in European culture all his life. Born to a wealthy family in rural Niigata prefecture in 1894, Nishiwaki spent his youth aspiring to be a painter and traveled to Tokyo in 1911 to study fused Japanese and European artistic traditions. After his father died in 1913, Nishiwaki studied economics at Keio University, but his real love was English literature. After graduating, he worked for several years as a reporter at the English-language *Japan Times* and as a teacher at Keio University.

Nishiwaki finally received the opportunity to concentrate on English literature in 1922, when Keio University sent him to Oxford University for three years. He spent this time reading literature in Old and Middle English and classical Greek and Latin. He became fluent in English, French, German, Latin, and Greek. While he was in England, Roaring Twenties modernism caught his eye, and the works of writers such as James Joyce, Ezra Pound, and T. S. Eliot were crucially important to his literary development. In 1925, Nishiwaki published his first book, *Spectrum,* a volume of poems written in English. He explained that English offered him much more freedom of expression than traditional Japanese poetic language.

Nishiwaki returned to Keio University in 1925 and became a professor of English literature, teaching linguistics, Old and Middle English, and the history of English literature. He remained active in modernist and avant-garde literary circles. In 1933 he published *Ambarvalia,* his first volume of poetry written in Japanese; this collection of surrealist verse ranged far and wide through European geography and history and included Japanese translations of Catullus, Sophocles, and Shakespeare. Angered by the Japanese government's fascist policies, Nishiwaki refused to write poetry during the Second World War. He spent the war years writing a dissertation on ancient Germanic literature.

After the war, Nishiwaki resumed his poetic pursuits and in 1947 published *Tabibito kaerazu,* in which he abandoned modernist language and returned to a classical Japanese poetic style but with his own postmodernist touch, incorporating both Eastern and Western literary traditions. In 1953, Nishiwaki published *Kindai no guuwa,* which critics consider his most poetically mature work. He spent his last years producing works of such writers as D. H. Lawrence, James Joyce, T. S. Eliot, Stéphane Mallarmé, Shakespeare, and Chaucer. Nishiwaki retired from Keio University in 1962, though he continued to teach and write poetry. Before his death in 1982, he received numerous honors and awards; he was appointed to the Japanese Academy of Arts and Sciences, named a Person of Cultural Merit, and nominated for the Nobel Prize by Ezra Pound. Critics today consider Nishiwaki to have exercised more influence on younger poets than any other Japanese poet since 1945.

12. Which one of the following most accurately states the main idea of the passage?

Ⓐ Nishiwaki was a Japanese poet who rebelled against the strictures of his country's government and protested its policies toward Europe during World War II.

Ⓑ Nishiwaki was a Japanese poet and literary critic who embraced European literature as a way of rebelling against the constraints of his family and traditional Japanese culture.

Ⓒ Nishiwaki was a Japanese poet and professor who spent his life trying to convince young Japanese students that European literary forms were superior to Japanese poetic styles.

Ⓓ Nishiwaki was a Japanese poet and linguist who throughout his life chose to write in English rather than Japanese.

Ⓔ Nishiwaki was a Japanese poet and scholar who spent his life specializing in European literature, which proved tremendously influential to his own work.

A process of elimination reveals the correct answer. Choice (A) is wrong: Though Nishiwaki did protest against his country's fascist policies during World War II, this fact isn't the main idea of the passage. Choice (B) is flat-out wrong: Although the first paragraph discusses Nishiwaki's departure from family and his country's literary insularity, the word *rebelling* is too harsh. Choice (C) is also wrong: The passage doesn't say that he tried to convince his students one way or the other. Choice (D) is wrong: The passage states only that his first book was in English and many others were in Japanese. Correct answer: Choice (E).

13. The author's attitude toward Nishiwaki's life and career can be best described as

Ⓐ Scholarly interest in the life and works of a significant literary figure

Ⓑ Mild surprise at Nishiwaki's choosing to write poetry in a language foreign to him

Ⓒ Open admiration for Nishiwaki's ability to function in several languages

Ⓓ Skepticism toward Nishiwaki's motives in refusing to write poetry during the Second World War

Ⓔ Envy of Nishiwaki's success in publishing and academia

Choices (B), (D), and (E) are wrong because the passage doesn't reflect surprise, skepticism, or envy. Choices (A) and (C) remain, but you can eliminate Choice (C): The passage is objective, not admiring, and Nishiwaki's multilingual ability is a supporting detail to his accomplishments. The correct answer is Choice (A).

14. The primary function of the first paragraph is to

Ⓐ Describe Nishiwaki's brief study of painting

Ⓑ Introduce Nishiwaki and his lifelong interest in European culture

Ⓒ Summarize Nishiwaki's contribution to Japanese literature

Ⓓ Explain why a Japanese man chose to specialize in English literature

Ⓔ Analyze European contributions to Japanese culture at the start of the 20th century

After rereading the first paragraph, you know that in a nutshell it introduces Nishiwaki as one who worked to bridge the literature gap separating Japan from Europe and America. It also summarizes Nishiwaki's interest in art through college and his early career years afterward. Most importantly, the first paragraph sets the stage for the rest of the essay. Armed with this perspective, only one possible answer remains: Choice (B).

15. Select the sentence in the third paragraph that explains why Nishiwaki stopped writing poetry during World War II.

Like most select-a-sentence questions, look for the correct sentence buried in the passage. Correct answer: "Angered by the Japanese government's fascist policies, Nishiwaki refused to write poetry during the Second World War."

16. The passage is primarily concerned with

Ⓐ Comparing Nishiwaki's poetry to that of other Japanese poets of the 20th century

Ⓑ Discussing the role of the avant-garde movement in Nishiwaki's writing

Ⓒ Providing a brief biography of Nishiwaki that explains the significance of his work

Ⓓ Explaining why writers can benefit from studying literature from other countries

Ⓔ Describing the transformation in Japanese poetic style during the post-war period

The key words in this question are *primarily concerned with*. The passage may suggest some of the points listed, but its *primary concern* is more explicit. Choice (A) is wrong because the author doesn't mention the work of other Japanese poets. Choice (B) is wrong because although the avant-garde movement was influential to Nishiwaki's writing, this point is hardly the primary concern. Choice (C) looks about right, but check the others just in case. Choice (D) is wrong because the author doesn't mention the benefits of studying foreign literature. Choice (E) is wrong because the passage doesn't mention changes in Japanese poetic style after the war. Correct answer: Choice (C).

17. According to the passage, which one of the following types of literature did *not* greatly interest Nishiwaki? Consider each of the three choices separately and select all that apply.

Ⓐ Old and Middle English literature such as *Beowulf* and *The Canterbury Tales*

Ⓑ Classical Greek works such as *Antigone*

Ⓒ Classical Japanese literature such as *The Tale of Genji*

From the first paragraph, you know that Nishiwaki's real love was English literature. From the second paragraph, you know that Nishiwaki spent his time at Oxford reading Old and Middle English and classical Greek and Latin. However, even though he may have had some interest in Japanese literature, it didn't *greatly* interest him as the question states. Only one correct answer: Choice (C).

18. Select the sentence in the second paragraph that explains why Nishiwaki chose to write his first published poems in English.

Though many sentences in the passage mention Nishiwaki's interest in English literature, in only one sentence does the passage provide Nishiwaki's explanation of why he chose to write his first published poems in English. Correct answer: "He explained that English offered him much more freedom of expression than traditional Japanese poetic language."

The social sciences passage redux

The previous three passages are good segues to the way the GRE thinks and phrases its questions. However, not all the passages are as *accessible* (easy) as these. Practice your chops on this challenging social sciences passage.

This passage is an excerpt from *The Wiley-Blackwell Companion to Sociology*, edited by George Ritzer (Wiley-Blackwell).

PLAY

Ritzer (2009) has recently argued that the focus on either production or consumption has always been misplaced and that all acts always involve both. That is, all acts of production and consumption are fundamentally acts of prosumption. The assembly-line worker is always consuming all sorts of things (parts, energy, tools) in the process of production, and conversely the consumer in, for example, a fast food restaurant is always producing (garnishes for a sandwich, soft drinks from the self-serve dispenser, the disposal of debris derived from the meal). This suggests a dramatic reorientation of theorizing about the economy away from production or consumption and in the direction of prosumption.

Prosumption is not only a historical reality, but it is becoming increasingly ubiquitous with the emergence on the internet of Web 2.0. Web 1.0 (e.g., AOL) typically involved sites that were created and managed by producers and used more or less passively by separable consumers. The latter not only did not produce the websites, but usually could not alter their content in any meaningful way. In contrast, Web 2.0 is defined by sites (e.g., Facebook, blogs) the contents of which are produced, wholly (blogs) or in part (Facebook), by the user. While everything about some 2.0 sites (a blog, for example) is likely produced by those who also consume them, on others (the Facebook page) the basic structure of the site is created by the producer, while all of the content comes from the consumer(s). Even though something of the distinction between producer and consumer remains in the latter case, it is clear that Web 2.0 is the paradigmatic domain of the prosumer. As the internet continues to evolve, we can expect to see more and more user-generated content and therefore an even greater role for the prosumer.

Of course, this shift to prosumption does not mean that sociological theorists should ignore production (the production end of the prosumption continuum) or consumption (the consumption end of that continuum). On the production side, there is certainly no end of issues to concern the theorist. Among others, there is David Harvey's (2005) interest in, and critique of, neoliberalism, as well as Hardt and Negri's (2000) interest in the transformation of the capitalist and proletariat into Empire and Multitude in the global age.

19. What does Ritzer argue is the difference between production and consumption?

Ⓐ Production is creating, and consuming is using.

Ⓑ Production is recent, and consumption is historical.

Ⓒ Production is permanent, and consumption is temporary.

Ⓓ They are opposite sides of the same spectrum.

Ⓔ They are not different.

In the first paragraph, Ritzer declares that "all acts always involve both" and that "all acts of production and consumption are fundamentally part of prosumption." Therefore, to Ritzer, they're part of the same spectrum. The correct choice is (D).

20. According to the passage, Unlike Web 1.0, Web 2.0 is specifically

Ⓐ Newer and therefore better

Ⓑ Fueled by content produced by the user

Ⓒ An asset to the neo-liberal market forces

Ⓓ A reflection of the distinction between the producer and the consumer

Ⓔ Designed for heavy reliance by the consumer

The second paragraph states that "Web 2.0 is defined by sites (e.g., Facebook, blogs) the contents of which are produced, wholly (blogs) or in part (Facebook), by the user," making the correct answer Choice (B).

21. According to the passage, the emergence of Web 2.0 is an example of

Ⓐ Production

Ⓑ Consumption

Ⓒ Prosumption

Ⓓ Neo-liberalism

Ⓔ Social networking

The second paragraph of Passage 1 states that "prosumption [. . .] is becoming increasingly ubiquitous with the emergence [. . .] of Web 2.0." The correct answer is Choice (C).

22. What is the primary purpose of the passage?

Ⓐ To explain the success of Web 2.0 sites such as Facebook

Ⓑ To describe the shift to prosumption and the accompanying emergence of Web 2.0

Ⓒ To portray the perspective of sociological theorists, such as Harvey, on neoliberalism

Ⓓ To depict the observation of sociological theorists, such as Hardt and Negri, on the transformation of the capitalist and proletariat into Empire and Multitude

Ⓔ To describe the inevitable path of the prosumer

The passage opens with the description of prosumption, then exemplifies it with Web 2.0, and then closes with the effects of prosumption. Though the passage mentions the topics of the other answer choices, none of these is the primary purpose of the passage, and the correct answer is Choice (B).

IN THIS CHAPTER

» Taking on Argument Analysis questions step-by-step

» Reading the passage analytically

» Honing in on what the question is asking for

» Thinking of your own answer first

» Eliminating wrong answers to find the right one

Chapter **7**

Critical Thinking: Argument Analysis Questions

You've probably heard the expression, "You can't believe everything you hear." That's what Argument Analysis is all about: challenging arguments and plans that you read in books, magazines, newspapers, and on the web; examining assertions that you see on the nightly news; and questioning claims that you hear from politicians, not to mention sales pitches. Graduate schools expect you not only to read with understanding but also to apply critical thinking to sort out what's supported by the facts and what isn't.

An *Argument Analysis* question asks you to determine what new fact strengthens, weakens, or completes the argument, along with some variations. This chapter shows you what to look for in the argument and how to approach the question and answer choices that follow it — a useful skill in day-to-day life, but this chapter is geared specifically toward the GRE take.

Expect about two Argument Analysis questions in each Verbal section. An Argument Analysis question consists of a short passage and a single question, though it may also appear as one of the Reading Comprehension questions. An argument is easy to spot because it presents a plan or a conclusion based on a set of facts.

TIP

The Argument Analysis question isn't much different from the Analyze an Argument essay. Both present a conclusion or a plan, and based on similar critical reasoning, you point out the unstated facts that would strengthen or weaken the outcome. Here you answer a question about it, and there you write an essay about it. Check out Chapter 16 for more on the Analyze an Argument essay — and when you get there, I refer you here for a refresher.

Use this five-step approach to take on an Argument Analysis question:

1. **Cover the answer choices.**
2. **Read the question for what it's asking.**
3. **Read the passage for what the question is asking.**
4. **Answer the question in your own words.**
5. **Eliminate each wrong answer.**

This chapter leads you through this five-step process and either transforms you into a critical thinker or makes you more of one.

Covering the Answer Choices

First, don't look at the answer choices. Avoiding the choices *facilitates* (eases) your ability to follow the argument, because all but one of the answer choices are wrong, and they clutter your brain with *superfluous* (nonessential) and *equivocal* (misleading) information. The wrong answer choices try to distract you, so don't let them. Instead, cover them with your hand or scratch paper.

Reading the Question for What It's Asking

Still covering the answer choices, read and understand the question so you know what to look for in the passage. The question typically asks you which answer choice does one of the following:

» Most seriously weakens the argument

» Best supports the argument

» Draws the most reasonable conclusion from the argument

» Identifies the assumption that must be true for the argument to be true

» Most accurately represents the premise on which the argument is based

The questions may not use the actual wording provided here; for example, instead of asking which choice most seriously *weakens* the argument, a question may ask which choice most effectively *undermines* (weakens) the argument. Don't get hung up on the wording — just be sure to understand what the question is looking for.

Reading the Passage for What the Question Is Asking

Now, knowing what the question is looking for, you're better equipped to *actively read* — read with a purpose. Instead of just reading the words, ask yourself critical questions, such as "How is the conclusion drawn?" "What would strengthen this argument?" "What would weaken this argument?" and "What's the author assuming?"

Having read the question first, you can take this critical reading step because you know what to look for. The active reading is guided, because the exam gives you the *one* question to answer, and you read it before reading the argument.

The following sections provide guidance on what to look for in a passage when answering different types of Argument Analysis questions.

Identifying the "because" and "therefore"

Think of a logical argument as an if-then statement, where *because* of a certain set of facts, *therefore* you will have this result or plan. When reading an argument, break it down into these two parts:

>> **Because:** The *because* (the *if* part) is facts or reasons that support the therefore, including observations, statistics, reasonable generalizations, and anecdotes.

>> **Therefore:** The *therefore* (the *then* part), which is the result of the because, is the argument's main point, plan, or assertion.

After identifying the *because* and *therefore*, you have what you need to begin your argument analysis, as I explain in the next few sections. Consider this simple argument:

PLAY

> Our dog Rover came in from the backyard, and the flower bed is all dug up! Rover must have dug up the flower bed.

To analyze this argument, place it in the *because/therefore* template. You can paraphrase the argument:

>> **Because** Rover was in the backyard,

>> **Therefore** he dug up the flower bed.

This single, simple restatement of the argument helps you evaluate the answer choices without having to reread the entire passage.

TIP

Look for the following words to identify the conclusion: *then, therefore, thus, hence, so, consequently, as a result, must have,* and *in conclusion.* However, don't rely solely on these words; they may be implied rather than stated.

However, this simple argument is flawed. You could *weaken* it by introducing new evidence that suggests Rover *didn't* dig up the flower bed. You could also *strengthen* it by introducing new evidence that suggests he *did* dig up the bed.

Start with the *assumption* of the argument, which isn't stated in the passage. What do you think the assumption is? That no other kids or dogs were in the yard, leaving Rover responsible. I discuss finding this further in the next section.

What new evidence *weakens* the argument? Rover wasn't alone in the backyard — Ginger (the neighbor's dog) and the kids were also in the backyard! In this case, Rover *may* have dug up the flower garden, or he may not have. You *can't* be sure.

What new evidence *strengthens* the argument? Rover *was* alone in the backyard — no other dogs or kids (or anything else that tends to dig). In this case, Rover *must* have dug up the yard, because there's no other plausible explanation. You *can* be sure.

Whether you introduce new evidence that *weakens* or *strengthens* the argument depends on what the question asks. With a longer, more complicated argument, it really helps if you know what you're trying to do as you read the passage — and this is why you read the question first!

Finding the unstated assumption

An *assumption* is a claim that the passage makes without stating it directly. The assumption is based on the *because* part and suggests that the argument has only one reasonable conclusion. When asked to identify an assumption, think of what *must* be true for the argument to work. This is the part that isn't *stated* in the passage, so it takes some critical thinking.

PLAY

> Employees in the sales department had special training, and now they perform better than they did before. This special training should thus be given to the employees in all other departments to improve their performance also.

Like many arguments, this argument has more than one *because* and *therefore*, each with its own unstated assumption.

First because and therefore in this argument

> » **Because** sales employees had special training,
>
> » **Therefore** they now perform better.

Between this first *because* and the *therefore* is the unstated assumption that the improved performance in the sales department is a direct result of the special training. What is the assumption? That nothing else happened that improved their performance.

To *strengthen* or *weaken* the argument, go for the assumption. You could *weaken* it by introducing new evidence that suggests the training *didn't* improve the sales employees' performance. You could also *strengthen* it by introducing new evidence that suggests it *did* improve the performance.

What new evidence *weakens* the argument? A lot of things would work: The salespeople were novices, and they learned on the job. They got new leadership. They got lots of new leads. The product went down in price and improved in quality. The competition went out of business. The demand increased, for whatever reason. You get the point — the performance improvement may not have been a result of the special training.

What new evidence *strengthens* the argument? That none of these previously mentioned factors changed: The leadership, leads, product, competition, and demand *didn't* change. In this case, the improved performance probably was from the special training.

Second because and therefore in this argument

> » **Because** sales employees had special training and now perform better,
>
> » **Therefore** this special training should be given to the other employees so they also perform better.

Between this second *because* and the *therefore* is the unstated assumption that the training that is effective for the sales department will also be effective for the other departments. What is the assumption? That the training is universally effective.

To *strengthen* or *weaken* the argument at this point, go for this assumption. You could *weaken* it by introducing new evidence that suggests the training *only* affects the sales department. You could *strengthen* it by introducing new evidence that suggests that the training is beneficial for *all* departments.

What new evidence *weakens* the argument? You could make it about the special training — it's specific to sales; it fits the salesperson demographic; it addresses anything specific to the sales department. In other words, this training *wouldn't* have much of an effect on the other departments.

What new evidence *strengthens* the argument? Basically the opposite of what weakens it: The special training is for general employee skills; it's effective for all demographics and job types; basically it's *not* specific to sales. In this case, the special training *would* help other departments.

For this plan to work, both assumptions must be true. You don't need to think about them to the level described previously, and typically the answer choices mention *one* assumption — but now you know what to look for and how to critically approach an argument or plan.

TIP

Writing the Analyze an Argument essay is *exactly* like this — only instead of answering a question, you write an essay. Basically, each paragraph covers one assumption.

Exploring common logical fallacies

Arguments may seem logical and fair on the surface but actually be *fallacious* (erroneous, flawed). The following sections reveal some of the more common logical fallacies you're likely to find on the exam. By spotting these, you identify weaknesses in arguments and gather the knowledge required to determine which statements best support or refute the argument.

Erroneous cause-and-effect

An erroneous cause-and-effect assumes that because two events happened, one must have caused the other. For example — true story — a study came out saying that taking selfies makes you more confident. How did these brilliant researchers arrive at such a profound conclusion? Apparently, people who take lots of selfies are more confident — so it must be that the selfies bring confidence. What do you think of this? Personally, I think that people take selfies *because* they're confident, not the other way around.

Sweeping generalization

A *sweeping generalization* applies a general rule to a specific case. It suggests that a plan that works in one context will work in another. For example, because the addition of sharp-turn warning signs to roads in Town *X* reduced the rate of accidents, adding these signs to the roads in Town *Y* will surely have the same effect. This argument uses a sweeping generalization by assuming that the roads in the two towns are similar. However, is it possible that the two towns are different? It could be that Town *X* has lots of curvy mountain roads, while Town *Y* has only straight, flat roads. Because sharp-turn warning signs don't make straight roads safer, the addition of these signs to roads in Town *Y* will not have the intended effect.

Misplaced motive

A *misplaced motive* assumes that someone did something on purpose when really that person didn't have an option. For example, if the play director is selecting students to act in the high-school play, and the director comes back with a list of only seniors, the assumption may be that the director has a motive to work with seniors, for whatever reason: They're experienced, mature, taller, afflicted with senioritis, or any other reason. Is it possible that the director had no such motive? It could be that only seniors applied to act in the play — no juniors, sophomores, or freshmen wanted to participate — so the director only had seniors to choose from. It wasn't the director's motive at all: It was just the limited options.

REMEMBER

Of course, these logical fallacies are just broad categories. GRE Argument Analysis fallacies include these but also can be more varied and specific — but looking for these common fallacies helps you get started in critically approaching the Argument passages. If you don't see one of these example fallacies, you'll probably find something *else* that you can use to strengthen or weaken the argument.

Answering the Question in Your Own Words

After you have a clear understanding of the argument's premise and conclusion, which make up the Because and Therefore, and you've identified the assumption that the argument hinges upon, answer the question in your own words. For one thing, this gives the wrong answer choices less power to lead you astray. Use the question as your focal point. For example, if the question asks you to weaken the argument, you can use the skills you just learned to identify the assumption and think of new evidence that weakens the assumption.

Following are the different question types and what you need to ask yourself and answer before looking at the answer choices:

>> **Weakening the plan or argument:** What new information that's not in the plan or argument would weaken it? Does the argument commit a logical fallacy? If so, which one?

>> **Strengthening the plan argument:** What new information that's not in the plan or argument would strengthen it? It could be that there's no other relevant information, so the assumption is probably true.

>> **Identifying the assumption:** What assumption does the plan or argument hinge on that, if proven untrue, would render the conclusion false?

WARNING

Be sure to stay away from the answer choices until you've answered the question in your own words. Even though the right answer is in there, there are also four wrong answers designed to distract and mislead you.

Eliminating Each Wrong Answer

After you've answered the question in your own words, the next step is to eliminate wrong answer choices. Your answer won't match the correct answer, but it doesn't have to. The purpose of answering the question yourself is less to get a sense of what the correct answer looks like and more to make the clearly wrong answers stand out, so that you can eliminate them.

WARNING

Avoid the trap that I've seen too many students fall into. *Don't change your own answer based on the answer choices!* Four of the answer choices are wrong, and changing your answer defeats the whole strategy. Even if your own answer is wrong, it'll be close enough for you to spot and eliminate the wrong answers.

This strategy is relevant to most of the Verbal questions on the GRE — eliminating the obviously wrong answers and working with what's left. The following sections show you how to eliminate wrong answers and highlight some common traps to avoid.

Applying the process of elimination

GRE developers take pleasure in intentionally misleading you, the test-taker. To defend yourself against this underhanded *chicanery* (deceit), brush up on these common traps.

Beware of "some"

If an argument applies a sweeping generalization, it's understood that the generalization may not apply to the entire population. For example, if the argument is to reduce jaywalking by issuing tickets, and the question asks you to weaken the argument, a trap answer would read, "Some jaywalkers don't care about paying the tickets." This may be true, but *most* jaywalkers *do* care about paying the tickets, and the argument/plan would still reduce jaywalking even if some jaywalkers don't care.

Stay in scope

A trap answer choice may contain information that's irrelevant to the argument. For example, if the argument is that dolphins absorb too much mercury because they eat too much fish, and the question asks you to weaken the argument, a trap answer would be that seals also eat too much fish but don't absorb mercury. Whether you're strengthening or weakening this argument, you can eliminate this answer choice, because whatever happens with seals is out of scope of dolphins.

Don't go with an answer just because it's true

The correct answer will be true, but a trap answer is also true — so make sure it answers the question. In the preceding two examples, the sample trap answers, "Some jaywalkers don't care about paying the tickets" and "Seals also eat too much fish," are certainly true — but they don't answer the question, so they're wrong.

Don't be tempted by opposites

If you're asked to weaken or support the argument, the answer choices almost always contain at least one statement that does the exact opposite. It may make sense because it contains the elements that you're looking for, but make sure it goes in the right direction. If you're strengthening an argument, for example, this trap answer will fit perfectly but actually weaken the argument.

Testing your skills

Here are some sample questions to test your skills, followed by the best approach for choosing the right answer.

PLAY

A recent study of the Alhambra High School District shows a two-point increase in truancy in its high schools from the previous year to 14.5 percent. Participation in after-school programs has decreased by 22 percent. The Alhambra High School District is obviously failing in its mission to improve academic success.

The argument that the Alhambra High School District is failing to improve academic success is based on which of the following assumptions?

Set up the *because* and *therefore* premise:

>> **Because** truancy increased and after-school participation declined,

>> **Therefore** the high school is failing in its mission to improve academic success.

The argument assumes that academic success is tied to truancy and after-school participation.

Ⓐ The Alhambra High School District doesn't have sufficient funding to enforce attendance or improve after-school programs.

Ⓑ Attendance has remained unchanged at the elementary and middle-school levels.

Ⓒ Private schools and charter schools have had significantly improved academic success.

Ⓓ Attendance and after-school participation are accurate measures of academic success.

Ⓔ The Alhambra High School District has increased focus to improving its athletic program.

Now eliminate each choice, one by one:

>> Choice (A) is wrong, because funding is outside the scope of the argument.

>> Choice (B) is wrong, because elementary and middle schools are also outside the scope of the argument.

>> Choice (C) is wrong, because private and charter schools are outside the scope of the argument.

>> Choice (D) is correct, because the argument uses reduced attendance and after-school participation as its evidence that academic success is failing.

>> Choice (E) is wrong because the athletic program is out of scope of the argument.

The correct answer is Choice (D).

PLAY

For healthcare and health insurance to become less expensive, the federal government first needs to implement cost-control measures in the healthcare industry. Tort reform is the obvious place to start. The costs of medical malpractice insurance and lawsuits are skyrocketing, and medical professionals simply increase the cost of their services to keep pace. Tort reform would significantly reduce the number of frivolous malpractice claims, limit the damage awarded to plaintiffs, and reduce the cost of malpractice insurance. Healthcare providers and insurance companies could then pass the savings along to consumers. Until some sort of tort reform effectively addresses this issue, healthcare will continue to be expensive regardless of whether people are paying out of pocket or through a government-administered program.

Which of the following statements most accurately identifies the assumption that must be true for the argument to be true?

Set up the *because* and *therefore* premise:

> ❯❯ **Because** malpractice insurance and lawsuits are expensive,

> ❯❯ **Therefore** reducing these costs will bring down the price of healthcare.

The argument assumes that malpractice insurance and lawsuits are the key drivers of inflated healthcare costs.

Ⓐ Medical insurance will increase the cost of healthcare services.

Ⓑ Medical insurance costs are rising.

Ⓒ The costs of malpractice insurance and lawsuits drive up the healthcare costs.

Ⓓ Providers are responsible for the high healthcare costs.

Ⓔ Tort reform would reduce medical malpractice litigation and limit damages awarded to plaintiffs.

Now eliminate each choice, one by one:

> ❯❯ Choice (A) is wrong, because it merely repeats information stated in the passage.

> ❯❯ Choice (B) is wrong, because it simply restates the problem.

> ❯❯ Choice (C) is correct, because it restates the assumption: that insurance and lawsuits drive up the cost of healthcare.

> ❯❯ Choice (D) is wrong, because it's too vague — it doesn't describe how providers drive up the costs.

> ❯❯ Choice (E) is wrong because it restates the argument, but it doesn't say *how* tort reform would help.

The correct answer is Choice (C).

PLAY

In earlier versions of the GRE, approximately 6 percent of test-takers achieved perfect quantitative scores, while almost no test-takers answered more than 60 percent of the verbal questions correctly. Because approximately one in 17 test-takers scored perfect quantitative scores of 800 (based on the old scoring scale), **a perfect or near-perfect GRE quantitative score did not help distinguish a truly competitive applicant.** The current version of the GRE, released in 2011, resolves this discrepancy by **featuring more challenging questions in the quantitative sections** and simplifying the verbal sections.

In the argument given, the two **bolded phrases** play which of the following roles?

Set up the *because* and *therefore* premise:

> ❯❯ **Because** on the old GRE, too many test-takers achieved perfect quantitative scores,

> ❯❯ **Therefore** the current GRE features a more challenging quantitative section.

TIP

This is a different and less common format of the Analyzing an Argument question, but the premise is exactly the same. As long as you establish the *Because/Therefore* relationship and answer the question yourself, the wrong answers are easy to eliminate.

Ⓐ The first describes a hypothesis which the second opposes; the second is an alternative explanation.

Ⓑ The first describes the result of a problem; the second describes a solution to that problem.

Ⓒ The first proposes a solution to a problem described by the second; the second is that problem.

Ⓓ The first is a claim of the result of a problem described by the second; the second is a problem with the claim described by the first.

Ⓔ The first describes a requirement of the argument to revise its initial formulation of the position it seeks to establish; the second presents that position in a revised form.

Now eliminate each choice, one by one:

TIP

>> Choice (A) is wrong, because the second phrase doesn't oppose the first one.

Choice (A) is a standard wrong answer. Typically, a few of the answer choices will suggest that the two phrases "oppose" or "counter" each other. This may be true, but you can quickly scan the passage to make sure the phrases agree, and if they do, you can eliminate any answer choices that suggest they contradict.

>> Choice (B) is correct, because the first phrase describes the problem with the easy quantitative section, and the second phrase describes the solution that ETS put into place.

>> Choice (C) is wrong, because it gets the phrases backwards — the first phrase describes a problem, and the second phrase proposes a solution.

>> Choice (D) is wrong, because it hardly makes sense — a true tactic of this question format, suggesting it's a trap answer designed to take up your time.

>> Choice (E) is wrong for the same reason as Choice (D) — it's a wordy, nonsense trap designed to absorb your time.

TIP

Choices (D) and (E) illustrate why it's imperative to *answer the question yourself first* — so that when you see a nonsensical, wordy answer, you don't spend a whole lot of time checking whether it's true.

The correct answer is Choice (B).

Chapter **8**

Expanding Your Vocabulary to Boost Your Score

You can't get around it: You absolutely *must* know vocabulary to do well on the GRE. Regardless of your conversational expertise, the GRE tests your grasp of commonly used academic and intellectual vocabulary words. Many of the words used on the GRE probably aren't words you use on a daily basis, but you've most likely heard them somewhere before. You can't know for certain which words are going to appear on the test, but the odds are good that you'll see some of the vocab words presented in this chapter.

REMEMBER

Mastering new vocabulary words is more than just reading this chapter. You need to make it part of your daily practice. Study daily. Revisit the words you think you already know. Knowing as many vocabulary words as possible helps immensely with the Verbal section. You can also improve your vocabulary by reading novels, articles, and so on.

This chapter helps you get a firmer grasp on vocabulary words used on the GRE. I provide a detailed discussion of prefixes, suffixes, and roots, which can help you significantly improve your vocabulary. I also provide a long list of common vocabulary words that you need to know.

Brushing Up on Prefixes, Suffixes, and Roots

Mastering prefixes, suffixes, and roots can bump up your Verbal score significantly. Although prefixes and suffixes abound, the ones in the following sections are the most common. Take the time to memorize them.

Prefixes

A *prefix* is one or more letters at the beginning of a word that alters its meaning. For example, if a feat is *possible*, then you can do it. With a simple prefix, you can change that feat to *im*possible, meaning you can't do it. Knowing that in this case *im-* means not, you can narrow down the possible meanings of a word starting with *im-*, such as *impermeable*. Whatever the word is, the *im-* usually stands for not. (Because *permeate* means to pass through, *impermeable* means not capable of being passed through.) Following are the most common prefixes you need to know with several related examples:

>> **a-/an-** = not or without: Someone *amoral* is without morals or conscience; someone *atypical* isn't typical or normal. Someone *apathetic* is uncaring or without feeling. Similarly, an *anaerobic* environment is without oxygen, and *anarchy* is without rule or government.

>> **ambi-** = dual: Someone *ambidextrous* uses both left and right hands equally well; an *ambivert* is both introverted and extroverted. Something *ambiguous* has dual meanings, but that word typically refers to something that's unclear.

>> **ante-** = before: When the clock reads 5 a.m., the *a.m.* stands for *ante meridiem*, which means before the middle of the day. *Antebellum* means before the war. Tara in *Gone with the Wind* was an antebellum mansion, built before the Civil War.

>> **ben-/bon-** = good: A *benefit* is something that has a good result, an advantage. Someone *benevolent* is good and kind. *Bon voyage* means have a good voyage; a *bon vivant* is a person who lives the good life.

>> **contra-** = against: A medical treatment that's *contraindicated* for a certain condition is something that would make the condition worse, not better. *Contravene* means to deny or oppose.

>> **de-** = down from, away from (to put down): To *descend* or *depart* is to go down from or away from. To *denounce* is to put down or to speak badly of, and *demote* means to reduce in rank or stature.

Many unknown words on the GRE that start with *de-* mean to put down in the sense of to criticize or bad-mouth. Here are a few more: *demean, denounce, denigrate, derogate, deprecate,* and *decry*.

>> **eu-** = good: A *eulogy* is a good speech, usually given for the dearly departed at a funeral. A *euphemism* is a good way of saying something or a polite expression, like saying, "Oh, dang!" instead of using certain other words.

>> **ex-** = out of, away from: An *exit* is literally out of or away from *it* — *ex*-it. (The word *exit* is probably one of the most logical words around.) To *extricate* is to get out of something. To *exculpate* is to let off the hook — literally to make away from guilt, as *culp* means guilt.

>> **im-/in-** = not: Something *impossible* isn't possible — it just can't happen. Someone *immortal* isn't going to die but will live forever, because *mortal* means able to die. Someone *implacable* can't be calmed down, because *placate* means to ease one's anger. Similarly, something *inappropriate* isn't appropriate, and someone *inept* isn't adept, meaning he's not skillful. Someone who's *insolvent* has no money and is bankrupt, like most students after four years of college.

Note that *im-* and *in-* can also mean into — (*immerse* means to put into), inside (*innate* means something born inside of you), or beginning (as in *initial*) — but these meanings are less common.

>> **ne-/mal-** = bad: Something *negative* is bad, like a negative attitude. Someone *nefarious* is full of bad, or wicked and evil; you may read about a nefarious wizard in a fantasy novel. Something *malicious* also is full of bad, or wicked and harmful, such as a malicious rumor.

>> **post-** = after: When the clock reads 5 p.m., the *p.m.* stands for *post meridiem*, which means after the middle of the day. Something *postmortem* occurs after death.

EPONYMOUS WORDS

An *eponym* is a word derived from the name of a person. For example, the cardigan sweater got its name from the Earl of Cardigan. Here are a few eponyms to add to your GRE vocabulary:

- **bowdlerize:** To omit indecent words or phrases in a book or piece of writing (you bowdlerize a love letter before you let your roommate read it). In 1818, Dr. Thomas Bowdler, an English physician, published a ten-volume edition of Shakespeare's plays called *The Family Shakespeare.* He left out all the dirty parts. For example, instead of "Out, damn'd spot!" the line reads, "Out, crimson spot!" They had different standards back then.

- **boycott:** Withdraw or ban participation. Charles Boycott was a retired English army captain who refused to lower rents to his farmer tenants after a few bad harvests and was accused of exploiting the poor. The locals harassed him, stealing his crops and refusing to sell his products in their stores, until he was hounded out of the county. Today, when you refuse to have anything to do with something, you're said to boycott it.

- **draconian:** Extremely harsh and severe, harking all the way back to about 620 BC. Draco was an Athenian who wrote a code of laws that made nearly every crime punishable by death. The word *draconian* came to describe any law that is too cruel or strict.

- **maverick:** An individualist; an unconventional person. Samuel Maverick, who lived during the 1800s, was a Texas rancher whose unbranded cattle roamed free. Maverick's neighbors refused to hand back his strays, claiming that because they were unbranded, he had no proof they were his. The word eventually came to be used to describe people or ideas that are unconventional, independent, or defiant.

- **quisling:** A traitor. Vidkun Quisling was a Norwegian politician who turned traitor in World War II, siding with Hitler. He was executed by a firing squad at the end of the war, but his name lives on to torment GRE-takers.

- **simony:** The buying or selling of religious or sacred objects or privileges. Simon Magus (who's often described as a reformed wizard) offered St. Peter and St. John money to give him their religious abilities. *Simony* was especially popular in the Middle Ages, when people sold pardons, indulgences, and the like.

You probably already know these words, but did you know they're also eponyms?

- **august:** Respected and powerful, named for Augustus, the first Emperor of the Roman Empire.

- **diesel:** A type of engine, named for Rudolf Diesel, a German engineer.

- **mausoleum:** A large tomb or memorial, named for King Mausolus, King of Calia in ancient Greece, circa 370 BC.

- **nicotine:** The addictive stuff in tobacco, named for French diplomat Jean Nicot.

- **quixotic:** A person or disposition that's excessively chivalrous, romantic, impractical, and impulsive, such as the character Don Quixote in Cervantes's novel *The Ingenious Gentleman Don Quixote of La Mancha.*

- **saxophone:** A musical instrument, invented by and named after Adolphe Sax, a Belgian musician of the early to mid 1800s. People refer to the saxophone as a *sax,* so the word has turned a full circle.

- **shrapnel:** Fragments thrown out by a shell or a bomb, invented in 1802 by Lt. Gen. Henry Shrapnel, an English army officer.

- **silhouette:** Profile or shadow of a face, named after Étienne de Silhouette, a French finance minister.

WARNING

There's an exception to every prefix. For example, *a-/an-* may mean the opposite in most contexts, but with the word *aver*, it does not refer to the opposite of *ver*, which means truth. The prefix *ambi-* may refer to dual, as in *ambidextrious*, but someone *ambitious* doesn't necessarily have dual goals.

Suffixes

A *suffix* is usually three or four letters at the end of a word that give the word a specific inflection or change its type, such as from a verb to an adjective; for example, to transform the verb *study* into the adjective *studious*, you change the *y* to *i* and add the suffix *-ous*. Following are some common suffixes along with related examples:

- » *-ate* = to make: To *duplicate* is to make double. To *renovate* is to make new again (*nov* means new). To *placate* is to make peaceful or calm (*plac* means peace or calm).

- » *-ette* = little: A *cigarette* is a little cigar. A *dinette* table is a little dining table. A *coquette* is a little flirt (literally, a little chicken, but that doesn't sound as pretty).

- » *-illo* = little: An *armadillo* is a little armored animal. A *peccadillo* is a little sin. (You might know that *pecar* means "to sin.")

- » *-ify (-efy)* = to make: To *beautify* is to make beautiful. To *ossify* is to become rigid or make bone. (If you break your wrist, it takes weeks to ossify again, or for the bone to regenerate.) To *deify* is to make into a deity, a god. To *liquefy* is to turn a solid into a liquid.

- » *-ist* = a person: A *typist* is a person who types. A *pugilist* is a person who fights, a boxer (*pug* means war or fight). A *pacifist* is a person who believes in peace, a noncombatant (*pac* means peace or calm).

- » *-ity* = a noun suffix that doesn't actually mean anything; it just turns a word into a noun: *Anxiety* is the noun form of anxious. *Serenity* is the noun form of serene. *Timidity* is the noun form of timid.

- » *-ize* = to make: To *alphabetize* is to make alphabetical. To *immunize* is to make immune. To *ostracize* is to make separate from the group, or to shun.

- » *-ous* = full of (very): Someone *joyous* is full of joy. Someone *amorous* is full of *amour*, or love. Someone *pulchritudinous* is full of beauty and, therefore, beautiful. Try saying that to your loved one.

Roots

A *root* is the core part of a word that gives the word its basic meaning. Recognizing a common root helps you discern the meaning of an unfamiliar word. For example, knowing that *ver* means truth, as in *verify*, you can recognize that the unfamiliar word *aver* has something to do with truth. *Aver* means to hold true or affirm the truth. Following are some common roots along with related examples:

- » *ambu* = walk, move: In a hospital, patients are either bedridden (they can't move) or *ambulatory* (they can walk and move about). A *somnambulist* is a sleepwalker. *Som-* means sleep, *-ist* is a person, and *ambu* is to walk or move.

- » *andro* = man: An *android* is a robot shaped like a man. Someone *androgynous* exhibits both male (*andro*) and female (*gyn*) characteristics.

- » *anthro* = human or mankind: *Anthropology* is the study of humans, and a *misanthrope* hates humans.

bellu / belli = fight

» **bellu, belli** = war, fight: If you're *belligerent,* you're ready to fight — and an *antebellum* mansion, mentioned above with prefixes, was created before the Civil War. (Remember that *ante-* means before.)

» **cred** = trust or belief: Something *incredible* is unbelievable, such as the excuse "I would've picked you up on time, but there was a 15-car pileup on the freeway. I barely got out of there!" Saying something is *incredible* is like saying it's unbelievable, and if you're *credulous,* you're trusting and *naive* (literally, full of trust).

Be careful not to confuse the words *credible* and *credulous.* Something *credible* is trustable or believable, whereas *credulous* means trusting, naive, or gullible. Furthermore, if you're *incredulous,* then you doubt something is true.

» **gnos** = knowledge: A doctor shows his or her knowledge by making a *diagnosis* (analysis of the situation) or a *prognosis* (prediction about the future of the illness). An *agnostic* is a person who doesn't know whether a god exists. Differentiate an agnostic from an atheist: An *atheist* is literally without god, a person who believes there's no god. An *agnostic* hasn't decided yet.

gnos = know

» **greg** = group, herd: A *congregation* is a group of people. A *gregarious* person likes to be part of a group — he or she is sociable. To *segregate* is literally to make away from the group. (*Se-* means apart or away from, as in *separate, sever, sequester,* and *seclusion.*)

greg = group

» **gyn** = woman: A *gynecologist* is a physician who treats conditions and ailments specific to women. A *misogynist* is a person who hates women.

gyn = woman

» **loq, log, loc, lix** = speech or talk: Someone *prolix* or *loquacious* talks a lot. A *dialogue* is talk or conversation between two or more people. *Elocution* is proper speech.

loq log } speech
loc lix }

» **luc, lum, lus** = light, clear: Something *luminous* is shiny and full of light. Ask the teacher to *elucidate* something you don't understand (literally, to make clear). *Lustrous* hair reflects the light and is sleek and glossy.

» **meta** = beyond, after: A *metamorphosis* is a change of shape beyond the present shape.

» **morph** = shape: Something *amorphous* is without shape, while *morphology* is the study of shape.

morph = shape

» **mut** = change: Something *mutates* from one state to the next, and something *immutable* isn't changeable; it remains constant. Don't confuse *mut* (change) with *mute* (silent).

mut = change

» **pac** = peace, calm: Why do you give a baby a *pacifier?* To calm him or her down. To get its name, the *Pacific* Ocean must have appeared calm at the time it was discovered.

» **path** = feeling: Something *pathetic* arouses feeling or pity. To *sympathize* is to share the feelings (literally, to make the same feeling). *Antipathy* is a dislike — literally, a feeling against.

» **phon** = sound: *Phonics* helps you to sound out words. *Cacophony* is bad sound; *euphony* is good sound. *Homophones* are words that sound the same, such as *red* and *read.* And of course, there's the *phone* you use to talk to someone.

» **plac** = peace, calm: To *placate* someone is to calm him or her down or to make peace with that person. Someone *implacable* can't be calmed down.

» **pro** = big, much: *Profuse* apologies are big, or much — in essence, a *lot* of apologies. A *prolific* writer produces a great deal of material.

pro = big & before & for (as in pro/con)

Pro has two additional meanings less commonly used on the GRE. It can mean *before,* as in "A *prologue* comes before a play." Similarly, to *prognosticate* is to make knowledge before, or to predict. A *prognosticator* is a fortune-teller. *Pro* can also mean *for.* Someone who is *pro* freedom of speech is in favor of freedom of speech. Someone with a *proclivity* toward a certain activity is for that activity or has a natural tendency toward it.

pug = war, fight: Someone *pugnacious* is ready to fight. A *pugilist* is a person who likes to fight, such as a professional boxer. Also, the large sticks that marines train with in hand-to-hand combat are called *pugil sticks.*

scien = knowledge: A *scientist* is a person with knowledge. Someone *prescient* has forethought or knowledge ahead of time — for example, a prognosticator. (A fortune-teller, remember?) One who is *omniscient* is all-knowing.

somn = sleep: If you have *insomnia,* you can't sleep. (The prefix *in-* means not.)

son = sound: A *sonic* boom breaks the sound barrier. *Dissonance* is clashing sounds. A *sonorous* voice has a good sound.

Memorizing the GRE's Most Common Vocabulary Words

This section features the most commonly occurring words on the GRE. Besides reviewing the words and their definitions in this section, track down words that you don't know while practicing the Verbal section of the GRE. When you get stuck on a word, look it up and list it for review.

REMEMBER

Note that some of these words have other definitions besides the ones listed here. For example, the word *base* has several meanings, but the GRE typically uses the obscure meaning of boring and simple, like the base model of a car. Also, the word *accessible,* which normally means that you can reach something, typically means understandable on the GRE. These are the definitions that I provide.

Keep in mind too that words have different forms, so learning to spot variations based on suffixes and prefixes is an excellent way to discern an unfamiliar word. For example, if you've learned the meaning of *equivocal* as an adjective, you should be able to interpret *equivocate* as a verb.

TIP

As you review these words, pay attention to the word parts (prefixes, suffixes, and roots) from the lists earlier in this chapter. Try covering up the definitions and discerning the word meanings from these parts. You can also make note cards and highlight the word parts. With practice, interpreting new words becomes much easier.

aberrant	Abnormal; different from the accepted norm
abeyance	State of suspension; temporary inaction
abscond	To sneak away
abstemious	Indicative of self-denial, particularly with food or drink
abstruse	Difficult to comprehend
accessible -	Easy to understand, especially by a certain group
acquiescent	Agreeing without protest
acrid	Bitter; harsh
acrimonious	Bitter in temper, manner, and speech
acumen	Keenness; quickness of intellectual insight
admonition	A gentle ~~reproof~~ *disapproval*

	affect (noun)	Emotion that influences behavior
	affront	To deliberately offend, as with a gesture
	aggrandize	To widen in scope or make bigger or greater
	aggregate	Amounting to a whole
	allay	To reduce the intensity of
	amalgamate	To mix or blend together in a homogenous body
	ameliorate	To make better or improve
	anachronous	Out of place in time
	anecdote	A short account of an interesting incident
	archipelago	A large group of islands
	articulate	Well-spoken, eloquent
	artifice	Cleverness or skill
	artless	Without deceit or cunning; sincere
	ascetic	Representative of severe self-denial
	assiduous	Persistent, unceasing
	astute	Keen; wise
	audacious	Fearless, bold
	augment	To increase in measure or intensity
	austere	Unadorned; severely simple
	avarice	Extreme greed and hoarding
	aver	To declare or profess
	banal	Trite; commonplace
	base	Simple and boring
	belie	To present a false front
	beset	To surround, as in an attack
	blatant	Very obvious, offensively loud, or coarsely conspicuous
	bolster	To support; to reinforce
	bombastic	Using inflated language; pompous
	boon	A timely benefit; a blessing
	brevity	Briefness or conciseness
	browbeat	To intimidate in an overbearing manner
	bumptious	Offensively self-assertive; pushy
	bungle	To perform clumsily or inadequately; botch
	burgeon	To grow forth; to send out buds
	cacophony	A disagreeable, harsh, or discordant sound or tone

(continued)

callous	Insensitive; indifferent
calumniate	To make false and malicious statements about; to slander
candor	The quality of being open and sincere
cantankerous	Bad-tempered and uncooperative
carp	To complain unreasonably
chaos	A state of disorder and confusion
chicanery	Trickery, deception, especially through the use of questionable logic
churl	A rude, boorish, or surly person
coda	Concluding section of a musical or literary piece; something that summarizes
codify	To assemble related laws or principles into a systematic collection
cognizant	Aware; taking notice
cohort	A companion or associate
colloquial	Pertaining to common speech
commensurate	Corresponding in amount, quality, or degree
complacency	A feeling of quiet security; satisfaction
conciliatory	A state of seeking to reconcile or make peace
concrete	Actual, irrefutable, as in concrete evidence
confidante	One to whom secrets are confided
congruous	Appropriate or fitting
consternation	Unsettling dismay or amazement
consummate	To bring to completion
contentious	Quarrelsome
contrite	Penitent, apologetic
contumacious	Rebellious
cordial	Polite in a pleasant way
corroborate	To make more certain; confirm
countenance	Appearance, especially the look or expression of the face
counter	To go against or attempt to undermine an action
counterpart	A person or thing resembling or complementing another
craven	Cowardly
credulity	Willingness to behave or trust too readily
cronyism	The practice of favoring one's friends, especially in political appointments
curmudgeon	An ill-tempered person
cursory	Hasty, superficial, as of a review of something
dearth	An inadequate supply; scarcity; lack

debacle	A complete collapse or failure
decorum	Orderliness and good taste in manners
deferent	In a state of giving in out of respect for another person
deleterious	Hurtful, morally or physically
delineate	To represent by sketch or diagram; to describe precisely in words
depravity	The state of being morally bad or evil
deride	To ridicule; to make fun of
derision	Ridicule
derivative	Something obtained or developed from a source
desultory	Aimless; haphazard
diatribe	Bitter or malicious criticism
didactic	For the purpose of teaching
diffidence	Lacking confidence
dilatory	Causing delay
disconcert	To disturb the composure of
discretion	Using one's own judgment; being discreet
disingenuous	Insincere, phony
disquiet	Lack of calm, peace, or ease
dissemble	To disguise or pretend in order to deceive or mislead
dissolution	Breaking up of a union of persons
dissonant	Out of harmony, incongruous
divergent	Deviating from a certain course
divest	To strip; to deprive, often in terms of property
divulge	To tell or make known, generally of something secret or private
doctrinaire	A person who's fanatical about enforcing a certain principle, regardless of its practicality
dogmatic	Forceful and unwavering, allowing no room for interpretation or dissent
doldrums	A state of inactivity or low spirits
dubious	Doubtful
dupe	Someone who's easily fooled; to fool someone
duplicity	Deceitfulness
ebullient	Showing great enthusiasm or exhilaration
eclectic	Drawn from multiple sources or based on multiple styles
efficacious	Capable of producing the intended result
efficacy	Power to produce an intended effect
effrontery	Shameless boldness; impudence

(continued)

egregious	Seriously bad or wrong
egress	Exit
elegy	A poem lamenting the dead
elicit	To extract (usually information, a reaction, or an emotional response) without the use of force; to learn through discussion
elitism	Consciousness or pride in belonging to a select group
embellish	To beautify or enhance with additional features or information
empirical	Proven by observed occurrence or existence
emulate	Imitate
endemic	Characteristic of a specific place or culture
enervate	To weaken
engender	To produce or to make something come into existence
enigmatic	Mysterious, perplexing
ennui	Boredom
ephemeral	Short-lived; fleeting
equable	Free from many changes or variations
equanimity	Evenness of mind or temper
equivocal	Ambiguous
equivocate	To use ambiguous or unclear expressions, usually to avoid commitment or to mislead
eradicate	To destroy completely
erudite	Very well-educated
eschew	To keep clear of, avoid
esoteric	Hard to understand; known only by a few
euphemism	A nice way of saying something that's otherwise unpleasant
exacerbate	To make sharper or more severe; to make worse
exculpate	To free from blame
exigency	Urgent situation
expatiate	To speak or write at some length on a given topic or theme
expiation	The means by which atonement or reparation is made
extenuating	The state of explaining or justifying in order to lessen the seriousness of an action
extirpate	To root out; to eradicate
extrapolation	To infer an unknown from something that's known
facetious	Not intended to be taken seriously
facilitate	To make easier
fallacious	Illogical

fatuous	Idiotic
felicitous	Appropriate or suitable for the situation or circumstances
ferret out	To track down, discover
fervor	Ardor or intensity of feeling
fledgling	Inexperienced
foment	To instigate or encourage negative behavior, such as violence
forestall	To prevent by taking action in advance
fortification	The act of strengthening or protecting
frugal	Thrifty
fulminate	To cause to explode; to detonate
fumble	To feel or grope about clumsily
gaffe	A social blunder; faux pas
gainsay	To contradict or oppose
garrulous	Prone to trivial talking
generosity	The state of giving freely
germane	Relevant
goad	To urge on
grandiloquent	Speaking or expressing oneself in a lofty style
grandstand	To conduct oneself or perform showily in an attempt to impress onlookers
gregarious	Sociable; outgoing
grouse	To complain or grumble
guileless	Without deceit
gullible	Easily deceived
halcyon	Calm
haphazard	Characterized by a lack of order or planning
harangue	A tirade
harbinger	Anything or anyone who makes known the coming of a person or future event; an omen
hedge	A barrier or boundary; an act of preventing complete loss of a bet or investment
heresy	Opinion or doctrine subversive of settled or accepted beliefs
homogeneous	Of the same kind
hyperbole	Exaggeration or overstatement
iconoclast	A person who attacks and destroys religious images or accepted beliefs or traditions
ignominious	Shameful, disgraceful
imbroglio	Entanglement, as in a situation
immense	Very large

(continued)

impartial	Objective, open-minded
impecunious	Having no money; broke
impede	To hinder; to block
impenitent	Not feeling regret about one's sins
imperious	Domineering, overbearing; urgent
imperturbable	Calm
impervious	Impenetrable
impetuous	Impulsive
implicit	Implied
importune	To harass with persistent demands
impugn	To challenge as false with arguments or accusations
inadvertently	Unintentionally
inane	A nicer word for describing someone or something as stupid or idiotic
incensed	Angered
inchoate	Recently begun, not fully developed or organized
inconstant	Changeable; fickle; variable
indigenous	Originating in a particular place or region
indigent	Lacking necessities, such as food, clothing, and shelter
indolence	Laziness
ineffable	Incapable of being expressed in words; unutterable
inert	Inactive; lacking power to move or react
inexorable	Not subject to change; not able to be persuaded or convinced
ingenuous	Innocent, sincere
ingratiating	Charming, agreeable
innocuous	Harmless
insensible	Incapable of perceiving or feeling
insinuate	To suggest or hint slyly
insipid	Bland
insouciant	Free from worry or concern; carefree
intimation	Something indicated or made known indirectly
intrepid	Fearless and bold
inure	To harden or toughen by use, exercise, or exposure
invidious	Showing or feeling envy
irascible	Easily angered
ironic	To convey the opposite of an expression's literal meaning

itinerant	Travelling from place to place
jingoism	Professing one's patriotism loudly and excessively
killjoy	A person who spoils the joy or pleasure of others
laconic	Brief and to the point; concise
lampoon	To make fun of; to mock or ridicule
latent	Dormant
laud	To praise
laudable	Praiseworthy
licentious	Unrestrained by laws or rules, especially those related to sexuality
liken	To represent as similar to someone or something
loquacious	Talkative
lucid	Easily understood; clear
lugubrious	Gloomy, depressing
magnanimity	Generosity
malingerer	One who feigns illness to escape duty
malleable	Pliant; able to be reshaped
masticate	To chew or reduce to a pulp
maverick	Rebel; nonconformist
mealymouthed	Insincere, deceitful
mediocrity	The state or quality of being barely adequate
mendacious	Untruthful, deceitful
mendicant	A beggar or homeless person
metamorphosis	Change of form
meticulous	Very thorough and precise
misanthrope	One who hates people
mitigate	To lessen in intensity; to appease
modicum	A small amount
mollify	To soothe
morbidity	Related to illness or disease, in a certain population or geographical area
mordant	Sarcastic; harsh
moribund	Near death or extinction
morose	Ill-humored; sullen
mundane	Ordinary; dull
myopic	Shortsighted or narrow-minded
narcissism	Excessive fascination with oneself

(continued)

nefarious	Extremely wicked
negate	To cancel out; to nullify
neophyte	Beginner
nepotism	Favoritism on the basis of family relationship
obdurate	Stubborn
obfuscate	To darken or conceal
obsequious	Servile; ready to serve
obviate	To make unnecessary
odious	Hateful
officious	Aggressively authoritative in offering help or advice, especially when dealing with trivial matters
onus	Burden
opprobrium	Infamy that results from shameful behavior
oscillate	To waver or switch between different positions or beliefs
ostentation	A display of vanity; showiness
painstaking	Characterized by being very careful and diligent
palpable	Readily seen, heard, or perceived
panache	A grand or flamboyant manner or style
parable	A short story designed to teach a lesson
paragon	Model of perfection
parsimonious	Sparing in spending of money; stingy
partisan	One-sided; committed to one party
pathos	Having a quality that rouses emotion or sympathy
paucity	Scarcity, insufficiency
pejorative	Having a disparaging or derogatory effect
penchant	Strong inclination
penurious	Excessively sparing in the use of money; extremely stingy
perennial	Something long-lasting
perfidy	Treachery, betrayal
permeable	Penetrable; porous
pernicious	Tending to kill or hurt
pervasive	Spread throughout
phlegmatic	Slow moving; not easily roused to feeling or emotion
pious	Religious
placate	To soothe; to bring from a hostile state to a calm one
placid	Peaceful

platitude	Trite or commonplace statement
plethora	Excess; abundance
plumb	To make vertical; to reach the deepest point
polarize	To divide into sharply opposing factions
pompous	Ostentatiously lofty or arrogant
ponder	To consider something thoroughly and thoughtfully
ponderous	Massive, awkward, unwieldy
pontificate	Express an opinion in an annoying fashion
porous	Full of holes; spongy, absorbent
portend	Foretell
poseur	A person who attempts to impress others by assuming a manner other than his true one
pragmatic	Practical
precarious	Hazardous, perilous
precipitate	To hasten the occurrence of
precocious	Mature beyond one's age, typically in respect to mental abilities, talents, or skills
preeminent	A step above others; distinguished, renowned
prescience	Knowledge of events before they happen
presentiment	A feeling or impression that something is about to happen
prevaricate	To use ambiguous language for the purpose of deceiving
proclivity	Natural inclination
prodigal	Wasteful or lavish
prodigious	Immense
prodigy	A person, usually a child, having extraordinary talent
profound	Deep, significant
prognosticate	To predict something in the future
proliferate	To grow rapidly
propensity	Natural inclination
prophetic	Ability to predict the future
propitious	Presenting favorable conditions
prosaic	Commonplace or dull
protean	Changeable in shape or form
prudence	Cautious wisdom
puerile	Childish
pugnacious	Quarrelsome or combative
pungent	Stinging; sharp in taste or smell

(continued)

pusillanimous	Cowardly; fainthearted
qualms	Misgivings; uneasy fears
quibble	Minor objection or complaint
quiescence	Being quiet or still; inactivity
quintessential	The perfect representation of something
quixotic	Idealistic; romantic to a ridiculous degree
recant	To formally withdraw a statement
recidivism	The tendency toward repeated or habitual relapse
recondite	Beyond ordinary knowledge or understanding; profound
redress	To set right by compensation or punishment
refutation	An act of disproving a statement or charge
refute	To disprove
repose	The state of being at rest
reprobate	A sinful and depraved person
repudiate	To refuse to have anything to do with
rescind	To repeal, revoke, or void
resilience	The ability to recover from a setback
respite	Interval of rest
restive	Impatient or stubborn
reticent	Reluctant or inclined to silence
reverent	Respectful
rhetoric	The art of effective communication
rout	To drive out; to stampede
rueful	Causing sorrow or pity
ruminate	To chew over and over again; to think over, ponder
sagacious	Wise
salacious	Lustful; sexually indecent
salubrious	Healthful
sanction	To approve; in legal circles, a law that enacts a penalty for disobedience or a reward for obedience
sanguine	Cheerfully confident; optimistic; bloody, ruddy, or reddish
satiate	To satisfy or fulfill the appetite or desire of
savor	To enjoy fully
scanty	Scarce in quantity or amount
secrete	To hide away
security	Safety

sedulous	Persistent in effort or endeavor
seethe	To be in a state of excitement or agitation
seminal	Influencing future developments
shard	Fragment
shirk	To avoid
shoddy	Not genuine; inferior
sinuous	Curving in and out
skeptic	Doubter
skepticism	Doubt or disbelief
skittish	Lively; restless
slander	Defamation
slothful	Slow-moving, lazy
solecism	A minor mistake in grammar or usage; a breach of good manners
solicitous	Worried or concerned; eager to receive approval from others
sonorous	Loud, deep, or resonant, as a sound
soporific	Causing sleep
spate	A sudden, almost overwhelming outpouring
specious	Seemingly reasonable but incorrect
spendthrift	Someone who wastes money
spurious	Not genuine
stentorian	Extremely loud
stigma	A token of disgrace
stint	A period of time (noun); to be thrifty (verb)
stipulate	To make specific conditions
stoic	Lacking in emotional response, especially with pain or adversity
stolid	Dull; impassive
stratify	To form or place in layers
striated	Marked with parallel bands
strut	A pompous walk
sublime	Supreme or outstanding; elevated
subterfuge	Evasion
supercilious	Showing careless contempt; arrogant
superfluous	More than what's needed
supersede	To replace or supplant
supine	Lying on one's back face upward

(continued)

(continued)

sybarite	A person devoted to luxury and pleasure
sycophant	A self-seeking, servile flatterer
tacit	Understood
taciturn	Stern; silent
tangential	Only slightly connected or related
tantamount	Equivalent in significance, effect, or value
tawdry	Showy, in a cheap way
temerity	Recklessness
tempestuous	Stormy; impassioned
tenacious	Holding fast
tendentious	Having or showing a definite tendency, bias, or purpose
tenuous	Thin; slim
tepid	Lukewarm
thrall	A state of being enslaved or held captive physically, mentally, or morally
thwart	To frustrate
tilt	To lean forward, as if to attack
timidity	Lacking in self-assurance or courage
tirade	A long, passionate speech against something
titillate	To excite or arouse
titular	Holding a position in name (title) only without the power or responsibility that usually comes with that position
torpid	Dull; sluggish; inactive
tortuous	Abounding in irregular bends or turns; unpleasantly complicated
tractable	Docile; easily controlled or shaped
transgression	Violation; sin
transience	A temporary state
transmute	To change
transparent	Easily detected
transpire	To happen, to be revealed
trepidation	Nervous feeling; fear
truculence	Ferocity
truculent	Harsh, brutal
turgid	Inflated, overblown, or pompous; literally swollen to the point of being firm
tutelage	The act of training or being under instruction
tyro	Beginner, novice
ubiquitous	Being present everywhere

umbrage	Sense of having been injured
unassuaged	Not soothed or relieved
uncouth	Clumsy; rude
undermine	To weaken or derail
unerringly	Without fail
ungainly	Awkward; clumsy
unison	Complete accord
unruly	Disobedient
untenable	Indefensible
upbraid	To reproach as deserving blame
urbanity	Refined courtesy or politeness
vacillate	To waver; to fluctuate
vagabond	Wanderer
vainglorious	Excessive; pretentious
valorous	Courageous
vantage	Position giving advantage
vapid	Having lost quality and flavor; dull; lifeless
variegated	Many-colored
vehement	Forceful
veneer	A thin covering to improve the appearance of something
venerate	To look upon with deep respect
veracious	Truthful
verbiage	Use of many words
verbose	Wordy
vestigial	Occurring or persisting as a rudimentary or degenerate structure
viable	Capable of living or succeeding
vicissitude	Change of condition or circumstances, generally of fortune
vigor	Strength; stamina; power
virtuosity	Having the character or ability of an expert
virulence	Intense sharpness of anger; intensity
visage	Face, especially in terms of its features or expression
viscous	Sticky; gluey
vituperate	Overwhelm with wordy abuse
vociferous	Making a loud outcry
volatile	Changeable; explosive

(continued)

volition	A willful choice or decision
voluble	Fluent; talkative
warranted	Justified
wary	Very cautious
welter	Turmoil (noun); to roll, tumble, or toss about (verb)
whet	To sharpen or stimulate
whimsical	Fanciful
whorl	A circular or spiral arrangement
winsome	Attractive; charming
wreak	Inflict
writhe	Twist
yore	Time past
zealot	Fanatic
zeitgeist	Intellectual and moral tendencies of any age

TIP

As you study for the exam and encounter new vocab words, create your own vocabulary list, complete with each word's definition. There are plenty of flash-card apps, some that even read words to you so you can study in the car. And don't overlook low-tech but effective vocabulary-building tools and techniques, like good ol' paper flash cards.

FINDING GRE VOCAB WORDS IN LITERATURE

Question: What do the GRE and *Moby Dick* have in common?

Answer: They both feature these vocabulary words:

antediluvian	fastidious	omnipotent
blunder	fathom	precipice
cadge	floundering	prodigious
conflagration	heinous	ruefully
depict	incensed	sagacious
descry	incredulous	superficial
disparaging	indiscriminate	tyro
dogged	inert	voracious
effulgent	leviathan	wretched

3

Math You Thought You'd Never Need Again

Chapter **9**

Raising Your Best GRE Math Score

G RE math may seem to be expansive, but fortunately, the exam has a scope of topics that you'll see and topics you won't see. For example, you can expect plenty of geometry but rule out trigonometry. You'll see exponents but no logarithms. And even closer than that, you'll see square roots but not of −1.

Don't worry about discerning which topics to brush up on. I got this, and of course, you will too. If a math topic isn't covered in these chapters, you probably don't need it.

REMEMBER

There are some 200 math topics within the GRE's purview, and thus within these pages. Will you see all these topics on the exam? Of course not. With only 40 scored math questions (and possibly 20 more unscored questions), you'll see maybe 25 percent of these topics. A lot of this refresher is provided *just in case* it appears on the exam.

Also, the GRE occasionally breaks its own rules. If you do great on the first math section, likely because you have *GRE For Dummies,* the second math section becomes more challenging. (For more on this, review Chapter 1.) This is good, because your score is on track to be nice and high, but you're also more likely to see a GRE curveball on a math topic that doesn't often appear on the exam.

Does it make sense to study math outside this book? No. There are way too many topics, and your priority is those that you know are within scope of the exam. Of the 40 math questions that count toward your score, you *might* see one that's off topic, but the other 39 are well explored here.

And if you do see a math question from a topic outside this book, it's probably because you performed so well on the *first* math section that the GRE is trying to challenge you on the *second* one, which means that you're in very good shape. Again, for more on how this works, see Chapter 1.

Managing Your Time

Here's the rule: *Don't spend more than one minute on any single question.* But wait — you get 35 minutes for 20 questions! That's (hold on while I check Chapter 10) almost two minutes per question. Why stick with *one* minute?

Because. For one thing, it's easy to lose track of time, especially while you're focusing. Two minutes go by, and you hardly notice. That's okay. Stick with the one-minute rule for *most* questions, and you'll be fine. Also, if you're close to solving a math problem, and you're past a minute, finish solving it! But three core ideas drive this one-minute rule:

» **Make sure you don't get stuck.** If you spend five minutes on a question and get it right, you'll run out of time and miss the last few questions at the end. Not worth it! Instead, what do you do? The tired class, in unison: "Take a guess, mark it for review, and come back to it later."

» **Save time for the graphs questions.** Embedded in each section of 20 math questions (or 25 in the old paper-based version) is a group of 3 (or 4 on paper) questions based on a single set of graphs. These questions aren't harder, but they take more time to figure out because of the graphs. *Always work these questions last.* You'll need a few extra minutes for these, so save up a little time. For more on graphs questions and to read the take-a-guess mantra again, pay a visit to Chapter 14.

» **Save time for questions that are marked for review.** After spending a minute (give or take) on each question and a few more minutes on the graph questions, you still have questions that you want to return to and that are marked for review. Now's your chance! You'd better hope that you still have a few minutes. On the bright side, often when you return to a stuck question, the answer comes to you. On the flip side, if you didn't save time to go back, at least you took a guess and have a shot at getting it right. Oh, wait — that's also a bright side.

Typing an Answer

Some GRE math questions aren't multiple-choice. Instead, you type the answer into a box. This process isn't much different from a multiple-choice question: You still have to answer it, but instead of selecting your answer from a list, you type it into a box. The difference is no biggie, but you should be aware of a few things:

» **Rounding:** The question may ask for the answer to be rounded, such as to the nearest *whole number,* as in 13 instead of 12.8, or the nearest *tenth,* as in 3.7 instead of 3.72. Watch for these instructions, and remember that 0.5 rounds *up.* 4.135 rounds to 4.14, not 4.13.

» **Fractions:** If the answer is in the form of a fraction, such as 2 over 3, the answer entry will have two boxes, one over the other. Naturally, with this example, you'd place 2 in the top box and 3 in the bottom one. Note that an equivalent fraction is considered to be correct: If you type 4 over 6, or 20 over 30, you'll get the answer right.

» **Possible answers:** Sometimes a question has more than one correct answer, commonly in algebra topics. If x can equal 2 *or* 3, simply enter *one* of the answers in the box, and don't worry about the other answer. Your answer will be correct. Note that the question typically reads something like this: "What is one possible value of x?"

>> **Answers with percentage or dollar signs:** If the answer is $42 or 37 percent, the question typically instructs you to disregard the percentage or dollar sign when entering your answer. The dollar sign is a no-brainer; simply enter 42 for $42. But the percentage can trip you up. Remember that 37 percent as a decimal is 0.37, *not* 37. Pay attention to whether the question asks for the answer *as a percentage* so that you're sure to answer correctly.

>> **Calculator's Transfer Display button:** The GRE onscreen calculator has a button marked Transfer Display. You click this button, and the computer transfers the number from the calculator's display right into the typed answer box. Amazing! But be careful. To expand on the previous point about not mixing decimals with percentages, if the answer needs to be a percentage, and you correctly calculate 0.15, clicking Transfer Display places 0.15 in the answer box, whereas the computer is expecting the equivalent answer of 15 percent, which you should enter as 15.

Selecting Two or More Answers

Other GRE questions go overboard with multiple-choice. You can select more than one answer, and you have to get them exactly right: A missed answer or an extra answer costs you the point, and there's no partial credit. The instructions always tell you what to do (whether to pick *one* or *all* correct answers), but you can also easily tell by how the answer choices are marked:

Ⓐ An answer choice with an oval indicates exactly one correct answer.

Ⓑ An answer choice with a square indicates one or more correct answers.

Note that with the squares, there could be one right answer, or two or more, or even all of them. The correct answer will never be *none* of the choices, though: You always have to select *something*. The next few sections show how this process works.

Choosing among three answers

With three answer choices, you typically check each answer separately. Try this simple example, just to get the idea:

PLAY

If $\frac{x}{5}$ is an integer, which of the following *could* be the value of x?

Ⓐ 5

Ⓑ 8

Ⓒ 10

Try each answer separately, and place the possible value of x over 5:

Ⓐ $\frac{(5)}{5} = 1$ (Integer)

Ⓑ $\frac{(8)}{5} = 1.6$ (Not an integer)

Ⓒ $\frac{(10)}{5} = 2$ (Integer)

In this example, the correct answers are (A) and (C).

Choosing among more than three answers

When you have more than three answer choices, you typically check for a range of answers. Here's another simple example so that when you encounter the real thing, you'll know how it works.

PLAY

If Billy earns between $20 and $30 per lawn, which of the following *could* be the amount he earned on the neighbor's lawn?

A $19

B $22

C $26

D $28

E $29

F $31

You know that Billy earns between $20 and $30, so he *could* have earned any amount within that range: (B), (C), (D), and (E).

The question may have the word *inclusive*, like this:

PLAY

If Giselle earns from $45 to $60 per game, <u>inclusive</u>, as a sports announcer, which of the following *could* be the amount she earned last week at <u>the</u> State game?

A $42

B $45

C $48

D $60

E $62

F $65

Because the question has the word *inclusive*, you know that she *could* have earned $45 or $60 in addition to any amount in between: (B), (C), and (D).

Selecting the Quantity That's Greater

GRE math also features the Quantitative Comparison format, in which you review two quantities side by side and select the one that's greater. The answer choices never change, so memorize them now:

Ⓐ Quantity A is greater.

Ⓑ Quantity B is greater.

Ⓒ The two quantities are equal.

Ⓓ The relationship cannot be determined from the information given.

These questions tend to be based more on the math concept than the math calculation. Try this simple example:

PLAY

**Quantity A**	_**Quantity B**_
$(-1)^2$	1

Ⓐ Quantity A is greater.

Ⓑ Quantity B is greater.

Ⓒ The two quantities are equal.

Ⓓ The relationship cannot be determined from the information given.

You know that −1 times itself is 1, making the quantities equal and the correct answer (C). This which-quantity-is-greater format, along with specific traps and tricks, is explored further in Chapter 15.

These simple examples just show you how the questions work. On the GRE, of course, they're more challenging, but they're nothing that you won't be able to handle.

TIP

These variations are straightforward enough when you encounter them, so be sure to encounter and practice them _before_ the exam.

Also, begin practicing your time management skills now by keeping to the one-minute rule and marking questions to return to so that on the day of the exam, this strategy is built into the way that you work, and you can focus on the questions themselves.

While practicing on the computer, or the actual test on the computer, there is a timer in the corner which you can use to track your time. While practicing on paper, use your wristwatch or even a timer. The one-minute rule is approximate, so don't go counting the seconds.

Chapter **10**

Working with Numbers and Operations

This chapter takes you way back . . . all the way to middle school. Although many of the basic math concepts covered in this chapter are fairly simple, you may not have touched them for a while, and you do need a firm grasp of these for GRE math. Fortunately, you've seen this stuff before, so this chapter is a refresher.

This chapter covers most of the basic arithmetic concepts featured in the GRE, including whole numbers, units of measurement, decimals, fractions, percentages, and ratios. After reading this chapter and practicing these concepts, you'll be good to go for any basic math question the GRE throws at you. More important, these math concepts are the foundation of the GRE math topics in the other chapters of this book.

Working with Integers, Factors, and Multiples

GRE math questions may use some math terminology when referring to values. A question might read "*x* is an integer" or "*x* is a factor of 21." You're expected to know what these terms mean:

» **Integer:** Any number, positive or negative, but not a fraction or decimal, is an *integer*. Zero is neither positive nor negative, but still an integer. Examples of integers include –3, –2, –1, 0, 1, 2, and 3.

» **Whole number:** Any integer that's not negative is a *whole number*. Basically, a whole number is any positive integer or zero.

» **Real number:** Any number, whether positive or negative, that goes on the number line is a *real number*. Real numbers include every fraction in which the number on the bottom is *not* zero, decimals, and whole numbers, along with π, zero, and the square root of any positive number.

» **Non-real number:** Any number that can't exist in real math is a *non-real number*. The only one you need to worry about for the GRE is the square root of a negative number, covered further in Chapter 11.

>> **Factor:** Any integer that you get from dividing an integer by another integer is a *factor*. If you divide 15 by 5, you get 3, so 5 and 3 are factors of 15. Note that 1 is a factor of every integer, and each integer is a factor of itself. For example, both 1 and 15 are factors of 15.

>> **Multiple:** Any integer you get from multiplying an integer by another integer is a *multiple*. Multiples of 3 begin with 3, 6, 9, 12, and 15, and they go on forever. Every integer is a multiple of itself. For example, 8 is a multiple of 8.

>> **Prime number:** Any integer that has exactly two factors (1 and itself) is a *prime number*. For example, 3 is prime, and its only factors are 1 and 3. Prime numbers are explored further in the next section.

Working with Math Terms

The GRE may describe the steps you take with the math. Instead of a nice, simple "5 − 4 =," the GRE asks something like "What is the difference of five and four?" That's fine as long as you know what it's asking. Just to be sure, here are some common math terms:

>> **Sum:** The *sum* means adding numbers. The sum of 2, 3, 4, and 5 is the same as $2 + 3 + 4 + 5$.

>> **Product:** The *product* means multiplying numbers. The product of 3, 4, and 10 is the same as $3 \times 4 \times 10$.

>> **Difference:** The *difference* means subtracting numbers. The difference of 22 and 8 is the same as $22 - 8$.

>> **Quotient:** The *quotient* means dividing numbers. The quotient of 20 and 5 is the same as $20 \div 5$ or $\frac{20}{5}$.

Working with Prime and Composite Numbers

Any whole number greater than 1 is either prime or composite. A *prime number* is a whole number that has exactly two positive factors: 1 and itself. Examples of prime numbers include 2, 3, 5, 7, and 11.

The GRE expects you to know these key specifics when dealing with prime numbers:

TIP

>> Zero isn't prime because it's not positive and can't be factored.

>> One isn't prime because it has only *one* factor: itself. (A prime number has *two* factors.)

>> Two is the *only even* prime number because it's the only even number with exactly two factors: 1 and itself.

Meanwhile, a *composite number* has more than two factors, meaning that it can be divided into smaller integers and primes. Examples of composite numbers include 4, 6, 8, and 9.

Any composite number factors to prime numbers. 12 factors to $2 \times 2 \times 3$; 84 factors to $2 \times 2 \times 3 \times 7$; and 125 factors to $5 \times 5 \times 5$. This process is called *prime factorization*.

REMEMBER

Here's an example GRE question that challenges your grasp of prime numbers:

PLAY

Quantity A	**_Quantity B_**
The number of prime numbers from 0 to 10, inclusive	The number of prime numbers from 11 to 20, inclusive

1 3 5 7   *11   13   17   19*

Ⓐ Quantity A is greater.

Ⓑ Quantity B is greater.

Ⓒ The two quantities are equal.

Ⓓ The relationship cannot be determined from the information given.

In Quantity A, the prime numbers from 0 to 10, inclusive, are 2, 3, 5, and 7. In Quantity B, the prime numbers from 11 to 20, inclusive, are 11, 13, 17, and 19. Both quantities have four prime numbers, but counting 0 or 1 as prime (which you know not to do) would lead you to choose (A), which is incorrect. The correct answer is (C).

Working with the Units Digit

The *units digit* is the single number before the decimal or the ending number of any integer. In the number 654.37, for example, the units digit is 4, and in 298, the units digit is 8. When you multiply two integers, the units digit of the product comes from the units digit of the numbers multiplied.

Any integer ending in a 4 times any integer ending in a 3 results in an integer ending in a 2, because $4 \times 3 = 12$, and 12 ends in a 2. Check out these examples:

$$14 \times 13 = 182$$
$$24 \times 43 = 1,032$$
$$204 \times 103 = 21,012$$

Whatever integers you multiply, if one ends in a 4 and the other ends in a 3, the product ends in a 2. But this is true with all integers, not just 4 and 3. Integers ending in 6 and 3, for example, result in a product ending in 8, because $6 \times 3 = 18$:

Pick any two integers, and the result ends in the product of the two integers. $9 \times 7 = 63$, so $5,779 \times 4,477$ ends in (you guessed it) a 3:

$$5,779 \times 4,477 = 58,872,583$$

Who knew? Anyway, this comes up in the GRE, so try these examples.

$$n = (99)^2$$

PLAY

Quantity A	**_Quantity B_**
The units digit of *n*	1

8
99
× 99
1
0

Ⓐ Quantity A is greater.

Ⓑ Quantity B is greater.

Ⓒ The two quantities are equal.

Ⓓ The relationship cannot be determined from the information given.

You could multiply the 99s, but you don't have to. Instead, just multiply the units digits: $9 \times 9 = 81$, so the units digit of n is 1 and the answer is (C).

Try a variation of this theme.

PLAY

If $h = (4)^g$, where g is an even integer, what is the units digit of h?

Ⓐ 0
Ⓑ 2
Ⓒ 4
Ⓓ 6
Ⓔ 8

Try g as the lowest even integer, 2: $(4)^2 = 16$, making the correct answer (C). Just to be sure, what if g is 4: $(4)^4 = 256$, nice. What happens if g is odd, such as 3 or 5: $(4)^3 = 64$ and $(4)^5 = 1{,}024$, so you're good.

Here's one more along the same avenue as that last one.

If $n = (99)^p$, where p is an integer, which of the following *could* be the units digit of n?

Select all possible answers:

Ⓐ 1
Ⓑ 3
Ⓒ 5
Ⓓ 7
Ⓔ 9

To find possible units digits of $(99)^p$, go with $(9)^p$, because of course, you just need the units digit. Try some low values of p and see what happens. Good thing for the ol' calc:

$(9)^1 = 9$

$(9)^2 = 81$, so go with 1

$(9)^3 = (9)^2 \times 9$, so go with $1 \times 9 = 9$

$(9)^4 = (9)^3 \times 9$, so go with $9 \times 9 = 81 \rightarrow 1$

$(9)^5 = (9)^4 \times 9$, so go with $1 \times 9 = 9$

Seems that the units digit of $(9)^p$, and thus $(99)^p$, alternates between 1 and 9. There you go, for correct answers (A) and (E).

REMEMBER

GRE math is *always simple*, even if it looks like a long night. Look at the tricky-looking question, and if you understand the math concept, you can spot the *simple* way to solve it.

Working with Absolute Value

The *absolute value*, indicated by two vertical parallel lines, is the positive form of a number. Technically, *absolute value* refers to the expression's distance from 0 on the number line. Because −7 is 7 units from 0, the absolute value of −7, written as $|{-7}|$, is 7.

Working with one absolute value

The GRE likes to play with absolute values and catch you with double negatives. $-|-3|$ is the same thing as $-(+3)$, which equals -3. The trick is taking the calculations step by step. The absolute value of -3 is 3, which you make negative to get -3.

Try this one:

$$-|+||-5|| = \qquad -5$$

Take this example step by step, from the inside out. Say to yourself, "The absolute value of -5 is 5. Then the negative of that is -5. Then the absolute value of that is 5. And finally, the negative of that is -5."

This example is like a sentence that reads, "The committee voted against stopping the proposition from not happening." Wait — was the committee *for* or *against* the proposition? Break the sentence (or equation) down piece by piece to resolve the double negatives.

If x is a negative number, which of the following must be a positive number?

 Ⓐ $x|x|$ —
 Ⓑ $x|x^2|x||$ —
 Ⓒ $2x|x|$ —
 Ⓓ $2x^2|x|$
 Ⓔ $2x^3|x|$ —

Pick a negative number for x, such as -2, and place that -2 for x in each answer choice:

 Ⓐ $x|x| \rightarrow (-2)|(-2)| = -2|2| = -4$ (negative)
 Ⓑ $x|x^2|x|| \rightarrow (-2)|(-2)^2|(-2)|| = -2|4|2|| = -16$ (negative)
 Ⓒ $2x|x| \rightarrow 2(-2)|(-2)| = -4|2| = -8$ (negative)
 Ⓓ $2x^2|x| \rightarrow 2(-2)^2|(-2)| = 2(4)|2| = 16$ (positive!)
 Ⓔ $2x^3|x| \rightarrow 2(-2)^3|(-2)| = 2(-8)|2| = -32$ (negative)

Breaking it down step by step, you find that the answer is (D).

Be sure to simplify any expression *inside* the absolute value bars first. If you're working with $|3-4|$, calculate that first, for $|3-4| = |-1|$, and only *then* take the absolute value, which in this case is 1.

Working with two absolute values

If you have an x or another unknown inside the absolute-value expression, it means that the expression is that distance from 0 on the number line and typically could be in two separate places. For example,

 $|x| = 7$

tells you that x is 7 away from 0 on the number line, but you don't know whether it's on the positive or negative side, so x could equal 7 or -7. Couple of things just to be clear:

>> **Any x has *one* value.** You don't know which one it is without more information. (With $|x| = 7$, something like $x > 0$ would do the trick.)

>> **Any absolute value is always *positive*.** A number can't be a negative distance from 0, so an equation like $|x| = -5$ is impossible or, in math, has *no solution*.

With an expression like $|x+2| = 5$, you know that $x+2$ is 5 away from 0 on the number line, but you don't know whether on the positive or negative side. Therefore, you actually have two equations: $x+2 = 5$ and $x+2 = -5$. Solve them separately for the two possible values of x:

$$x+2 = 5 \quad \text{and} \quad x+2 = -5$$
$$x = 3 \qquad\qquad x = -7$$

(Be sure not to use the ± symbol, as in $x+2 = \pm5$. Although that is technically true, students always lose the negative value and miss one of the possible answers.) Anyway, given $|x+2| = 5$, you know that x could equal either 3 or −7. Now try an example.

PLAY

In the equation $|x-4| = 3$, x could equal

(enter an answer)

_____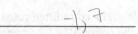

If $x-4$ is 3 away from 0, solve this equation as two separate equations:

$$x-4 = 3 \quad \text{and} \quad x-4 = -3$$
$$x = 7 \qquad\qquad x = 1$$

Enter either 1 or 7, and you got this one right.

REMEMBER

The value of x can't be both 7 *and* 1. x has one value, and that's why the question reads "*x could equal*."

Working with Order of Operations

When you encounter a question on the GRE that includes several operations (addition, subtraction, multiplication, division, squaring, and so on), you must perform those operations in the following order to arrive at the correct answer:

1. Parentheses

   Start with what's inside the parentheses. If they're nested (meaning parentheses inside other parentheses), work the inside parentheses first.

2. Exponents

   Any exponents are next.

3. Multiplication or division

   Work multiplication and division next.

4. Addition or subtraction

   Finally, add or subtract.

REMEMBER

Use the mnemonic *Please Excuse My Dear Aunt Sally (PEMDAS)*, which of course is *Parentheses, Exponents, Multiplication, Division, Addition, and Subtraction.*

PLAY

Use PEMDAS for this problem:

$$10(3-5)^2$$

$\text{\it (handwritten: } (-2)^2 = 4 = 40 \text{)}$

Start with what's inside the parentheses: $3-5=-2$. Then move on to the exponents: -2 squared equals 4. Finally, do the multiplication: $4 \times 10 = 40$. The correct answer is 40.

REMEMBER

The GRE tests your ability to approach these questions *analytically*, which means thinking outside the established methods. Blindly following any rule, including PEMDAS, can lead you into a trap. Instead, take a high-level look at any math question before jumping to a strategy.

For example, take this problem:

PLAY

$$\left(\frac{600}{5}\right)^0 =$$

$\text{\it (handwritten: } 1 \text{)}$

You could begin with dividing 600 by 5 before raising it to the 0 power. That will work. But wait a second — anything to the 0 power equals 1! By taking a high-level look at the question before trying to solve it, you save yourself the effort of working the parentheses first. (Exponents are covered further in Chapter 11.)

Working with Fractions

You probably got fractions just fine back in middle school. This section helps you refresh what you learned.

Adding and subtracting

REMEMBER

You can add and subtract fractions with a *common denominator* (the same bottom part of the fraction). If the fractions don't have a common denominator, give them one; then add or subtract them with the *numerator* (the top part of the fraction).

PLAY

$$\frac{2}{5}+\frac{3}{7}=$$

$\text{\it (handwritten: } \frac{14 + 15}{35} = \frac{29}{35} \text{)}$

Here, 5 and 7 are different denominators, so you can't add these two fractions. Make the denominators the same, however, and then you *can* add the fractions.

To change the denominator without changing the fraction's value, multiply the fraction's top and bottom by the same number. You're not changing the fraction's value because you're essentially multiplying each fraction by 1:

$$\frac{7}{7}=1 \quad \text{and} \quad \frac{5}{5}=1$$

Use this method to give the fractions common denominators:

$$\frac{2}{5}\times\frac{7}{7}=\frac{14}{35} \quad \text{and} \quad \frac{3}{7}\times\frac{5}{5}=\frac{15}{35}$$

Now that the denominators are the same, add the fractions:

$$\frac{14}{35} + \frac{15}{35} = \frac{29}{35}$$

PLAY

Try this one.

$$\frac{2}{5} - \frac{1}{3} =$$

$$\frac{6-5}{15} = \frac{1}{15}$$

Give the fractions common denominators:

$$\frac{2}{5} \times \frac{3}{3} = \frac{6}{15} \quad \text{and} \quad \frac{1}{3} \times \frac{5}{5} = \frac{5}{15}$$

Now that the denominators are the same, subtract the fractions:

$$\frac{6}{15} - \frac{5}{15} = \frac{1}{15}$$

REMEMBER

Don't just multiply the denominators for a common denominator. That will work, but you might get clunky fractions that aren't easy to work with. Instead, look for the *lowest* number that *both* denominators go into:

$$\frac{1}{6} - \frac{1}{15} =$$

$$\frac{5-2}{30} = \frac{3}{30} \quad \frac{1}{10}$$

You can multiply 15×6 for a common denominator, but that's not the *lowest* common denominator, so it creates a lot of extra work:

$$\frac{1}{6} - \frac{1}{15} =$$

$$\left(\frac{1}{6} \times \frac{15}{15}\right) - \left(\frac{1}{15} \times \frac{6}{6}\right) =$$

$$\frac{15}{90} - \frac{6}{90} =$$

$$\frac{9}{90} = \frac{1}{10}$$

Instead, count by 15s, because 15 is the larger of the two numbers.

Check each multiple of 15 for divisibility by 6. Does 15 work? No, 6 doesn't go into 15. How about 30? Yes, both 15 and 6 go into 30. There you have it: The lowest common denominator is 30.

Now multiply the top and bottom of each fraction by the number that makes that fraction's denominator equal to 30. Multiply the first fraction by 5 over 5 and the second fraction by 2 over 2. Then subtract and simplify for the answer:

PLAY

Simplify this expression: $\left(\frac{2}{3} - \frac{1}{5}\right) + \left(\frac{1}{3} - \frac{2}{5}\right)$

Ⓐ $\frac{1}{5}$

Ⓑ $\frac{2}{5}$

Ⓒ $\frac{3}{5}$

Ⓓ $\frac{4}{5}$

Ⓔ 1

$$\frac{3}{3} - \frac{3}{5} = 1 - \frac{3}{5}$$

$$= \frac{2}{5}$$

Before jumping into PEMDAS, take a look at the expression. You could subtract the fractions within the parentheses and then add the results, but is there a simpler way to do this?

Instead, drop the parentheses:

$$\frac{2}{3} - \frac{1}{5} + \frac{1}{3} - \frac{2}{5}$$

Place the like-denominator fractions near each other (along with the + or −)

$$\frac{2}{3} + \frac{1}{3} - \frac{2}{5} - \frac{1}{5}$$

and solve them as two separate equations:

$$\frac{2}{3} + \frac{1}{3} = 1 \quad \text{and} \quad -\frac{2}{5} - \frac{1}{5} = -\frac{3}{5}$$

Now combine the two resulting fractions:

$$1 - \frac{3}{5} = \frac{2}{5}$$

The correct answer is (B).

WARNING

No strategy applies to *every* question of that type. The strategy — in this case, PEMDAS — gets you started, but you still have to take a critical look.

Multiplying

To multiply fractions, just go straight across, multiplying the numerators together and the denominators together:

$$\frac{2}{5} \times \frac{3}{7} = \frac{2 \times 3}{5 \times 7} = \frac{6}{35}$$

TIP

Always check whether you can cancel out common factors between a numerator and a denominator before you begin multiplying. This approach simplifies the work and makes it easier to reduce fractions at the end. Typical GRE math questions are set up to do this.

To multiply these fractions:

$$\frac{6}{5} \times \frac{4}{9}$$

You could just multiply straight across, which will work, but note that the 6 and the 9 are each divisible by 3. It's easier to cancel those 3s from the numerator and denominator and *then* multiply:

$$\frac{{}^2\cancel{6}}{5} \times \frac{4}{\cancel{9}_3} = \frac{2}{5} \times \frac{4}{3} = \frac{8}{15}$$

Or with this example:

$$\frac{4}{15} \times \frac{5}{8}$$

Before you multiply these, reduce the 4 and the 8 (each is divisible by 4), along with the 15 and the 5 (both by 5), simplifying the problem:

$$\frac{{}^{1}\cancel{4}}{\cancel{15}_{3}} \times \frac{{}^{1}\cancel{5}}{\cancel{8}_{2}} = \frac{1}{3} \times \frac{1}{2} = \frac{1}{6}$$

Dividing

To divide two fractions, you *reciprocate* the second fraction (flip it over) and then multiply them:

$$\frac{1}{3} \div \frac{2}{5} = \frac{1}{3} \times \frac{5}{2} = \frac{5}{6}$$

Working with mixed numbers and improper fractions

A *mixed number* is a whole number with a fraction, such as $2\frac{1}{3}$ or $4\frac{2}{5}$. Before you can add, subtract, multiply, or divide a mixed number, you have to get it into fraction form. To do this, multiply the denominator (bottom number) by the whole number and add that to the numerator (top number); then put the sum over the denominator:

>> $2\frac{1}{3} = \frac{(3 \times 2) + 1}{3} = \frac{7}{3}$

>> $4\frac{2}{5} = \frac{(5 \times 4) + 2}{5} = \frac{22}{5}$

The result is an *improper fraction,* in which the numerator is larger than the denominator. Converting an improper fraction back to a mixed number is less common, but to do so, divide the numerator by the denominator, write down the whole number, and then place the remainder over the denominator.

To convert the improper fraction $\frac{22}{7}$ to a mixed number, divide the 7 into 22, and you get 3 with a remainder of 1. The 7 stays as the denominator, and the resulting mixed number is $3\frac{1}{7}$.

Cross-multiplying

To cross-multiply, multiply the top of one fraction by the bottom of the other fraction, and set the quantities equal to each other:

$$\frac{4}{5} = \frac{2}{3x}$$
$$(4 \cdot 3x) = (5 \cdot 2)$$
$$12x = 10$$
$$x = \frac{5}{6}$$

If you have a fraction and a nonfraction, simply place a 1 under the nonfraction and *then* cross-multiply:

$$\frac{2x}{5} = 4$$
$$\frac{2x}{5} = \frac{4}{1}$$
$$2x = 20$$
$$x = 10$$

This process of course is the same as multiplying both sides by the denominator:

$$\frac{2x}{5} = 4$$

$$(5)\frac{2x}{5} = 4(5)$$

$$\cancel{5}\frac{2x}{\cancel{5}} = 20$$

$$x = 10$$

PLAY

If $\frac{2a-1}{4b-1} = 1$, which of the following is also true?

Ⓐ $a = b$

Ⓑ $a = 2b$

Ⓒ $2a = b$

Ⓓ $2a = 3b$

Ⓔ $2a = 3b$

Multiply both sides by the denominator and then simplify:

$$\frac{2a-1}{4b-1} = 1$$

$$(4b-1)\frac{2a-1}{4b-1} = 1(4b-1)$$

$$2a - 1 = 4b - 1$$

$$2a = 4b$$

$$a = 2b$$

The answer is (B).

Working with Decimals

Working with decimals is simple with a few key points:

>> Line up the decimal points when adding or subtracting.

>> Count the decimal places when multiplying.

>> Move the decimal points of both numbers when dividing.

WARNING

Yes, you get an onscreen calculator, but don't rely on it. It's better to understand how the math works. Besides, I see *way* more typos on the calculator — which you're likely to miss — than mistakes on scratch paper — which you're likely to catch.

The following sections walk you through adding, subtracting, multiplying, and dividing decimals.

Adding and subtracting

To add or subtract decimals, first line up the decimal points. Then add or subtract as usual, placing the decimal point in the answer right below where it falls in the original numbers:

$$\begin{array}{r} 4.16 \\ + 0.1 \\ \hline 4.26 \end{array}$$

Multiplying

When multiplying decimals, multiply the numbers first; then count the decimal spaces. Be sure that the number of decimal places in the answer is the same as the *total* number of decimal places in the numbers you're multiplying:

$$0.06 \times 0.03 = 0.0018$$

You know that 6×3 is 18. But the 0.06 and the 0.03 each has two decimal places, for a total of four. Therefore, the final answer also has four decimal places: 0.0018.

Here's a variation:

$$0.04 \times 0.05 = 0.0020$$

You know that 4×5 is 20, so be sure to include the entire 20 (two and zero) when counting the decimal places. After you have the decimal set correctly, you can drop the right-side zero, giving you 0.002.

If a positive number with three decimal places is multiplied by another positive number with three decimal places, which of the following is the *least* product possible?

Ⓐ 0.01

Ⓑ 0.001

Ⓒ 0.0001

Ⓓ 0.00001

Ⓔ 0.000001

For the least product possible, what is the smallest positive number with three decimal places? Probably 0.001. No, definitely 0.001. Anyway, you have two of these numbers, so multiply them starting with the 1s, $1 \times 1 = 1$, and count the six decimal places for 0.000001. The answer is (E).

Now try a variation on this theme:

If a positive number with three decimal places is multiplied by another positive number with three decimal places, which of the following is *closest* to the *greatest* product possible?

Ⓐ 1

Ⓑ 0.1

Ⓒ 0.01

Ⓓ 0.001

Ⓔ 0.0001

For the *greatest* product possible, use the largest number with three decimal places, 0.999, and you have two (because you're multiplying two of them). Before you multiply these numbers, note that you don't need an *exact* answer. The question asks for which is *closest*, so round the pair of 0.999s to 1, and multiply $1 \times 1 = 1$ for answer (A).

Dividing

To divide decimals, move the decimal points of both numbers to the right, the same number of spaces, until the denominator is a whole number.

A tricky $\frac{0.032}{0.008}$ becomes an easy $\frac{0032.}{0008.}$, or $\frac{32}{8}$, for a final answer of 4.

PLAY

Try these on for size:

1. $\frac{0.012}{0.004} = 3 =$

2. $\frac{0.0028}{0.0007} = 4$

3. $\frac{0.360}{0.009} = 40$

$\frac{0.012}{0.004}$ becomes $\frac{0012.}{0004.}$, or $\frac{12}{4}$, for a final answer of 3. For the other two,

» $\frac{0.0028}{0.0007} = \frac{00028.}{00007.} = \frac{28}{7} = 4$

» $\frac{0.36}{0.009} = \frac{0360.}{0009.} = \frac{360}{9} = 40$

See? You don't need a calculator.

REMEMBER

The same thing goes for large numbers with extra zeros on the right: Cancel them, which means moving the decimal point to the *left*, except that here, you don't see the decimal point:

$$\frac{18,000}{3,000} = \frac{18}{3} = 6$$

PLAY

Which of the following has the greatest value?

Ⓐ $\frac{100}{0.1}$

Ⓑ $\frac{10}{0.01}$

Ⓒ $\frac{100}{0.01}$

Ⓓ $\frac{10}{0.001}$

Ⓔ $\frac{100}{0.001}$

With each answer choice, move the decimal points of both numbers to the right, the same number of spaces until the denominator is a whole number:

Ⓐ $\frac{100}{0.1} \rightarrow \frac{1,000}{1} = 1,000$

Ⓑ $\frac{10}{0.01} \rightarrow \frac{1,000}{1} = 1,000$

Ⓒ $\frac{100}{0.01} \rightarrow \frac{10,000}{1} = 10,000$

Ⓓ $\frac{10}{0.001} \rightarrow \frac{10,000}{1} = 10,000$

Ⓔ $\frac{10}{0.0001} \rightarrow \frac{100,000}{1} = 100,000$

Without needing a calculator, you find that the greatest value is (E).

Simplify this expression: $\dfrac{(0.06)(0.014)}{(0.007)(0.003)}$

Ⓐ 400

Ⓑ 40

Ⓒ 4

Ⓓ 0.4

Ⓔ 0.04

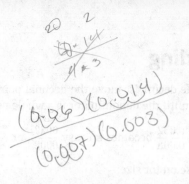

You have a few ways to work this problem, but here's a way that won't mix you up as you're solving it. The steps are simple; the trick is placing the decimal. Note the answers are exactly the same except for the decimal placement.

Start by swapping the top numbers so that the numbers you'll cancel are lined up. Remember that with multiplying, the order doesn't matter:

$$\dfrac{(0.06)(0.014)}{(0.007)(0.003)} \text{ becomes } \dfrac{(0.014)(0.06)}{(0.007)(0.003)}$$

Now you can separate fractions into two separate fractions:

$$\dfrac{(0.014)}{(0.007)} \quad \text{and} \quad \dfrac{(0.06)}{(0.003)}$$

With each fraction separately, move the decimal points to the right until the numbers are integers. With each fraction, move *both* decimals the *same number of spaces*:

$$\dfrac{(0.014)}{(0.007)} \rightarrow \dfrac{(0014.)}{(0007.)} = \dfrac{14}{7}$$

$$\dfrac{(0.06)}{(0.003)} \rightarrow \dfrac{(0060.)}{(0003.)} = \dfrac{60}{3}$$

Now simplify both fractions and multiply:

$$\dfrac{14}{7} = 2 \quad \text{and} \quad \dfrac{60}{3} = 20$$

$$2 \times 20 = 40$$

The correct answer is (B).

Working with Percentages

A percentage is a fraction of 100 — hence the name *per cent*. In this example,

$$24\% = \dfrac{24}{100} = \dfrac{6}{25}$$

100% is 1, and anything over 100% is more than 1:

$$150\% = \dfrac{150}{100} = \dfrac{3}{2} = 1.5$$

The next section shows you how to work these conversions quickly.

Converting

To answer a percentage-based math question, depending on the question, it may be easier to convert the percentage to a decimal or fraction. You may need to convert it back to a percentage to put the answer in the right form, but that happens later. Start with this:

>> **To convert a percentage to a decimal:** Move the decimal point two places to the left and drop the % sign:

$$35\% = 0.35 \qquad 6\% = 0.06 \qquad 50\% = 0.5 \qquad 3.33\% = 0.0333$$

>> **To convert a decimal to a percentage:** Move the decimal point two places to the right and add the % sign:

$$0.32 = 32\% \qquad 0.185 = 18.5\% \qquad 0.05 = 5\%$$

>> **To convert a percentage to a fraction:** Place the number over 100, drop the % sign, and reduce if possible:

$$50\% = \frac{50}{100} = \frac{1}{2} \qquad 125\% = \frac{125}{100} = \frac{5}{4} \qquad 4\% = \frac{4}{100} = \frac{1}{25}$$

>> **To convert a fraction to a percentage:** Set the fraction equal to x over 100 and cross-multiply to find x. The x is your percentage. Set $\frac{27}{50}$ up as

$$\frac{27}{50} = \frac{x}{100}$$

Now cross-multiply to find x:

$$\frac{27}{50} = \frac{x}{100}$$
$$50x = 2{,}700$$
$$5x = 270$$
$$x = 54$$

The fraction equals 54%.

Calculating percentage of change

A question may ask for a percentage of change from an original amount. To find this change, use the following formula:

$$\text{Percent of change} = \frac{\text{Amount of change}}{\text{Original amount}}$$

Finding the percentage of change requires a few simple steps:

1. **Find the number that increased or decreased, and from this number, the *amount* of change.**

If a baseball team won 25 games last year and 30 games this year, the amount of change is 5, because the baseball team won 5 more games this year than last. If a salesperson earned $10,000 last year and $8,000 this year, the amount of change is $2,000.

The *amount* of change is always positive, whether the value has increased or decreased. The salesperson's amount of change is still $2,000 (not –$2,000): He simply earned $2,000 *less* than he did last year.

2. **Place the amount of change over the original amount.**

If the team won 25 games last year and 30 games this year, the original amount is 25. If the salesperson earned $10,000 last year and $8,000 this year, the original amount is $10,000.

3. **Divide and write the answer as a percentage.**

For the baseball team, $\frac{5}{25} = \frac{1}{5} = 20\%$. Divide 1 by 5 to get 0.20, move the decimal point two places to the right, and add the % sign to make it a percentage.

For the *hapless* (meaning *unfortunate*, the opposite of *happy*) salesman, $\frac{2,000}{10,000} = \frac{20}{100} = 20\%$.

Again, divide 20 by 100 to get 0.20, move the decimal point two places to the right, and add the % sign to make it a percentage.

PLAY

Last season, Coach Jamieson's baseball team won 50 games. This season, the team won 30 games. What was the percentage decrease?

Ⓐ 10
Ⓑ 20
Ⓒ 30
Ⓓ 40
Ⓔ 50

Handwritten: $\frac{20}{50} = 40\%$ $50 - 30 = 20$ $\frac{20}{50}$

The number of games that Coach Jamieson's team won decreased by 20 (from 50 to 30). Place the 20 over the original amount of 50 for a decrease of 40%. The correct answer is (D).

PLAY

Carissa has three quarters. Her father gives her three more quarters. Carissa's wealth has increased by what percentage?

Ⓐ 50%
Ⓑ 100%
Ⓒ 200%
Ⓓ 300%
Ⓔ 500%

Did you fall for the trap answer, (C)? Carissa's wealth has doubled, to be sure, but the percentage increase is only 100%, which you can prove with the percentage-of-change formula. The number increase is 0.75 (she has three more quarters, or 75 cents), and her original whole was 0.75. So if you follow the formula, you get $\frac{75}{75} = 100\%$. The right answer is (B).

TIP

When you double something, you increase it by 100%. When you triple something, you increase it by 200%. You're looking for the percentage of *change*, not the *result*. If you turned $3 into $9, the *result* is 300%, but the increase — the *change* — is 200%.

PLAY

The share price of a certain stock was *x* at the end of Wednesday's trading. The price went up 25% at the close of Thursday's trading and then down 20% at the close of Friday's trading.

Quantity A	*Quantity B*
The share price of that stock at the close of Friday's trading.	*x*

Handwritten: $(1.25x)0.8$ $1.25(0.8)$ =

Ⓐ Quantity A is greater.
Ⓑ Quantity B is greater.
Ⓒ The two quantities are equal.
Ⓓ The relationship cannot be determined from the information given.

As a general rule, when the GRE gives you a letter to represent a number, pick a number to use for the letter. In this case, because you're dealing with percentages of change, go with 100.

If the share price was up 25% from Wednesday to Thursday, that price is

$$\$100 + (\$100 \times 25\%) = \$125, \text{ or } \$100 \times 125\% = \$125$$

If the share price was down 20% from Thursday to Friday, that price is

$$\$125 - (\$125 \times 20\%) = \$100, \text{ or } \$125 \times 80\% = \$100$$

The quantities are the same for the correct answer, (C).

TIP

Did you get the right share price for Thursday but use $100 to find Friday's price? No test-taker has *ever* made that mistake. None. The key with these tricky GRE questions is staying organized.

Working with Factorials

The *factorial* is used heavily in counting methods, as explored further in Chapter 13, but it also appears as part of a fraction. It's indicated by an exclamation point (!) and represents the product of integers up to and including a specific integer. 4!, which stands for "four factorial," is $4 \times 3 \times 2 \times 1$, which of course is 24. So $4! = 24$.

There are many variations of the factorial, but the GRE keeps it simple. Just know these:

>> You won't see a fraction, decimal, or exponent factorial — no $6.5!$, $7\frac{1}{4}!$, or $8^{3!}$.

>> The negative factorial is a non-real number, so you won't see that either — no $-2!$.

>> The zero factorial, also known as 0!, equals 1, just as 1! equals 1, so $0! = 1!$.

TIP

When simplifying a factorial, *multiply the numbers last.* Here's an example of how to simplify a factorial in a fraction:

$$\frac{10!}{8!}$$

Because $10! = 10 \times 9 \times 8 \times 7 \times 6 \times 5 \times 4 \times 3 \times 2 \times 1$ and $8! = 8 \times 7 \times 6 \times 5 \times 4 \times 3 \times 2 \times 1$, cancel the matching numbers first:

$$\frac{10 \times 9 \times \cancel{8!}}{\cancel{8!}}$$

Then multiply: $10 \times 9 = 90$.

It wouldn't be beneath the GRE to present something like this:

$$\frac{100!}{98!}$$

Instead of panicking like the test-taker next to you who didn't read *GRE Prep 2023 For Dummies,* you can laugh out loud (well, not *too* loud, because you want to be kind) and heartily slash apart the fraction:

$$\frac{100 \times 99 \times \cancel{98!}}{\cancel{98!}}$$

This is why you multiply the numbers *last*: $100 \times 99 = 9,900$. See? You *don't* need the calculator.

PLAY

The fraction $\frac{1,000!}{998!}$ is equivalent to

Ⓐ 999,000

Ⓑ 988,000

Ⓒ 99,000

Ⓓ 98,000

Ⓔ 9,000

The calculator would actually make this problem harder. Factor out the 998! and cancel:

$$\frac{1,000 \times 999 \times 998!}{998!}$$

$$\frac{1,000 \times 999 \times \cancel{998!}}{\cancel{998!}}$$

$$1,000 \times 999$$

$$999,000$$

The answer is (A).

Working with Ratios

A *ratio* is a relationship between two similar numbers or quantities. A ratio acts like a fraction, written as either dogs : cats or $\frac{dogs}{cats}$. Here are a couple of examples:

>> The ratio *of* umbrellas *to* people is $\frac{umbrellas}{people}$.
>> The ratio *of* yachts *to* sailboats is yachts : sailboats.

When you know the tricks, ratios are some of the easiest problems to answer quickly. The following sections show you two ways to solve simple ratios and the best way to handle combined ratios.

Working with total numbers

Because ratios compare two amounts, the *total* number of items is a multiple of the sum of the numbers in the ratio. In other words, if the ratio is 3 dogs for every 2 cats, the total number of animals has to be a multiple of 5, such as 5, 10, or 15.

Try these exercises.

PLAY

At last night's game, the ratio of your team's fans to the other team's fans was 4 : 5. Which of the following *could* be the total number of fans at the game?

Ⓐ 8

Ⓑ 12

Ⓒ 16

Ⓓ 25

Ⓔ 54

To solve this ratio problem, first add the numbers in the ratio: $4 + 5 = 9$. The total number of fans must be a multiple of 9 (9, 18, 27, 36, and so on). Can the total, for example, be 54? Yes, because 9 goes evenly into 54. Can it be 12? No, because 9 doesn't go evenly into 12. The correct answer is (E).

TIP

These GRE-style questions ask for numbers that *could* be true. But the GRE also asks for numbers that *must* be true or *cannot* be true. Be sure to double-check when selecting your answer, *especially* for questions with more than one answer.

PLAY

To create his special dish, Thomas uses 7 teaspoons of sriracha for every 5 teaspoons of soy sauce. Which of the following *could* be the total number of teaspoons of sriracha and soy sauce in this dish? Select *all* correct answers.

[A] 75
[B] 60
[C] 57
[D] 48
[E] 36
[F] 24

$$\frac{5sr}{7ss} \qquad 12$$

Add the numbers in the ratio: $7 + 5 = 12$. The total must be a multiple of 12 (meaning that it must be evenly divisible by 12), which in this list are 60, 48, 36, and 24, making (B), (D), (E), and (F) the correct answers.

PLAY

The ratio of his CDs to her CDs is 2:9.

Quantity A	*Quantity B*
Total number of CDs	11

Ⓐ Quantity A is greater.
Ⓑ Quantity B is greater.
Ⓒ The two quantities are equal.
Ⓓ The relationship cannot be determined from the information given.

You know the total must be a multiple of 11, but it could be many things: 11, 22, 33, 44, 55, and so on. This type of trap has caught many a test-taker. Quantity A may be equal to *or* greater than Quantity B, but you don't have enough information to decide that. The correct answer is (D).

PLAY

After a rough hockey game, Toni checks her uniform and finds 3 smudges for every 5 tears. Which of the following could be the total number of smudges and tears on her uniform?

Ⓐ 53
Ⓑ 45
Ⓒ 35
Ⓓ 33
Ⓔ 32

Add the numbers in the ratio: $3 + 5 = 8$. The total must be a multiple of 8 (or, looking at it another way, the total must be evenly divisible by 8). Only (E) is a multiple of 8 ($8 \times 4 = 32$). The correct answer is (E).

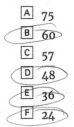

Working with amounts in the ratio

Suppose that you're given a ratio and a total and are asked to find an amount in the ratio. The ratio of doughnut holes to doughnuts is $5:3$, and there are 32 total snacks. How many doughnut holes are there? One way to find the answer is the following:

1. Add the numbers in the ratio.

There are 5 doughnut holes for every 3 doughnuts, so $5 + 3 = 8$.

2. Divide the total number of items by that sum.

There are 32 items total, so $\frac{32}{8} = 4$.

3. Multiply the result from Step 2 by each term in the ratio.

Multiply 4 by 5 for 20 doughnut holes and 4 by 3 for 12 doughnuts.

4. Add the answers to make sure that they match the total.

Make sure that the 20 doughnut holes and 12 doughnuts total 32 items, which they do.

You can also set up the solution with this equation:

$$5x + 3x = 32$$
$$8x = 32$$
$$x = 4$$

And place 4 for x back in the equation:

$$5(4) + 3(4) = 32$$
$$20 + 12 = 32$$

There you have it: 20 doughnut holes and 12 doughnuts. Nice! Have some coffee.

With practice, this technique becomes second nature. Try this example:

PLAY

To congratulate his team, which just won the last game in an undefeated season, the ecstatic coach took his team to the local pizza joint, where each player ordered either a deep-dish pizza or a calzone. If there were 3 deep-dish pizzas for every 4 calzones, if there were 28 players on the team, and if each player ordered one or the other, but not both, how many deep-dish pizzas were there?

There were 3 deep-dish pizzas for every 4 calzones, so set up the solution with the equation

$$3x + 4x = 28$$
$$7x = 28$$
$$x = 4$$

Place 4 for x back in the equation:

$$3(4) + 4(4) = 28$$
$$12 + 16 = 28$$

So the team had 12 deep-dish pizzas and 16 calzones.

Maintaining the ratio

If the GRE math problem has a ratio, and you have to change the number of items while maintaining the ratio, you can calculate the number of items you need by setting the two ratios equal.

Make the existing ratio (as a fraction) equal the new items (also as a fraction), and cross-multiply to find the missing value.

Your college has to maintain its current ratio of 3 graduate assistants for every 40 students. If 240 new students are expected this fall, how many new graduate assistants does the school need to hire to maintain the ratio?

Solve the problem as follows:

1. Set up the existing ratio as a fraction:

$$\frac{\text{Assistants}}{\text{Students}} = \frac{3}{40}$$

2. Set up the new additions as a fraction, with *x* as the unknown value:

$$\frac{\text{Needed Assistants}}{\text{New Students}} = \frac{x}{240}$$

3. Set the fractions equal:

$$\frac{3}{40} = \frac{x}{240}$$

4. Cross-multiply to solve for *x*.

Multiply the numerator of each fraction by the denominator of the other:

$$40x = 720$$
$$4x = 72$$
$$x = 18$$

Thus, 18 new graduate assistants are needed to maintain the ratio.

Now try this one:

The aviary keeps on hand a ratio of 4 sacks of seed for every 30 birds. If the aviary currently has 180 birds, how many sacks of seed does it need on hand to maintain the ratio?

Ⓐ 12
Ⓑ 18
Ⓒ 24
Ⓓ 27
Ⓔ 30

4:30
×6 ×6

Solve the problem as follows:

1. Set up the existing ratio as a fraction:

$$\frac{\text{seed}}{\text{birds}} = \frac{4}{30}$$

2. Set up the new additions as a fraction, with *x* as the unknown value:

$$\frac{\text{Needed seed}}{\text{Existing birds}} = \frac{x}{180}$$

3. Set the fractions equal:

$$\frac{4}{30} = \frac{x}{180}$$

4. **Cross-multiply to solve for *x*.**

Multiply the numerator of each fraction by the denominator of the other:

$$30x = 720$$
$$3x = 72$$
$$x = 24$$

Thus, 24 sacks of seed are needed to maintain the ratio, for answer (C).

Banker's Credit Union has 7 call-center reps on hand for every 200 customers. With an aggressive marketing campaign, the bank just signed an additional 1,400 customers. How many new reps should the bank hire to maintain this ratio?

Ⓐ 14

Ⓑ 20

Ⓒ 35

Ⓓ 49

Ⓔ 50

Set up the equation:

$$\frac{\text{Reps}}{\text{Customers}} = \frac{7}{200} = \frac{x}{1,400}$$

Cross-multiply, and you find that $x = 49$. The correct answer is (D).

Combining ratios

Sometimes, the GRE provides two separate ratios that have a common item. You can use that common item to combine the ratios for a single three-part ratio.

Combining ratios is a little like adding fractions. When adding fractions, you find the lowest common denominator. When combining ratios, find the lowest multiple of the item they have in common, just like a common denominator. Here's how you do that:

Sam's jazz shop has 6 saxophones for every 5 drum kits and 2 drum kits for every 3 trombones. What's the ratio of saxophones to trombones?

Solve the problem as follows:

1. **Set up the ratios as $A:B$.**

Place the item that the ratios have in common (drum kits) in a column.

Saxes		Drums		Trombones
6	:	5		
		2	:	3

2. **Find a common multiple of the item that these ratios have in common.**

In this instance, both ratios include drum kits. The least common multiple of 5 and 2 (the numbers of drum kits) is 10.

3. **Multiply each ratio term so the quantity of the common item equals the common multiple (from Step 2).**

Find the common ratio exactly as though you were adding fractions, with drum kits as the common denominator:

$$\frac{6}{5} + \frac{3}{2} = \frac{6(2)}{5(2)} + \frac{3(5)}{2(5)} = \frac{12}{10} + \frac{15}{10}$$

You aren't adding fractions, of course, but you treat the ratios the same way. You want the number of drum kits to equal 10. Multiply both terms in the first ratio by 2, and multiply both terms in the second ratio by 5.

Saxes		Drums	Trombones
6(2)	:	5(2)	
		2(5)	: 3(5)

Saxes		Drums	Trombones
12	:	10	
		10	: 15

4. **Write out a combined ratio.**

The combined ratio of saxophones to drum kits to trombones is $12:10:15$. To answer the question, give only the ratio of saxophones to trombones, which is $12:15$, or $4:5$.

PLAY

A sports shop has 3 jerseys for every 2 helmets and 6 kneepads for every 5 jerseys. What's the ratio of helmets to kneepads?

Ⓐ $1:3$

Ⓑ $4:9$

Ⓒ $5:9$

Ⓓ $2:3$

Ⓔ $7:9$

Set up the ratios:

Jerseys		Helmets	Kneepads
3	:	2	
5	:		6

Find a common multiple of jerseys. A common multiple of 3 and 5 is 15, so multiply each term of the first ratio by 5 and each term of the second by 3:

Jerseys		Helmets	Kneepads
15	:	10	
15	:		18

Now write these ratios out as a combined ratio:

Jerseys		Helmets		Kneepads
15	:	10		
15		:		18
15	:	10	:	18

The ratio of helmets to kneepads is $10:18$, or $5:9$, for the correct answer is (C).

Chapter 11

Solving Algebra and Functions

lgebra and functions use letters and abstract operations to represent mathematics to solve for an unknown value, usually represented by *x*. You probably solved algebra in junior high and high school, and perhaps even in college, but here's a refresher on the details that may have escaped over time, in the context of the GRE.

This chapter reveals everything you need to know about algebra to be fully prepared for the test. It starts slowly, with bases, exponents, and good ol' *x* and *y*, and gradually moves on to more complicated concepts. Although you may be tempted to skip around, you may want to go through this chapter from start to finish.

Solving Bases and Exponents

When you multiply a number repeatedly by itself, you raise that number to a certain power. Here's an example: 3 to the power of 4, or 3^4, is $3 \times 3 \times 3 \times 3 = 81$. In this example, 3 is the base, and 4 is the exponent. The *exponent* simply tells you how many times to multiply the *base* (number) by itself. Here are a few more examples:

» $10^2 = 10 \times 10 = 100$

» $5^3 = 5 \times 5 \times 5 = 125$

» $x^4 = x \cdot x \cdot x \cdot x$

Remember these rules of bases and exponents:

Any number to the zero power equals 1:

$$x^0 = 1 \qquad 5^0 = 1 \qquad 129^0 = 1$$

Any number to a negative exponent is the reciprocal of that number to its positive exponent:

$$y^{-4} = \frac{1}{y^4} \qquad 6^{-3} = \frac{1}{6^3} \qquad 325^{-1} = \frac{1}{325}$$

REMEMBER

A number with a negative exponent isn't negative. When you flip it, you get the reciprocal, and the negative goes away:

$$5^{-3} = \frac{1}{5^3} = \frac{1}{125}$$

When you raise 10 to a power, you get 1 followed by the number of zeros equal to that power:

» $10^2 = 100$ (two zeros)

» $10^3 = 1,000$ (three zeros)

» $10^4 = 10,000$ (four zeros)

because $10^4 = 10,000$, 5×10^4 is $5 \times 10,000$, which equals 50,000.

To multiply like bases, add the exponents:

» $\left(x^3\right)\left(x^2\right) = x^{(3+2)} = x^5$

» $5^3 \times 5^4 = 5^{(3+4)} = 5^7$

» $150^5 \times 150^7 = 150^{(5+7)} = 150^{12}$

WARNING

You can't multiply *different* bases. $x^2 \cdot y^3$ stays $x^2 \cdot y^3$, and $14^3 \times 15^5$ stays $14^3 \times 15^5$.

To divide like bases, subtract the exponents:

» $x^5 \div x^3 = x^{(5-3)} = x^2$

» $\frac{5^8}{5^4} = 5^{(8-4)} = 5^4$

» $150^4 \div 150^0 = 150^{(4-0)} = 150^4$

WARNING

Did you look at the second example, and think that the answer is 5^2? Falling into the trap of dividing exponents rather than subtracting them can happen, especially when you see numbers that divide easily, such as 8 and 4. Common mistake, but don't let it get you.

Multiply the exponents of a base inside and outside parentheses:

» $\left(x^2\right)^3 = x^{(2 \times 3)} = x^6$

» $\left(5^3\right)^3 = 5^{(3 \times 3)} = 5^9$

» $\left(175^0\right)^3 = 175^{(0 \times 3)} = 175^0 = 1$

REMEMBER

This rule is true even with negative exponents:

» $\left(x^{-2}\right)^3 = x^{(-2 \times 3)} = x^{-6}$

» $\left(x^4\right)^{-5} = x^{(4 \times -5)} = x^{-20}$

» $\left(x^{-2}\right)^{-4} = x^{(-2 \times -4)} = x^8$

To add or subtract like bases with like powers, add or subtract the numerical coefficients of the bases.

The *numerical coefficient* is the number to the left of the base. In $15y^2$, y is the base, and 15 is the numerical coefficient. Note that the exponent 2 applies only to the y, not the whole $15y$. To subtract:

$$15y^2 - 10y^2$$
$$(15 - 10)y^2$$
$$5y^2$$

WARNING

You can't add or subtract the numerical coefficients when the bases are different. $16x^2 - 4y^2$ stays $16x^2 - 4y^2$. Furthermore, you can't add or subtract like bases with *different* exponents. $14x^3 - 9x^2$ stays $14x^3 - 9x^2$. The bases *and* exponents must be the same for you to add or subtract the terms.

To make sure that you're comfortable with the variations, try these Quantitative Comparison (QC) questions with bases and exponents. (In a QC question, you compare the contents in two columns, explored further in see Chapter 15.)

PLAY

Quantity A	*Quantity B*
x^3	$\dfrac{x^7}{x^4}$

Ⓐ Quantity A is greater.

Ⓑ Quantity B is greater.

Ⓒ The two quantities are equal.

Ⓓ The relationship cannot be determined from the information given.

Remember that when you divide, you subtract the exponents, so $x^{(7-4)} = x^3$, regardless of the value of x. The correct answer is (C).

PLAY

Quantity A	*Quantity B*
$(x^3)^4$	x^{12}

Ⓐ Quantity A is greater.

Ⓑ Quantity B is greater.

Ⓒ The two quantities are equal.

Ⓓ The relationship cannot be determined from the information given.

Because you multiply exponents together when you take an exponent to a higher power, the two quantities are the same, regardless of x: $x^{(3\times4)} = x^{12}$. The correct answer is (C).

PLAY

Quantity A	*Quantity B*
$(x^3)^4$	12

Ⓐ Quantity A is greater.

Ⓑ Quantity B is greater.

Ⓒ The two quantities are equal.

Ⓓ The relationship cannot be determined from the information given.

Because you don't know the value of x, you can't tell which quantity is greater. You may think that anything to the 12th power is a large number, making (A) the correct answer, but it depends on the value of x. If x equals 2, you'd be right. If x equals $\frac{1}{2}$, you'd be wrong. This is an easy mistake to fall for. See Chapter 13 for more on trying different values of x for different results. The correct answer is (D).

PLAY

Quantity A	_Quantity B_
$16x^4 - 4x^3$	$12x$

Ⓐ Quantity A is greater.

Ⓑ Quantity B is greater.

Ⓒ The two quantities are equal.

Ⓓ The relationship cannot be determined from the information given.

Because you don't know what x is, as in the preceding question, try different values for x to see which quantity is greater. If you selected (C), you fell for the trap. The correct answer is (D).

PLAY

Quantity A	_Quantity B_
$10x^3 - 2y^3$	$8xy$

Ⓐ Quantity A is greater.

Ⓑ Quantity B is greater.

Ⓒ The two quantities are equal.

Ⓓ The relationship cannot be determined from the information given.

Because you don't know what x or y is, you can't tell which quantity is greater. The correct answer is (D).

Solving Math Operators

You see a problem with a strange symbol — a triangle, a star, or a circle with a dot, as in the following example. You've never seen it before, and you're not sure what it means. It's probably a math operator, such as +, −, ×, or ÷, but it's a new one that the GRE uses just for this one math question. Don't worry — the GRE always tells you what the symbol means (or sets up the question so you can figure it out).

The approach is simple: Place a number for the variable. The math itself is *always* easy. The trick is knowing how to set up the equation.

The symbol may be part of an equation, like this:

$$a \odot b \odot c = \frac{(a+b)}{(b+c)}$$

A question follows the explanation, like this:

$$3 \odot 4 \odot 5 =$$

Here's how you solve it:

1. Substitute the numbers for the letters.

For this problem, substitute 3, 4, and 5 for *a*, *b*, and *c*, respectively:

$$3 \odot 4 \odot 5 = \frac{(3+4)}{(4+5)}$$

2. Solve the equation:

$$\frac{3+4}{4+5} = \frac{7}{9}$$

The GRE keeps things interesting with variations like this:

PLAY

$$\text{If } [[x]] = \frac{2x}{x+2}, \text{ then } [[-4]] =$$

To solve, substitute −4 for *x*:

$$[[-4]] = \frac{2(-4)}{(-4)+2}$$

Then solve the equation for your answer:

$$\frac{2(-4)}{(-4)+2} = \frac{-8}{-2} = 4$$

Here's another variation to get through:

PLAY

If $3 \oplus 4 = \frac{6}{7}$, which of the following could be an expression for $x \oplus y$?

Ⓐ $x \oplus y = \frac{x+y}{2y}$

Ⓑ $x \oplus y = \frac{2y}{x+y}$

Ⓒ $x \oplus y = \frac{2x}{x+y}$

Ⓓ $x \oplus y = \frac{x+y}{2x}$

Ⓔ $x \oplus y = \frac{x}{y}$

$$3 \oplus 4 = \frac{2(3)}{3+4}$$

Looks crazy, right? Not if you know what to do. Place 3 for *x* and 4 for *y* in each answer choice, which seems like a lot of work, but the simple math goes fast. You'll see that only answer (C) works:

$$x \oplus y = \frac{2x}{x+y}$$
$$(3) \oplus (4) = \frac{2(3)}{(3)+(4)}$$
$$= \frac{6}{7}$$

Solving for *X*

Solving for x is just that: turning something like $2x + 3 = 5$ into $2x = 2$ and finally $x = 1$. Simple, right? But the GRE, being what it is, varies this idea in ways you haven't seen since your SAT or ACT and you won't see again until your kids need help with their SATs. But that's another story.

The GRE, still being what it is, stays within its scope of math topics and sets the questions up for easy answering if you know how to answer them. This section takes you through these GRE-level topics and shows you how to answer each question in less than a minute.

Solving for *x* with a number

To solve for x or any other variable that the question asks for, move that variable to one side of the equation, and divide both sides of the equation by the coefficient. Where $4x = x + 6$, subtract x from both sides of the equation for $3x = 6$. Divide both sides by 3, for $x = 2$, and the solution is 2.

Try it with the equation

$$3x + 7 = 9x - 5$$

1. **Move all the *x*'s to the left side of the equation.**

   Anything on the right side that's tied to an x, in this case $9x$, is subtracted — from *both* sides. The $9x$ get canceled from the right and subtracted from the left side.

   $$\begin{array}{r} 3x + 7 = 9x - 5 \\ \underline{-9x \quad\quad -9x} \\ -6x + 7 = -5 \end{array}$$

2. **Move all the numbers to the right side of the equation.**

   This step is just like Step 1 except that you're subtracting the number, in this case 7, from both sides. The 7 is canceled from the left and subtracted from the right.

   $$\begin{array}{r} -6x + 7 = -5 \\ \underline{-7 \quad -7} \\ -6x = -12 \end{array}$$

3. **Divide both sides by the coefficient.**

   The *coefficient* is the number near the x.

   $$\frac{-6x}{-6} = \frac{-12}{-6}$$
   $$x = 2$$

   Just to be sure, place the 2 back in the original equation to check that it works:

   $$\begin{array}{r} 3x + 7 = 9x - 5 \\ 3(2) + 7 = 9(2) - 5 \\ 6 + 7 = 18 - 5 \\ 13 = 13 \end{array}$$

TIP

GRE algebra questions are typically simple to solve, but once in a while, there's a question where it's easier to try the answer choices. Always go for solving the problem first, but if that seems to be tricky, trying out answers may be the way to go.

PLAY

Solve for x:

$$5^{\frac{x}{5}} + \frac{x}{2} = 30$$

Ⓐ 7

Ⓑ 8

Ⓒ 10

Ⓓ 12

Ⓔ 14

You *could* solve for x, but I wouldn't. Instead, start with the answer choice number that's easiest to work with, in this case probably 10. Then the process goes like this:

$$5^{\frac{(10)}{5}} + \frac{(10)}{2} = 30$$
$$5^2 + 5 = 30$$
$$25 + 5 = 30$$

See? Almost too easy. Solving for x would have been a nightmare, but this way it's an easy $x = 10$. Correct answer: (C).

Solving with the FOIL method

When you're multiplying any number by a *binomial* (two numbers in parentheses), use the *distributive property*, which means multiplying all the values inside the parentheses by the number to the left of the parentheses. Here's an example:

$$9(3x + 2y)$$
$$9(3x) + 9(2y)$$
$$27x + 18y$$

When you're multiplying two binomials, such as $(a+b)(a-b)$, you basically multiply everything in one set of parentheses by everything in the other set of parentheses and then add up all the results. This technique is also known as the *FOIL method*, which stands for *First, Outer, Inner, Last*. Try it with the equation

$$(a+b)(a-b)$$

1. **Multiply the *First* variables:**

   $a \times a = a^2$

2. **Multiply the *Outer* variables:**

   $a \times (-b) = -ab$

3. **Multiply the *Inner* variables:**

   $b \times a = ba$ (which is the same as *ab*).

4. **Multiply the *Last* variables:**

   $b \times (-b) = -b^2$

5. **Combine like terms:**

   $a^2 - ab + ab - b^2$ (Here, the *−ab* and *+ab* cancel out.)
   $a^2 - b^2$

Like terms are two or more terms with the same variable(s) and exponent. $3x^3$ and $2x^3$ are like terms, and you may combine them as follows: $3x^3 + 2x^3 = 5x^3$. You can't combine $3x^3$ and $3y^3$ because the variables differ, nor $3x^3$ and $3x^5$ because the exponents differ.

REMEMBER

When you're multiplying, the order doesn't matter, as in $5 \times 3 = 3 \times 5$ and $ab = ba$.

Try another equation: $(3a + b)(a - 2b)$.

1. **Multiply the *First* terms:**

$$3a \times a = 3a^2$$

2. **Multiply the *Outer* terms:**

$$3a \times (-2b) = -6ab$$

3. **Multiply the *Inner* terms:**

$b \times a = ba$ (which is the same as ab)

4. **Multiply the *Last* terms:**

$$b \times (-2b) = -2b^2$$

5. **Combine like terms for the final answer:**

$$3a^2 - 6ab + ab - 2b^2$$
$$3a^2 - 5ab - 2b^2.$$

Try the following FOIL-based question. The secret is to do what you can. You can FOIL the expressions, so start with that:

PLAY

If $(x + 3y)(x - 3y) = 10$, what is the value of $x^2 - 9y^2$?

Ⓐ 5

Ⓑ 10

Ⓒ 15

Ⓓ 20

Ⓔ 25

Don't get stuck. FOIL it:

$$(x + 3y)(x - 3y) = 10$$
$$x^2 - 3xy + 3xy - 9y^2 = 10$$
$$x^2 - 9y^2 = 10$$

That's it? I mean, that's it! The answer is (B).

TIP

Memorize the following three common FOIL equations so you can save time by not working them out each time:

$$(a - b)(a + b) = a^2 - b^2$$

You can also prove this equation with FOIL: $(a - b)(a + b)$.

TIP

1. **Multiply the *First* terms:**

   $a \times a = a^2$

2. **Multiply the *Outer* terms:**

   $a \times b = ab$

3. **Multiply the *Inner* terms:**

   $(-b) \times a = -ba$ (which is the same as *-ab*)

4. **Multiply the *Last* terms:**

   $(-b) \times b = -b^2$

5. **Combine like terms for the final answer:** $ab - ab = 0$, so $a^2 - b^2$

The *only* time the middle term cancels out is when the binomials are the same except that one has a plus and the other a minus, such as $(a-b)(a+b)$, resulting in a perfect square minus a perfect square: $(a^2 - b^2)$. When a question has a perfect square minus a perfect square, you can quickly do the reverse and factor it: $(x^2 - 25) = (x-5)(x+5)$. For more on factoring, see the next section, "Factoring back out."

$$(a+b)^2 = a^2 + 2ab + b^2$$

You can prove this equation by using FOIL: $(a+b)(a+b)$.

1. **Multiply the *First* terms:**

   $a \times a = a^2$

2. **Multiply the *Outer* terms:**

   $a \times b = ab$

3. **Multiply the *Inner* terms:**

   $b \times a = ba$ (which is the same as *ab*)

4. **Multiply the *Last* terms:**

   $b \times b = b^2$

5. **Combine like terms for the final answer:**

   $ab + ab = 2ab$, so $a^2 + 2ab + b^2$

   $$(a-b)^2 = a^2 - 2ab + b^2$$

You can also prove this equation by using FOIL: $(a-b)(a-b)$.

1. **Multiply the *First* terms:**

   $a \times a = a^2$

2. **Multiply the *Outer* terms:**

   $a \times (-b) = -ab$

3. **Multiply the *Inner* terms:**

   $(-b) \times a = -ba$ (which is the same as *-ab*)

4. **Multiply the *Last* terms:**

$$(-b) \times (-b) = b^2$$

5. **Combine like terms for the final answer:**

$$-ab + -ab = -2ab, \text{ so } a^2 - 2ab + b^2$$

Note that the b^2 at the end is positive because it's from a negative times a negative.

Factoring back out

As often as you FOIL on the GRE, you also *factor*, which is the opposite of FOILing. Factoring takes an algebraic expression from its final form back to its original form of two binomials. You perform this operation when an equation contains x^2 to find the two possible values of x.

REMEMBER

x (or any letter in the equation) always has *one* value. Most equations with an x squared have two *possible* values for x, but x actually has one value. If $x^2 = 25$, you know that x equals 5 *or* −5, but *not both*. If $y^2 = 9$, the two *possible* solutions are 3 and −3, but the *value* of y is *either* 3 *or* −3. These possible values of x or y are also called the *solutions* or the *roots* of the equation.

TIP

When solving for x^2, also known as a *quadratic equation* (though you won't need the quadratic formula, so put that right back on the shelf), the first thing to do is set the equation equal to zero. If the GRE gives you $48 = x^2 + 2x$, make it $x^2 + 2x - 48 = 0$. If the exam gives you $20 = h^2 - h$, don't think about it; make it $h^2 - h - 20 = 0$.

Given $x^2 - 4x - 12 = 0$, what are the two possible values of x? Factor the answer one step at a time:

1. **Draw two sets of parentheses:**

$$(\quad)(\quad) = 0$$

2. **Fill in the *First* terms.**

To get x^2, the *first* terms have to be x and x:

$$(x\quad)(x\quad) = 0$$

3. **Fill in the *Last* terms.**

You need two numbers that equal −12 when multiplied and −4 when added. Start with the multiplied number, in this case −12: You have 3×4, 2×6, and 1×12. Keep in mind that one of these terms is negative, for the −12, so which two numbers add up to −4? After a few tries, you find that −6 and +2 do the trick. Multiplied, they equal −12, and added, they equal −4. Now you can complete the equation:

$$(x - 6)(x + 2) = 0$$

REMEMBER

Whether you write it as $(x - 6)(x + 2)$ or $(x + 2)(x - 6)$ doesn't matter. These expressions are multiplied, so they can be in either order.

Now solve for x as two separate equations: $(x - 6) = 0$ and $(x + 2) = 0$, for x values of 6 and −2. Remember that x doesn't equal *both* 6 and −2; it equals one *or* the other. That's why the question is phrased "What are the two *possible* values for x?"

REMEMBER

Factoring becomes more complicated when a number is in front of the x^2, as in $6x^2 - x - 2 = 0$, but that almost never happens on the GRE, so there's no need to cover it here. The equations that you factor will almost always be very simple: The GRE is testing whether you understand the concept, not whether you can go knee-deep in the math.

If $x^2 + 2x = 15$, what are the two possible values of x?

Ⓐ 3 and 5
Ⓑ 3 and −5
Ⓒ −3 and 5
Ⓓ −3 and −5
Ⓔ −3 and 3

Factor this one, but first set the equation equal to zero:

$$x^2 + 2x = 15$$
$$x^2 + 2x - 15 = 0$$
$$(x + 5)(x - 3) = 0$$

$$(x + 5) = 0$$
$$(x - 3) = 0$$

The two possible values of x are 3 and −5, which is answer (B).

Don't always go straight for factoring. Sometimes, there's an easier way.

One of the roots of the equation $x^2 + kx - 10 = 0$ is 5, and k is a constant. What is the value of k?

Ⓐ 5
Ⓑ 3
Ⓒ 2
Ⓓ −3
Ⓔ −5

Now you *could* factor it, and that *will* work, but there's a better way. Don't treat it like a math problem; treat it like a puzzle.

If one of the roots is 5, one of the possible values of x is 5, so place 5 for x in the equation:

$$x^2 + kx - 10 = 0$$
$$(5)^2 + k(5) - 10 = 0$$
$$25 + 5k - 10 = 0$$
$$5k + 15 = 0$$
$$5k = -15$$
$$k = -3$$

There you have it, for answer (D).

Solving Square Roots and Radicals

You're likely to see math problems on the GRE that include square roots or radicals. A *square root* is a number that's multiplied by itself for a result. 3 is the square root of 9, because $3 \times 3 = 9$. A *radical* is another way of expressing a square root. The square root of 9 may be represented as $\sqrt{9}$. Though higher-level roots exist in math, the *square* root is the root you most commonly see on the GRE.

REMEMBER

A square root can be on only a *positive* number, such as $\sqrt{25}$, and never $\sqrt{-25}$, because a negative number multiplied by itself results in a positive answer. If you see a square root on a negative number, then this number isn't real, which means that the equation with the number won't work. $\sqrt{-25}$ isn't -5, because the square root is from the *same* number multiplied by itself (squared), and -5 times itself is $+25$.

The following sections review the math problems you may encounter on the exam related to roots and radicals. But first, you need to know how to simplify them.

Simplifying

When possible, simplify radicals to get rid of them. *Simplifying* basically means reducing the radical to its most manageable form, often getting rid of the radical. To simplify a radical, factor the number inside and pull out pairs of factors. Here are a few examples:

» $\sqrt{1} = \sqrt{1 \times 1} = 1$

» $\sqrt{4} = \sqrt{2 \times 2} = 2$

» $\sqrt{9} = \sqrt{3 \times 3} = 3$

» $\sqrt{16} = \sqrt{4 \times 4} = 4$

» $\sqrt{25} = \sqrt{5 \times 5} = 5$

In some cases, part of the radical remains, but you can still reduce it to make the number easier to work with. In these problems, the GRE simply expects you to reduce the radical as far as you can, and the correct answer will typically include a radical. Here's an example of a radical that you can't reduce to an integer but can simplify:

$$\sqrt{300} = \sqrt{10 \times 10 \times 3}$$
$$= \sqrt{10 \times 10} \times \sqrt{3}$$
$$= 10 \times \sqrt{3}$$
$$= 10\sqrt{3}$$

In this example, the square root of 100 is 10, so the 10 comes out of the radical. The 3, however, stays inside the radical, and the two numbers (10 and $\sqrt{3}$) are multiplied for a result of $10\sqrt{3}$. The answer choice will typically look like $10\sqrt{3}$, and you won't have to estimate the value.

To take the square root of a fraction, such as $\sqrt{\dfrac{9}{25}}$, take the roots of the top and bottom separately.

You know that $\sqrt{9} = 3$ and $\sqrt{25} = 5$, so $\sqrt{\dfrac{9}{25}} = \dfrac{\sqrt{9}}{\sqrt{25}} = \dfrac{3}{5}$.

PLAY

If $a = \sqrt{\dfrac{1}{16}}$, what is the value of $\sqrt{a}$?

Ⓐ $\dfrac{1}{16}$

Ⓑ $\dfrac{1}{8}$

Ⓒ $\dfrac{1}{4}$

Ⓓ $\dfrac{1}{2}$

Ⓔ 1

Start with the value of *a*:

$$a = \sqrt{\frac{1}{16}}$$

$$= \frac{1}{4}$$

Take the square root of that:

$$\sqrt{a} = \sqrt{\frac{1}{4}}$$

$$= \frac{1}{2}$$

There you have it, for answer (D).

If you work a problem and end up with a radical such as $3\sqrt{5}$, never calculate it. Instead, check the answer choices. Typically, $3\sqrt{5}$ is waiting in the list, so you can leave your answer at that.

Adding and subtracting

To add and subtract numbers with radicals, stick with these rules:

REMEMBER

>> **You can add or subtract *similar* radicals.** Just add or subtract the number in front of the radical:

$$2\sqrt{7} + 3\sqrt{7} = 5\sqrt{7}$$

$$4\sqrt{5} - \sqrt{5} = 3\sqrt{5}$$

This works just like adding or subtracting numbers with *x*: $2x + 3x = 5x$ and $4y - y = 3y$.

>> **You *can't* add or subtract *different* radicals.** $6\sqrt{5} + 4\sqrt{3}$ stays the same, just as $4x + 5y$ stays the same.

If the radicals aren't similar, you may still be able to add or subtract them. Try to simplify one radical to make it similar to the other:

$$\sqrt{28} + \sqrt{7} =$$
$$\sqrt{4 \times 7} + \sqrt{7} =$$
$$2\sqrt{7} + \sqrt{7} = 3\sqrt{7}$$

PLAY

Try these problems: $\sqrt{25}\ \sqrt{2} + \sqrt{2} = 6\sqrt{2}$

1. $\sqrt{50} + \sqrt{2} =$

2. $\sqrt{27} + 5\sqrt{12} =$ $3\sqrt{3} + 10\sqrt{3} = 13\sqrt{3}$

     3   9   3   4

Here are the answers:

1.

$$\sqrt{50} + \sqrt{2} =$$
$$\sqrt{5 \times 5 \times 2} + \sqrt{2} =$$
$$5\sqrt{2} + \sqrt{2} = 6\sqrt{2}$$

2.

$$\sqrt{27} + 5\sqrt{12} =$$
$$\sqrt{3 \times 3 \times 3} + 5\sqrt{2 \times 2 \times 3} =$$
$$3\sqrt{3} + \left(5 \times 2\sqrt{3}\right) =$$
$$3\sqrt{3} + 10\sqrt{3} = 13\sqrt{3}$$

Multiplying and dividing

To multiply and divide numbers with radicals, follow these rules:

>> **Put all the numbers inside one radical and then multiply or divide the numbers:**

$$\sqrt{5} \times \sqrt{6} \rightarrow \sqrt{5 \times 6} = \sqrt{30}$$
$$\frac{\sqrt{15}}{\sqrt{5}} \rightarrow \sqrt{\frac{15}{5}} = \sqrt{3}$$

>> **If numbers are in front of the radicals, multiply or divide them separately.** Because the order doesn't matter when multiplying, move the pieces around to make them easier to multiply.

$$6\sqrt{3} \times 4\sqrt{2} \rightarrow (6 \times 4)\left(\sqrt{3} \times \sqrt{2}\right)$$
$$= (24)\left(\sqrt{6}\right)$$
$$= 24\sqrt{6}$$

Dividing works pretty much the same way. Divide the numbers in front of the radicals separately from the radicals themselves:

$$6\sqrt{10} \div 2\sqrt{5} \rightarrow (6 \div 2)\left(\sqrt{10 \div 5}\right)$$
$$= (3)\left(\sqrt{2}\right)$$
$$= 3\sqrt{2}$$

PLAY

$7\sqrt{5} \times 3\sqrt{6} =$

Ⓐ $10\sqrt{11}$

Ⓑ $10\sqrt{30}$

Ⓒ $21\sqrt{11}$

Ⓓ $21\sqrt{30}$

Ⓔ 630

You know that $7 \times 3 = 21$ and $\sqrt{5} \times \sqrt{6} = \sqrt{30}$, so the answer is $21\sqrt{30}$. This one is straight multiplication. The correct answer is (D).

Simplifying first

If you can simplify what's under the radical, do that first; then take the square root of the answer. Here's an example:

$$\sqrt{\frac{1}{3} + \frac{1}{9}}$$

First, simplify the fractions: $\frac{1}{3} + \frac{1}{9} = \frac{4}{9}$. Next, take the square roots of the top and bottom separately:

$$\sqrt{\frac{4}{9}} = \frac{\sqrt{4}}{\sqrt{9}} = \frac{2}{3}$$

And the answer is $\frac{2}{3}$.

Solving Coordinate Geometry

Coordinate geometry is where algebra and geometry meet — a method of describing points, lines, and shapes with algebra. It all happens on a grid known as the *coordinate plane*.

The coordinate plane, also known as the *xy rectangular grid* or *xy plane,* is a two-dimensional area defined by a horizontal *x*-axis and a vertical *y*-axis that intersect at a *point of origin* labeled (0, 0). Each point is labeled using an *ordered pair (x, y)* with the first number in the parentheses indicating how far to the right or left of (0, 0) the point is and the second number indicating how far above or below (0, 0) the point is. This point has an *x*-value of 2 and a *y*-value of 1, for the coordinates (2, 1):

© John Wiley & Sons, Inc.

Here's what you need for the coordinate geometry questions on the GRE.

Solving common problems

Most questions on coordinate geometry involve the *linear equation,* thoroughly explored in the following sections. Before you get there, however, here are other common coordinate geometry topics along with practice questions and instructions for solving them.

Distance between two points

To find the distance between two points on the grid, you can use the *distance formula,* which is based on the Pythagorean theorem (see Chapter 12). In a right triangle, using the lengths of the two shorter sides, the formula lets you determine the length of the longest side (the *hypotenuse*); in equation form, $a^2 + b^2 = c^2$, where a and b are the lengths of the shorter sides and c is the length of the longest side.

In coordinate geometry, you use this formula along with the coordinates of two points to specify the lengths of the sides. Given two points, one with coordinates (x_1, y_1) and the other with coordinates (x_2, y_2), the length of one of the shorter sides is $x_2 - x_1$, and the length of the other shorter side is $y_2 - y_1$.

The distance formula involves drawing a right triangle from the points on the grid and using the Pythagorean theorem to find the hypotenuse.

Suppose that you're asked to calculate the distance between two points with coordinates (1, 2) and (7, 10). On the coordinate system, the right triangle would look like the following drawing, where the length of one short side would be $x_2 - x_1 = 7 - 1 = 6$, and the length of the other short side would be $y_2 - y_1 = 10 - 2 = 8$.

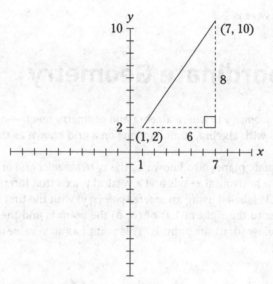

© John Wiley & Sons, Inc.

Place these lengths in the distance formula for a distance of 10:

$$a^2 + b^2 = c^2$$
$$(6)^2 + (8)^2 = c^2$$
$$36 + 64 = c^2$$
$$100 = c^2$$
$$10 = c$$

The distance formula provides another approach for answering questions such as these. With the coordinates of the two points, you can use the following formula to calculate the distance between the two points:

$$\text{distance} = \sqrt{(x_2 - x_1)^2 + (y_2 - y_1)^2}$$
$$= \sqrt{((7) - (1))^2 + ((10) - (2))^2}$$
$$= \sqrt{6^2 + 8^2}$$
$$= \sqrt{36 + 64}$$
$$= \sqrt{100}$$
$$= 10$$

TIP

You can use the distance formula or draw the grid and triangle; both approaches use the Pythagorean theorem to find the length of the hypotenuse in a right triangle when given the lengths of the two shorter sides.

PLAY

Find the distance from (9, 4) to (8, 6).

Just put the distance formula to work:

$$\text{distance} = \sqrt{(x_2 - x_1)^2 + (y_2 - y_1)^2}$$
$$= \sqrt{((8)-(9))^2 + ((6)-(4))^2}$$
$$= \sqrt{(-1)^2 + 2^2}$$
$$= \sqrt{1+4}$$
$$= \sqrt{5}$$

Slope of a line

The *slope of a line* can be found with "rise over run," which refers to the distance that a segment of the line moves vertically (its "rise") divided by the distance it moves horizontally (its "run"). To find the slope of the line that goes through the points (1, 2) and (7, 10) (from the preceding section), note that the line rises 8 and runs 6. The slope is $\frac{8}{6}$, which reduces to $\frac{4}{3}$.

TIP

Don't worry about positive versus negative when using rise over run. Just place the rise on top and the run on the bottom; *then* decide whether it's positive or negative: Going left to right, if the line goes *up*, the slope is positive; if the line goes *down*, the slope is negative. If the line is *flat*, the slope is 0, and if the line goes straight up and down, the slope is undefined.

Another way to calculate the slope of a line that goes through the points (x_1, y_1) and (x_2, y_2) is to use the *slope formula*:

$$\text{slope} = \frac{y_2 - y_1}{x_2 - x_1}$$

PLAY

What is the slope of the line connecting the points $(-1, -2)$ and $(4, 6)$?

The slope formula can get this one for you:

$$\text{slope} = \frac{y_2 - y_1}{x_2 - x_1}$$
$$= \frac{(6)-(-2)}{(4)-(-1)}$$
$$= \frac{6+2}{4+1}$$
$$= \frac{8}{5}$$

Midpoint formula

To find the midpoint of a line segment defined by the coordinates of two points on the graph, you can use the *midpoint formula*:

$$\text{midpoint} = \left(\frac{x_1 + x_2}{2}, \frac{y_1 + y_2}{2} \right)$$

In this formula, (x_1, y_1) are the coordinates of one of the line segment's endpoints, and (x_2, y_2) are the coordinates of the other endpoint. It takes the average of the *x* coordinates and the average of the *y* coordinates to find the *x, y* coordinates in the middle. Try an example.

In the xy-coordinate grid, which is the midpoint of the segment defined by the points $(200,50)$ and $(-40,-30)$?

Ⓐ $(160,20)$

Ⓑ $(120,40)$

Ⓒ $(100,25)$

Ⓓ $(80,10)$

Ⓔ $(20,15)$

Take the average of the x- and y- coordinates or place them in the midpoint formula, which does the same thing:

$$\text{midpoint} = \left(\frac{x_1 + x_2}{2}, \frac{y_1 + y_2}{2}\right)$$

$$= \left(\frac{(200) + (-40)}{2}, \frac{(50) + (-30)}{2}\right)$$

$$= \left(\frac{160}{2}, \frac{20}{2}\right)$$

$$= (80,10)$$

The answer is (D).

Solving linear equations

A *linear equation* is any equation with two letters, usually x and y, and no exponents, such as $2x + y = 5$. The *slope-intercept* form shows it as solved for y, such as $y = -2x + 5$, or $y = mx + b$. This form is called *slope-intercept* because it shows the slope and y-intercept right there in the equation: m is the slope, and b is the y-intercept (the point at which the line representing the equation intersects the y-axis).

In the xy-coordinate grid, which is the slope of the line with the equation $2y - 3x = 6$?

Ⓐ $\frac{2}{3}$

Ⓑ $\frac{3}{2}$

Ⓒ $\frac{4}{3}$

Ⓓ $\frac{3}{4}$

Ⓔ 1

Convert the equation $2y - 3x = 6$ to its *slope-intercept* form, which means that you solve for y. Then the x-coefficient is the slope of the line:

$$2y - 3x = 6$$

$$2y = 3x + 6$$

$$y = \frac{3x}{2} + 3$$

The answer is (B).

Questions on the GRE that involve the slope-intercept form may provide the coordinates of a point through which the line passes and require you to calculate the y-intercept. The line $y = 7x + b$ passes through point $(4, 15)$. At what point does the line cross the y-axis? To get the answer, place 4 for x and 15 for y and then solve the equation:

$$y = 7x + b$$
$$(15) = 7(4) + b$$
$$15 = 28 + b$$
$$15 - 28 = b$$
$$b = -13$$

So the line crosses the y-axis at the point $(0, -13)$.

You can also use the slope-intercept form to find the slope of a line when given its y-intercept and the coordinates of any point on the line. Suppose that a line crosses the y-axis at $y = 5$ and goes through the point $(4, 13)$, and you need to determine its slope. Simply place the given values in the slope-intercept form:

$$y = mx + b$$
$$(13) = m(4) + (5)$$
$$13 - 5 = 4m$$
$$8 = 4m$$
$$m = 2$$

Given the equation $2x + 3y = 24$, find an ordered pair (the x-y coordinates of a point) that makes the equation true. To test this, place in values for x and y, and make sure the equation works. In this case, the ordered pairs $(0, 8)$, $(6, 4)$, and $(-3, 10)$ make the equation true.

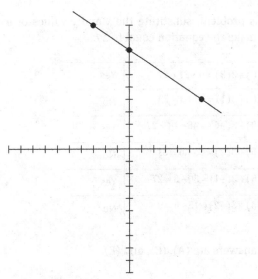

As you now know, a linear equation may appear in a different format. Instead of $2x + 3y = 24$, you may see $3y = 24 - 2x$ or $2x = 24 - 3y$. Regardless of the format, you can usually find two points on the line by setting x equal to 0 and solving for y and then setting y equal to 0 and solving for x. Use this method to find two ordered pairs for the equation $2x + 3y = 24$. Here's y if $x = 0$:

$$2x + 3y = 24$$
$$2(0) + 3y = 24$$
$$3y = 24$$
$$y = 8$$

So one point is $(0, 8)$. And here's x if $y = 0$:

$$2x + 3(0) = 24$$
$$2x = 24$$
$$x = 12$$

The other point is $(12, 0)$.

PLAY

Identify the (x, y) coordinates that make the equation $5x + 3y = 27$ true.

Select all correct answers.

A (0, 9)
B (6, 1)
C (9, −6)
D (5, 2)
E (6, −1)
F (3, −2)

To solve this problem, substitute the x and y values of each answer into $5x + 3y = 27$, and see which ones make the equation equal to 27:

A	$5(0) + 3(9) = 0 + 27 = 27$	Yes
B	$5(6) + 3(1) = 30 + 3 = 33$	No
C	$5(9) + 3(-6) = 45 - 18 = 27$	Yes
D	$5(5) + 3(2) = 25 + 6 = 31$	No
E	$5(6) + 3(-1) = 30 - 3 = 27$	Yes
F	$5(3) + 3(-2) = 15 - 6 = 9$	No

The correct answers are (A), (C), and (E).

Solving two linear equations

Any linear equation has endless solutions, because for each value of x, there's a corresponding value of y. With *two* linear equations, also called *simultaneous equations*, the equations usually depict lines that cross, which means there is a single set of x and y values where the lines cross. These single values for x and y are called the *solutions* to the equation. There are two ways to find these solutions: addition and substitution.

Addition method

The addition method (also known as the *elimination method*) is easy and works best for simpler equations, which means most of the time on the GRE. Suppose that you're solving this problem:

PLAY

$$5x - 2y = 4$$
$$x + 2y = 8$$

Make sure that the *x*s and *y*s (or whichever letters are in the equations), the numbers, and the equal signs are lined up. Then add (or subtract) to cancel one unknown and solve for the other:

$$\begin{array}{r} 5x - 2y = \ 4 \\ + \ x + 2y = \ 8 \\ \hline 6x + \ \ 0 = 12 \\ x = \ 2 \end{array}$$

Now place the newly discovered value of *x* in an original equation to find the value of *y*. You should get the same value of *y* from either equation:

$$5(2) - 2y = 4$$
$$10 - 2y = 4$$
$$-2y = -6$$
$$y = 3$$

If you were to graph the two equations, the lines would meet at $(2,3)$.

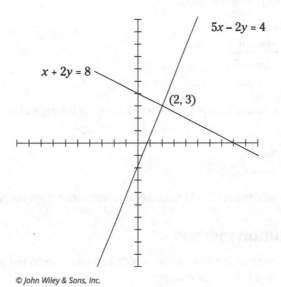

© *John Wiley & Sons, Inc.*

PLAY

Fit these equations together for the solutions:

1. $2x + y = 9$
  $- \ x + y = 5$ $x = 4$

2. $3a + 4b = 5$
  $+ \ 2a - 2b = 5b$ $5a = 15 \Rightarrow a = 3$
  $\overline{ 5a = 15}$

You're sure to encounter linear equation pairs on the GRE, so make sure you're comfortable with these variations on the theme.

1. In this one, you don't add the equations; you subtract them:

$$2x + y = 9$$
$$\underline{-(x + y = 5)}$$
$$x = 4$$

Armed with x as 4, place it back in for y in one of the equations:

$$(4) + y = 5$$
$$y = 1$$

2. What can you add or subtract to cancel something out? First, multiply the second equation by 2 to cancel the bs or 3 to cancel the as. Either way is fine, so here's an example of multiplying the second equation by a 2:

$$3a + 4b = 5$$
$$2(a - 2b = 5)$$

And the pair of equations become this:

$$3a + 4b = 5$$
$$2a - 4b = 10$$

Then it's business as usual:

$$3a + 4b = 5$$
$$\underline{+(2a - 4b = 10)}$$
$$5a = 15$$
$$a = 3$$

You did all that for $a = 3$. Place it back in one of the original equations:

$$(3) - 2b = 5$$
$$-2b = 2$$
$$b = -1$$

The lines cross at $(3, -1)$, because linear equations don't always use x and y.

Substitution method

The other method is substitution, which has more steps but works better for some complicated equations. Just follow these steps:

1. **In one equation, solve for the first unknown in terms of the second unknown.**

2. **Substitute the result from Step 1 for the first unknown in the other equation and solve for the second unknown.**

3. **Place the value for the second unknown into either equation, and solve for the first unknown.**

PLAY

It's easier than it sounds. Try this example:

$$5x - 2y = 4$$
$$+ \quad x + 2y = 8$$

(handwritten) OR $x = -2y + 8 \Rightarrow$ $5(8-2y) - 2y = 4$ $\quad x + (6) = 8$
$40 - 10y - 2y$
$6x \quad 12 \Rightarrow x = 2$ $\Rightarrow -12y = -36 \Rightarrow y = 3$ $\quad y = 2$

In this example, the second equation is simpler, so start with that. Solve for x in terms of y:

$$x + 2y = 8$$
$$x = 8 - 2y$$

Now substitute $8 - 2y$ for x in the first equation and solve for y:

$$5(8 - 2y) - 2y = 4$$
$$40 - 10y - 2y = 4$$
$$-12y = 4 - 40$$
$$-12y = -36$$
$$y = 3$$

Finally, place the value for y into one of the original equations to find the value of x:

$$x + 2y = 8$$
$$x + 2(3) = 8$$
$$x + 6 = 8$$
$$x = 2$$

The solution is $(2, 3)$.

The addition method is usually faster and simpler, especially when everything lines up (the *x*s, the *y*s, and the equal signs). If the *x* is on the left of the equal sign in one equation and on the right side in the other, you may want to use substitution. Don't sweat this choice, though: Both methods work well and fast to give you the same result.

You'll find simultaneous equations in word problems, which I cover in Chapter 13. Here's an example of a problem where substitution works nicely:

PLAY

Andy is 5 years older than Betsy. If Andy will be twice Betsy's age in 3 years, how old are Andy and Betsy now?

Ⓐ 7 and 2
Ⓑ 6 and 3
Ⓒ 8 and 5
Ⓓ 10 and 2
Ⓔ 10 and 5

(handwritten) $A = B + 5$ $\quad (B + B + 5 = 2B + 3$
$A + 3 = 2(B + 3)$ $\quad 2 = B$
$\quad\quad 2B + 6$ $\quad A = 7$
$A = 2B + 3$ $\quad B + 5 = 15$

First, set up the equations. Remember that words like *is*, *are*, and *will be* serve as equal signs. "Andy is 5 years older than Betsy" becomes $a = b + 5$, and "he'll be twice her age in 3 years" becomes $a + 3 = 2(b + 3)$. Only the GRE could turn kids into linear equations. Anyway, because $a = b + 5$ from the first equation, substitute $(b + 5)$ for a in the second equation, like this:

$$(b + 5) + 3 = 2(b + 3)$$

Now solve for b:

$$b + 8 = 2b + 6$$
$$-b = -2$$
$$b = 2$$

So if Betsy is two years old, use 2 for b in the first equation to find Andy's age:

$$a = (2) + 5$$
$$a = 7$$

The kids are young, which makes the math easier. Correct answer: (A).

Solving graphed circles

A *graphed circle* is a circle drawn on the x/y plane from an equation. The equation is like a contorted linear equation; there are an x and a y, but they're twisted and squared instead of a nice, simple equation. Don't worry, though. In the classroom, the teachers vary the heck out of this concept, but on the GRE, there's only one flavor. This is the equation for the graphed circle:

$$(x-h)^2 + (y-k)^2 = r^2$$

In this equation, h and k are the x and y values of the center, and r is the radius. The way you remember is that the x and y values of the center become negative (or positive, if they're already negative), and the radius is squared. Suppose that you have a circle in which the (x, y) coordinates of the center are $(3, -2)$ and the radius is 5.

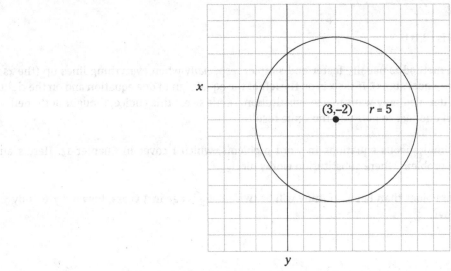

© John Wiley & Sons, Inc.

Thus, the equation of this circle is $(x-3)^2 + (y+2)^2 = 5^2$. It also may appear as $(x-3)^2 + (y+2)^2 = 25$, but the radius is still 5.

PLAY

A circle is drawn in the x/y coordinate grid. If the radius is 3 and the (x, y) coordinates of the center are $(-2.5, 0.5)$, which of the following is the equation for the circle?

Ⓐ $(x+2.5)^2 + (y-0.5)^2 = 3$

Ⓑ $(x-2.5)^2 - (y+0.5)^2 = 3$

Ⓒ $(x-2.5)^2 + (y+0.5)^2 = 3^2$

Ⓓ $(x+2.5)^2 - (y-0.5)^2 = 3^2$

Ⓔ $(x+2.5)^2 + (y-0.5)^2 = 3^2$

Knowing the equation of the circle is $(x-h)^2 + (y-k)^2 = r^2$, just place −2.5 for x, 0.5 for y, and 3 for r, like this:

$$(x-h)^2 + (y-k)^2 = r^2$$
$$(x-(-2.5))^2 + (y-(0.5))^2 = (3)^2$$
$$(x+2.5)^2 + (y-0.5)^2 = 3^2$$

Watch out for trap answers in which x and y have the wrong sign or r isn't squared. Correct answer: (E).

Solving Patterns in a Sequence

A GRE sequence question has you interpret a numeric pattern from an equation. The term is indicated by a letter, such as a, and counted with a subscript number, such as: $a_1, a_2, a_3, a_4, a_5, ..., a_n$.

You're typically given one value for a, such as $a_1 = 10$. The 1 in a_1 means "the *first a*," and the statement tells you that the first a has a value of 10. Be sure not to confuse the subscript number, in this case the 1 in a_1, with the value of that particular a, in this case 10.

Next, you're given an equation that describes the relationship between the sequential terms — in other words, the value of the next a, such as

$$a_{n+1} = a_n + 3$$

Though the value of n (the subscript of a) changes, it has only one value at a time in the equation. If $n = 1$, $= n + 1 = 2$. Thus, the equation can be rewritten as

$$a_2 = a_1 + 3$$

Don't get caught up in the math. Under all that subscript, what it tells you is simple. The *next a* is 3 more than the *previous a*. The second a, which is a_2, is 3 more than the first a, which is a_1.

The next iteration of the equation, with 1 added to n again, looks like this:

$$a_3 = a_2 + 3$$

It tells you that the *third a*, a_3, is 3 more than the *second a*, a_2. In other words, if $a_1 = 10$, then $a_2 = 13$, $a_3 = 16$, and so forth. That's the pattern, and the question is based on this pattern, such as "What is the value of a_6?" Just keep adding 3 until you reach the sixth a:

$$a_1 = 10$$
$$a_2 = 13$$
$$a_3 = 16$$
$$a_4 = 19$$
$$a_5 = 22$$
$$a_6 = 25$$

PLAY

In the sequence $b_{n+1} = b_n - 4$, for all integers b and n, where $b_3 = 12$, what is the value of b_5?

Ⓐ 20
Ⓑ 16
Ⓒ 8
Ⓓ 4
Ⓔ 0

$b_4 = b_3 - 4$
↓
8
↓
4

Start with the equation $b_{n+1} = b_n - 4$, which translates to English as "The *next b* is 4 less than *this b*." If *this b*, or b_3, is 12, then the *next b*, b_4 is 8, and b_5 is 4. Correct answer: (D).

PLAY

In the sequence $h_{m-1} = h_m - 5$, for all integers h and m, where $h_6 = 8$, what is the value of m when $h_m = -2$?

$\underbrace{8 - 5}_{5} = \underbrace{3 - 5}_{4} = -2$

(A) 4

(B) 2

(C) 0

(D) −1

(E) −2

Start with the equation $h_{m-1} = h_m - 5$, which is GRE for "The *previous h* is 5 less than *this h*." Instead of counting the little numbers up, you count them down. If *this h*, or h_6, is 8, the *previous h*, h_5 is 3, and the one before that, h_4, is −2. But there's a twist: The question doesn't ask for the value of *h*; it asks for the value of *m* when $h_m = -2$. The GRE does stuff like this. Correct answer: (A).

Solving f(x) Functions

A *function* is a graphed equation, such as $y = 2x + 3$. Instead of y, however, there's an $f(x)$, like this: $f(x) = 2x + 3$. The $f(x)$ represents the resulting y value, and you place a value for x by substituting the number in the $f(x)$. If $x = 5$, $f(5) = 2(5) + 3$, and $f(5) = 13$. Note that the function may use other letters, such as $g(h)$.

TIP

Sometimes the $f(x)$ question is easier to solve by trying out the answer choices.

Questions on the GRE that involve $f(x)$ typically give you an equation where you place the values for x for the answer. Here's how you get started:

1. Place the value of x from the $f(x)$ into each x in the equation.

2. Watch for variations in the $f(x)$ or the equation.

Plenty of these are on the GRE, so here are some examples of variations:

PLAY

$f(x) = (2x)^3$. Solve for $f(2)$. $= (2(2))^3$ 4^3

To solve, substitute the number in parentheses for the letter in parentheses (in this case, place in 2 for x):

$$f(2) = (2(2))^3 = 4^3 = 64$$

Try another one:

PLAY

When $f(x) = x^2 + 2x$, what is the value of $f(3)$?

Just place in 3 for x in the equation:

$$f(x) = x^2 + 2x$$
$$f(3) = (3)^2 + 2(3)$$
$$= 9 + 6$$
$$= 15$$

PLAY

When $f(x) = x^2 + 2x$, what is the value of $2f(5)$?

[handwritten: $25 + 10 \sim (35)2 = 70$]

First find the value of $f(5)$:

$$f(x) = x^2 + 2x$$
$$f(5) = (5)^2 + 2(5)$$
$$= 25 + 10$$
$$= 35$$

Now that you know what $f(5)$ is, double it for $2f(5)$:

$$f(5) = 35$$
$$2f(5) = 70$$

PLAY

When $f(x) = x^2 + 2x$, what are the two values of x when $f(x) = 48$?

[handwritten figure and: $0 = x^2 + 2x - 48$, $-2 \pm \sqrt{2^2 - 4(-48)}$ over 2, $8 \cdot 6$, $y = -8, +6$]

If $f(x) = 48$, place 48 for $f(x)$ and solve as a quadratic:

$$f(x) = x^2 + 2x$$
$$(48) = x^2 + 2x$$
$$x^2 + 2x - 48 = 0$$
$$(x + 8)(x - 6) = 0$$
$$x = -8 \text{ or } 6$$

See? That's all there is to it. Now try this one:

PLAY

$f(x) = x + x^2 + x^3$. Solve for $f(10)$.

[handwritten: $10 + 100 + 1000 \quad 1110$]

Just substitute the 10 for the x:

$$f(10) = (10) + (10)^2 + (10)^3 = 10 + 100 + 1{,}000 = 1{,}110$$

You seem to like these, so here's another. (Just kidding, I can't tell.)

PLAY

If $g(h) = 2h + 3$ and $g(k) = 17$, what is the value of k?

[handwritten: $2k + 3 = 17$, $2k = 14$, $h = 7$]

Ⓐ 4
Ⓑ 5
Ⓒ 6
Ⓓ 7
Ⓔ 8

Place k for h in the first equation, and set that equal to 17:

$$g(k) = 2(k) + 3 = 17$$

Now drop the $g(k)$ and solve for k:

$$2(k) + 3 = 17$$
$$2k = 14$$
$$k = 7$$

See, the math is *always* simple but it *looks* menacing. Just remember that there's always a simple trick, but it helps if you've seen it before and know what to do — and practice. The answer is (D).

This one is more challenging to set up, but the actual math is just as simple:

PLAY

The function g is defined as $g(h) = \dfrac{h^2 - h}{2}$ for all real numbers h. If j is a number such that $g(-j) = 10$, which two of the following could be the number j?

Indicate *two* such numbers.

A. −5

B. −3

C. −1

D. 2

E. 4

F. 6

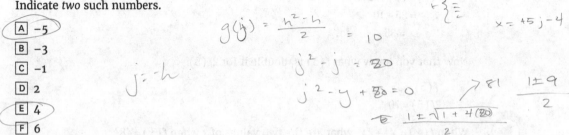

Start with finding the possible values of h when $g(h)$ equals 10, which is another quadratic:

$$g(h) = \frac{h^2 - h}{2}$$

$$10 = \frac{h^2 - h}{2}$$

$$20 = h^2 - h$$

$$h^2 - h - 20 = 0$$

$$(h - 5)(h + 4) = 0$$

$$h = -4 \text{ or } 5$$

Now, here's the twisted part. h could be −4 or 5, but the question asks for possible values of j, which is equal to $-h$. Simple math, but tricky question. Correct answers: (A) and (E).

Chapter **12**

Drawing Geometry

G RE geometry is all about basic shapes that you know and understand, along with familiar details that need refreshing but come back to you in no time. As with all GRE math, you could see a specific scope of topics see (such as parts of a circle), and outside that scope are topics that you aren't likely to see (such as cones and spheres). This chapter covers the topics you need to understand and gives you hands-on practice answering targeted practice questions.

Drawing Lines and Angles

The main parts of most of these shapes are lines and angles.

REMEMBER

GRE images are *typically* drawn to scale, well enough for you to get a sense of what's going on in the drawing. The drawing or the description will always tell you everything that you need (such as side lengths, parallel sides, and right-angle boxes), so whether it's drawn to scale really doesn't matter. You wouldn't eyeball the answer anyway (except in graphs, explored in Chapter 14), so always look in the description for clues to unravel the drawing. On that note, if the drawing has a label that reads, "Figure not drawn to scale," it's *way* off.

Drawing lines

A *line* is straight and continuous. If it curves, it's not a line, and if it ends, it's a *segment* (running between two points) or a *ray* (going in only one direction, like an arrow). For the most part, don't worry about this distinction, but if you see these terms, you know what they are.

Parallel lines don't cross and are represented by the symbol ∥. *Perpendicular lines* cross at right angles and are represented by the symbol ⊥ or in a drawing by the right-angle indicator ⌐. Find more on right angles in the next section. A *perpendicular bisector* is a line that passes through the midpoint of a line segment and is perpendicular to it.

Drawing angles

An *angle* is the space between two lines or segments that cross or share an endpoint. Fortunately, there's not much to understanding angles when you know the types of angles and a few key concepts.

Finding an angle is usually a matter of simple addition or subtraction. Besides the rules in the following sections, these three rules apply to the angles on the GRE:

» An angle can't be negative.

» An angle can't be 0 degrees or 180 degrees.

» Fractional angles, such as $44\frac{1}{2}$ degrees or 179.5 degrees, are rare on the GRE. An angle is typically a whole number and rounded to be easy to work with. If you're placing a number for an angle, use a whole number, such as 30, 45, or 90.

Right angle

A *right angle* equals 90 degrees and is represented by perpendicular lines with a small box where the two lines meet.

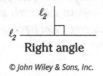

Right angle

© John Wiley & Sons, Inc.

WARNING

Watch out for lines that appear to be perpendicular but really aren't. An angle is a right angle *only* if the description reads, "The lines (or segments) are perpendicular," you see the box in the angle, or you're told the shape is a square, rectangle, or right triangle. Otherwise, you can't assume that the angle is 90 degrees.

TIP

Other than the words *right angle* and *bisect*, you probably won't see the following terms, so don't worry about memorizing words such as *obtuse* and *supplementary*. But review the definitions so that you understand how the angles work, because that's the key to solving almost any GRE angle problem.

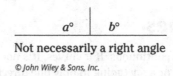

Not necessarily a right angle

© John Wiley & Sons, Inc.

Acute angle

An *acute angle* is any angle between 0 and 90 degrees.

30°

Acute angle

© John Wiley & Sons, Inc.

Obtuse angle

An *obtuse angle* is any angle between 90 and 180 degrees.

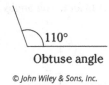

Obtuse angle

© John Wiley & Sons, Inc.

Complementary angles

Complementary angles add to 90 degrees to form a right angle.

Complementary angles

© John Wiley & Sons, Inc.

Supplementary angles

Supplementary angles add to 180 degrees to form a straight line.

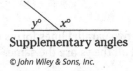

Supplementary angles

© John Wiley & Sons, Inc.

Vertical angles

Vertical angles always have equal measures and are the resulting opposite angles when two lines cross.

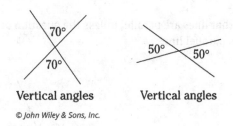

Vertical angles   Vertical angles

© John Wiley & Sons, Inc.

Bisectors

A *bisector*, or line that bisects, cuts directly down the middle. You need to know this term. If a line (or segment) bisects an angle, it divides that angle into two equal angles; if a first segment bisects a second segment, the first one cuts the second one perfectly in half. And if the first segment bisects the second segment at 90 degrees, it's a *perpendicular bisector*, and yes, the GRE expects you to know that. Don't worry — there will almost always be a drawing.

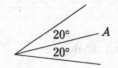

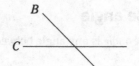

Segment *A* bisects the angle   Segment *B* bisects segment *C*

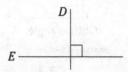

Segment *D* perpendicularly bisects segment *E*

© John Wiley & Sons, Inc.

Other key points

Angles around a point total 360 degrees, just as in a circle.

360°

© John Wiley & Sons, Inc.

A line that cuts through two parallel lines forms two sets of four equal angles. In this drawing, all the *x*s are the same, and all the *y*s are the same.

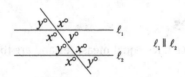

$\ell_1 \parallel \ell_2$

© John Wiley & Sons, Inc.

WARNING

Never assume that lines are parallel unless the question or image states that they are. The symbol $\ell_1 \parallel \ell_2$ indicates parallel lines.

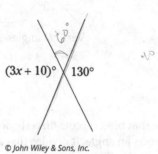

$(3x + 10)°$ 130°

© John Wiley & Sons, Inc.

PLAY

In the preceding figure, the value of *x* is

(A) 20

(B) 30

(C) 40

(D) 50

(E) 60

The opposite angles are *vertical*, meaning that they equal each other. Because the left-side angle equals the right-side angle, set up the equation like this:

$$(3x + 10)° = 130°$$
$$3x + 10 = 130$$
$$3x = 120$$
$$x = 40$$

The correct answer is (C). By the way, this is why you solve algebra before drawing geometry: Algebra is *patent* (apparent) throughout geometry.

Measuring Polygons

A *polygon* is any closed shape consisting of line segments, from a *triangle* (three sides) to a *dodecagon* (a dozen sides) and beyond. (Don't worry about knowing the dodecagon.) The polygons you're most likely going to encounter on the GRE are triangles and *quadrilaterals* (with four sides). Table 12-1 lists the names of polygons you may bump into, but don't get caught up with the names; these problems almost always include a drawing, so you can count the sides.

TABLE 12-1 ## Polygons

Number of Sides	Name
3	Triangle
4	Quadrilateral (including the square, rectangle, trapezoid, and parallelogram)
5	Pentagon
6	Hexagon (think of x in six and x in hex)
7	Heptagon
8	Octagon
9	Nonagon
10	Decagon

REMEMBER

A polygon with all sides equal and all angles equal is a *regular polygon*. An equilateral triangle is a regular triangle, and a square is a regular quadrilateral. *Equilateral* refers to equal side lengths, as in a diamond (rhombus), and *equiangular* refers to equal angles, as in a rectangle. With the equilateral triangle, the equal sides give it equal angles, but this isn't the case with other shapes.

If two polygons are *congruent*, they're identical. If they're *similar*, they have identical angles but different sizes. The following sections explain what you need to know about polygons for the GRE.

Measuring total interior angles

Because you may be asked to find the total interior angle measure of a particular polygon, keep this formula in mind (where *n* stands for the number of sides):

$$\text{Angle total} = (n-2)180°$$

Here are the sums of the interior angles of the following polygons:

- » **Triangle:** $(3-2)180° = 1 \times 180° = 180°$
- » **Quadrilateral:** $(4-2)180° = 2 \times 180° = 360°$
- » **Pentagon:** $(5-2)180° = 3 \times 180° = 540°$
- » **Hexagon:** $(6-2)180° = 4 \times 180° = 720°$
- » **Heptagon:** $(7-2)180° = 5 \times 180° = 900°$
- » **Octagon:** $(8-2)180° = 6 \times 180° = 1,080°$
- » **Nonagon:** $(9-2)180° = 7 \times 180° = 1,260°$
- » **Decagon:** $(10-2)180° = 8 \times 180° = 1,440°$

TIP

If you can't remember the formula, start with a triangle, where three sides have an angle total of 180°, and add 180 for each additional side.

Measuring one interior angle

I've seen GRE problems asking for the measure of *one* interior angle of a *regular* polygon. If you see one of these problems, here's what you do:

$$\frac{(n-2)180°}{n}$$

Remember that *n* stands for the number of sides (which is the same as the number of angles), so here's how to find a single angle measure of a regular pentagon:

$$\frac{(5-2)180°}{5} = \frac{(3)180°}{5} = \frac{540°}{5} = 108°$$

WARNING

Be sure that the polygon is *regular* or *equiangular*. The question will typically state this, but if it doesn't, look for some other clue in the question to find the measure of that angle.

PLAY

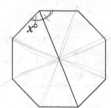

© John Wiley & Sons, Inc.

The preceding drawing shows a regular 8-sided polygon. What is the value of x?

Ⓐ 52.5

Ⓑ 55

Ⓒ 62.5

Ⓓ 65

Ⓔ 67.5

The term *regular* means that all the sides and angles are the same. First, find the measure of one angle: Take the total of all the angles, and divide by the number of angles, which in this case is 8. The equation sums it all up:

$$\frac{(n-2)180°}{n}$$
$$\frac{((8)-2)180°}{(8)}$$
$$\frac{(6)180°}{8}$$
$$\frac{1080°}{8}$$
$$135°$$

Next, you know the segment bisects the angle because shape is regular, so divide this angle measure in half:

$$\frac{135°}{2} = 67.5°$$

So the answer is (E). See, even though the drawing is to scale, you can't just eyeball the answer. You have to know the rules and constructs of geometry.

Drawing Triangles

The *triangle* has three sides and is a key figure in GRE geometry. Understanding how triangles work helps you understand other polygons. The following sections introduce you to certain common triangles and explain how to do the related math.

Drawing three types of triangles

Three common types of triangle are equilateral, isosceles, and right.

Equilateral triangle

An *equilateral triangle* has three equal sides and three equal angles. Though technically it's also a *regular* or *equiangular triangle*, it's known as equilateral.

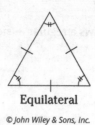

Equilateral

© John Wiley & Sons, Inc.

In these figures, the curved lines with the double lines through them inside the triangle tell you that the angles are equal. The short lines through the sides of the triangle tell you that the sides are equal.

Isosceles triangle

An *isosceles triangle* has two equal sides and two equal angles. Note that any triangle that's *equilateral* (with three equal sides) is also *isosceles* (with two equal sides).

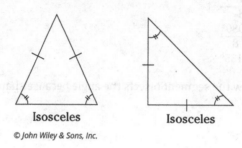

Isosceles   **Isosceles**

© John Wiley & Sons, Inc.

Right triangle

A *right* triangle has one 90-degree angle.

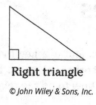

Right triangle

© John Wiley & Sons, Inc.

The little box in the bottom-left corner of the triangle tells you that the angle is 90 degrees. If the triangle *looks* like a right triangle but the question or drawing doesn't clearly state that it is (that is, with the box in the corner of the drawing), don't assume that it's a right triangle.

Measuring key characteristics

Triangles have some characteristics that help you field some questions on the exam. These may be intuitive, but study them just to be sure:

» **The largest angle is opposite the longest side.** Conversely, the smallest angle is opposite the shortest side. (Remember that $\sqrt{3}$ is between 1 and 2.)

© John Wiley & Sons, Inc.

» **The sum of any two side lengths is greater than any third side length.** This idea can be written as $a + b > c$, where *a*, *b*, and *c* are the sides of the triangle.

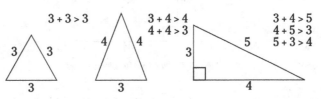

© John Wiley & Sons, Inc.

» **The sum of the interior angles is *always* 180 degrees.** No matter what the triangle looks like or how big it is, the angles total 180 degrees.

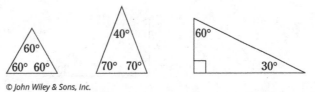

© John Wiley & Sons, Inc.

PLAY

If two sides of a triangle have lengths 7 and 8, the length of the third side must be between

Ⓐ 0 and 7

Ⓑ 1 and 8

Ⓒ 1 and 15

Ⓓ 7 and 15

Ⓔ 8 and 15

Start with 7 and 8 as *a* and *b*, and find the longest that the third side can be:

$$a + b > c$$
$$(7) + (8) > c$$
$$15 > c$$

So the third side, *c* in this case, has to be less than 15. So what's the *shortest* that it can be? Use the same equation, this time with 7 and 8 as *a* and *c*:

$$a + b > c$$
$$(7) + b > (8)$$
$$b > 1$$

The third side, *b* in this case, has to be greater than 1, which makes the answer (C).

Drawing perimeter and area

You may encounter at least one question that asks for the perimeter or area of a triangle. The following sections can help you clear that hurdle.

Drawing the perimeter

Perimeter is the distance around the triangle, so add up the lengths of the sides. This is true for any shape.

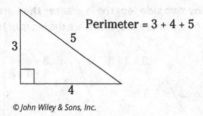

© John Wiley & Sons, Inc.

Shading the area

The area of a triangle is $\frac{\text{base} \times \text{height}}{2}$. The height is a line perpendicular to the base, and in a right triangle, it's one of the sides. This formula works *only* on a triangle.

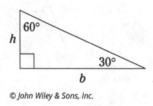

© John Wiley & Sons, Inc.

The height may be inside the triangle, represented by a dashed line and a 90-degree box.

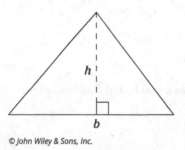

© John Wiley & Sons, Inc.

TIP

The height may also be outside the triangle, because the GRE is trying to trick you. Regardless, the area is the same formula:

$$\frac{\text{base} \times \text{height}}{2}$$

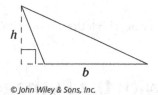

© John Wiley & Sons, Inc.

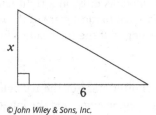

© John Wiley & Sons, Inc.

PLAY

The area of the triangle is 12. What is the value of x?

Enter your answer:

$a = \frac{1}{2}bh$

$a = 3h$

_____ 4

Did you automatically answer 2, as though the triangle were a rectangle? A rectangle's area is *length* times *width*, which in this case would be $2 \times 6 = 12$, covered further in "Drawing Quadrilaterals." As a *triangle*, the area is $\frac{\text{base} \times \text{height}}{2}$, so place the numbers from the drawing, where x is the height:

$$a = \frac{\text{base} \times \text{height}}{2}$$
$$(12) = \frac{(6) \times \text{height}}{2}$$
$$24 = 6 \times \text{height}$$
$$4 = \text{height}$$

The answer is 4. Don't feel bad. I had an engineer miss this one.

An *equilateral* triangle has a specific formula for the area. $\frac{\text{base} \times \text{height}}{2}$ certainly works, but you need the height, and if the GRE doesn't give you the height, use $\frac{s^2\sqrt{3}}{4}$, where s is a side length.

PLAY

What is the area of an equilateral triangle with a side length of 8?

Ⓐ 8

Ⓑ $8\sqrt{3}$

Ⓒ 16

Ⓓ $16\sqrt{3}$

Ⓔ 32

$\frac{1}{2}(4)(4\sqrt{3}) \times 2 = 16\sqrt{3}$

Place 8 for s in the trusty formula $\frac{s^2\sqrt{3}}{4}$ and solve for the area:

$$A = \frac{s^2\sqrt{3}}{4}$$
$$= \frac{(8)^2\sqrt{3}}{4}$$
$$= \frac{64\sqrt{3}}{4}$$
$$= 16\sqrt{3}$$

The answer is (D). As a rule, check the answer choices before finding the exact decimal value of something like $16\sqrt{3}$.

Measuring with the Pythagorean theorem

The *Pythagorean theorem* works only on a right triangle. It states that the sum of the squares of the two shorter sides is equal to the square of the hypotenuse. If you know the lengths of any two sides, you can find the length of the third side, with this formula:

$$a^2 + b^2 = c^2$$

Here, *a* and *b* are the shorter sides of the triangle, and *c* is the hypotenuse. The hypotenuse is always opposite the 90-degree angle and the longest side of the triangle.

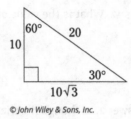

© John Wiley & Sons, Inc.

PLAY

Suppose that you're asked for the length of the base of this right triangle:

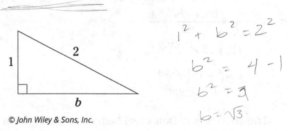

© John Wiley & Sons, Inc.

To find the unknown length of the third side, start with the Pythagorean theorem:

$$a^2 + b^2 = c^2$$

In this case, you know the *a* and the *c*, but you're missing the *b*. Place the side lengths that you have, and solve for the missing side:

$$a^2 + b^2 = c^2$$
$$(1)^2 + b^2 = (2)^2$$
$$1 + b^2 = 4$$
$$b^2 = 3$$
$$b = \sqrt{3}$$

REMEMBER

Before calculating the value of $\sqrt{3}$, check the answer choices. They will almost always be in terms of the radical. In this case, the calculator isn't your friend: If you're all set with the answer 1.732, and the answer choices are $\sqrt{2}$, $\sqrt{3}$, and $\sqrt{5}$, you'll have to start over.

Suppose that you're asked for the length of the hypotenuse of this triangle:

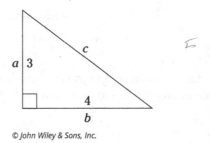

© John Wiley & Sons, Inc.

Here are the calculations:

$$a^2 + b^2 = c^2$$
$$(3)^2 + (4)^2 = c^2$$
$$9 + 16 = c^2$$
$$25 = c^2$$
$$5 = c$$

Drawing common right triangles

The two preceding triangles are examples of *common right triangles*. With a common right triangle, you don't need to work the Pythagorean theorem every time you need the third side length. These next sections show you four common right triangles that save you a lot of scratch work.

3:4:5

If one side of a right triangle is 3 and the other is 4, the hypotenuse must be 5. Likewise, if the hypotenuse is 5 and the length of one side is 4, the other side must be 3. I proved this relationship with the Pythagorean theorem in the preceding section.

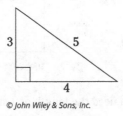

© John Wiley & Sons, Inc.

TIP

These side lengths are a ratio, so the sides of a right triangle can be in any multiple of these numbers, including $6:8:10$ (multiplied by 2), $9:12:15$ (multiplied by 3), and $15:20:25$ (multiplied by 5). Note that the 3:4:5 triangle and its ratios are common in the GRE. Good thing it's simple.

5:12:13

If one side of a right triangle is 5 and another side is 12, the hypotenuse must be 13. Likewise, if the hypotenuse is 13 and one of the sides is 5, the other side must be 12. You don't need the Pythagorean theorem for this one. This triangle isn't as common as the ubiquitous 3:4:5, and it almost never appears in multiples such as $10:24:26$, though it could.

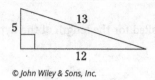

© John Wiley & Sons, Inc.

$$s : s : s\sqrt{2}$$

This ratio is for an *isosceles right triangle*, also known as the 45-45-90 triangle (containing 45-45-90-degree angles), where *s* stands for *side*. If one side is 2 and a second side is also 2, the hypotenuse is $2\sqrt{2}$.

© John Wiley & Sons, Inc.

TIP

This ratio also helps when working with squares. If the side of a square is 5, and you need its diagonal, you know right away that said diagonal is $5\sqrt{2}$, because a square's diagonal cuts the square into two isosceles right triangles. This is true regardless of the size of the square: If a side length is 64, snap your fingers, and the diagonal is $64\sqrt{2}$. If the side length is $\frac{1}{2}$, the diagonal is $\frac{1}{2}\sqrt{2}$.

If you're given the length of the hypotenuse of an isosceles right triangle and need to find the length of the other two sides, use this formula, where *h* is the hypotenuse:

$$\frac{h}{\sqrt{2}} : \frac{h}{\sqrt{2}} : h$$

PLAY

If the diagonal of a square is 5, what is the area of the square?

© John Wiley & Sons, Inc.

To find the area, first you need the length of a side. If the diagonal is 5, right away, you know the side length is $\frac{5}{\sqrt{2}}$, and the side-length ratio of the embedded 45-45-90 triangle is

$$\frac{5}{\sqrt{2}} : \frac{5}{\sqrt{2}} : 5$$

This means that each side of the square is $\frac{5}{\sqrt{2}}$. The area of any square is $a = s^2$ (discussed further in "Drawing Quadrilaterals"), making the area of this square

$$\left(\frac{5}{\sqrt{2}}\right)^2 = \frac{25}{2} = 12.5$$

$$s : s\sqrt{3} : 2s$$

This is a special ratio for the sides of a 30-60-90 triangle, with angles measuring 30, 60, and 90 degrees. s is the length of the short side (opposite the 30-degree angle), $s\sqrt{3}$ is the longer side, and $2s$ is the hypotenuse.

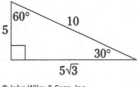

© John Wiley & Sons, Inc.

It's an equilateral triangle cut perfectly in half. As you know, an equilateral triangle has three 60-degree angles. If you have one where each side length is 2, and you cut it perfectly in half, you get two 30-60-90 triangles having side lengths of 1, $\sqrt{3}$, and 2.

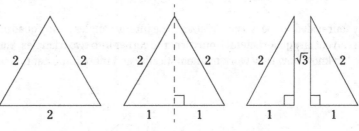

© John Wiley & Sons, Inc.

This type of triangle is a favorite of the test-makers. Keep in mind that the hypotenuse is twice the length of the *shorter* side (opposite the 30-degree angle). If you encounter a question that reads "Given a 30-60-90 triangle with a hypotenuse of 20, find the area," or "Given a 30-60-90 triangle with a hypotenuse of 100, find the perimeter," you can do this easily because you can quickly find the lengths of the other sides.

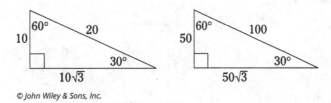

© John Wiley & Sons, Inc.

TIP

One commonly appearing side-length ratio of the 30-60-90 triangle is

$$\frac{1}{2} : \frac{\sqrt{3}}{2} : 1$$

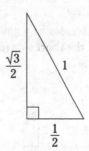

The hypotenuse 1 and shorter side $\frac{1}{2}$ are easy to reconcile, but everyone — *everyone* — except you, that is — messes up the longer side and clicks $\sqrt{3}$ instead of the correct $\frac{\sqrt{3}}{2}$.

Drawing Quadrilaterals

Any four-sided shape is a *quadrilateral*. The interior angles of any quadrilateral total 360 degrees, and you can cut any quadrilateral from corner to corner into two triangles. You know these shapes, but you need to know how they work mathematically, and more important, how they appear in GRE Math.

Quadrilateral

>> **Square:** The *square* has four equal sides and four right angles. The area of a square is length × width, but because *length* and *width* are the same, they're called *sides*, and the area is side^2.

Square

>> **Rhombus:** A *rhombus* has four equal sides but angles that aren't right angles, like a square that got stepped on. It looks like a diamond, and its area is $\frac{1}{2}d_1d_2$, or $\left(\frac{1}{2}\text{diagonal}_1 \times \text{diagonal}_2\right)$. The rhombus isn't a common shape in GRE Math.

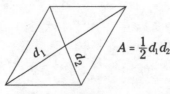

Rhombus

>> **Rectangle:** A *rectangle* has four right angles and opposite sides that are equal, and its area is length × width (which is the same as base × height).

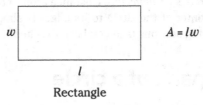

$A = lw$

Rectangle

>> **Parallelogram:** A *parallelogram* is like a rectangle with opposite sides that are equal, but the angles aren't necessarily right angles, like a rectangle that got stepped on. The area of a parallelogram is base × height, but the height is the distance between the two bases, not the length of one of the sides. The height is represented by a dotted line that's a right angle from one of the bases.

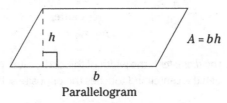

$A = bh$

Parallelogram

>> **Trapezoid:** A *trapezoid* has two sides that are parallel and two sides that are not parallel. The area of a trapezoid is like base × height, but because the bases have different lengths, you average them first captured by the clunky formula $\frac{base_1 + base_2}{2}$ × height. Just remember that it's simply base × height with the bases averaged.

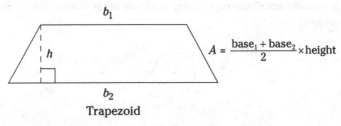

$A = \dfrac{base_1 + base_2}{2} \times \text{height}$

Trapezoid

>> **Other quadrilaterals:** Some quadrilaterals don't have specific shapes or names, but regardless, with 4 sides, the angles *always* total 360 degrees, the perimeter is *always* the distance around it, and if the question asks for the area, you can typically cut the shape into two triangles and measure those.

Drawing Circles

Determining a circle's *circumference* (distance around the circle) or area using its *radius* (the distance from the center of the circle to its edge) is simple with the formulas and features of the circle. The following sections take you back to school.

Drawing parts of a circle

The parts of a circle have specific names, and the GRE expects you to know these:

>> **Center:** The *center* is the point in the middle of the circle. If a question refers to the circle by a capital letter, that's both the circle's center and its name.

Circle *M*

Center

>> **Diameter:** The *diameter* is the width of the circle, often represented by a line segment that passes through the center and touches the opposite sides. The diameter is equal to twice the radius.

Diameter

>> **Circumference:** Known as a *perimeter* with other shapes, the *circumference* is the distance around the circle.

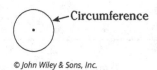

>> **π, or pi:** Pronounced "pie," π is the ratio of the circumference to the diameter. It equals approximately 3.14, but circle-based questions usually have answer choices in terms of π, such as 2π, rather than 6.28.

>> **Radius:** The *radius* is the distance from the center of the circle to the edge of the circle. The radius of a circle is half the diameter.

Radius

The radius is the same length regardless of which part of the edge of the circle it touches. This means that if a triangle is formed from two *radii* (the plural of radius) inside one circle, it's *always* isosceles and *could be* equilateral.

© John Wiley & Sons, Inc.

» **Tangent:** A *tangent* is a line outside a circle that touches the circle at one point.

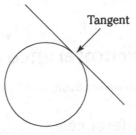

Tangent

© John Wiley & Sons, Inc.

» **Chord:** A *chord* is a line or segment that crosses through the circle and connects it on two points. The diameter is the circle's longest chord.

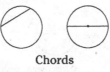

Chords

© John Wiley & Sons, Inc.

PLAY

Quantity A	*Quantity B*
Area of a circle of radius 6	Area of a circle with a longest chord of 12

Ⓐ Quantity A is greater.

Ⓑ Quantity B is greater.

Ⓒ The two quantities are equal.

Ⓓ The relationship cannot be determined from the information given.

The *longest chord* of a circle is the diameter. Because the diameter is twice the radius, a circle with diameter 12 has a radius of 6. In other words, the circles are the same size and have the same area. (Don't worry about solving for that area; you know the two circles are the same.) The correct answer is (C).

Quantity A	*Quantity B*
Area of a circle with a radius of 10	Area of a circle with a chord of 20

Ⓐ Quantity A is greater.

Ⓑ Quantity B is greater.

Ⓒ The two quantities are equal.

Ⓓ The relationship cannot be determined from the information given.

A chord connects any two points on a circle, but you don't know whether this particular chord is the diameter. Quantity B doesn't specify the *longest* chord. If it did, the quantities would be equal, but it doesn't, so you don't know the size of the circle in Quantity B. The correct answer is (D).

These Quantity Comparison questions play on your assumptions. There's more on spotting these traps in Chapter 15.

Drawing the circumference and area

You knew these equations, mastered them, and then forgot them. That's okay; they're right here.

Drawing the circumference

The *circumference* is the distance around a circle, found with the equation $C = 2\pi r$ (where C is the circumference and r is radius). Because diameter is twice the radius, you may also use the equation $C = \pi d$ (where d is the diameter).

Circumference

© John Wiley & Sons, Inc.

The circumference of a circle with a radius of 3 is

$$2\pi r = 2 \times \pi \times 3 = 6\pi$$

The answer choices to circle problems are almost always in terms of π, so here you'd select 6π. If you do encounter a problem with the answer choices in regular numbers, such as "How far did a wheel with a 3-inch radius travel if it rolled 6 times," you can replace π with 3.14 and multiply it, but first, look at the answer choices.

A wagon has a wheel radius of 6 inches. If the wagon wheel travels 100 revolutions, approximately how many feet has the wagon rolled?

Ⓐ 325

Ⓑ 315

Ⓒ 255

Ⓓ 210

Ⓔ 180

The question gives the radius in inches, but the answer choices are all in feet, so the first order of business is to convert inches into feet: $6 \div 12 = 0.5$ feet. One revolution of the wheel carries the wagon a distance of one circumference of the wheel, so find the circumference of the circle in feet:

$$C = 2\pi r$$
$$C = 2\pi(0.5)$$
$$C = \pi$$

Next, multiply by the number of revolutions:

$$\pi \times 100 = 100\pi \text{ feet}$$

Finally, check the answer choices, which are in real numbers, so replace π with 3.14 and multiply:

$$100 \times 3.14 = 314 \text{ feet}$$

Because the question reads *approximately*, go with 315 as an approximate of 314, so the correct answer is (B).

Shading the area

Area is the space inside the circle. The formula is $A = \pi r^2$, so if a circle has a radius of 4, you can find the area like this:

$$A = \pi(4)^2 = 16\pi$$

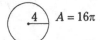

$A = 16\pi$

© John Wiley & Sons, Inc.

PLAY

What's the total approximate area, in square inches, of two 10-inch-diameter pizzas?

Ⓐ 40

Ⓑ 60

Ⓒ 100

Ⓓ 120

Ⓔ 160

Only the GRE can make a math question out of a pizza. Actually, the SAT does this too. Anyway, the area equation takes the radius, but the question gives the diameter, so start by dividing the diameter in half for that radius: $10 \div 2 = 5$ inches.

Next, place that 5 in the area equation:

$$A = \pi r^2$$
$$A = \pi(5)^2$$
$$A = 25\pi$$

Check the answer choices, which are in real numbers, so replace π with 3.14 and multiply:

$$25 \times 3.14 = 78.5 \text{ inches}$$

Finally (and this is where the GRE trips testers up), the question asks about *two* pizzas, so take that answer and double it: $78.5 \times 2 = 157$. Because the question reads *approximately*, go with 160 as the closest approximate of 157. The correct answer is (E).

Note there's no answer choice for 80, which is another GRE tactic: It doesn't set a trap for a mis-read question. If you don't find your answer among the choices, don't just check your math — check the question.

Drawing the arc and sector

The *arc* is part of the circumference of a circle, and *sector* is part of the area. To measure these parts, first find either the circumference or the area of the whole circle, depending on the question, then multiply by the fraction in the question. In this section, I guide you through some practice and variations.

Drawing the arc

An *arc* is a part of the circumference of a circle and is typically formed by either a *central angle* or an *inscribed angle*:

» **Central angle:** A central angle has its vertex at the center of a circle and its endpoints on the circumference. The degree measure of a central angle is the same as the degree measure of its *minor arc* (the smaller arc).

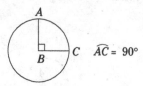

Central angle

© John Wiley & Sons, Inc.

» **Inscribed angle:** An inscribed angle has both its vertex and endpoints on the circumference. The degree measure of an inscribed angle is half the degree measure of its intercepted arc, as shown in the figure. The intercepted arc is 80 degrees, and the inscribed angle is half of that, at 40 degrees.

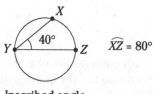

Inscribed angle

© John Wiley & Sons, Inc.

Even a drawing that looks like a dream-catcher, with lines all over, isn't so bad if you know how the vertices, arcs, and angles work.

PLAY

In this figure, if minor arc $XY = 60°$, what is the sum of the degree measures of angles a, b, c, d, and e?

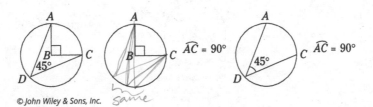

© John Wiley & Sons, Inc.

Ⓐ 60

Ⓑ 90

Ⓒ 120

Ⓓ 150

Ⓔ 180

The angles a, b, c, d, and e are *inscribed angles*, meaning each angle has half the degree measure of its intercepted arc. You know from the drawing that the endpoints of each angle are X and Y, and the problem tells you that arc XY measures 60 degrees. This means that each angle is 30 degrees, for a total of $30 \times 5 = 150$. The correct answer is (D).

REMEMBER

With a *central* angle, the resulting arc has the *same* degree measure as the angle. With an *inscribed* angle, the resulting arc has *twice* the degree measure of the angle.

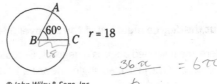

© John Wiley & Sons, Inc.

To find the length of an arc when you have its degree measure, follow these steps:

1. **Find the circumference of the entire circle.**

2. **Put the degree measure of the arc over 360 and reduce the fraction.**

3. **Multiply the circumference by the fraction.**

 PLAY

Find the length of minor arc *AC*:

B 60° C $r = 18$

© John Wiley & Sons, Inc.

Ⓐ 36π

Ⓑ 27π

Ⓒ 18π

Ⓓ 12π

Ⓔ 6π

Take the steps one at a time:

1. **Find the circumference of the entire circle:**

$$C = 2\pi r$$
$$= 2\pi(18)$$
$$= 36\pi$$

Don't multiply π out; the answer choices are in terms of π.

2. **Put the degree measure of the arc over 360 and reduce the fraction.**

The degree measure of the arc is the same as its central angle, 60 degrees:

$$\frac{60}{360} = \frac{6}{36} = \frac{1}{6}$$

3. **Multiply the circumference by the fraction:**

$$36\pi \times \frac{1}{6} = 6\pi$$

The correct answer is (E).

Try another one. Make it intuitive.

PLAY

Find the length of minor arc *RS* in this figure:

$r = 5$

Angle *ROS* = 6°

© John Wiley & Sons, Inc.

Ⓐ $\frac{1}{3}\pi$

Ⓑ π

Ⓒ 3π

Ⓓ 4π

Ⓔ 12

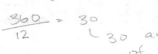

1. **Find the circumference of the entire circle:**

$$C = 2\pi r$$
$$= 2\pi(5)$$
$$= 10\pi$$

2. **Put the degree measure of the arc over 360°, and reduce the fraction.**

Here, the inscribed angle is 6 degrees. Because the intercepted arc has twice the degree measure of the inscribed angle, the arc is 12 degrees:

$$\frac{12°}{360°} = \frac{1}{30}$$

3. **Multiply the circumference by the fraction:**

$$10\pi \times \frac{1}{30} = \frac{10}{30}\pi = \frac{1}{3}\pi$$

The correct answer is (A).

WARNING

Be careful not to confuse the arc's *degree measure* with its *length*. The length is always part of the circumference and usually has a π in it. If you picked (E), 12, you found the degree measure instead.

Shading the sector

A *sector* is part of the area of a circle that comes from a central angle. The degree measure of a sector is the same as the degree measure of the that angle. On the GRE, you always see a sector from a *central* angle, never an *inscribed* angle.

To find the area of a sector, do the following:

1. Find the area of the entire circle.

2. Put the degree measure of the sector over 360 and reduce the fraction.

3. Multiply the area by the fraction.

Finding the area of a sector is similar to finding the length of an arc. The only difference is in the first step: You find the circle's *area*, not *circumference*. With this in mind, try a few sample sector problems:

PLAY

Find the area of minor sector *ABC*.

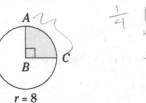

$r = 8$

© John Wiley & Sons, Inc.

Ⓐ 64π
Ⓑ 36π
Ⓒ 16π
Ⓓ 12π
Ⓔ 6π

Use the steps listed previously:

1. Find the area of the entire circle.

$A = \pi r^2 = \pi (8)^2 = 64\pi$

2. Put the degree measure of the sector over 360°, and reduce the fraction.

The sector is 90 degrees, same as its central angle:

$\dfrac{90°}{360°} = \dfrac{1}{4}$

3. Multiply the area by the fraction:

$64\pi \times \dfrac{1}{4} = 16\pi$

The correct answer is (C).

Find the area of minor sector *XYZ* in this figure:

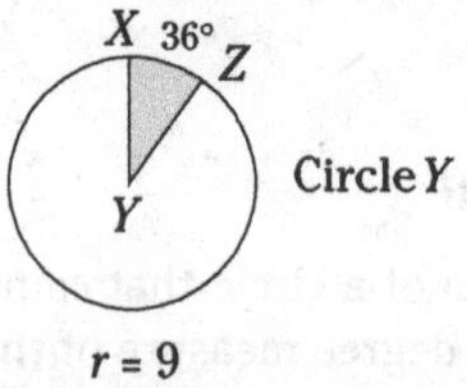

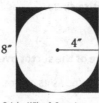

X 36° Z

Circle *Y*

Y

r = 9

© John Wiley & Sons, Inc.

(handwritten) 10 slices

$\pi(9^2)$

$\dfrac{81\pi}{10}$

Ⓐ 9.0π

Ⓑ 8.1π *(circled)*

Ⓒ 7.2π

Ⓓ 6.3π

Ⓔ 5.4π

1. **Find the area of the entire circle.**

$A = \pi r^2 = \pi(9)^2 = 81\pi$

2. **Put the degree measure of the sector over 360°, and reduce the fraction.**

A sector has the same degree measure as its intercepted arc:

$$\frac{36°}{360°} = \frac{1}{10}$$

3. **Multiply the area by the fraction:**

$$81\pi \times \frac{1}{10} = 8.1\pi$$

The correct answer is (B).

Drawing overlapping shapes

A question may present two shapes where one overlaps the other. The visible part of the shape underneath may be shaded, and the question typically asks you to calculate that shaded area. You don't always find an exact number, especially when one of the shapes is a circle.

PLAY

A circle of radius 4 inches is centered over an 8-inch square. Find the total shaded area.

8″   4″

(handwritten) □rea = 64

Orea = 16π

64 − 16π

© John Wiley & Sons, Inc.

Here are two basic shapes where one overlaps the other. This is how to find that shaded part:

1. **Calculate the total area of the outside shape.**

Each side of the square is 8 inches:

$8 \times 8 = 64$

2. Calculate the area of the inside shape.

$$\pi r^2 = \pi(4)^2 = 16\pi$$

3. Subtract the area of the inside shape from the area of the outside shape.

The difference between the two shapes is the shaded area.

$64 - 16\pi$ ✓

And that's it! No calculating the exact number.

Here's another one:

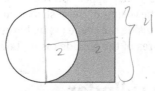

© John Wiley & Sons, Inc.

PLAY

In the preceding drawing, exactly half the circle overlaps the square. If the square has a side length of 4 and the circle has a radius of 2, what is the area of the shaded region?

Ⓐ $8 - \pi$

Ⓑ $8 - 2\pi$

Ⓒ $16 - \pi$

Ⓓ $16 - 2\pi$

Ⓔ $16 - 4\pi$

$16 - \frac{1}{2}\left(\pi(2^2)\right)$

2π

The key here is that *half* the circle overlaps the square, so you need to calculate the area of the *sector* to subtract from the area of the square. The circle has a radius of 2, so its area is $\pi r^2 = \pi(2)^2 = 4\pi$. Only half the circle overlaps the square, so the area that you subtract is half the circle: 2π. The square has an area of 16, so the difference between the two shapes is $16 - 2\pi$: The correct answer is (D).

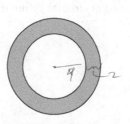

© John Wiley & Sons, Inc.

$a = \pi(6^2)$

big r = 6
small = 4

$\pi(4^2)$

PLAY

The preceding drawing shows a circular rock garden surrounded by a sidewalk. If the rock garden has a diameter of 8 and the sidewalk is exactly 2 feet wide, what is the area of the sidewalk?

Ⓐ 20π

Ⓑ 24π

Ⓒ 30π

Ⓓ 32π

Ⓔ 36π

$100\pi - 64\pi$
$= 36\pi$

$36\pi - 16\pi$
$= 20\pi$

This problem is exactly the same as the others, only you're subtracting two circles. The small circle has a diameter of 8, so its radius is 4. The visible part of the large circle has a width of 2, so combined with the small circle's radius of 4, it has a total radius of 6. Now find the areas so you can subtract them. The large circle has an area of $\pi r^2 = \pi(6)^2 = 36\pi$, while the small circle has an area of $\pi r^2 = \pi(4)^2 = 16\pi$. Subtract them for a sidewalk area of $36\pi - 16\pi = 20\pi$. The correct answer is (A).

Drawing 3D Shapes

Three 3D shapes regularly appear on the GRE: the cylinder, the rectangular solid, and the cube. You typically find the *volume* of these shapes, and you may find the *surface area* of the cube. *Volume* refers to the space inside the shape (as in, how much water goes into a fish aquarium), and *surface area* refers to the area of the outside (as in, how much paper you would need to wrap a gift).

Drawing a cylinder

The GRE calls its cylinders *right circular cylinders*, meaning that the top and bottom circles are the same size and perpendicular to the curved side, unlike, say, a cheerleading cone. Don't get caught up in it; it's basically a can of soup.

The volume of a cylinder is $V = \pi r^2 h$. Here's how you remember that: The base of the cylinder, as a circle, has an area of πr^2, times the height, h.

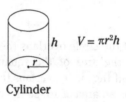

Cylinder

© John Wiley & Sons, Inc.

PLAY

What is the volume of a right circular cylinder having a radius of 3 and a height of 5?

Ⓐ 15π

Ⓑ 30π

Ⓒ 45π

Ⓓ 60π

Ⓔ 75π

The volume of a cylinder is $V = \pi r^2 h$. Just place the radius and height, and find the volume:

$$V = \pi r^2 h$$
$$= \pi(3)^2(5)$$
$$= 45\pi$$

The correct answer is (C).

What is the height of a right circular cylinder having a volume of 24π and a radius of $\sqrt{6}$?

Ⓐ 2
Ⓑ 3
Ⓒ 4
Ⓓ 5
Ⓔ 6

This is a common variation on the GRE. If it seems to laugh at you, just laugh right back: Place the volume and radius into the formula and solve for the height:

$$V = \pi r^2 h$$
$$(24\pi) = \pi\left(\sqrt{6}\right)^2 h$$
$$24\pi = \pi 6 h$$
$$24 = 6h$$
$$4 = h$$

The correct answer is (C).

Drawing a rectangular solid

A rectangular solid on the GRE has six sides that are rectangles, basically like a shoebox. Multiply the lengths of the length, width, and height for the volume: $V = l \times w \times h$.

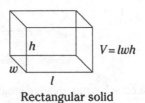

Rectangular solid

© John Wiley & Sons, Inc.

What is the volume of a rectangular shoebox having a length of 6, a width of 3, and a depth of 4?

Ⓐ 72
Ⓑ 60
Ⓒ 48
Ⓓ 36
Ⓔ 24

Simple practice. Multiply out the dimensions for your answer: $V = 6 \times 3 \times 4 = 72$.

The correct answer is (A).

If a rectangular salt-water aquarium has a volume of 14,400 cubic inches, and the surface area of each end is 120 square inches, what is its length, in feet?

Ⓐ 10
Ⓑ 12
Ⓒ 15
Ⓓ 18
Ⓔ 20

You know that the volume of a rectangular solid is $V = l \times w \times h$ and in this case is 14,400. You don't have the width and height, so just place 120 for $w \times h$ in the equation. First find the length in inches; then convert it to feet:

$$V = l \times w \times h$$
$$(14,400) = l \times (120)$$
$$l = 120$$

Good thing you get an on-screen calculator. Anyway, if the length is 120 inches, at 12 inches per foot, the length is 10 feet for (A).

Drawing a cube

A *cube* is a rectangular solid where the dimensions are the same, like a six-sided *die* (one of a pair of dice). Because the *length*, *width*, and *height* are the same, they're called *edges* and represented by the letter *e*.

Drawing the volume

Like the rectangular solid, the volume of a cube is $V = l \times w \times h$. However, because the edges are the same and referred to as *e*, the volume of a cube is thus $V = e^3$.

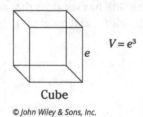

Cube

© John Wiley & Sons, Inc.

PLAY

What is the volume of a cube having an edge length of 4?

Ⓐ 16
Ⓑ 24
Ⓒ 32
Ⓓ 48
Ⓔ 64

Consider this question to be your *hors d'oeuvre*, or appetizer, for the GRE-type cube questions coming up. You have the edge length, so place that in the equation:

$$V = e^3$$
$$= (4)^3$$
$$= 64$$

The correct answer is (E).

PLAY

What is the edge length of a cube having volume of 1?

Ⓐ $\frac{1}{3}$

Ⓑ $\frac{1}{2}$

Ⓒ 1

Ⓓ 2

Ⓔ 3

Don't get all cognitive on this one. Just go through the steps. You have the volume, so place that in the equation:

$$V = e^3$$
$$(1) = e^3$$
$$1 = e$$

The correct answer is (C). Trick question? Not for you.

Shading the surface area

The cube is typically the only shape where the GRE asks for the surface area. In fact, it'll give you the cube's volume, and you back-solve to find the surface area — or vice versa. Don't worry — it's just as doable as everything else in this chapter.

A cube has six identical faces, and each face is a square. The area of a square is side², or because each side is an *edge*, edge². And because the cube has six faces, the surface area is $6 \times$ edge², or $6e^2$.

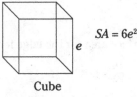

$SA = 6e^2$

Cube

© John Wiley & Sons, Inc.

PLAY

What is the surface area of a cube having an edge length of 3?

Ⓐ 18

Ⓑ 27

Ⓒ 36

Ⓓ 45

Ⓔ 54

Another *hors d'oeuvre*. You have the edge length, so place that in the equation:

$$SA = 6e^2$$
$$= 6(3)^2$$
$$= 54$$

The correct answer is (E).

PLAY

If a cube has a volume of 8, what is its surface area?

Ⓐ 8

Ⓑ 12

Ⓒ 16

Ⓓ 24

Ⓔ 32

Now, *this* is more like it. First, back-solve the volume for the edge length:

$$V = e^3$$
$$8 = e^3$$
$$2 = e$$

And place that in the surface area equation:

$$SA = 6e^2$$
$$= 6(2)^2$$
$$= 24$$

The correct answer is (D).

PLAY

If a cube has a surface area of 600, what is its volume?

Ⓐ 10

Ⓑ 60

Ⓒ 100

Ⓓ 600

Ⓔ 1,000

First, back-solve the surface area for the edge length:

$$SA = 6e^2$$
$$(600) = 6e^2$$
$$100 = e^2$$
$$10 = e$$

Now place that puppy right back into the volume formula:

$$V = e^3$$
$$= (10)^3$$
$$= 1,000$$

The correct answer is (E).

All right, one more, just to mix in overlapping shapes:

If a cube with an edge length of 2 is placed inside an empty cylinder with a radius of 2 and a height of 3, what is the volume of the unoccupied portion of the cylinder?

PLAY

Ⓐ $3\pi - 2$

Ⓑ $6\pi - 4$

Ⓒ $8\pi - 6$

Ⓓ $12\pi - 8$

Ⓔ $16\pi - 12$

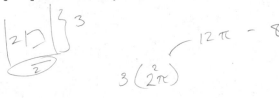

Think of an ice cube placed inside a drinking glass. How much water can you put in? This is just an overlapping shapes question, only with volume instead of area.

First, find the volume of the cylinder:

$$V = \pi r^2 h$$
$$= \pi (2)^2 (3)$$
$$= 12\pi$$

Next, find the volume of the cube:

$$V = e^3$$
$$= (2)^3$$
$$= 8$$

Finally, subtract the cube from the cylinder, $12\pi - 8$, for answer (D).

Chapter **13**
Simplifying Word Problems

Most GRE Math is front and center, but sometimes you need to extract the math from a narrative in the form of a word problem. Fortunately, like all other GRE Math, you solve most word problems with one or more standard strategies. If you can recognize the type of problem and corresponding strategy, you'll do just fine. This chapter introduces common word problems along with those strategies for getting them right, fast.

Simplifying the Steps

When you're up against a word problem, knowing where to start is the key. Begin with the part that you know, and this will clarify the part that you don't know. You can solve almost all word problems with the following step-by-step approach:

1. **Check what kind of word problem it is.**

   Word problems tend to be formula-heavy. If you recognize what kind of word problem it is, you automatically know which formula to use and thus how to solve it. That's what this chapter does for you.

2. **Write down the base formula.**

   Most word problems are based on some formula, so write that down so you can fill in the blanks next. Sometimes you vary the formula based on your understanding of the word problem.

3. **Place what you know into the formula.**

   The question provides info mixed into a story, and the formula gives you the framework to place the numbers as you **curate** (collect) the details. It also helps you stay organized. Just place what you know into the formula and solve for the rest.

TIP

When you write the equation from a sentence, remember that the word *is* becomes an equal sign. "Carly's age *is* twice David's age" becomes $c = 2d$. The same is true with variations of *is*, including *could be, would be,* and, of course, *was.*

When you have two unknowns, don't use both *x* and *y* if you can use *x* for both, especially when knowing one means you automatically know the other. For example, if Sally got some of 100 marbles and Alice got the rest, don't use *s* and *a* to represent the marbles given to Sally and Alice. Instead, use *s* and 100 − *s*. The moment you know how many marbles Sally got, you automatically know how many went to Alice. If Sally got 40 marbles, you automatically know that Alice got 60.

4. **Solve for what's missing.**

   Once you have everything in place, do the math. On the GRE, if you set the equation up properly, the math is *always* simple.

5. **Make sure your answer fits the reality check.**

   If you have Grandma driving to LA at 200 miles per hour, check your work. Most word problems are in the context of a story, so you can reality-check to see whether the answer makes sense. My grandma got a speeding ticket — in a school zone. True story.

REMEMBER

Yes, it's a timed test. If you're prepared, meaning you know what to do, you can be methodical and careful so that timing is *never* an issue. Practice working the problems in this chapter so that the steps are fluid, and you'll know what to do and won't get stuck.

Simplifying Time and Distance

No math set would be complete without two trains headed somewhere from Chattanooga. You'll probably encounter at least one question on the GRE that deals with distance, rate, and time. The question typically provides segments of a trip and asks for the average speed. To find this, place the total distance over the total time, and reduce the fraction to one hour (or whatever unit of time the question asks for). Solve it with this:

$$\frac{\text{total \# miles}}{\text{total \# hours}} = \frac{\text{miles (per hour)}}{1 \text{ hour}}$$

In its simplest form, if you drive 180 miles to Winslow in 3 hours, what was your average speed?

$$\frac{180 \text{ miles}}{3 \text{ hours}} = \frac{60 \text{ miles}}{1 \text{ hour}}$$

Your average speed was 60 miles per hour. On the trickier GRE-level questions, just total up the distance and place that over the total time. (You may have to convert minutes to hours.)

PLAY

Jennifer drives 40 miles an hour for two and a half hours, and then 60 miles per hour for one and a half hours. What is her average speed?

Finding Jennifer's total time is easier, so start with that: Per the story, she drove $2\frac{1}{2} + 1\frac{1}{2} = 4$ hours total. To find her total distance, work one part at a time. If she went 40 miles per hour for 2½ hours, then she went $40 \times 2\frac{1}{2} = 100$ miles for the first part, and 60 miles per hour for 1½ hours is $60 \times 1\frac{1}{2} = 90$ miles, for a total of $100 + 90 = 190$ miles. Set up the fraction and reduce it to 1 hour, like this:

$$\frac{190 \text{ miles}}{4 \text{ hours}} = \frac{47.5 \text{ miles}}{1 \text{ hour}}$$

Jennifer drove at an average speed of 47.5 miles per hour, which makes sense: You would expect the answer to fall between 40 and 60 miles per hour.

PLAY

Harry rides his bike uphill 14 miles in 70 minutes, and then turns around and rides the same distance downhill in 50 minutes. What was his average speed, in miles per hour?

(A) 14

(B) 21

(C) 28

(D) 35

(E) 42

Set up the fraction with total distance on the top and total time on the bottom. Remember that Harry rode 14 miles each way for a total of 28 miles, and the total time is $70 + 50 = 120$ minutes:

$$\frac{28\ miles}{120\ minutes} = \frac{28\ miles}{2\ hours} = \frac{14\ miles}{1\ hour}$$

The correct answer is Choice (A).

Simplifying Units of Measurement

In a conversion question, the GRE gives you the relationship between the units of measurement, *except* for units of time (for example, you won't be told that 60 seconds is 1 minute). If you're asked how many ounces are in 5 pounds, the question tells you that 1 pound is 16 ounces. To solve the problem, take the following steps:

1. **Set up the conversion equations as fractions, with the terms (in this case, lbs) on opposite sides of the fraction.**

$$\left(\frac{5\ lb}{1}\right)\left(\frac{16\ oz}{1\ lb}\right)$$

2. **Cancel the common terms.**

In this example, the *lb* units appear in the numerator and the denominator, so they cancel:

$$\left(\frac{5\ \cancel{lb}}{1}\right)\left(\frac{16\ oz}{1\ \cancel{lb}}\right)$$

3. **Multiply the fractions.**

$$\left(\frac{80\ oz}{1}\right) = 80\ oz$$

WARNING

Be sure that the *l* in *lbs* doesn't look like the number 1, making "3 lbs" look like "31 bs." Instead, write your l like this: ℓ. Also, write your t with a curved bottom so it doesn't look like a plus: +. Lastly, don't use m to abbreviate because it could stand for *meters*, *miles*, or *minutes*. I've never seen students mess this up.

PLAY

If Murray runs at a constant rate of 15 kilometers per hour, how many meters does he run in two minutes? (1 kilometer = 1,000 meters)

(A) 200

(B) 500

(C) 8,000

(D) 16,000

(E) 18,000

First, find the meters he runs in *one* minute:

1. **Set up the conversion equations as fractions, with the terms opposite.**

$$\left(\frac{15 \text{ km}}{1 \text{ hour}}\right)\left(\frac{1,000 \text{ meters}}{1 \text{ km}}\right)\left(\frac{1 \text{ hour}}{60 \text{ minutes}}\right)$$

2. **Cancel the common terms.**

$$\left(\frac{15}{1}\right)\left(\frac{1,000 \text{ meters}}{1}\right)\left(\frac{1}{60 \text{ minutes}}\right)$$

3. **Multiply the fractions.**

$$\frac{15,000 \text{ meters}}{60 \text{ minutes}} = \frac{250 \text{ meters}}{1 \text{ minute}}$$

Now double your 250-meters-per-minute result for his two-minute distance of 500 meters and Choice (B).

Simplifying Averages

You can always find the average in the way your teacher taught you in fifth grade: Add the terms together and divide by the number of terms. Say you want to find the average of 5, 11, 17, 23, and 29. First, add them all up:

$$5 + 11 + 17 + 23 + 29 = 85$$

Next, divide the total by the number of terms, which is 5:

$$\frac{85}{5} = 17$$

This method works every time, regardless of the numbers.

The following sections reveal shortcuts for tackling problems that are variations on this theme, including questions about missing-term averages and weighted averages.

Simplifying missing-term averages

For these types of questions, the GRE turns things around: It gives you the average and asks you for one of the missing terms. Say it tells you that the average is 10, and three of the numbers are 1, 8, and 13, so what's the missing number? You know what to do. Start with the formula:

$$\text{Average} = \frac{a + b + c + d}{4}$$

Place the numbers that you know into the formula, like this:

$$10 = \frac{1 + 8 + 13 + d}{4}$$

Then solve for d:

$$10 = \frac{22 + d}{4}$$
$$40 = 22 + d$$
$$d = 18$$

PLAY

A student takes seven exams. Her scores on the first six are 91, 89, 85, 92, 90, and 88. What score does she need on the *seventh* exam for an average of <u>90</u> to get an A?

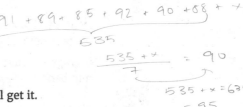

Set up the formula with x as the seventh exam score:

$$90 = \frac{91 + 89 + 85 + 92 + 90 + 88 + x}{7}$$

Then solve for x by adding the numbers and multiplying by 7:

$$90 = \frac{535 + x}{7}$$
$$630 = 535 + x$$
$$x = 95$$

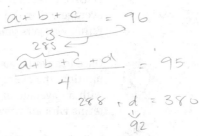

The student's seventh exam score needs to be 95 for that A. They'll get it.

PLAY

A student takes four exams for an average exam score of 95. Three of the exams have an average score of 96. What is his fourth exam score?

This works just like the last one: Set up the equation and solve for x:

$$95 = \frac{(3)96 + x}{4}$$
$$95 = \frac{288 + x}{4}$$
$$380 = 288 + x$$
$$x = 92$$

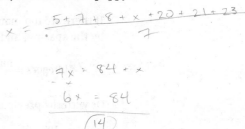

The fourth exam score was 92.

PLAY

If x is the mean of the numbers 5, 7, 8, x, 20, 21, and 23, what is the value of x?

Don't be intimidated by the extra x. These all work the same way: Set up the formula with x as one of the numbers *and* x as the average, just as the question describes, and solve that puppy:

$$x = \frac{5 + 7 + 8 + x + 20 + 21 + 23}{7}$$
$$x = \frac{84 + x}{7}$$
$$7x = 84 + x$$
$$6x = 84$$
$$x = 14$$

See? After all that, it was nothing. x equals 14.

Simplifying evenly spaced integers

You can quickly find the average when the integers are evenly spaced, including consecutive. *Consecutive* means that the numbers come one right after another, as in {2, 3, 4, 5}. *Evenly spaced* means that the terms are the same distance apart, as in {5, 10, 15, 20}. Whether the terms are consecutive or evenly spaced, use one of these methods to find the average:

>> If the number of terms is odd, the average is equal to the middle term. For example, {3, 4, 5, 6, 7} has an average of 5.

>> If the number of terms is even, the average is equal to the average of the two middle terms. For example, {10, 12, 14, 16} has an average of 13 because $\frac{12 + 14}{2} = \frac{26}{2} = 13$.

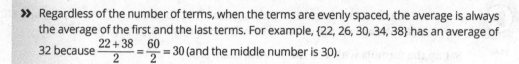

>> Regardless of the number of terms, when the terms are evenly spaced, the average is always the average of the first and the last terms. For example, {22, 26, 30, 34, 38} has an average of 32 because $\frac{22+38}{2} = \frac{60}{2} = 30$ (and the middle number is 30).

PLAY

Find the average of these evenly spaced numbers:

{50, 59, 68, 77, 86}

Don't reach for your pencil. Instead, use the fact that the terms are evenly spaced. Because the set contains an odd number of terms, go for the middle number: The average is 68. You could also average the first and last numbers: $\frac{50+86}{2} = 68$. Either way is less work than averaging *all* the numbers.

PLAY

Find the average of these consecutive even integers:

{18, 20, 22, 24, 26, 28, 30, 32}

Consecutive even integers are numbers evenly spaced by two. Since there isn't a middle number, average either the middle two numbers (24 and 26) or the first and last numbers (18 and 32). Either way gets you an average of 25.

TIP

Once in a while, you may need the total of the consecutive or evenly spaced integers. To find this, multiply the average by the number of terms. In the preceding example, there are eight terms with an average of 25, so the total is $8 \times 25 = 200$. In the example before that one, there are five terms with an average of 68, so the total is $68 \times 5 = 340$. Try this one out:

PLAY

Find the sum of the consecutive odd integers from 95 to 105.

Start with the average, which is $\frac{95+105}{2} = 100$. For the number of integers, count on your fingers: 95, 97, 99, 101, 103, 105 — six! Now multiply 'em: $100 \times 6 = 600$.

If there are too many to count, there's another trick: Subtract the lowest from the highest, divide by the spacing, and add one. In other words,

$$\# \text{integers} = \frac{\text{highest} - \text{lowest}}{\text{spacing}} + 1$$

Or with the previous example,

$$6 = \frac{105 - 95}{2} + 1$$

Simplifying weighted averages

A *weighted average* is the average of groups, where you have the average value for each group. For example, five juniors have an average score of 120, and ten seniors have an average score of 90. The larger the group, the more it affects — weights — the total average. The ten seniors affect the total average more than the five juniors do because the group of seniors is larger, regardless of the test scores.

TIP

If the larger group has a greater effect on the average, then the average is always closer to the larger group. With the preceding example, there are more seniors than juniors, so you know right away — without doing *any* math — that the students' total average score is closer to the seniors' average of 90 than to the juniors' average of 120.

To calculate a weighted average, multiply each value (each specific score) by the number in the group (the number of students who got that score). Do this for each group, add the products together, and divide this sum by the total number in all the groups (here, the total number of students).

PLAY

Find the weighted average score for 15 students with the following scores:

Number of Students	Score
5	120
10	90

Because 5 students got a 120, multiply $5 \times 120 = 600$. Do the same with the other score: $10 \times 90 = 900$. Now add them up:

$$600 + 900 = 1{,}500$$

You now have the total number of points that all the students earned. To find the total average, divide the 1,500 by the total number of students, which is $5 + 10 = 15$:

$$\frac{1{,}500}{15} = 100$$

The average score is 100.

It's good to know how to calculate the weighted average, but you won't have to do this very often. It's more common that you're tested on how well you *understand* it — specifically, that the total average is closer to the larger group. Try this one:

PLAY

Tree Species	Number of Trees	Average Height
Navel Orange	42 — *largest*	30.5 feet
Pomelo	31	48.0 feet
White Oak	12	81.5 feet

The average height of all 85 trees, in feet, is

Ⓐ less than 30.5
Ⓑ between 30.5 and 48.0 ← *larger group method*
Ⓒ exactly 48.0
Ⓓ between 48.0 and 81.5
Ⓔ greater than 81.5

You didn't *calculate* this, did you? Remember that the total average is closer to the *larger* group. Which group is the largest? Not the oaks, which are taller, but at 12 are the smallest group. The largest group is the navel orange, at 42 trees. So the total average is closer to the navel orange's height, 30.5, but not *less* than or *equal* to 30.5. It's more than 30.5 but less the pomelo at 48.0, for answer Choice (B). If you really want to calculate this, the total average is 44, but honestly there's no need. Trust the larger group method.

Simplifying Work Problems

Work problems typically tell you how long individuals take to complete a task working alone and then ask you how long they'd take to complete the task working together. To solve a work problem, use this formula:

$$\frac{1}{\text{Time}_A} + \frac{1}{\text{Time}_B} = \frac{1}{\text{Time}_{\text{Total}}}$$

where Time_A is the time it takes the first person (A), Time_B is the time it takes the second person (B), and so on. This formula works with as many people as could be in a GRE question. $\text{Time}_{\text{Total}}$ is the total time it takes all of them working together. If you have more than two people working, just put 1 over the time each one takes and add that to the total.

PLAY

If Jonathan can paint a house in six days and David can paint the same house in eight days, how many days does it take them, working together, to paint the house?

To solve this problem, place the numbers and do the math:

$$\frac{1}{\text{Time}_A} + \frac{1}{\text{Time}_B} = \frac{1}{\text{Time}_{\text{Total}}}$$

$$\left(\frac{1}{6}\right) + \left(\frac{1}{8}\right) = \frac{1}{\text{Time}_{\text{Total}}}$$

$$\frac{8}{48} + \frac{6}{48} =$$

$$\frac{14}{48} =$$

$$\frac{7}{24} =$$

Then reciprocate the fractions and simplify:

$$\frac{7}{24} = \frac{1}{\text{Time}_{\text{Total}}}$$

$$\frac{24}{7} = \text{Time}_{\text{Total}}$$

$$3\frac{3}{7} = \text{Time}_{\text{Total}}$$

Working together, Jonathan and David would take $3\frac{3}{7}$ days to paint the house.

WARNING

Be sure to reality-check your answer. If you get an answer of ten days, for example, you know there's a mistake because the two of them working *together* should take *less* time than either one working alone.

PLAY

If Tommy, Billy, and Joey take three, five, and six hours, respectively, to mow the neighbor's lawn, then how much time would it take them working together to mow the lawn?

Set up the equation with one extra fraction:

$$\frac{1}{3} + \frac{1}{5} + \frac{1}{6} = \frac{1}{\text{Time}_{\text{Total}}}$$

Then solve for total time:

$$\frac{21}{30} = \frac{1}{\text{Time}_{\text{Total}}}$$

$$\frac{30}{21} = \text{Time}_{\text{Total}}$$

$$\frac{10}{7}$$

$$1\frac{3}{7}$$

The GRE won't ask you to convert $1\frac{3}{7}$ days into hours and minutes. The answer is in the form that you solve it. Which is good.

Simplifying Team-Work Problems

A *team-work problem* gives you a team of workers (or machines) where each works at the same rate, and the problem tells you that the team accomplishes a certain task in a certain amount of time. For example, 12 factory workers accomplish a certain task in 10 days. Then the problem asks for either the new number of days required with a different number of workers or the new number of workers required with a different number of days. Either way, you solve it exactly the same way, with this formula:

(old # workers)(old # days) = (new # workers)(new # days)

If 12 workers can accomplish a certain task in 10 days, how many days are needed to accomplish the same task with only 8 workers?

Use the formula, with x as the new number of days:

(old # workers)(old # days) = (new # workers)(new # days)

$$(12)(10) = (8)(x)$$
$$120 = 8x$$
$$x = 15$$

handwritten: 12w in 10d ; 12(10) = 8x ; $\frac{120}{8} = x$

8 workers would require 15 days to accomplish the same task.

If 18 workers can accomplish a certain task in 3 days, how many workers are needed to accomplish the same task in 9 days?

Use the formula, with x as the new number of workers:

(old # workers)(old # days) = (new # workers)(new # days)

$$(18)(3) = (x)(9)$$
$$54 = 9x$$
$$x = 6$$

handwritten: 18(3) = x(9) ; x = 6

Accomplishing this task in 9 days would require 6 workers.

Besides describing machines instead of workers, the problem may describe hours instead of days. Solve it exactly the same way, and don't worry about converting.

Instead of saying, "to do a certain task," the problem may read, "to produce 240 drones." If that number doesn't change, don't worry about it; if that number *does* change, apply the ratio of the change to your answer. For example, if the factory now needs 480 drones, which is twice the original 240, then double your answer.

TIP

If six machines can produce 240 drones in 10 hours, how many machines are needed to produce 480 drones in 15 hours?

PLAY

Ⓐ 4

Ⓑ 8

Ⓒ 10

Ⓓ 12

Ⓔ 16

Use the formula, with x as the new number of machines, to accomplish the original task of producing 240 drones:

$$(\text{old \# machines})(\text{old \# hours}) = (\text{new \# machines})(\text{new \# hours})$$
$$(6)(10) = (x)(15)$$
$$60 = 15x$$
$$x = 4$$

If four machines require 15 hours to produce 240 drones, then to produce twice the number of drones, 480, the factory would require twice the number of machines. Correct answer: Choice (B).

If 16 kids can eat 800 French fries in three minutes, how much time would be required for 12 of these kids to eat 400 fries?

PLAY

Ⓐ 2

Ⓑ 3

Ⓒ 4

Ⓓ 8

Ⓔ 12

Use the formula, with x as the new number of kids, to accomplish the original task of eating 800 French fries:

$$(\text{old \# kids})(\text{old \# minutes}) = (\text{new \# kids})(\text{new \# minutes})$$
$$(16)(3) = (12)(x)$$
$$48 = 12x$$
$$x = 4$$

If 12 kids require four minutes to eat 800 French fries, then eating half the fries would only require half the time. Correct answer: Choice (A).

This last example is silly, but I want to make the point that regardless of the task, the workers, or the units of time, the process is exactly the same. Besides, anyone who has kids knows that they eat fries quickly.

REMEMBER

Simplifying Mixture Problems

A mixture problem looks more confusing than it actually is. The key to solving it is to set up a table that accounts for both the total mix and the component parts, as in the following example.

PLAY

Carolyn wants to mix 40 pounds of almonds selling for 30 cents a pound with x pounds of dark chocolate selling for 80 cents a pound. She wants to pay 40 cents per pound for the final mix. How many pounds of dark chocolate should she use?

The hardest part for most test-takers is knowing where to begin. Begin with these steps:

1. **Make a table and start with the labels for all the data you have.**

	Pounds	Price	Total
Almonds			
Dark Chocolate			
Mixture			

Handwritten notes:
40 lbs   3a
30¢/lb
x lbs   3c
80¢/lb
x lbs
$\frac{40}{x}$

2. **Fill in the values that the test question gives you.**

Almonds are 40 pounds at 30 cents a pound, and dark chocolate is 80 cents per pound. Carolyn wants the mixture to cost 40 cents a pound.

	Pounds	Price	Total
Almonds	40	$0.30	
Dark Chocolate		$0.80	
Mixture		$0.40	

Handwritten notes:
12
40 × 0.3
+ x · 0.8
(40 + x) · 0.4
12 + .8x = .4(40+x)

3. **Use x for your unknown value.**

If Carolyn starts with 40 pounds of almonds and adds x pounds of dark chocolate, she ends up with $40 + x$ pounds of mixture.

	Pounds	Price	Total
Almonds	40	$0.30	
Dark Chocolate	x	$0.80	
Mixture	$40 + x$	$0.40	

4. **Multiply across the rows to fill in the Total column.**

The total cost of almonds is $40 \times \$0.30 = \$12.00$, the total cost of dark chocolate is $0.80 times x, and the total cost of the whole mixture is $0.40 times the total weight, which is $(40 + x)$.

	Pounds	Price	Total
Almonds	40	$0.30	$12.00
Dark Chocolate	x	$0.80	$0.80x
Mixture	$40 + x$	$0.40	$0.40(40+x)

Handwritten notes:
$12 + 0.8x = 0.4(40+x)$
$12 + .8x = 16 + .4x$
$.4x = 4$
$x = 10$

5. Solve for x.

In the Total column, the total cost of almonds plus the total cost of dark chocolate equals the total cost of the mixture, so the equation looks like this:

$$\$12.00 + \$0.80x = \$0.40(40 + x)$$

Next, distribute the $0.40 on the right, and it all falls into place:

$$\$12.00 + \$0.80x = \$16.00 + \$0.40x$$
$$\$0.40x = \$4.00$$
$$x = 10$$

Keep in mind that x stands for the number of pounds of dark chocolate, which is what the question asks for. See, that's the point of GRE word problems: Set up the formula, place what you know, and solve for the missing part.

Anyway, go back and double-check the answer by placing this value into the equation. You already know that Carolyn spent $12 on almonds. If she buys 10 pounds of dark chocolate for 80 cents per pound, she spends $8, for a total of $20. She spends that $20 on 50 pounds: $20.00 ÷ 50 = $0.40. Just like that.

Try another one:

PLAY

A chemistry student has one solution that's 25 percent saline and another that's 15 percent saline. Approximately how many liters of the 25 percent solution must be added to the 15 percent solution to make 10 liters of a solution that's 20 percent saline?

Ⓐ 2.5
Ⓑ 3.3
Ⓒ 5.0
Ⓓ 6.7
Ⓔ 7.5

To answer this question, first create the table with the details from the question:

	Amount of Solution	% Saline	Amount of Saline
25% solution	x	0.25	$0.25x$
15% solution	$10 - x$	0.15	$0.15(10-x)$
20% solution	10	0.20	2

Now, set up the equation and do the math to solve for x. The quantity of 15 percent saline solution plus the quantity of 25 percent saline solution equals the quantity of 20 percent saline solution, so the equation looks like this:

$$0.25x + 0.15(10 - x) = 2$$

Now do the math:

$$0.25x + 0.15(10 - x) = 2$$
$$0.25x + 1.5 - 0.15x = 2$$
$$0.10x = 0.5$$
$$x = 5$$

The student needs to add 5 liters of the 25 percent saline solution, for a correct answer of Choice (C).

Simplifying Sets and Groups

Sets and groups are problems that place numbers, objects, or any items whatsoever into groups and describe the relationships between those groups. For example, you may group students by juniors and seniors and have members of each group form a subset for athletes. The following sections show you what the GRE may ask and how to answer it.

REMEMBER

A *set* is a collection of numbers, values, or objects that are typically related in some way, like this: {1, 3, 5, 7, 9}. An *empty set,* also referred to as a *null set,* is a set with nothing in it, and it's noted by the symbol ∅ or by empty brackets { }. You don't see many null sets on the GRE.

Simplifying the Venn diagram

Some members of one set also belong to another set, and vice versa, creating an overlap. For example, some students in history class are also in physics class, and the *intersection* is the students taking both classes, shown by the upside-down *u*-shaped symbol: ∩. The right-side-up *u*-shaped symbol indicates a *union*, which is *all* the students: ∪.

» **Union:** The union of the sets A and B, using the symbol $A \cup B$, contains *all* the members of both sets. If Set $A = \{2, 3, 5\}$ and Set $B = \{3, 5, 7\}$, then $A \cup B = \{2, 3, 5, 7\}$.

» **Intersection:** The intersection of the sets A and B, using the symbol $A \cap B$, contains *only* members belonging to both sets. If Set $A = \{2, 3, 5\}$ and Set $B = \{3, 5, 7\}$, then $A \cap B = \{3, 5\}$.

A *Venn diagram* shows the relationship between sets, including the union and intersection. It always has two or three circles representing sets, and these circles overlap to show the relationships between members of the sets. If the problem describes two groups with some members in both groups, draw a Venn diagram to visualize it.

In this drawing, the shaded region depicts $A \cap B$.

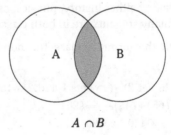

$A \cap B$

© John Wiley & Sons, Inc.

This next shaded region depicts $A \cup B$.

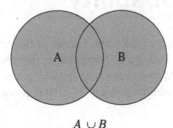

$A \cup B$

© John Wiley & Sons, Inc.

PLAY

What is in the intersection of sets A and B?

A = {cars, trucks, boats, vans}

B = {boats, vans, ATVs, motorcycles}

Ⓐ cars, trucks

Ⓑ nothing

Ⓒ cars, trucks, boats, vans, ATVs, motorcycles

Ⓓ boats, vans

Ⓔ A, B

The *intersection* of A and B has only the members that are in both sets. Only boats and vans are in both groups. The correct answer is Choice (D). If you picked Choice (C), you went with union instead of intersection.

Simplifying the sets formula

A Venn diagram is effective to count small numbers or to sort specific members within the groups. When the problem has you work with larger numbers in the groups, use the sets formula:

$$(\text{# in set 1}) + (\text{# in set 2}) - (\cap \text{ sets 1 and 2}) = \text{total #}$$

PLAY

Of all the company employees, 60 took advantage of educational benefits, 145 participated in the company retirement program, and 40 participated in both programs. How many employees took advantage of at least one program?

This group problem is about as straightforward as they get. Start with the formula, place the numbers that you know, and solve for what's missing:

$$(\text{# in set 1}) + (\text{# in set 2}) - (\cap \text{ sets 1 and 2}) = \text{total #}$$
$$(60) + (145) - (40) = x$$
$$x = 165$$

PLAY

Ninety students are taking either history, physics, or both. If 65 are taking history and 45 are taking physics, how many students are in both classes?

As always, start with the formula, place the numbers that you know, and solve for what's missing:

$$(\text{# in set 1}) + (\text{# in set 2}) - (\cap \text{ sets 1 and 2}) = \text{total #}$$
$$(65) + (45) - x = (90)$$
$$110 - x = 90$$
$$x = 20$$

Simplifying Probability

A *probability* question may ask your chances of throwing a pair of dice and getting a total of seven or snake eyes (1s on both dice). Fortunately, three simple steps can help you solve nearly every probability problem thrown your way, both in general and with multiple events. I also show you how to handle a probability problem involving sets and groups.

A probability is always a number between 0 and 1. A probability of 0 means that the event *won't* happen, and a probability of 1, or 100 percent, means it *will* happen. The probability that something *will* happen plus the probability that something *won't* happen always equals 1. A probability can't be negative or greater than 1.

Step #1: Set up the fraction

To find a probability, start with this formula to create a fraction:

$$\text{Probability} = \frac{\text{Number of desired outcomes}}{\text{Number of total outcomes}}$$

First, find the denominator, which is the total number of outcomes. For example, when you're rolling a six-sided die, there are six possible outcomes, giving you a denominator of 6. When you're pulling a card out of a standard deck, there are 52 possible outcomes (because a full deck has 52 cards), giving you a denominator of 52.

Next, find the numerator, which shows the total number of things you want. If you want to get a 5 when you roll a die, a die has exactly one 5 on it, so the numerator is 1. The probability of rolling a 5 is $\frac{1}{6}$. What's the probability of drawing a jack out of a standard deck of cards? The deck has 52 cards (the denominator) and 4 jacks (the numerator), so the probability is $\frac{4}{52}$, which reduces to $\frac{1}{13}$. The probability of drawing the jack of hearts, however, is only $\frac{1}{52}$ because a standard deck of cards contains only one jack of hearts.

PLAY

A jar of marbles has 8 yellow marbles, 6 black marbles, and 12 white marbles. What is the probability of drawing out a black marble?

With 26 marbles total and 6 black marbles, the probability is $\frac{6}{26}$, or $\frac{3}{13}$.

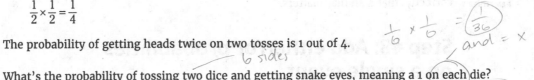

Step #2: Multiply consecutive probabilities

A *consecutive probability* is just a fancy term for events that happen more than once and don't affect each other (meaning they're *independent*). For example, if you flip a coin twice, the probability that it lands heads both times is a consecutive probability because the outcome of the first toss has no bearing on the outcome of the second toss. To find the probability of a specific set of events — that is, landing heads on both tosses — find the separate probability of each event and then multiply them.

The probability of landing heads is $\frac{1}{2}$ for the first toss and $\frac{1}{2}$ for the second, so multiply these together:

$$\frac{1}{2} \times \frac{1}{2} = \frac{1}{4}$$

The probability of getting heads twice on two tosses is 1 out of 4.

PLAY

What's the probability of tossing two dice and getting snake eyes, meaning a 1 on each die?

Because the outcomes are independent, meaning the score on one die has no bearing on the score on the other, treat each toss separately. The probability of getting a 1 is $\frac{1}{6}$ on the first die and $\frac{1}{6}$ on the second, so multiply these fractions for your answer:

$$\frac{1}{6} \times \frac{1}{6} = \frac{1}{36}$$

This probability is the same whether you toss one die twice or two dice together.

What's the probability of tossing two dice and getting a total of 7?

Because the outcomes have to match, meaning a 2 on one die doesn't count unless you have a 5 on the other, treat the tosses together. <u>Start with the denominator</u>: Because there are 6 sides to each die, the number of possible outcomes is $6 \times 6 = 36$.

How many ways can you get a total of 7? This table sums it up:

Die #1	Die #2	Total
1	6	7
2	5	7
3	4	7
4	3	7
5	2	7
6	1	7

(handwritten notes in margin: 1 6, 2 5, 3 4, AND, 6 tosses, 6/36)

Looks like there are 6 ways to get a total of 7, so place 6 as the numerator over 36 as the denominator. The probability of getting that lucky 7 is $\frac{6}{36} = \frac{1}{6}$.

If you're not sure whether to treat the tosses together or separately, don't worry: Either way is fine. Take the previous snake eyes example. I showed you how to treat the tosses separately, with $\frac{1}{6}$ per toss, for a snake eyes probability of $\frac{1}{6} \times \frac{1}{6} = \frac{1}{36}$. If you treat the tosses together, you get the same outcome: Start with the denominator, so with 6 sides to each die, the number of possible outcomes is $6 \times 6 = 36$. Now find the numerator, and with exactly 1 way to have both dice showing 1, the numerator is 1. The answer is the same as before: $\frac{1}{36}$.

With the lucky 7s example, you may ask, wouldn't a 2 plus 5 count the same as 5 plus 2? The answer is yes, and it follows that $1 + 6 = 6 + 1$ and $3 + 4 = 4 + 3$, meaning there would be exactly half the number of desired outcomes. There would also be exactly half the number of *possible* outcomes, where any combination would be canceled by its reflection, and the final answer would be exactly the same: $\frac{3}{18} = \frac{1}{6}$. So here's the takeaway: Don't worry about it. As long as you're *consistent*, either process is fine, and you get the right answer.

There's always more than one way to solve a problem. I show you the simplest way that's relevant to other GRE problems, but you can always find other ways that are just as fast and effective — or take longer and are effective. At the end of the day, as long as you solve the problem quickly and correctly, that's all that matters.

Step #3: Add either/or probabilities on a single event

An *either/or probability* on a single event is one in which either of two outcomes is desired. For example, if you reach into a bag containing 10 blue, 10 red, and 10 green marbles, what's the probability that you draw either a blue marble *or* a red marble? To solve this problem, find the probability of each event separately and then add them together. With 10 red marbles in a bag of 30, drawing a red marble has a 1 in 3 chance of occurring; drawing a blue marble is also 1 in 3:

$$\frac{1}{3} \text{ and } \frac{1}{3}$$

Add these together for the probability of drawing either a blue or a red marble:

$$\frac{1}{3} + \frac{1}{3} = \frac{2}{3}$$

You could also add the red and blue marbles first. To draw one of 10 blue marbles or 10 red marbles, there are 20 marbles total that would work, out of 30 marbles total in the bag, for the same answer:

$$\frac{20}{30} = \frac{2}{3}$$

PLAY

From the numbers 2, 3, 4, and 5, two different numbers are to be chosen at random. What is the probability that their product is either less than 9 or greater than 13?

Ⓐ $\frac{1}{6}$

Ⓑ $\frac{1}{3}$

Ⓒ $\frac{1}{2}$

Ⓓ $\frac{2}{3}$

Ⓔ $\frac{5}{6}$

Start with the total number of outcomes, which is the denominator. From the numbers 2, 3, 4, and 5, how many ways can you pick two numbers?

>> 2 and 3

>> 2 and 4

>> 2 and 5

>> 3 and 4

>> 3 and 5

>> 4 and 5

for 6 possibilities and a denominator of 6. Remember that *product* means multiply, so multiply those selections:

$$2 \times 3 = 6$$
$$2 \times 4 = 8$$
$$2 \times 5 = 10$$
$$3 \times 4 = 12$$
$$3 \times 5 = 15$$
$$4 \times 5 = 20$$

Looks like two are less than 9 and two are greater than 13, so place that total of 4 over 6, which reduces to 2 over 3, for answer Choice (D).

Simplifying probability in sets and groups

Sets and groups and probability (discussed in the previous sections) can be packaged into a single GRE question. Apply what you've already learned to answer these questions:

Of the 12 applicants for a job, 6 have master's degrees, 5 have tenure, and 4 have neither the degree nor the tenure. If one applicant is called at random, what is the probability that they have both a master's degree and tenure?

Ⓐ $\frac{1}{12}$

Ⓑ $\frac{1}{4}$

Ⓒ $\frac{1}{3}$

Ⓓ $\frac{5}{12}$

Ⓔ $\frac{1}{2}$

Start with the probability fraction:

$$\text{Probability} = \frac{\text{Number of desired outcomes}}{\text{Number of total outcomes}}$$

The number of total possible outcomes is easy: 12 candidates, so 12 is the denominator. The challenge is finding the number of possible desired outcomes. Because this example has members who are in neither group (having neither a master's degree nor tenure), use the sets formula, but add a third group for neither:

$$\text{Group}_1 + \text{Group}_2 + \text{Neither} - \text{Both} = \text{Total}$$
$$\text{Master's} + \text{Tenure} + \text{Neither} - \text{Both} = \text{Total}$$
$$(6) + (5) + (4) - x = 12$$
$$15 - x = 12$$
$$x = 3$$

Three applicants have both a master's degree and tenure. Place the 3 over the total number of applicants, 12:

$$\frac{3}{12} = \frac{1}{4}$$

The correct answer is Choice (B).

Simplifying Counting Methods

Counting certainly sounds easy enough, but when you're counting the number of ways different things can be arranged, counting becomes less intuitive. The following sections explain some methods to make complex counting intuitive again.

Basic counting methods

Suppose you have five shirts, two pairs of pants, and two jackets. How many different outfits can you put together? To answer this question, follow these steps:

1.   Make a space for each item that can change.

In this case, you have three spaces: one each for shirts, pants, and jackets.

2.   In each space, write down the number of options.

You now have something like this:

Shirts	Pants	Jackets
5	2	2

3.   Multiply the numbers.

$5 \times 2 \times 2 = 20$ different outfits.

This is how you count the possible combinations when rolling two six-sided dice. Each die has six possible outcomes, so the total number of different ways the numbers on the dice can be combined is $6 \times 6 = 36$.

PLAY

A gelato shop has ten no-sugar-added flavors, three types of cones, and two toppings. If your date gets one no-sugar-added flavor on a cone with one topping, how many possibilities are there?

3 and

10 f   3 c   2 t

10 × 3 × 2 = 60

- Ⓐ 60
- Ⓑ 50
- Ⓒ 40
- Ⓓ 30
- Ⓔ 20

Make a space for each item that can change. With ten flavors, three cones, and two toppings, your drawing looks like this:

$$\underline{10} \times \underline{3} \times \underline{2}$$

Serve up your answer:

$$\underline{10} \times \underline{3} \times \underline{2} = 60$$

The answer is a low-carb Choice (A).

PLAY

How many even four-digit numbers are there?

- Ⓐ 500
- Ⓑ 1,000
- Ⓒ 4,500
- Ⓓ 5,000
- Ⓔ 9,500

1000 → 9998

$$\begin{array}{r} 9998 \\ -1000 \\ \hline 8998 \end{array}$$

2

Make a space for each item that can change. There are four digits to the number, so make four spaces. Next, write down the number of options. The first space (the thousands digit) has 9 options, 1–9, because it can't be 0. (Zero would make it a 3-digit number.) The second and third spaces each has ten options, 0–9. The fourth space, which is the units digit, has only five options because it's even: 0, 2, 4, 6, and 8. So now your drawing looks like this:

$$\underline{9} \times \underline{10} \times \underline{10} \times \underline{5}$$

Multiply them for your answer:

$$\underline{9} \times \underline{10} \times \underline{10} \times \underline{5} = 4,500$$

The correct answer is Choice (C).

When order matters: Permutations

A *permutation* is a change in the arrangement of a given number of items or events. If the order in which items are arranged matters, you're looking at a permutation problem. One of the simplest examples looks at the possible number of ways the letters A, B, and C can be arranged (the possible number of permutations). The answer is six:

| ABC | BAC | CAB |
| ACB | BCA | CBA |

Based on the counting method discussed in the preceding section, you can figure this out without having to write out each possible permutation. The first event (or letter in this case) has three possible outcomes (A, B, or C), the second event has two possible outcomes (the remaining two letters), and the third event has only one possible outcome (the last remaining letter):

1st Letter	2nd Letter	3rd Letter
3	2	1

Multiplying gives you

$$3 \times 2 \times 1 = 6$$

When a question asks for the possible number of ways a certain number of objects may be arranged or events may occur, you can also use the factorial. (You can find more on factorials in Chapter 10.) The *factorial* is indicated by an exclamation point (!) and represents the product of integers up to and including a specific integer, so 3!, which stands for "three factorial," is $3 \times 2 \times 1 = 6$.

Remember that 0! is an exception: 0! = 1.

You can solve simple permutation problems using $n!$, where n represents the number of objects to arrange or the order of events.

Toby, Jill, Ashley, and Mark are racing bicycles. If there are no ties, in how many different orders can they finish the race?

Because there are four racers, the number of different orders in which they can finish is $4! = 4 \times 3 \times 2 \times 1 = 24$.

A permutation problem may ask about a small part of a larger group, such as the number of ways in which three kids out of a class of ten can be seated in the front row, or the number of ways in which three runners out of ten can place first, second, and third. Basically, if the order matters, it's a permutation problem.

There are two methods to solve this. The first method is to write the spaces for each item that can change, as you did in the previous section. Whether you're seating the three kids out of ten or placing three runners out of ten, the math is the same. There are ten possibilities for the first seat/place, nine possibilities for the second, and eight for the third:

$$\underline{10} \times \underline{9} \times \underline{8}$$

Multiply these for your answer:

$$\underline{10} \times \underline{9} \times \underline{8} = 720$$

This method is simple and works every time, but the second method uses a formula that leads to a better understanding of *combinations*, covered in the next section. The formula uses the factorial:

$$P_r^n = \frac{n!}{(n-r)!}$$

Where P is the number of permutations you're trying to determine, n is the total number of objects or events, and r is the subset of objects or events you're working with. (Note that near the P, the 10 below, and the n above, are not *exponents*: They're *indicators*.) In this example, $n = 10$ and $r = 3$. Place the numbers and do the math:

$$P_3^{10} = \frac{10!}{(10-3)!} = \frac{10!}{7!}$$

The numbers will always be simple and easy to multiply. You can make the calculations easier by reducing the fraction to its simplest terms first and then multiplying the remaining factors in the factorial:

$$P_3^{10} = \frac{10 \times 9 \times 8 \times 7!}{7!} = 720$$

WARNING

Be careful when reducing the fraction. The fraction $\frac{10!}{7!}$ doesn't equal $1\frac{3!}{7!}$, although that may be a trap answer choice. However, it does reduce to multiply easily:

$$\frac{10!}{7!} = \frac{10 \times 9 \times 8 \times 7!}{7!} = 10 \times 9 \times 8 = 720$$

PLAY

Nate is expecting eight families, each in a separate car, to attend the picnic. If there are only two parking spaces in front, and each space holds one car, how many ways can two cars park in front?

Because order matters, this is a permutation problem. In this example, you have eight total cars, but you're working with only two of those cars, so $n = 8$ and $r = 2$. Place the numbers and do the math:

$$P_2^8 = \frac{8!}{(8-2)!} = \frac{8!}{6!}$$

Reduce the fraction to its simplest terms and then multiply the remaining numbers:

$$P_2^8 = \frac{8 \times 7 \times 6!}{6!}$$
$$= 8 \times 7$$
$$= 56$$

When order doesn't matter: Combinations

A *combination* is a subset of objects or events in which order doesn't matter (for example, choosing 4 different business cards from a bowl containing 20 different cards). If a question asks about choosing a number of items and the order in which items are arranged or events occur doesn't matter, it's a combination problem. Use this formula:

$$C_r^n = \frac{n!}{r!(n-r)!}$$

where C is the number of combinations you're trying to determine, n is the total number of objects or events, and r is the number of objects or events you're choosing. (As with the Permutations formula, the n near the C is not an *exponent*: It's an *indicator*.)

PLAY

From a group of ten colleagues, Sally must choose three to serve on a committee. How many possible combinations does she have to choose from?

Because the order doesn't matter, this is a combination problem, so proceed as follows:

$$C_3^{10} = \frac{10!}{3!(10-3)!}$$
$$= \frac{(10)(^3\cancel{9})(^4\cancel{8})(\cancel{7!})}{(^1\cancel{3})(^1\cancel{2})(1)(\cancel{7!})}$$
$$= 120$$

PLAY

Joe buys a lottery ticket and picks two numbers out of 200. If the same number cannot be used twice and the order doesn't matter, what is the probability that his two numbers will match the two winning lottery numbers?

Here, Joe is choosing 2 out of 200, and the order doesn't matter, so first use the combinations formula to determine the total possible two-number combinations:

$$C_2^{200} = \frac{200!}{2!(200-2)!}$$
$$= \frac{200!}{2!(198!)}$$
$$= \frac{(200)(199)\cancel{(198!)}}{2!\cancel{(198!)}}$$
$$= \frac{(200)(199)}{2}$$
$$= \frac{(100)(199)}{1}$$
$$= 19{,}900$$

Joe has only one ticket, so his chances of winning are 1 out of 19,900, or $\frac{1}{19{,}900}$.

TIP

For more on reducing a fraction with factorials, turn to "Working with Factorials" in Chapter 10.

Chapter **14**

Interpreting Data and Graphs

Regardless of your area of study or your choice of grad school, you need a general understanding of how tables and graphs describe statistics and data. The folks who developed the GRE are well aware of this, so they include several questions in the math sections of the exam to test your skills in data analysis.

This chapter gets you up to speed on interpreting graphs and data as they appear in the GRE. In this chapter, you start with median, mode, range, mean, and standard deviation, and then you move on to reading tables and graphs to understand statistics and data.

Interpreting Basic Stats

With a few concepts, you can solve pretty much any basic statistics problem on the GRE. In this section, I cover the concepts of median, mode, range, mean, and standard deviation.

Interpreting the median

The *median* is the middle number when all the terms are arranged in order. Think of the median strip in the middle of a road. To find the median, place the numbers in order.

Find the median of $-3, 18, -4, \frac{1}{2}, 11$.

Ⓐ -3

Ⓑ 18

Ⓒ -4

Ⓓ $\frac{1}{2}$

Ⓔ 11

handwritten: $-4 \mid -3 \left(\frac{1}{2} \right) 11 \mid 18$

Put the numbers in order: $-4, -3, \frac{1}{2}, 11, 18$. The one in the middle, $\frac{1}{2}$, is the median. It's as simple as that. Correct answer: Choice (D).

If the list has an even number of terms, put them in order and find the middle two, and take the average of those two terms.

 Find the median of $5, 0, -3, -5, 1, 2, 8, 6$.

Ⓐ 0

Ⓑ 1

Ⓒ 1.5

Ⓓ 2

Ⓔ 5

handwritten: $-5 \mid -3 \mid 0 \; 1 \; 2 \mid 5 \; 6 \; 8$

Put the numbers in order: $-5, -3, 0, 1, 2, 5, 6, 8$. The middle two terms are 1 and 2, and their average is 1.5. That's it. Correct answer: Choice (C).

 This table shows the numbers and price ranges of 90 LED TVs sold at Harry's TV outlet. Which of the following *could* be the median TV sale price? Select *all* possible answers.

Number of LED TVs	Price range	
5	$200 – 299	5
15	$300 – 499	20
15	$500 – 699	35
15	$700 – 999	50
40	$999 – 1,300	90

Ⓐ $550

Ⓑ $650

Ⓒ $750

Ⓓ $850

Ⓔ $950

Ⓕ $1,050

The numbers are already in order, but you need to find which group has the median. Of 90 TVs, the middle two — the medians — are numbers 45 and 46. Looks like numbers 1–5 are in the first group, 6–20 are in the second, 21–35 are in the third, and 36–50 are in the fourth. If the two median TVs are in the fourth group, each price is somewhere between $700 and $999, and the prices *could* be anywhere in that range. Each price within that range has to be selected to get this one right because it's a price that the median TV *could* be. Correct answers: Choices (C), (D), and (E).

PLAY

Of the numbers 3, 3, 4, 4, 6, 6, 7, 7, and *x*, if *x* is an integer, which of the following *could* be the median? Select *all* possible answers.

- [A] 3
- [B] 4
- [C] 5
- [D] 6
- [E] 7
- [F] 8

The numbers are already in order, except possibly the *x*. The question asks which *could* be the median, so consider the different possible medians from the different values of *x*. If *x* is 4 or less, then the median is 4. If *x* is 5, then the median is 5, and if *x* is 6 or more, then the median is 6. Correct answers: Choices (B), (C), and (D).

Interpreting the mode

The *mode* is the most frequent number. Think *mode* rhymes (almost) with *most*. Put the numbers in order so you can more easily spot the number that shows up the most often — that's the mode.

PLAY

Find the mode of 11, 18, 29, 17, 18, −4, 0, 19, 0, 11, 18.

- (A) 11
- (B) 17
- (C) 18
- (D) 19
- (E) 29

The list of terms contains three 18s but no more than two of any other number. Correct answer: Choice (C).

PLAY

Find the modes of 6, 7, 8, 8, 8, 9, 10, 10, 11, 11, 11, 12, 15. Select *all* answers that apply.

- [A] 6
- [B] 8
- [C] 10
- [D] 11
- [E] 12
- [F] 15

A group of numbers can have more than one mode. In this case, the group of numbers contains three 8s and three 11s, so it has two modes. Correct answers: Choices (B) and (D).

REMEMBER

If the list has two modes, count them both. If the list has two medians (from an even number of values), average them.

Interpreting the range

The *range* is the distance from the smallest value to the largest value. You find the range by subtracting the smallest term from the largest term.

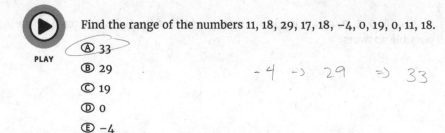

Find the range of the numbers 11, 18, 29, 17, 18, −4, 0, 19, 0, 11, 18.

Ⓐ 33

Ⓑ 29

Ⓒ 19

Ⓓ 0

Ⓔ −4

−4 → 29 ⇒ 33

To find the range, subtract the smallest number from the largest: $29 - (-4) = 33$. Correct answer: Choice (A).

If the range of the numbers 30, 40, 50, 70, 90, and x is 70, which of the following *could* be the value of x? Select <u>two</u> answers.

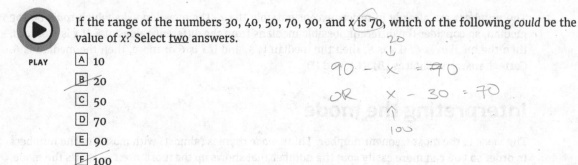

A 10

B 20

C 50

D 70

E 90

F 100

$$90 - x = 70$$
$$\text{OR} \quad x - 30 = 70$$

The range is the difference between the lowest and highest numbers. The lowest and highest numbers that you're given are 30 and 90, which have a difference of 60, so x has to be outside those numbers — either less than 30 or greater than 60. For a range of 70, x could be 20, because $90 - (20) = 70$, or it could be 100, because $(100) - 30 = 70$. The correct answers are Choices (B) and (F).

This is a common type of GRE range question, so try another:

If the range of the numbers 10, 15, 20, 30, 40, 55, and y is 50, which of the following *could* be the value of y? Select <u>two</u> answers.

A 5

B 10

C 20

D 40

E 60

F 80

$y = 5$ or 60

The lowest and highest numbers here are 10 and 55, with a difference of 45, so y has to be outside those numbers — either less than 10 or greater than 55. For a range of 50, y could be 5, because $55 - (5) = 50$, or it could be 60, because $(60) - 10 = 50$. The correct answers are Choices (A) and (E).

Interpreting the mean

Mean is another word for *average*, touched upon in Chapter 13, but it's also relevant to statistics, so here's a refresher. To calculate the mean, or average, add up all the values and divide by the number of values.

Suppose you have the numbers 1, 6, 8, 10, 12, and 17. To calculate the mean, do the following:

1. Add up all the values.

$$1+6+8+10+12+17=54$$

2. Divide this sum by the number of values.

$$\frac{54}{6}=9$$

The mean is 9. Try these out:

PLAY

Find the average of the numbers 12, 14, 22, 25, and 27.

Ⓐ 20

Ⓑ 22

Ⓒ 25

Ⓓ 27

Ⓔ 30

Set up the equation and solve for the average.

$$A=\frac{12+14+22+25+27}{5}$$
$$=\frac{100}{5}$$
$$=20$$

Correct answer: Choice (A).

PLAY

Billy scored an 89, 94, 85, and 90 on his first four algebra exams. If each exam counts the same, what is the minimum score that he needs on his fifth exam to squeak by with an average of 90 for an A?

Ⓐ 90

Ⓑ 92

Ⓒ 94

Ⓓ 96

Ⓔ 98

Set up the equation with *x* as the missing exam score:

$$90=\frac{89+94+85+90+x}{5}$$
$$90=\frac{358+x}{5}$$
$$450=358+x$$
$$x=92$$

Billy needs a 92 to get his A. He'll get it. Correct answer: Choice (B).

$$x + y + z = 5$$

Quantity A	*Quantity B*
The average of $(x+4y-z)$, $(x+2y+2z)$, and $(x-3y+2z+9)$	8

Ⓐ Quantity A is greater.

Ⓑ Quantity B is greater.

Ⓒ The two quantities are equal.

Ⓓ The relationship cannot be determined from the information given.

How do you find the average of three expressions? Add them up and divide by 3. Even though these aren't exactly numbers, it works the same way. First, set it up:

$$A = \frac{(x+4y-z)+(x+2y+2z)+(x-3y+2z+9)}{3}$$

Now drop the parentheses:

$$A = \frac{x+4y-z+x+2y+2z+x-3y+2z+9}{3}$$

I know it looks like madness. Remember how GRE Math works: If you set it up correctly, everything cancels out. Organize the madness by grouping the x's, y's, and z's:

$$A = \frac{x+x+x+4y+2y-3y-z+2z+2z+9}{3}$$
$$= \frac{3x+3y+3z+9}{3}$$

The question tells you that $x + y + z = 5$, so $3x + 3y + 3z = 15$. Plug that in and wrap this up:

$$A = \frac{15+9}{3}$$
$$= \frac{24}{3}$$
$$= 8$$

And that's the point: Don't be chilled by these crazy-looking equations. As long as you set them up correctly and don't drop a negative sign or make a silly mistake, you should have no problem solving them. The two quantities are equal, so the correct answer is Choice (C).

TIP

A good way to stay organized when simplifying $x+4y-z+x+2y+2z+x-3y+2z+9$ into $3x+3y+3z+9$ is to cross off the terms as you use them. For example, when you bring down all the y's, cross off the $4y$, $2y$, and $-3y$ as you write down $3y$. That way, you keep track of the terms that you've simplified and the ones that you haven't.

REMEMBER

If you find that the math is getting complicated, you either missed the concept or made a mistake. If this happens, *don't try to check your work.* Remember, the math moves fast and is simple, so instead, scrap your work and *start over.* Just takes a minute and goes *much* faster.

Interpreting standard deviation

Standard deviation for a set of numbers is a measure of the distance of each number from the mean. It's not quite the *mean* deviation, but it's similar. Outside the GRE, standard deviation can be complicated, but on the GRE, it's always simple.

Every set of numbers has a mean, and each number in that set is either on the mean or a distance from it. For example, with the numbers 3, 5, 7, 9, and 11, the mean is 7, and the other numbers are either 2 or 4 from the mean.

Through a complex calculation (which you don't need to worry about), the distances of these points from the mean are mixed together to find the standard deviation. Though you don't need to know how to calculate standard deviation, you do need to know what it is.

If a set of data has a mean of 100 and a standard deviation of 10, then anything 10 away from the mean, whether above or below, is *within* that standard deviation. For example, 95, being less than 10 away from the mean of 100, is within the standard deviation, and 115, being more than 10 away from the mean, is outside the standard deviation.

PLAY

Members of the June High football team have an average height of 6 feet, 3 inches, with a standard deviation of 2.5 inches. Which of the following players are within the standard deviation? Select *all* correct answers.

6'3" ± 2.5"

A Smith: 5 feet, 10 inches

B Barnes: 6 feet, 1 inch

C Carly: 6 feet, 3 inches

D Henry: 6 feet, 2 inches

E Edwin: 5 feet, 11 inches

F Astor: 6 feet

Within one standard deviation is between 6 feet, 0.5 inches (2.5 inches below the mean), and 6 feet, 5.5 inches (2.5 inches above the mean). Barnes, Carly, and Henry are within these heights. Correct answers: Choices (B), (C), and (D).

If the question asked for players whose heights are within *two* standard deviations, you'd look for heights 5 inches above and below the mean because $2 \times 2.5 = 5$.

PLAY

Mr. Jones's algebra class recently took a test and got an average score of 91.2 with a standard deviation of 5. Which of the following test scores are within 1.5 standard deviations? Select *all* correct answers.

91.2 ± 5×1.5
7.25

A 95

B 96

C 97

D 98

E 99

F 102 (with the bonus question)

If one standard deviation is 5, then 1.5 standard deviations is 7.5 because $5 \times 1.5 = 7.5$. You're looking for scores that are 7.5 above and below the class average of 91.2, so between 83.7 and 98.7 (91.2 plus and minus 7.5, respectively). Of the scores listed in the answer choices, 95, 96, 97, and 98 are within that range. Correct answers: Choices (A), (B), (C), and (D).

Eyeballing standard deviation

A question may ask you to compare two or more standard deviations of a graph or a data set. Eyeballing them typically does the trick: If the data is generally farther from the mean, it has a greater standard deviation; if it's generally closer to the mean, it has a lesser standard deviation. Eyeball these examples and see how it goes:

Quantity A	*Quantity B*
The standard deviation of 7, 8, 8, 8, 9, 11, 12	The standard deviation of 1, 2, 11, 12, 19, 25, 200

Ⓐ Quantity A is greater.

Ⓑ Quantity B is greater.

Ⓒ The two quantities are equal.

Ⓓ The relationship cannot be determined from the information given.

Which set of data is farther from the mean? You don't need to calculate the mean or measure the spread of the data. Just eyeball them, and you see that the Quantity B data set is spread out farther (from 1 to 200) than the Quantity A data (from 7 to 12) and thus has a greater standard deviation. Correct answer: Choice (B).

The GRE varies the standard deviation questions, so here are some more.

Quantity A	*Quantity B*
The standard deviation of 6, 8, 10, 12, 14	The standard deviation of 16, 18, 20, 22, 24

Ⓐ Quantity A is greater.

Ⓑ Quantity B is greater.

Ⓒ The two quantities are equal.

Ⓓ The relationship cannot be determined from the information given.

Standard deviation is not about the data itself; it's about its distance from the mean. Quantity B data is certainly greater, but that doesn't matter. How far are the numbers from the mean? Quantity A data has a mean of 10, and its numbers are either 2 or 4 from the mean. Quantity B data has a mean of 20, and its numbers are the *exact same* distance from its mean. The two standard deviations are equal. Correct answer: Choice (C).

n is a set of integers.

Quantity A	*Quantity B*
The standard deviation of *n*	The standard deviation of *n* if each number in *n* were increased by 5

Ⓐ Quantity A is greater.

Ⓑ Quantity B is greater.

Ⓒ The two quantities are equal.

Ⓓ The relationship cannot be determined from the information given.

So the numbers in *n* increased, but did the distances from the mean change? Probably not, since the mean *also* increased by 5. Say the numbers are 5, 7, and 9. The mean is 7, and the other two numbers are 2 from the mean. Now up the numbers by 5, for new values of 10, 12, and 14. The mean is now 12, and the other two numbers are *still* 2 from the mean. The standard deviation didn't change, so the quantities are equal. Correct answer: Choice (C).

Sometimes you have to compare the standard deviations of a set of graphs, like these:

PLAY

Graph A:

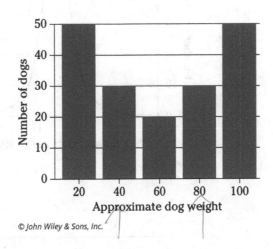

© John Wiley & Sons, Inc.

Graph B:

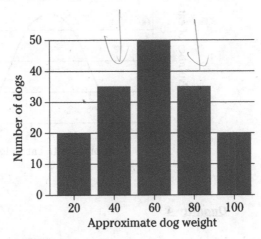

© John Wiley & Sons, Inc.

Quantity A	_Quantity B_
The standard deviation of the data in Graph A	The standard deviation of the data in Graph B

Ⓐ Quantity A is greater.

Ⓑ Quantity B is greater.

Ⓒ The two quantities are equal.

Ⓓ The relationship cannot be determined from the information given.

You're welcome to do the math, but you don't have to. Clearly the data in Graph A is spread out farther than the data in Graph B, so Graph A has a greater standard deviation. Correct answer: Choice (A).

PLAY

Graph A:

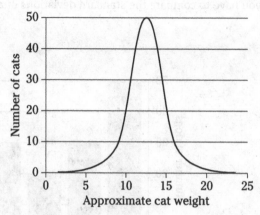

© John Wiley & Sons, Inc.

Graph B:

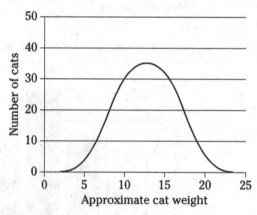

© John Wiley & Sons, Inc.

Quantity A	*Quantity B*
The standard deviation of the data in Graph A	The standard deviation of the data in Graph B

Ⓐ Quantity A is greater.

Ⓑ Quantity B is greater.

Ⓒ The two quantities are equal.

Ⓓ The relationship cannot be determined from the information given.

Here, you can't do the math, but again, you don't have to. The data in Graph B is spread out farther than the data in Graph A, so Graph B has the greater standard deviation. Correct answer: Choice (B).

Interpreting mean deviation

If you need to compare two or more standard deviations, and you don't trust eyeballing them, there's another way — you could estimate using *mean deviation*. Calculating actual standard deviation is more work than you'll ever have to do on a single GRE Math question, but *mean deviation* is simpler and works perfectly for this task on the GRE.

Here's how to find the mean deviation of the numbers 1, 6, 8, 10, 12, and 17:

1. **Find the average.**

$$\frac{1+6+8+10+12+17}{6} = \frac{54}{6} = 9$$

2. **Find the distance of *each value* from the mean.**

This distance is always *positive*.

In this example, the first value, 1, has a distance of 8 from the mean $(9-1=8)$. The second value, 6, has a distance of $3\,(9-6=3)$. The remaining values, 8, 10, 12, and 17, have respective distances of 1, 1, 3, and 8.

3. **Find the average of these distances.**

$$\frac{8+3+1+1+3+8}{6} = \frac{24}{6} = 4$$

The mean deviation for this set of data is 4.

So, basically, you have to *understand*, but *not calculate*, standard deviation. If you ever think you should calculate it — say, to check your estimation (when returning to the question at the end) — use *mean deviation* as a simple, reliable way to compare standard deviations.

Interpreting the distribution curve

The GRE expects you to understand the significance of the standard deviation. You don't have to calculate anything with this graph, but you do have to understand the normal distribution of data.

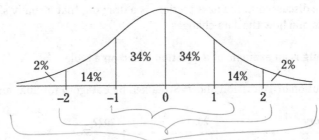

» Everything between –1 and 1 is within *one* standard deviation. With normal distribution, this is about 68% of the data.

» Everything between –2 and 2 is within *two* standard deviations and is about 95% of normal data.

» Everything between –3 and 3 is within *three* standard deviations and is just above 99% of normal data.

Of course, stats class explores this topic for at least a semester, and you may too, but for now, just understand the drawing and bullet points above, and you're good for just about any GRE question on this topic.

Interpreting Tables and Graphs

In each math section, the GRE presents a set of one or two tables and graphs along with three questions (on the computer-based exam) or four questions (on the paper-based one) — though there may also be a solo table/graph question here or there.

TIP

The three grouped table and graph questions aren't really more challenging than the other math questions, but they do take more time to sort out what's happening. Because you can go back and forth through the questions (see Chapter 1 for more on this), a good time-management strategy is to guess on the table/graph questions, mark them for review (or write the question numbers down), and return to them when you've finished the other questions in the section. These questions will take longer, so work them last. Try this strategy on a practice exam and be sure that it works for you.

REMEMBER

To handle the table and graph questions, you need an eye for detail and a knack for understanding what the data tells you. In other words, the GRE challenges you to determine the significance of the data. Take the following approach to answering any question that contains a table:

1. Look over the data for a sense of what it's describing.

2. Check for details, such as numbers versus percents, and if the data is over time, whether it's in days, months, or years.

3. Carefully read the question and understand *exactly* what it's asking.

4. Look at the answer choices: If they're far apart, you can estimate the answer.

5. From the table, find the details of what the question is asking.

6. Do your math and select the closest answer.

Interpreting tables

A *table* displays data in rows and columns, as in a channel guide or scoreboard. On the GRE, however, tables do more than help you find the game or the score: They contain details for analyzing the data.

A *graph,* discussed in the next section, is a drawing that visually shows the relationship between the data and how the data changes.

Following is an example of a question based on a table.

PLAY

Distribution of Television Shows Streamed by Category for 2021 and 2022

Category	2021	2022
Action	15.2%	13.7%
Comedy	18.9%	19.1%
Drama	7.4%	10.5%
Family	22.0%	19.2%
Foreign	4.8%	7.2%

Category	2021	2022
Independent	5.6%	9.3%
Romance	8.1%	5.2%
Sci-Fi	5.3%	4.0%
Thriller	12.7%	11.8%
Total	100.0%	100.0%
Total shows streamed	3,225	4,189

Based on the information in the table, which of the following statements can you infer? Select *all* that are true.

A In each of the years 2021 and 2022, TV shows streamed in the Action, Drama, and Thriller categories accounted for more than 35 percent of all TV shows streamed.

B The total number of Sci-Fi shows streamed increased from 2021 to 2022.

C From 2021 to 2022, the total number of shows streamed increased by more than 25 percent.

Check each answer choice separately:

>> For Choice (A), add the percentages in the Action, Drama, and Thriller categories for each year: $15.2 + 7.4 + 12.7 = 35.3\%$ and $13.7 + 10.5 + 11.8 = 36\%$, so Choice (A) is true.

>> For Choice (B), multiply the Sci-Fi percentage by the total number of shows streamed for each year and compare the numbers: $0.053 \times 3,225 = 171$ for 2021 and $0.04 \times 4,189 = 168$ for 2022, so Choice (B) is false — the number of Sci-Fi shows streamed actually decreased slightly.

>> For Choice (C), subtract 2021's total shows streamed from 2022's total shows streamed to determine how many more shows were streamed in 2022, and then divide by 2021's total shows streamed: $(4,189 - 3,225) \div 3,225 \times 100\% = 29\%$ (using the percent of change method from Chapter 10), so Choice (C) is true.

The correct answers are Choices (A) and (C).

Interpreting graphs

The following sections cover the graph types you're likely to encounter, provide some practice questions to test your graph-reading ability, and reveal a quicker method for estimating graph totals.

REMEMBER

The graphs are always drawn to scale, so you can rely on them as accurate visual representations of the data. To alleviate any doubt, the graphs typically include a note that says, "Graphs drawn to scale."

Different types of graphs

To make sense of data presented in a graph, familiarize yourself with the different graph types, as described in the following sections.

THE LINE GRAPH

A *line graph* consists of two or three axes with data points connected by a line, sort of like a connect-the-dots exercise. How data points are plotted on the graph depends on the graph type:

» **Two axes:** A typical line graph consists of an *x*- (horizontal) and *y*- (vertical) axis, each of which represents a different unit of measure. For example, the *x*-axis may represent years, while the *y*-axis represents profits in millions of dollars. In this example, each data point represents the profit for a specific year, and connecting the dots forms a line (hence the name *line* graph). In the following graph, the *x*-axis represents years, while the *y*-axis represents the number of dolphin sightings on Fort Myers Beach each year.

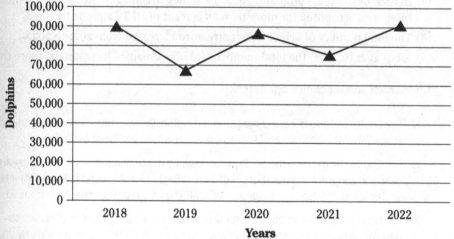

© John Wiley & Sons, Inc.

» **Three axes:** A graph with three axes contains a second *y*-axis on the right. In this example, the left axis represents the minutes per day spent exercising, and the right axis represents the pounds lost per month. You read the points on a three-axis graph the same way you do on a two-axis graph; just make sure you're clear on which *y*-axis each line refers to. Here's an example of a three-axis line graph:

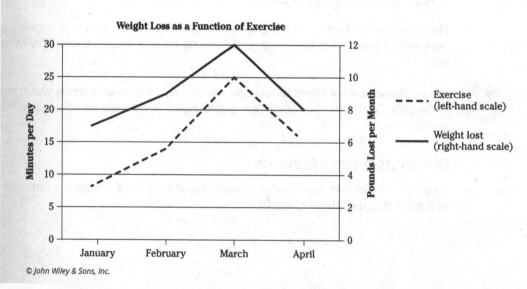

© John Wiley & Sons, Inc.

THE BAR GRAPH

A *bar graph*, also called a *column graph*, has vertical or horizontal bars that may represent actual numbers or percentages. Although they look significantly different from line graphs, they're very similar. The only difference is that the data points create bars instead of connecting to form a line. See the following example.

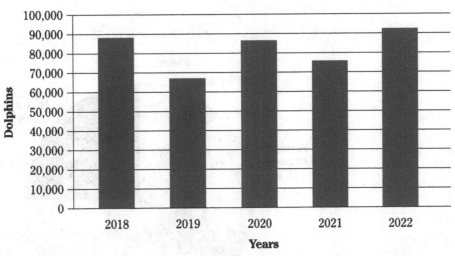

Number of Dolphin Sightings on
Fort Myers Beach, Florida
2018 – 2022

THE GANTT CHART

If you've worked as a project manager, you know this one well. Named for its inventor, Henry Gantt, the *Gantt chart* is a type of bar graph that tracks a timeline and shows the *sequence* and *dependency of events*, meaning one event has to conclude before the next one can begin. For example, you have to board the plane *before* you can fly to Hawaii. Your flight to Hawaii is *dependent* on you boarding that plane.

Here's a simple example:

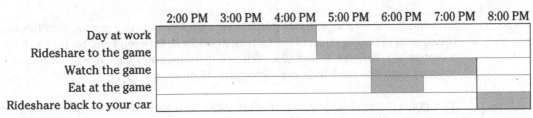

You finish your day at work, *then* you rideshare to the game, *then* you watch and eat at the game, and *then* you rideshare back to your car. Each event is in a sequence, and there are other ways to plan the evening, but per this plan, each event is *dependent* on the previous event. The exception is eating at the game, which could be delayed or skipped without affecting the plan — but it is dependent on your rideshare to the game.

THE PIE CHART

Each *pie chart* represents 100 percent of the whole, while portions of the graph represent parts of that circle or slices of that pie. To read such a graph, first make a mental note of what the whole circle or pie represents so you know what each portion represents.

For example, with the following pie chart, you may be told that 5,000 students graduated with PhDs in the year 2022. A 25 percent slice of the pie chart is labeled "History," so you know that the number of PhDs in History is 25 percent, or $\frac{1}{4}$, of 5,000, and $5,000 \times \frac{1}{4} = 1,250$ students. Check out this example of a pie chart:

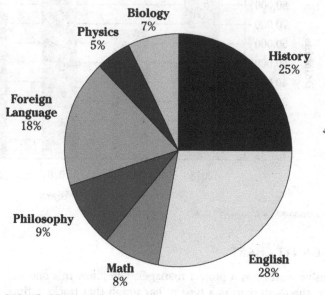

PhD Graduates per Major

THE LOGARITHMIC GRAPH

A *logarithmic graph* is a graph with an axis scale that changes by multiples of 10. The axis isn't labeled with consecutive numbers (1, 2, 3, 4) or an evenly spaced pattern (5, 10, 15, 20). Instead, each increment is equal to the previous increment multiplied by 10 (1, 10, 100, 1,000, and so on).

Each increment on a logarithmic graph is separated by nine tick marks. Each tick mark indicates the amount of change equal to the increment below it. Between 1 and 10, each tick mark indicates a change of 1. Between 10 and 100, each tick mark indicates a change of 10. Between 10,000 and 100,000, each tick mark indicates a change of 10,000.

This graph is useful for tracking small changes with small numbers but ignoring small changes with large numbers. Suppose, for example, you were to measure the populations of a handful of small Pacific islands. If Island A's population of 7 were to increase by 2, this 30 percent change would clearly show on the logarithmic graph. However, if Island D's population of 3,234 were to also increase by 2, this tiny percent change would not show on the logarithmic graph.

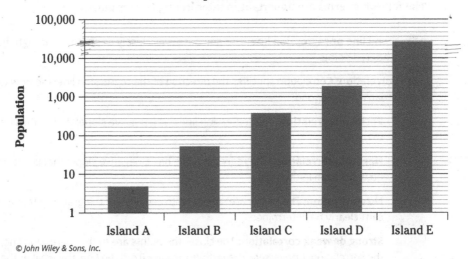

Population of Pacific Islands

© John Wiley & Sons, Inc.

The GRE may ask whether Island D has more than three times the population of Island C. At a glance, the answer appears to be no. However, with a grasp of how the logarithmic graph works, you know that Island C has approximately 600 residents, while Island D has roughly 3,000 residents, so the answer is yes. Be sure you understand how this works.

PLAY

According to the Population of Pacific Islands graph, the population of Island E is closest to

(A) 10,000

(B) 15,000

(C) 30,000

(D) 50,000

(E) 100,000

Each mark past 10,000 is equal to a 10,000-increment increase (until it reaches 100,000). The bar for Island E surpasses the 10,000 mark by four increments, so add 10,000 for each increment for a total of 50,000, which is answer Choice (D).

TIP

Note that the bar doesn't *quite* reach 50,000, so the population may actually be closer to 48,000. The question reads *closest to,* so among the answers, it's closest to 50,000. Note also that 40,000 isn't an answer choice, so if you're not sure whether to go with 40,000 or 50,000, it's a nonissue. The GRE isn't checking how good your optometrist is. It's checking whether you understand the concept of this graph.

THE SCATTER PLOT

A *scatter plot* is useful for spotting trends and making predictions. It's similar to a line graph in that it uses horizontal and vertical axes to display the values of the plotted points. With a scatter plot, however, instead of connecting the individual dots, you draw a line to show the flow of data and predict where the future data points are likely to fall. This line is called a *trend line* or *regression line*. Sometimes the trend line is drawn, and other times you estimate it based on the data flow.

The following terms are important in interpreting scatter plots:

» **Trend line or regression line:** This line passes as closely as possible through the middle of the scattered points.

» **Correlation:** Correlation specifies the direction of the regression line and how closely the two variables correspond:

- **Positive correlation:** The regression line has a positive slope; that is, the line rises from left to right.

- **Negative correlation:** The regression line has a negative slope; that is, the line runs downhill from left to right.

- **No correlation:** The points are simply scattered all over the graph so that a regression line can't clearly be determined.

- **Strong or weak correlation:** The closer the points are to the regression line, the stronger the correlation. Conversely, the farther they are from the line, the weaker the correlation.

PLAY

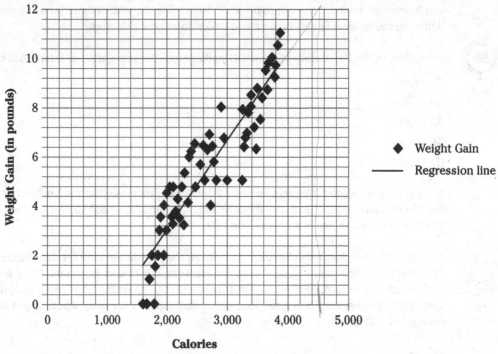

© John Wiley & Sons, Inc.

Based on the data in this scatter plot, about how many calories would need to be consumed to result in a 12-pound gain?

Ⓐ 3,000

Ⓑ 3,500

Ⓒ 4,000

Ⓓ 4,500

Ⓔ 5,000

Lay your pencil on top of the regression line and follow it to see where it intersects the graph at 12 pounds. Use the grid to follow the line down to the x-axis, and you have your answer: about 4,500 calories. Correct answer: Choice (D).

Interpreting two graphs

Some graph questions on the GRE contain two graphs, usually of different types. To answer the questions, you may need to extract data from one or both graphs.

Here's an example:

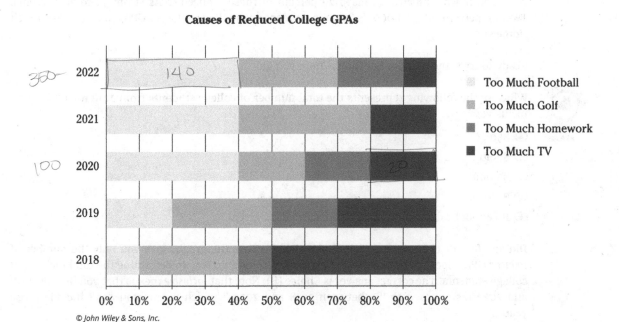

Causes of Reduced College GPAs

Legend:
- Too Much Football
- Too Much Golf
- Too Much Homework
- Too Much TV

© John Wiley & Sons, Inc.

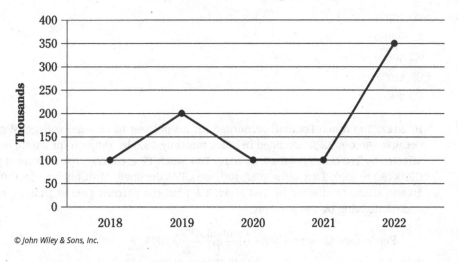

Number of Reduced College GPAs by Year

© John Wiley & Sons, Inc.

These two graphs are intended to be used in conjunction. The first graph is a bar graph that ranges from 0 to 100 percent. For this specific graph, calculate the impact of a cause of reduced GPAs by using the length of the bar segment. For example, for 2018, the Too Much Golf category (as a cause of reduced GPAs) begins at 10 percent and extends to 40 percent, for a range of 30 percent. If you say that in 2018, Too Much Golf was 40 percent, you're overlooking the 10-percent segment that is Too Much Football. Also, in 2022, Too Much Homework extends from 70 percent to 90 percent, for a range of 20 percent.

TIP

The second graph gives you the actual number of reduced GPAs in thousands. Be sure to look at the labels of the axes, which for the second graph says "Thousands." This means that in 2018, the GPAs of 100,000 study participants, not 100, went down.

Now, use the graphs together to find the number of students whose GPAs were reduced by a specific cause (or causes). For example, in 2019, 200,000 students had reduced GPAs. In that same year, Too Much Homework caused 20 percent of these reduced GPAs (from 50 to 70 percent). Twenty percent of 200,000 is 40,000 students who had reduced GPAs due to Too Much Homework.

Ready to try some practice questions? Here you go:

PLAY

Which of the following represents the total number of college students from 2018 to 2022, inclusive?

Ⓐ 850

Ⓑ 8,500

Ⓒ 85,000

Ⓓ 850,000

Ⓔ It cannot be determined from the information given.

Did you fall for the trap and pick Choice (D)? Because the graphs give you only the number of *reduced* GPAs (look at the titles of the graphs), you have no way to determine the total number of college students. The correct answer is Choice (E). Note that *inclusive* means that you include 2018 and 2022 (as opposed to "in between 2018 and 2022," which means you *don't* include those years).

PLAY

The number of GPAs in 2022 that declined due to Too Much Football was what percent greater than the number of GPAs in 2020 that declined due to Too Much TV?

Ⓐ 700%

Ⓑ 600%

Ⓒ 500%

Ⓓ 120%

Ⓔ 7%

In 2022, Too Much Football accounted for 40 percent of reduced college GPAs (from 0 to 40). Because 350,000 GPAs declined in 2022, multiply 0.40 by 350,000 for a total of 140,000 students affected by Too Much Football. In 2020, Too Much TV accounted for 20 percent of reduced college GPAs (80 to 100). That same year, 100,000 GPAs declined. Multiply 0.20 by 100,000 for a total of 20,000 students affected by Too Much TV. Find the percent greater than by reducing the zeros and multiplying by 100 percent:

$$\text{Percentage Greater Than} = \frac{\text{Football} - \text{TV}}{\text{TV}} \times 100\%$$

$$= \frac{(140,000) - (20,000)}{(20,000)} \times 100\%$$

$$= \frac{140,000 - 20,000}{20,000} \times 100\%$$

$$= \frac{12}{2} \times 100\%$$

$$= 600\%$$

Correct answer: Choice (B).

Estimating graph totals quickly

When choosing from answers that are far apart, consider rounding as you perform your calculations, especially if you're working with really big numbers and the question says "approximately" or "closest to." Here's an example:

PLAY

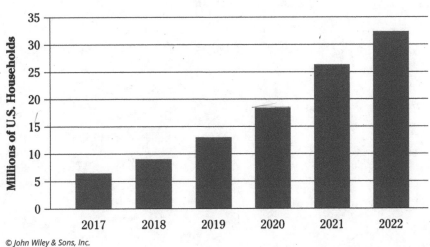

Broadband Subscriber Growth
(100 Mbps or higher)

© John Wiley & Sons, Inc.

If the average cost of broadband was $43 per month in 2020, which of the following is closest to the gross earnings for U.S. broadband companies in 2020?

Ⓐ $100,000,000

Ⓑ $1,000,000,000

Ⓒ $10,000,000,000

Ⓓ $100,000,000,000

Ⓔ $1,000,000,000,000

$43 \times 17mil \times 12$

$(43 \times 17 \times 12)\, mil$

$10,000\, mill$

To estimate the gross earnings for U.S. broadband companies in 2020, you have to multiply the monthly 2020 amount of $43 by the number of 2020 households with broadband, approximately 18 million as shown on the graph, and multiply by 12 to account for the 12 months of the year.

Now you're looking at something like this:

$$(43)(18)(10^6)(12)$$

Look at the answer choices: They're *really* far apart, so you just need to round the numbers to the nearest tens place:

$$(40)(20)(10^6)(10)$$

Multiply it all out:

$$(40)(20)(10^6)(10) = 8,000,000,000$$

TIP

You don't actually need to multiply $8,000 \times 10^6$, as long as you know that raising 10 to the sixth power gives you 1 with 6 zeros after it (a million); place those six zeros after the 8,000 for 8,000,000,000.

Because you rounded two numbers down and one number up, you know that this result is slightly shy of the actual answer, so look for an answer that's *slightly* higher than your result. 10,000,000,000 is the closest answer choice. Correct answer: Choice (C).

REMEMBER

Because the GRE provides a calculator, you can always just punch in the numbers. However, you're less likely to make a mistake by rounding and multiplying on paper than by entering all these numbers into the calculator. Also, the on-screen calculator errors out at numbers having nine or more digits, so you have to reach this answer on paper.

Chapter 15

Comparing Quantities

About a third of the GRE Math questions are quantitative comparison (QC), meaning the question provides two quantities, and you answer by determining which is greater, or whether they're the same or you need more information. You need to recognize common setups and know the strategies; otherwise, you'll end up working a lot of extra math. This chapter gives you the lowdown on QC questions and how to solve them, along with how to steer clear of common pitfalls.

REMEMBER

The two quantities, aptly named A and B, can contain numbers, variables, equations, scenarios, and so on. Fortunately, like all GRE Math, these questions use common, specific setups.

Comparing Exact Answer Choices

Each math section contains eight or so QC questions. The answer choices are always exactly the same, so glance at them on test day, but understand them now:

Ⓐ Quantity A is greater.

Ⓑ Quantity B is greater.

Ⓒ The two quantities are equal.

Ⓓ The relationship cannot be determined from the information given.

You don't need to read and interpret these answer choices each time you see them. Instead, paraphrase them to make them simpler:

Ⓐ A is greater.

Ⓑ B is greater.

Ⓒ They're equal.

Ⓓ You need more info.

Comparing Steps

The best way to begin *most* QC questions is with a simple three-step approach:

1. Simplify Quantity A.

Simplify may mean solve the equation, read through a word problem, or estimate.

2. Simplify Quantity B.

Sometimes Quantity B is simpler than Quantity A, but not always. Sometimes a ballpark estimate is sufficient, as I show you later in this chapter.

3. Compare the two quantities.

At this point, you know which quantity is larger.

Here are a few starter questions to get you warmed up:

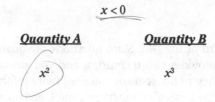

PLAY

$$x < 0$$

Quantity A	*Quantity B*
x^2	x^3

Ⓐ Quantity A is greater.

Ⓑ Quantity B is greater.

Ⓒ The two quantities are equal.

Ⓓ The relationship cannot be determined from the information given.

All you know is that x is negative. How can you answer this question? Well, you don't *need* to know what x is. If it's negative, then squared, it becomes positive, so Quantity A is positive. Cubed, it stays negative, so Quantity B is negative. Pick a number to try it out. Say $x = -2$: Quantity A is $(-2)(-2) = 4$ and Quantity B is $(-2)(-2)(-2) = -8$. Regardless of what x is, it's negative, so Quantity A is greater. Correct answer: Choice (A).

TIP

This simple example highlights a key point regarding QC questions: Many are based on the *concept* of the math, not the math itself. If you know basic number properties, such as how negative numbers multiply out, you'll save yourself a lot of pencil work on these questions. Revisit Chapter 10 for a refresher on number properties.

PLAY

Quantity A	*Quantity B*
40% of 340	340% of 40

Ⓐ Quantity A is greater.

Ⓑ Quantity B is greater.

Ⓒ The two quantities are equal.

Ⓓ The relationship cannot be determined from the information given.

To simplify Quantity A, multiply 40 percent by 340 for a value of 136. Simplify Quantity B by taking 340 percent of 40 for a value that is also 136. You can use the calculator, but you still have to know how the math works. The two quantities are equal, for a correct answer of Choice (C).

REMEMBER

This example highlights another key point of the QC questions: They're designed to make you take a step back, so just accept that they're simpler than they appear, like the Wizard of Oz using his shadow and a PA system to appear large, even though he's a small fellow. Just work on the part that you know, and the part that you don't know becomes clear.

PLAY

Quantity A	_Quantity B_
The number of miles hiked by Ken, who hiked at 3 mph for 6½ hours	18

ⓐ Quantity A is greater.

ⓑ Quantity B is greater.

ⓒ The two quantities are equal.

ⓓ The relationship cannot be determined from the information given.

Simplify A to find that Ken's miles hiked is 3 times 6.5 for 19.5, which is greater than 18, so Quantity A is greater. You can simply eyeball this one because you instantly know that 3 times 6 is 18, so 3 times anything greater than 6 is more than 18.

These questions seem simple enough, right? They're just tasters. There wouldn't be any point — or fun — if the questions didn't become more challenging.

Comparing via Strategy

With plenty of common setups and traps in the QC questions, I've included a separate section for each one, complete with examples and strategies for comparing them.

REMEMBER

Keep in mind that the following strategies aren't fail-safe. They _get you started_, but you still have to use your critical thinking, and when it makes sense, I include a practice question where the strategy alone doesn't do it. The GRE has far too many variations to anticipate them all, so never shut off your critical thinking in favor of a strategy.

Comparing similar appearances

If Quantities A and B appear to be equal, don't fall for it — a trap is almost always involved. Treat them like they're similar. Check out the following examples:

PLAY

Quantity A	_Quantity B_
2π	6.28

ⓐ Quantity A is greater.

ⓑ Quantity B is greater.

ⓒ The two quantities are equal.

ⓓ The relationship cannot be determined from the information given.

Your gut reaction may be to pick Choice (C) because both quantities appear to be equal at first glance. After all, wasn't it drilled into your head in school (and Chapter 12) that π is about 3.14, making 2π about 6.28? But hold the phone: The value of π is *slightly more* than 3.14. It's more like 3.1416, making π *greater than* 3.14 and 2π *greater than* 6.28, so Choice (A) is the right answer.

REMEMBER

The important thing is the math *concept,* not the math itself. You don't need to know the *exact* value of π, just that it's more than 3.14.

PLAY

Quantity A		Quantity B
$0.0062 \times 3,600$		$6,200 \times 0.3600$

Ⓐ Quantity A is greater.

Ⓑ Quantity B is greater.

Ⓒ The two quantities are equal.

Ⓓ The relationship cannot be determined from the information given.

You might have checked the number of digits and decimal places, which appear to be the same, and opted for Choice (C). But the trap here is that in Quantity B, the trailing zeros in 0.3600 don't count for anything, so that number is equivalent to 0.36, giving Quantity B fewer decimal places and making it greater. Quantity A equals 22.32, and Quantity B equals 2,232. It's good you fell for this trap *here, now,* when it *doesn't* matter — because you won't fall for it on the exam, when it does matter. If needed, Chapter 10 gives a refresher on how to multiply decimals. Correct answer: Choice (B).

Comparing drawings

Drawings in the GRE are typically drawn to scale, so you may be able to eyeball the correct answer. But if a figure contains the caveat "not drawn to scale," then it's *way* off. You can trust the right-angle box and that the angle touches the line on one point, as in this drawing, but you can't trust the dimensions.

PLAY

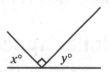

Note: Figure not drawn to scale.

Quantity A	Quantity B
x	y

Ⓐ Quantity A is greater.

Ⓑ Quantity B is greater.

Ⓒ The two quantities are equal.

Ⓓ The relationship cannot be determined from the information given.

Sure, x and y *appear* to be roughly 45 degrees each, but because the drawing isn't to scale, you can't make an estimate. You do know that x and y add up to 90 degrees because angles along a straight line add up to 180 degrees, and you already have a right angle: $180 - 90 = 90$. But you *don't* know how much of the 90 is x and how much is y. Correct answer: Choice (D).

Even if this drawing *were* to scale, you couldn't look at x and y and assume they're equal. You can *estimate*, but that's all it is — an estimate. It could be that x is 46 and y is 44, for example.

Only two types of drawings are scaled for you to typically answer the question from the drawing itself: the *xy*-coordinate grid and the data graph, covered respectively in Chapters 11 and 14. Other than that, you need to confirm that the shape is what it looks like. If you see a square, but the GRE doesn't tell you that it's a square, you can't assume that the angles are 90° or that the side lengths are the same.

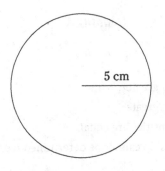

5 cm

Quantity A	**Quantity B**
The circumference of the circle $\quad 2(5)\pi$	30 cm
10π	

Ⓐ Quantity A is greater.

Ⓑ Quantity B is greater.

Ⓒ The two quantities are equal.

Ⓓ The relationship cannot be determined from the information given.

The circumference of a circle is $2\pi r$, making the circumference of this circle 10π. If π were equal to 3, then the answer would be Choice (C). However, because π is slightly greater than 3, 10π is greater than 30. You don't have to know the *exact* value of π, but you do have to know that it's slightly greater than 3. Correct answer: Choice (A).

Comparing concepts

Even though you can't always use the drawing to extract an exact measurement, you don't usually have to. The drawing tells you how the question is set up, and you *can* spot and use the math concepts. As with the earlier example with x^2 and x^3, the GRE challenges how well you get the math, not your ability to use the calculator.

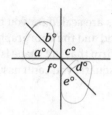

Quantity A	*Quantity B*
$a + b$	$d + e$

Ⓐ Quantity A is greater.

Ⓑ Quantity B is greater.

Ⓒ The two quantities are equal.

Ⓓ The relationship cannot be determined from the information given.

Angle *a* is *vertical* to angle *d*, meaning they're equal. Angle *b* is vertical to angle *e*, meaning they're also equal. Even though you can't tell the angle measures, you know these angle pairs are equal because of the math *concept*, and you can answer the question, regardless of whether the drawing is to scale. Because $a + b$ is equal to $d + e$, the quantities are equal, and the correct answer is Choice (C). For more on vertical angles, flip back to Chapter 12.

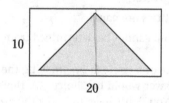

Quantity A	*Quantity B*
The area of the triangle	100

Ⓐ Quantity A is greater.

Ⓑ Quantity B is greater.

Ⓒ The two quantities are equal.

Ⓓ The relationship cannot be determined from the information given.

Don't pick Choice (D) just because you don't have the measurements of the triangle. Though the image isn't drawn to scale, you can use logic and critical thinking to compare the triangle to 100.

You know that the area of a triangle is $\frac{\text{base} \times \text{height}}{2}$. What's the base of this triangle? You can't tell, but you can see that the base of the triangle doesn't touch the sides of the rectangle, so it must be *less* than 20, which is the base of the rectangle. What's the height of this triangle? You can't tell that either, but you *can* see that it's less than 10, which is the height of the rectangle. Multiply less-than-10 by less-than-20 and divide that in half for less-than-100, making Quantity B greater and the correct answer Choice (B).

PLAY

The lengths of two sides of a certain triangle are 12 and 20.

Quantity A   **_Quantity B_**

The longest possible length of   32
the third side of the triangle

                                            12 + 20 = 32

Ⓐ Quantity A is greater.

Ⓑ Quantity B is greater.

Ⓒ The two quantities are equal.

Ⓓ The relationship cannot be determined from the information given.

Because the length of the third side of any triangle must be less than the sum of the lengths of the other two sides, the third side of this triangle must be less than 32. Correct answer: Choice (B).

PLAY

One angle of an isosceles triangle is 80°.

Quantity A   **_Quantity B_**

The measure of one of the other   50°
two angles of the triangle

Ⓐ Quantity A is greater.

Ⓑ Quantity B is greater.

Ⓒ The two quantities are equal.

Ⓓ The relationship cannot be determined from the information given.

An isosceles triangle has two identical angles. Problem is, you don't know whether the 80-degree angle is the solo angle or one of the twin angles. If the solo angle is 80 degrees, then the other two angles are each 50 degrees, for a total angle measure of 180 degrees and a correct answer of Choice (C). Or if the identical angles are each 80 degrees, the remaining angle is 20 degrees, for an angle total of 180 degrees and a correct answer of Choice (B). You don't know which is the case, so you can't tell which quantity is greater. Correct answer: Choice (D).

Comparing identical terms

When the quantities have identical terms, clear out the clutter by canceling them out so you can focus on the parts that are different. After all, a QC problem is like a balance: If something is the same on both sides, it doesn't affect the balance, so you can ignore it. Be careful that you cancel only *identical* terms. For example, you can't cancel −5 from one side and 5 from the other.

Quantity A		*Quantity B*
$x^2 - 21$	$>$	$x^2 - 35$

Ⓐ Quantity A is greater.

Ⓑ Quantity B is greater.

Ⓒ The two quantities are equal.

Ⓓ The relationship cannot be determined from the information given.

Cancel the x^2 in both quantities, and you're left with −21 and −35. Because −21 is greater than −35, the correct answer is Choice (A).

$$a < 0$$
$$b < 0$$

Quantity A	*Quantity B*
$(a+b)^2$	$(a-b)^2$

Ⓐ Quantity A is greater.

Ⓑ Quantity B is greater.

Ⓒ The two quantities are equal.

Ⓓ The relationship cannot be determined from the information given.

You can't just cancel out a and b on both sides because they're in expressions that need to be multiplied first. Go ahead and FOIL 'em, and *then* cancel:

$$(a+b)^2 = a^2 + 2ab + b^2 \qquad (a-b)^2 = a^2 - 2ab + b^2$$

Now you can cancel a^2 and b^2 from each quantity, and you're left with +2ab in Quantity A and −2ab in Quantity B. Because a and b are both negative, ab is positive, so Quantity A is greater. Correct answer: Choice (A). For more on FOILing, check out Chapter 11.

Sorting identical terms

Sometimes the identical terms are masked within the question. You can't just eyeball them and cancel — you need to figure out the identical terms that you can cancel. Try out this example:

Quantity A	*Quantity B*
The sum of all consecutive even integers from 14 to 28, inclusive.	The sum of all consecutive even integers from 18 to 30, inclusive.

Ⓐ Quantity A is greater.

Ⓑ Quantity B is greater.

Ⓒ The two quantities are equal.

Ⓓ The relationship cannot be determined from the information given.

Don't even *think* about adding up those numbers. What do the two quantities have in common that you can cancel? First, note that you *can't* cancel anything not on both sides: Only Quantity A has 14 and 16, while only Quantity B has 30. Because both quantities have 18, 20, 22, 24, 26, and 28, you can cancel those. Now the question looks like this:

>> Quantity A: 14+16

>> Quantity B: 30

To quote Billie Eilish: "Duh." The correct answer is Choice (C).

PLAY

Quantity A	**Quantity B**
The sum of all consecutive odd integers from 49 to 99, inclusive.	The sum of all consecutive odd integers from 53 to 101, inclusive.

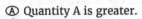

Ⓐ Quantity A is greater.

Ⓑ Quantity B is greater.

Ⓒ The two quantities are equal.

Ⓓ The relationship cannot be determined from the information given.

Okay, what's not on both sides: 49 and 51 are in Quantity A, while 101 is in Quantity B. All the other numbers cancel, so you're really looking at 49+51 for Quantity A and 101 for Quantity B. Sure, you have to add two numbers, but this is how you get to that point. Correct answer: Choice (B).

Practice makes perfect, so here's another one. This time, the quantities are *multiplied*, not added, but the approach is the same:

PLAY

Quantity A	**Quantity B**
The product of the consecutive integers from 99 to 9,899, inclusive.	The product of the consecutive integers from 101 to 9,900, inclusive.

Ⓐ Quantity A is greater.

Ⓑ Quantity B is greater.

Ⓒ The two quantities are equal.

Ⓓ The relationship cannot be determined from the information given.

Look for what's only on one side: 99 and 100 are only in Quantity A, while 9,900 is only in Quantity B. All the other numbers cancel, so you're really looking at 99×100 for Quantity A and 9,900 for Quantity B. Remember, *product* means multiply. $99 \times 100 = 9,900$, making these equal for a correct answer of Choice (C).

PLAY

Quantity A	Quantity B
The product of all consecutive integers from 10 to 109, inclusive.	The product of all consecutive integers from 12 to 110, inclusive.

Ⓐ Quantity A is greater.

Ⓑ Quantity B is greater.

Ⓒ The two quantities are equal.

Ⓓ The relationship cannot be determined from the information given.

Work all that math? Not a chance. Instead, focus your critical eye. Which numbers are on the left but not the right? 10 and 11. What's on the right but not the left? 110. The other numbers are identical, so cancel them out, and you're left with 110 on both sides because $10 \times 11 = 110$. Correct answer: Choice (C).

Making identical terms

The GRE goes even further and masks the terms so they don't appear identical. What you do is *make* them identical, and *then* you can cancel them. This goes back to knowing the math concept.

PLAY

Quantity A	Quantity B
$79 \times 80 \times 81 \times 82$	80^4

Ⓐ Quantity A is greater.

Ⓑ Quantity B is greater.

Ⓒ The two quantities are equal.

Ⓓ The relationship cannot be determined from the information given.

Make the terms identical so you can cancel them. $80^4 = 80 \times 80 \times 80 \times 80$, so cancel the 80 from each side. Now you're left with this:

>> Quantity A: $79 \times 81 \times 82$

>> Quantity B: $80 \times 80 \times 80$

Even though it's simpler, still don't do that math. Though 79 in Quantity A is slightly less than 80 in Quantity B, the 81 and 82 in Quantity A are greater than the other two 80s in Quantity B, by a larger amount. Correct answer: Choice (A).

Quantity A	Quantity B
$\sqrt{(98)(99)(100)(101)}$	99^2

Ⓐ Quantity A is greater.

Ⓑ Quantity B is greater.

Ⓒ The two quantities are equal.

Ⓓ The relationship cannot be determined from the information given.

Another one where you make the terms identical. There are a few ways to do this, but probably the simplest is to make Quantity B identical to Quantity A. You know how $\left(\sqrt{2}\right)\left(\sqrt{2}\right)=2$, right? Well, take that backwards, where 2 becomes $\left(\sqrt{2}\right)\left(\sqrt{2}\right)$. With this, make Quantity B identical to Quantity A:

$$= 99^2$$
$$= (99)(99)$$
$$= \sqrt{(99)}\sqrt{(99)}\sqrt{(99)}\sqrt{(99)}$$
$$= \sqrt{(99)(99)(99)(99)}$$

Now that these are identical, cancel one $\sqrt{(99)}$ from each side. The remaining $\sqrt{(98)}$ in Quantity A is slightly less than one $\sqrt{(99)}$ in Quantity B, but the $\sqrt{(100)(101)}$ in Quantity A is greater than the $\sqrt{(99)(99)}$ in Quantity B by a larger amount, making the correct answer Choice (A).

Quantity A	Quantity B
$\dfrac{500!}{498!}$	499^2

Ⓐ Quantity A is greater.

Ⓑ Quantity B is greater.

Ⓒ The two quantities are equal.

Ⓓ The relationship cannot be determined from the information given.

Laughing yet? You will be. Remember how to divide factorials from Chapter 13: You cancel them out. Reduce Quantity A to $\dfrac{500 \times 499 \times 498!}{498!} = 500 \times 499$, while Quantity B is 499×499. Then cancel 499 from each side, making Quantities A and B into 500 and 499, respectively. Quantity A is greater. A not-too-bad correct answer: Choice (A).

Quantity A	Quantity B
5^{-8}	25^{-4}

Ⓐ Quantity A is greater.

Ⓑ Quantity B is greater.

Ⓒ The two quantities are equal.

Ⓓ The relationship cannot be determined from the information given.

Remember that 25^{-4} can also be expressed as $(25)^{-4}$, which becomes $(5^2)^{-4}$ and then 5^{-8}. Now the terms are both identical and equal. Correct answer: Choice (C). For more on exponents, go to Chapter 11.

Comparing ranges

Sometimes the QC question tells you that x has a *range* of values. For example, it might tell you that x is between 2 and 10. Don't bother trying x as 4.5, 9.99, or any of the other dozens of numbers that it could be. You don't have all day. Just try x as the lowest and the highest that it could be. For example, when x is between 2 and 10, try $x = 2$ and $x = 10$, and you're done (usually).

PLAY

$$2 < x < 10$$

Quantity A	*Quantity B*
$\dfrac{x}{2}$	$2x$
$1 \to 5$	$4 \to 20$

Ⓐ Quantity A is greater.

Ⓑ Quantity B is greater.

Ⓒ The two quantities are equal.

Ⓓ The relationship cannot be determined from the information given.

First, try $x = 2$, making Quantity A equal 1 and Quantity B equal 4. Next, try $x = 10$, making Quantity A equal 5 and Quantity B equal 20. Either way, Quantity B is greater, and you don't have to try any other possible values of x for the correct answer of Choice B.

PLAY

$$4 < x < 5$$

Quantity A	*Quantity B*
x^3	125

Ⓐ Quantity A is greater.

Ⓑ Quantity B is greater.

Ⓒ The two quantities are equal.

Ⓓ The relationship cannot be determined from the information given.

Try $x = 4$, making Quantity A equal 64, and $x = 5$, making Quantity A equal 125. Seems like Choice D, right? But wait. If x is *less than* 5, then x^3 must be *less than* 125. Remember, these strategies only get you *started*, but you still have to apply your critical thinking. Correct answer: Choice (B).

Comparing estimates

Pretend the QC problem is a balance scale, where you compare Quantity A to Quantity B. If Quantity A is heavier than Quantity B, Quantity A is greater.

PLAY

Quantity A	*Quantity B*
$\dfrac{17}{21} + \dfrac{47}{80}$	$\dfrac{19}{81} + \dfrac{23}{97}$

Ⓐ Quantity A is greater.

Ⓑ Quantity B is greater.

Ⓒ The two quantities are equal.

Ⓓ The relationship cannot be determined from the information given.

You don't need your pencil for this one. Compare each part of Quantity A to its counterpart in Quantity B. Whereas the Quantity A fractions are each more than one-half, the Quantity B fractions are each roughly a quarter, so they're less than one-half. Two more-than-halves on the left; two less-than-halves on the right. Correct answer: Choice (A).

REMEMBER

The GRE is also testing how resourceful you are. Do you just blindly jump in and start working, or do you assess the elements and see if there's another way? Before working any math, check whether it's a trap that consumes your time.

PLAY

At a certain factory, machines A and B have a maximum per-day production capacity of p and q parts, respectively, where $p < q < 100$.

Quantity A	*Quantity B*
The number of days required for machine A, working at maximum capacity, to fill an order of 1,000 parts	The number of days required for machine B, working at maximum capacity, to fill an order of 1,000 parts

Ⓐ Quantity A is greater.

Ⓑ Quantity B is greater.

Ⓒ The two quantities are equal.

Ⓓ The relationship cannot be determined from the information given.

It's easy to get lost in the description, picking numbers and trying math. Actually, after you get past the verbiage, this question is very simple. Basically, machine A works slower than machine B, so machine A takes more days to complete the order. Correct answer: Choice (A).

Comparing with Four Square

When x or some other letter represents numbers, and there's no way to tell what these numbers are, one strategy is to use the *Four Square*: 2, −2, $\frac{1}{2}$, and −$\frac{1}{2}$. (You could use 0.5 and −0.5 instead of $\frac{1}{2}$ and −$\frac{1}{2}$.) The Four Square covers most possibilities, and you'll see whether the quantity that seems greater flips or stays the same.

PLAY

Quantity A	*Quantity B*
x^2	x^4

Ⓒ Quantity A is greater.

Ⓓ Quantity B is greater.

Ⓔ The two quantities are equal.

Ⓕ The relationship cannot be determined from the information given.

Remember, both x's have the *same* value at any one time. The trap answer is Choice (B). Certainly a number to the fourth power is greater than the same number squared, right? Positive or negative, no matter.

But wait — what happens when you use the Four Square? Sure, 2 and −2 make Choice (B) seem correct, but $\frac{1}{2}$ and −$\frac{1}{2}$ make it Choice (A). Together, they make it a correct Choice (D).

TIP

You don't always have to go through the entire Four Square. As soon as two numbers give you two different answer choices, you can stop. In this example, just trying 2 and $\frac{1}{2}$ would have done the trick.

REMEMBER

If you happen to find that the quantities could be equal *or* one could be greater, don't go with the one that could be greater — go with Choice (D).

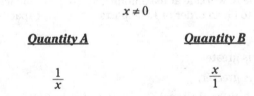

PLAY

$$x \neq 0$$

Quantity A	*Quantity B*
$\dfrac{1}{x}$	$\dfrac{x}{1}$

Ⓒ Quantity A is greater.

Ⓓ Quantity B is greater.

Ⓔ The two quantities are equal.

Ⓕ The relationship cannot be determined from the information given.

Choice (B) is the trap answer. If $x = 2$, Quantity A is a fraction less than 1, while Quantity B is greater than 1. However, this trap doesn't catch *you*. Use the Four Square: Go on to try $x = -2$, $x = \frac{1}{2}$, and $x = -\frac{1}{2}$ to vary which quantity is greater. Because you can make either one greater, you know that the correct answer is Choice (D).

PLAY

$$x > 0$$

Quantity A	**_Quantity B_**
x^2	0.5

Ⓐ Quantity A is greater.

Ⓑ Quantity B is greater.

Ⓒ The two quantities are equal.

Ⓓ The relationship cannot be determined from the information given.

If *x* is an integer, then any value squared would be more than 0.5. However, *x* could be a decimal; if *x* equals 0.2, x^2 would equal 0.04. Because you can't assume that *x* is an integer, you can't tell which value is higher. Correct answer: Choice (D).

PLAY

x and *y* are integers

Quantity A	**_Quantity B_**
The average of *x* and *y*	The sum of *x* and *y*

Ⓐ Quantity A is greater.

Ⓑ Quantity B is greater.

Ⓒ The two quantities are equal.

Ⓓ The relationship cannot be determined from the information given.

positive
OR negative

You could try the Four Square, but this one is even simpler. If *x* and *y* are positive integers, the correct answer is Choice (A). If they're negative, then the correct answer is Choice (B). If they're equal to zero, which is also an integer, the correct answer is Choice (C). Because you don't know, the relationship can't be determined. Correct answer: Choice (D).

Like any strategy, the Four Square is just a starting point, and you still have to use your critical thinking. Here's an example:

PLAY

$$x \neq 0$$

Quantity A	**_Quantity B_**
$\dfrac{1}{x}$	3

Ⓐ Quantity A is greater.

Ⓑ Quantity B is greater.

Ⓒ The two quantities are equal.

Ⓓ The relationship cannot be determined from the information given.

With the entire Four Square, Quantity B remains greater. However, *x* isn't limited to these values: The Four Square is just a starting point, and more important, it shows you how the problem works. With that, try a number *outside* the Four Square for *x* that makes Quantity A greater, such as 0.1, making Quantity A 10 and greater than Quantity B, and Choice (D) the clearly correct answer.

Comparing with a hundred

If a question deals with dollars or percentages, start with 100 to make it an easier number. Remember that the key is simplifying the math.

A book bag costs x dollars.

Quantity A	*Quantity B*
Cost of the book bag on sale at 60% off	$0.6x$

Ⓐ Quantity A is greater.

Ⓑ Quantity B is greater.

Ⓒ The two quantities are equal.

Ⓓ The relationship cannot be determined from the information given.

If you make $x = \$100$, you can easily determine that 60 percent of 100 is 60; subtract 60 from 100, and you get 40. In Quantity B, $0.6(100) = 60$. The answer is Choice (B).

This type of problem is easy to miss because of carelessness. Other test-takers automatically opt for Choice (C), but not you. When both sides have a percent of x, start with 100 for x and do the math.

Quantity A	*Quantity B*
One year's interest on x dollars at 6% annual interest	$12

Ⓐ Quantity A is greater.

Ⓑ Quantity B is greater.

Ⓒ The two quantities are equal.

Ⓓ The relationship cannot be determined from the information given.

If you make $x = \$100$, you know that Quantity A is $6, while Quantity B is $12, making the answer Choice (B). But wait — there's no x in Quantity B. Throwing down 100 (for x) is only a starting strategy. If $x = \$200$, the quantities are the same, and anything greater than $200 makes Quantity A greater. As with any strategy, you still have to use your judgment. Correct answer: Choice (D).

Comparing multiple unknowns

Some questions may provide you with multiple unknowns. In that case, try numbers that are close together and then numbers that are far apart. For example, with three unknowns, try consecutive numbers such as 1, 2, and 3, and then try spread-out numbers such as 2, 5, and 200. If this doesn't change which quantity is greater, you could try negative numbers. On these questions, you can usually skip trying fractions.

$$a < b < c$$

Quantity A	**Quantity B**
$\dfrac{a+c}{2}$	b

Ⓐ Quantity A is greater.

Ⓑ Quantity B is greater.

Ⓒ The two quantities are equal.

Ⓓ The relationship cannot be determined from the information given.

Start with consecutive numbers 1, 2, and 3, making Quantity A $\dfrac{1+3}{2} = 2$ and Quantity B equal 2, so they're equal. But you're not done: Mix it up with numbers that are farther apart, such as 2, 5, and 200. Now Quantity A is $\dfrac{2+200}{2} = 101$, and Quantity B is 5, making the answer Choice (A). If the correct answer changes from the values you place into the variables, you know it's Choice (D).

$$x > y > z$$

Quantity A	**Quantity B**
$y + z$	x

Ⓐ Quantity A is greater.

Ⓑ Quantity B is greater.

Ⓒ The two quantities are equal.

Ⓓ The relationship cannot be determined from the information given.

The trap answer is Choice (C), but you know better. Because x, y, and z can be anything, the right answer is *probably* Choice (D), but try it out just to be sure. Start with 3, 2, and 1 for x, y, and z, respectively. Quantity A is $2+1$ and Quantity B is 3, making them equal. But when you mix it up with very different numbers — say, 100, 5, and 1 — Quantity A is $y + z = 5 + 1 = 6$, and Quantity B, x, is 100, making Quantity B larger. Because you're able to change the correct answer, go with Choice (D).

4
Getting the Essays Right

Chapter **16**

Writing the Essays Well and Fast

The GRE starts with two essay-writing tasks: Analyze an Issue and Analyze an Argument. You're given 30 minutes each, for a total of 60 minutes of intense writing before you encounter any other test question. As you prepare for the essay-writing portion, remember these overall goals:

» Write two well-organized, insightful essays that showcase your perspective and critical thinking.

» Pace yourself and complete each essay within 30 minutes.

» Write well and clearly, with few errors.

» Conserve your energy for the rest of the test.

Thirty minutes for each essay is plenty of time *if* you know what to do and *if* you've practiced. The more you practice, the more comfortable you'll become with organizing your thoughts and expressing them in words within the time limit and under the pressure of the exam. Find out how to do this here, in this chapter, and then take a trial run writing practice essays using the Issue and Argument topics presented in Chapter 17. You can check your work against sample essays in that chapter.

In this chapter, I explain what evaluators look for and how they ultimately score your essay. I then guide you through the process of writing each essay, paragraph by paragraph.

REMEMBER

On the GRE, you type your essays in a text box not unlike Windows Notepad or Mac TextEdit with formatting turned off. It features cut, copy, paste, and undo, but that's it — no spell check, grammar check, or automated anything, so the burden of proofreading is on you.

Setting Your Sights on a Perfect 6

Before you can score well on the GRE essays, you need to know how this section is graded. Your essays are graded one at a time, first by a trained evaluator and then by a computerized ETS system. Your final score for each essay is the average of the two scores. If those two scores differ by more than a couple points, which doesn't happen very often, then your essay goes to a third, human evaluator, and your score for that essay is the average of the two humans' scores. You get one score for each essay (0 to 6, with 6 being the best), and your final writing score is the average of the two essay scores.

Following is an overview of how the essays are scored along with tips for improving your score.

What the essay scores really mean

Here are basic evaluator descriptions associated with each essay score. In this chapter, I show you the mechanics of achieving a 6 or at least a 5.

>> **Outstanding (6):** The Issue essay demonstrates your ability to take a position on a topic, support personal views and insights, and write with clarity, focus, and interest — in other words, you don't sound bored. The Argument essay demonstrates your ability to identify strengths and weaknesses of an argument or a plan. Either essay may have a grammar or spelling error but otherwise is well-written with control of the language, good **diction** (word choice), and variety of sentence structure.

>> **Strong (5):** The essay demonstrates your thoughtful analysis of the argument or presentation of the issue. Presentation is logical, and main points are well-supported. The essay may have minor errors in grammar and spelling but demonstrates control of the language, good diction, and variety of sentence structure.

>> **Adequate (4):** The essay demonstrates your overall competence in analyzing the argument or presenting the issue, along with organizing and supporting your thoughts and expressing them clearly. It may not flow smoothly due to a lack of effective transitions, and it may contain some errors, but it demonstrates sufficient control of the language.

>> **Limited (3):** Competent but flawed, the essay (not yours, of course — someone else's) misses the main point or ideas in the argument or presents the issue poorly, lacks order, offers little or no support for the ideas presented, and contains occasional glaring errors or lots of minor errors in grammar, diction, and mechanics.

>> **Seriously flawed (2):** This person's essay completely misses the point, presents the author's point of view with no support or irrelevant support, is poorly organized, and has plenty of errors in grammar, word use, mechanics, and sentence construction.

>> **Fundamentally deficient (1):** The essay demonstrates little or no evidence of the author's ability to understand or address the issue or analyze the argument. In addition, the essay contains extensive errors in grammar, word use, mechanics, and sentence structure.

>> **No essay (0):** The essay is blank or only garbage is typed in.

The essay section demonstrates your ability to communicate and convey your critical-thinking skills. Regardless of whether your target school places emphasis on the essay scores, these scores reflect on you as an applicant. Furthermore, the essays are *first*, so if you get flustered during this hour of two essays, your performance on the rest of the test will be affected. Essay-writing strategies are easy to master, and with a little guidance and practice, you'll write excellent essays that reflect well on you and carry you through the test.

Key methods to scoring well

Essay writing (and scoring) is subjective to some degree. There's no right or wrong answer, and each essay is different, based on the test-taker's perspective, knowledge, experience, writing style, and so on. Evaluators, however, have a specific rubric for grading your essay. To perform well, be sure to do the following:

>> **Follow the instructions.** The prompt tells you what to do. For example, an Issue prompt may ask you to consider ways in which the statement may or may not hold true, or to describe circumstances in which taking a certain course of action would or would not be best. An Argument essay may ask you to state the questions needed to evaluate the passage or to describe the assumptions the statement relies upon. To score well, you need to follow those instructions and write about what the prompt asks for.

>> **Get to the point in each paragraph.** The evaluator will always look for your point in the first two lines of each paragraph, so don't try to be clever and write a paragraph with a surprise ending or twist. State the point of the paragraph clearly and unequivocally in the first line of each paragraph. Then spend the rest of the paragraph supporting that point.

>> **Stay on topic.** After stating your position in the introductory paragraph, make sure each succeeding paragraph supports that position instead of wandering off topic. If the issue is low commodity prices versus quality of workmanship, for example, and you're discussing factory output, don't go off topic and start writing about offshore labor — as I once had a student do on that very subject. Each paragraph should have a sentence (preferably at the end), like a thesis statement that restates your main point and ties the paragraph directly to your position statement.

>> **Avoid fluff.** Though a longer essay typically earns a higher score, that higher score is the result of you exploring and supporting the topic to an appropriate level, not rambling on and on. Your essay isn't judged on your number of words; it's judged on the use of your words.

>> **Manage your time.** A clock in the corner of the screen tells you how much time is left. When you have about eight minutes to go, wrap up what you're writing, write your conclusion (basically a reworded copy of your introduction), and proof your essay.

>> **Proof your essay.** Leave yourself a few minutes to read through your text and ensure everything flows and makes sense. It doesn't have to be flawless, but it has to be good. Check your grammar and clarify any unclear pronouns. For example, in the sentence "Claire and Kathy went out, and she drove," it's not clear who *she* refers to — and that will cost you points.

>> **Watch the details.** If you don't know how to spell a word, *use a different word*. A typo here or there is okay, but reversing the *i* and the *e* in common words will cost you. I once had a student misspell "illustrate" about five times in an essay. That won't fly.

>> **Maintain a professional tone.** The essay section isn't for creative writing. It's more like business writing, so avoid off-color language, slang, and inappropriate humor. Creativity, done well, will be appreciated by the evaluators, but be appropriate. And no bullet points.

Is that enough? Time to get down to an essay.

Writing the Issue Essay

In the Analyze an Issue task, the GRE gives you an issue statement and asks you to introduce and then support your position on that issue. The format is like this:

TIME: 30 minutes

"Today's cheap, mass-produced goods lack the precision and quality of yesterday's hand-built, carefully crafted products."

DIRECTIONS: Write an essay in response to the preceding statement in which you discuss the extent to which you agree or disagree with the statement. Explain your reasoning in a clear, well-organized essay that supports your position. Consider both sides of the issue when developing your response.

Where do you begin? What do they want? Only 29 minutes left! Getting started is the hardest part, and staying focused is the most important. With a game plan and a structure in place, you're equipped to do both. There are many strategies for writing a good essay, but this approach is effective and you can quickly master it:

1. Read and understand the prompt.

2. Identify examples you already know about the issue.

3. Take a position that's in line with your examples.

4. Write a four- to five-paragraph essay using the following outline as your guide:

- **First paragraph:** Introduction stating your position

- **Second paragraph:** Your best supporting detail

- **Third and possibly fourth paragraphs:** One or two more supporting details

- **Final paragraph:** Conclusion reiterating your position statement from your introduction

Step 1: Read and understand the prompt

The Issue Analysis essay prompt consists of an issue statement followed by instructions that tell you exactly what to do. The issue statements vary, and so do the accompanying instructions. Here are a few examples that illustrate how the instructions in Issue Analysis prompts may differ:

>> Write a response expressing your agreement or disagreement with this statement and the reasoning you followed to arrive at your position. Be sure to consider ways in which the statement may or may not be true and how these considerations influence your position.

>> Write a response expressing your agreement or disagreement with this statement and addressing the most compelling reasons and/or examples that may challenge your position.

>> The prompt may consist of a statement and a response, like a brief two-part conversation. In that case, the instructions may look like this:

Which do you find more compelling: Group A's assertion or Group B's response to it? Write a response in which you take a position and explain the reasoning you followed to arrive at your position.

TIP

At the time of this writing, ETS has made its entire pool of Issue Analysis topics available at `https://www.ets.org/content/dam/ets-org/pdfs/gre/issue-pool.pdf`. You don't have to type this whole address in your browser. Just include the word "pool" in your online search: "GRE issue essay *pool*." The list contains all the issue statements along with examples of the instructions that accompany those statements so you can develop a better feel for how the prompts may be worded and what they're likely to instruct you to do.

You can use this list for extra practice, but don't get bogged down by trying to practice on every topic — there are a *lot* of topics. Just read through some of them so you know what to expect. (We play a game in class called "topic roulette," where we scroll through the list, randomly pick a topic, and then as a group discuss the essay. I've had students tell me later that the prompt they got on the exam was one we reviewed in class!)

Step 2: Identify examples you already know about the issue

Your first inclination may be to state your position on the issue and then try to come up with data to support it. This may work, but it may also backfire. I've seen students take a stand and then struggle to support it. You don't have time for soul-searching or rewriting your intro a bunch of times. On the actual GRE, this approach would earn you an essay score of 2. Instead, find your supporting details and then base your position on those details. This way, no matter what, you can support the point you're making, and the evaluators check off the first thing on their list.

Before taking a position, use your scratch paper to write down five supporting details related to the issue statement. Along with each supporting detail, write down which side of the issue you think it supports. For the earlier prompt on handmade versus mass-produced goods, such a list may look something like this:

>> Your mass-produced Casio wristwatch versus your uncle's handmade Patek Philippe — favors cheap manufacturing

>> An off-the-rack suit versus a tailored suit — favors handmade quality

>> Your HP computer versus your friend's custom-built PC from catalog-ordered parts — can go either way

>> The $60 Raspberry Pi pocket-sized computer — can go either way

>> Your Toyota 4Runner versus your great grandpa's Ford Model T — favors mass production, but this example can easily be refuted by discussing the technology

Don't worry if your examples aren't perfect — you're racing the clock, so just throw down some ideas. You need only two or three examples, so writing down five gives you room to discard a couple.

Your examples can be taken from personal or professional experiences, your reading, or other general background knowledge you possess. What have you seen, done, or heard that formed your opinion on this issue? You may find that your examples support the opposite of your initial response; you want to discover that before writing the introduction.

Step 3: Take a position that's in line with your examples

From your examples, formulate your position. I know, you may feel like you're working backwards, but you want to take the position that you know you can support. This essay isn't a personal statement — it's a test of your ability to compose a clear, coherent train of thought. In this case, your best examples favor cheap manufacturing over handmade quality. So run with that, even if you personally disagree. If necessary, adjust your personal position for the essay. Your goal isn't self-expression; it's to score a perfect 6.

You're not making a commitment here. You're simply writing an essay to be graded. No one is going to bring this essay up in ten years when you're running for office. In fact, no one sees your essays ever again, and believe me, students and I have tried. If your supporting examples don't fit your inherent position, this half hour isn't the time for self-discovery about why or why not. Your task is *one thing*: Write a Level 6 essay. It's okay to declare something that you don't feel. Just look at your examples and write from a position that these examples can support.

The examples you wrote in Step 2 give you a good sense of where your essay will go. Now that your examples are down on paper and you've gathered your thoughts, you're ready to write your introduction.

Step 4: Write your Issue essay

You've laid the groundwork for writing your essay. You've read the statement and the instructions, identified supporting details, and shaped your position. The time has come to write your essay. The easiest approach to composing a great essay is to structure it around a very basic four- or five-paragraph outline, as explained in the following sections.

First paragraph: The introduction

Use the first paragraph of your essay (the introduction) to demonstrate your understanding of the issue and clearly state your position. Structure the paragraph as follows:

>> **First sentence:** Introduce the issue and state your position as a response to the prompt.

Take a *clear stand* in your essay — it's one of the things they grade you on. Arguing both sides of an issue, discussing strengths and weaknesses, or writing "It depends on the situation" is fine, but you must — *must* — make your position clear and be *consistent* throughout your essay.

>> **Second sentence:** Acknowledge the presence of both sides of the issue and that you, in fact, anticipate and address objections to your point of view while alluding to your brilliant logic and reasoning.

>> **Next few sentences:** Prepare the reader for your supporting details.

>> **Final sentence:** Write your thesis statement, which *uses words from the prompt*.

Repeat your thesis, with varied wording, at the end of each paragraph. You get points for being organized, and this is a good way for you to check that your example is on topic.

Refer to this bulleted list as you read the following example to see how I use this structure.

The broad assertion that all mass-produced goods are inferior to handcrafted products is clearly overreaching, and I disagree with the statement. Certainly, in some instances handcrafted products are superior, but in other instances mass production yields more precise, higher-quality products. A few real-world examples, including a wristwatch, a suit, and a personal computer, demonstrate why many, but not all, of today's cheaper, mass-produced goods have better quality and precision than yesterday's hand-built, carefully crafted products.

A common pitfall is launching into the examples while you're still in your introduction. Then, when you get to the paragraph where you describe the example, you have nothing left to say. Such an approach demonstrates a lack of organizational skills and will tank your score. Instead, allude to your examples by mentioning what you *will* talk about in just a few words. Look at the sample introduction to see what I mean.

As you write your introductory paragraph, adhere to the following guidelines:

>> **State your position clearly and succinctly.** The evaluators favor a concise writing style. If you can clearly state your point with fewer words, do it. That said, be thorough when making your point.

>> **Convey confidence.** You're stating a position and supporting it with relevant examples. You know you're right, so act like it.

>> **Stay on topic.** Digressing and expanding your scope to support your position is tempting, but keep your discussion within the scope of the issue topic. For example, mass production may lower the cost to reach a broader market, but the issue is about quality, not cost or sales. Anything outside the scope of the issue will result in a lower score.

>> **Reference key terms.** The essay prompt describes mass production, quality, and precision, so use those terms whenever possible, especially in your thesis as the concluding sentence of each paragraph. Doing so signals that you're responding directly to the prompt.

Second paragraph: Your best example

For the second paragraph, pick your best example and use it to write a single paragraph that supports your position. Structure the paragraph as follows:

>> **First sentence:** Present that example and mention that it supports your position as stated in the introduction.

>> **Next several sentences:** Describe your example in greater detail.

>> **Next sentence or two:** Show how your example supports your position as stated in the introduction.

>> **Last sentence:** State unequivocally that the example you just presented clearly supports your position or refutes the counterargument.

TIP

Make sure one sentence (preferably the last sentence) of each paragraph connects back to your thesis in the introduction. This assures the evaluator that you're on track and your thoughts are organized. Check out the following example and compare it to the preceding list to see how I structured this second paragraph.

A wristwatch is a perfect example of a product that is better when mass-produced. My Casio watch was mass-produced with probably 10,000 other identical units. I purchased this watch five years ago, and it has consistently worked perfectly, with the occasional interruption for a battery replacement. The quality is fine, and the precision couldn't be better. Contrast this with my uncle's Patek Philippe, which was handmade with maybe a dozen others. Due to the motion-generated winding feature, his watch stops working when he doesn't wear it for more than two days! Clearly, this is neither precise timekeeping nor quality of utility. At any given moment, the Casio will always show the correct time, while the Patek's precision is a coin toss. The claim that mass-produced products lack the precision and quality of handmade goods, in this commonly occurring context, is clearly wrong.

Your examples don't need to be 100 percent correct. They serve to demonstrate how your powers of observation and insight support your point. The evaluators understand that you can't research anything while writing the essay. However, don't create examples out of thin air because they're likely to sound phony.

REMEMBER

A clever writing style, as in describing the Patek's accuracy as "a coin toss," is encouraged. Again, though, be appropriate.

WARNING

Make sure your examples aren't easily refutable. For example, if you're claiming that mass-produced goods are both better and cheaper, don't compare your mass-produced, affordable 4Runner to your great-grandfather's hand-built, now-priceless Model T. In this case, the 100 years of improved technology, not the method of production, is clearly the reason for the Toyota's superior performance and reliability. This comparison is a poor example because it's too easily refuted.

Third and fourth paragraphs: Your next best examples

The third and fourth paragraphs of your essay are similar to the second paragraph. Each presents a single supporting example from your notes, shows how the example supports your position, and refers back to the introduction.

> However, some products, such as gentlemen's suits, are better as handmade items than as mass-produced commodities. For example, I wore an off-the-rack two-piece suit to my high school graduation. The jacket was slightly large, but the next size smaller was too small. The workmanship was mediocre, with loose threads and a misplaced stitch. It wasn't cheap, but it was mass-produced, and thus had neither quality nor precision. Contrast this with the handmade, professionally tailored suit that I bought last year. The precise fit is flawless and the quality is unparalleled. Though the claim that mass-produced products lack the quality and precision of handmade goods is true in this example, the claim still cannot be applied to all products.

Here's another example paragraph:

> Furthermore, some products can feature high or low quality and precision regardless of whether they are mass-produced or handmade. Computers are a good example of this. My mass-produced HP laptop demonstrates both precision and quality, while the Compaq computer I bought in 2016 lacked the quality to last more than 18 months. On the other hand, my friend hand-built a computer from parts ordered online, and his computer works with extremely high quality and precision. I have heard stories, however, of hand-built computers that didn't fare as well. Therefore, the general claim that mass-produced products lack the quality and precision of handmade goods is clearly flawed, because in this case, whether the product is handmade or mass-produced doesn't determine the outcome.

TIP

You don't need to always take *one* side of the issue. These examples of the wristwatch, gentlemen's suit, and computer clearly show different sides of the issue. However, the examples are consistent with the thesis, which is that a general claim of precision and quality cannot be applied to everything.

Final paragraph: The conclusion

Think of the final paragraph, the conclusion, as the closing bracket of your essay, with the introduction as the opening bracket. Your conclusion should mirror your introduction while leaving the evaluator with a sense of closure. Structure your concluding paragraph as follows:

>> **First sentence:** Restate your position on the issue presented in the prompt.

>> **Middle sentence or two:** Remind the reader of the supporting details and/or examples you presented and the logical conclusion those details and examples support.

>> **Final sentence:** Summarize why you agree or disagree with the issue statement presented on the test, and touch upon or restate your thesis statement.

TIP

You can refer to the introduction when you write the conclusion. They basically say the same thing, but the conclusion should be more robust because now you've explored the topic.

The following conclusion demonstrates how to follow these instructions:

> To sum up, one cannot correctly claim that all mass-produced products are inferior to handmade goods. The examples describing the wristwatch, the gentlemen's suit, and the personal computer clearly demonstrate that the claim may or may not be true, depending on the context and product. A claim that is sometimes true and sometimes not is an invalid claim, and this statement implies that it is always true. For this reason, I disagree with the statement, and I contend that some, but not all, mass-produced goods have better quality and precision than hand-built, carefully crafted products.

Tying everything together with smooth transitions

As you write, work toward transitioning smoothly from one paragraph to the next. Strong transitions connect the points you're making, especially when your examples take different sides of the issue. Transitions contribute greatly to the organization and coherence of your essay, and they demonstrate control of the language. Here are a few examples of commonly used transitions:

» Closely related to this idea is . . .

» Conversely, . . .

» On the other hand, . . .

» However, . . .

» In contrast, . . .

» Similarly, . . .

Besides transitions, a more subtle technique for tying everything together and staying on point is to repeat key terms throughout the essay. Identify key terms in the issue statement. For example, in the following issue statement, you may identify these as key terms: *cheap, mass-produced, precision, quality,* and *hand-built.*

> Today's **cheap, mass-produced** goods lack the **precision** and **quality** of yesterday's **hand-built,** carefully crafted products.

Here's the sample second paragraph again, with the repetition of key terms drawn directly from the issue statement highlighted in bold type:

> A wristwatch is a perfect example of a product that is better when **mass-produced.** My Casio watch was **mass-produced** with probably 10,000 other identical units. I purchased this watch five years ago, and it has consistently worked perfectly, with the occasional interruption for a battery replacement. The **quality** is fine, and the **precision** couldn't be better. Contrast this with my uncle's Patek Philippe, which was **handmade** with maybe a dozen others. Due to the motion-generated winding feature, his watch stops working when he doesn't wear it for more than two days! Clearly, this is neither **precise** timekeeping nor **quality** of utility. At any given moment, the Casio will always show the correct time, while the Patek's accuracy is a coin toss. The claim that **mass-produced** products lack the **precision** and **quality** of **handmade** goods, in this commonly occurring context, is clearly wrong.

Writing the Argument Essay

Okay, next! The second essay is called Analyze an Argument. The essay prompt is a paragraph that states a position and provides several reasons in support of it. Your job is to analyze the argument and its reasoning and evidence, and describe the additional evidence that's missing and how this evidence would affect the argument. Here's an example:

TIME: 30 minutes

The following memorandum appeared in an investor newsletter: "Many considerations point to the conclusion that Flint's restaurant should be changed from a youth-oriented, family-style restaurant to a Western-style saloon serving alcoholic beverages and featuring country bands. First, few families live in the area surrounding the restaurant; most have moved farther out into the suburbs. Second, Flint owns and operates two other saloons that have liquor licenses, making him experienced in the field. And finally, alcohol has a higher profit margin than does food."

DIRECTIONS: Write a response to the memorandum that analyzes its stated or implied assumptions, reveals how the argument's position depends on the assumptions, and explains the effect of any flawed assumptions on the argument's validity.

The clock's ticking, so you need to work fast, but you also need to analyze the argument before you start writing. By having a plan of attack and a structure in place, you're better equipped to produce an outstanding essay in the allotted time. The following steps provide the basis for writing a good essay:

1. Read and understand the prompt.

2. Identify the position stated in the argument.

3. List the reasons given to support the stated position.

4. Identify the flawed assumptions behind each reason.

5. Write a four- or five-paragraph essay using the following outline as your guide:

   - Introductory paragraph demonstrating your understanding of the position stated in the argument and whether you think the evidence provided supports that position

   - Two or three paragraphs, each of which refutes a faulty assumption/conclusion presented in the argument or, if you agree with the stated position, provides additional evidence to support it

   - Concluding paragraph that recaps your essay and reinforces why the argument is or isn't valid

REMEMBER

Unlike the Issue essay, which is based on your opinion, the Argument essay isn't based on your opinion at all. It's based on your analysis of the argument. For example, in this essay, your personal preference of family restaurants to saloons shouldn't affect what you write.

Step 1: Read and understand the prompt

The Argument essay prompt contains a brief argument or plan along with instructions that tell you exactly what to do. The instructions vary, so read them carefully and understand what you're being asked to do. Here are a few examples:

>> Write a response that evaluates the <u>stated or unstated assumptions</u> on which this argument is based. Explain how the argument relies on these assumptions and how any of the assumptions, if proven to be untrue, would affect the validity of the argument.

>> Write a response explaining the types of <u>evidence needed</u> to evaluate the argument and how the evidence might weaken or strengthen the argument.

>> Write a response presenting the types of <u>questions that need to be answered</u> in order to determine whether the recommended course of action would be advisable and whether the argument on which the recommended course of action is based is reasonable.

They're basically the same: Call out the key assumptions and describe how new information would support or weaken the argument or plan. The difference is usually how you phrase it. Be sure to read the instructions because they vary, and you want to follow them exactly. Also, be sure to frame your writing as an analysis of stated or unstated assumptions, the evidence needed, or the questions that need to be answered, per the instructions. Note that I underlined these key words for you in the above examples, but they aren't underlined in the exam.

TIP

Finding the evidence that's missing from the Analyze an Argument prompt is similar to strengthening, weakening, or finding the assumption of an Argument Analysis question in the GRE's Verbal section. Visit Chapter 7 for more targeted practice on spotting the assumption and ways that new information can strengthen or weaken it.

REMEMBER

Like the Issue essay topics, at the time of this writing, the entire set of Analyze an Argument topics is available online courtesy of ETS. Just be sure to include the word "pool" in your online search, as in "GRE argument essay *pool*," or visit this link: https://www.ets.org/content/dam/ets-org/pdfs/gre/argument-pool.pdf. The list contains all the argument statements along with examples of the accompanying instructions, so you can practice finding the evidence that's needed to support or weaken an argument. Don't try to practice *every* topic — just read through some of them so you know what to expect. (In class, we also play "topic roulette" with the argument topics.)

Step 2: Identify the position stated in the argument

The position statement is the point of the argument. It may be in the first sentence, or it may be offset by "therefore" or "for this reason," like the conclusion of an argument. In this example, the position is

> Flint's restaurant should be changed from a youth-oriented, family-style restaurant to a Western-style saloon serving alcoholic beverages and featuring country bands.

Identifying the position stated in the argument is a crucial first step because in the paragraphs that follow, you need to show how new information can support or weaken that position.

Step 3: List the reasons given to support the stated position

Every argument includes a list of facts to support the position. In this Flint's restaurant example, the facts are easy to pick out because they're identified by number:

>> **First:** Few families live in the area surrounding the restaurant; most have moved farther out into the suburbs.

>> **Second:** Flint owns and operates two other saloons that have liquor licenses, making him experienced in the field.

>> **Third:** Alcohol has a higher profit margin than food.

Step 4: Identify the flawed assumptions behind each reason

As you begin to write your essay, look for the author's flawed assumption(s) — anything the author claims or implies without providing sufficient evidence to back it up. (See Chapter 7 for more about assumptions.) For example, stating that "alcohol has a higher profit margin than does food" is a fact — but that doesn't mean serving alcohol is more profitable than serving food.

While taking this on, keep in mind that you can argue assumptions, but you can't argue facts. Alcohol *does* have a higher profit margin — you can't challenge that. Instead, suggest that the profitability depends on the number of local residents who drink or that it may be offset by the loss of revenue from food sales. Pose these as questions that need to be answered or evidence that needs to be presented — whichever is stated in the essay instructions — before determining that the higher profit margin from alcohol will lead to increased profits at Flint's. This is new evidence that refutes the flawed assumption.

On your scratch paper, jot down about five assumptions and new facts that, going either way, would support or refute those assumptions. Write down only key words — save your prose for the essay. The following list is an example of assumptions and new facts that affect the argument:

>> **Faulty assumption:** Families won't make the drive from the distant suburbs.

   New fact: Though families don't live nearby, they may drive to the area for other reasons, such as shopping or recreation.

>> **Faulty assumption:** Because Flint's other two saloons are successful, this new saloon will also be successful.

   New fact: Make sure this new saloon shares the factors that contribute to the success of the two other saloons, such as a nearby sports stadium or a theater.

>> **Faulty assumption:** Flint's experience with saloons will make this newly converted saloon a success.

   New fact: Other factors, including other saloons in the area, affect success. There could be five saloons across the street from this restaurant but no other family restaurants within 5 miles.

>> **Faulty assumption:** A liquor license that brings success to one locale will bring success to another.

   New fact: Regions are different. A liquor license in Dallas may be more lucrative than one in Salt Lake City.

>> **Faulty assumption:** Alcohol's higher profit margin will lead to higher overall profits because the level of sales will be the same.

   New fact: Though alcohol has a higher profit margin than food, the sales volume could be lower. Selling 200 dinners at a profit margin of 40 percent is more profitable than selling 24 beers at a profit margin of 60 percent.

You don't have to describe all the faulty assumptions. Two or three are good, which is especially comforting if you can think of only a few. Regardless, start with the strongest faulty assumption and work your way down. With only 30 minutes, having three well-developed points is very good, and it's far better than having five sketchy ideas.

Step 5: Write your essay

You always want to outline an essay, and this outline is simple: an introduction that sums up the faulty assumptions, two or three body paragraphs that each explores a faulty assumption, and a conclusion that restates the introduction.

Introductory paragraph

The first paragraph of your Analyze an Argument essay (the introduction) must demonstrate your understanding of the argument and whether you think the argument is valid. Structure the paragraph as follows:

>> **First sentence or two:** Briefly describe the argument you're analyzing and underscore that it's based on key information that's missing.

>> **Middle sentences:** Touch upon the faulty assumptions and mention that they don't fully support the argument. You *could* briefly mention all the assumptions in your list and then write that you will explore the assumptions with the most glaring flaws.

>> **Final sentence:** State your thesis, which for the Analyze an Argument essay, is typically something to the effect of "Without knowing these answers (or 'Without this additional evidence'), there is no way to know whether this argument is true."

As you read the following example introductory paragraph, refer to the preceding list and see how I apply this structure.

The author provides a compelling, though flawed, argument for Flint to convert his family restaurant to a saloon. Converting the restaurant may or may not be a wise course of action, and the assumptions used to support the argument lack sufficient evidence and are therefore flawed. A great deal of information is missing that would validate or weaken the assumptions, such as whether how far away the families live makes a difference, whether success in one location promises success in another, and whether profit margins alone determine success. Without knowing these answers, there is no way to know that this plan will succeed, and Flint would be unwise to risk his business without first finding out these facts.

Paragraphs two, three, and possibly four

Each of your example paragraphs covers one of the argument's reasons or faulty assumptions and presents a new fact or reason to support or refute it. Start with your strongest point and structure each paragraph as follows:

>> **First sentence or two:** Present one of the argument's reasons/assumptions in your own words.

>> **Next sentence:** Transition to the new fact that supports or refutes this particular reason or assumption.

>> **Remaining sentences:** Provide additional details to support your new fact.

>> **Last sentence:** Summarize how your new fact supports or refutes this reason or assumption.

Read these sample second, third, and fourth paragraphs and compare them to this list to see how I use this structure.

First of all, the memorandum states that most families live too far away. This may be true, but it doesn't mean families won't eat there. The author assumes that because families live so far away, they'll never be in the area. This may not be the case, because families may take a day trip into town and want to stop somewhere to eat. The author doesn't mention whether the restaurant is near a children's museum or shopping mall that caters to families. The restaurant could be near plenty of family-based traffic, even though the suburbs are far from the restaurant. Without knowing whether families will still be visiting the area, it's impossible to know whether the families' living far away will affect the success of the restaurant.

Note the transition words at the beginning of each of the following essay paragraphs that help smooth the movement from one paragraph to the next.

Next, the memorandum suggests that because Flint runs two successful saloons, this new saloon will also be successful. The author assumes that the conditions are the same at all locations. What works at one location, however, may not necessarily work at another. For example, the two saloons could be near sports arenas, where saloons thrive, and the restaurant could be near an amusement park, which wouldn't be as welcoming to a new saloon. Without knowing the factors that lead to the other saloons' success, there is no way to know whether converting Flint's restaurant to a third saloon would be profitable.

In addition, the memorandum mentions the higher profit margin of alcohol as key to increased profits. The memo assumes, however, that sales of alcohol will be the same. No information is provided to suggest liquor sales will be comparable to food sales. Although profit margin is key to profits, sales volume is also important. A 20 percent profit from $500,000 in sales is worth more than a 30 percent profit from $100,000 in sales. The level of potential alcohol sales needs to be known before Flint abandons his existing food sales for a throw-of-the-dice level of alcohol sales, regardless of the profit margin.

As you write the body paragraphs, be sure to stick to these fine points:

>> Spell out exactly why each reason is valid or why each assumption is invalid. Don't expect the evaluators to draw conclusions from your description — make it clear.

>> Cover only *one* faulty assumption per paragraph.

>> Use transition words at the beginning of each subsequent paragraph to move from one paragraph to the next. For more about transitions, see the section "Tying everything together with smooth transitions" earlier in this chapter.

Concluding paragraph

The last step in writing the Analyze an Argument essay is to compose the final paragraph, which is the conclusion. This is the closing bracket of your essay, with the introduction being the opening bracket. Your conclusion should mirror your introduction while leaving the evaluator with a sense of closure. It should also be more robust than the intro because by now you've fully explored the faulty assumptions. Structure your concluding paragraph as follows:

- » **First sentence:** Acknowledge the main point of the argument or plan and generally explain why you think it has or hasn't been adequately proven.

- » **Next sentence or two:** Remind the reader of the reasons or assumptions that you think support or question that main point.

- » **Closing:** The closing need not be a separate sentence, but it should complete your essay, leaving the evaluator with a sense of closure.

Read this example conclusion for how I use the preceding list to draft the sentences.

> Though the author provides a strong argument for converting Flint's restaurant to a saloon, the argument relies on several assumptions that are based on uncertain facts. These uncertain facts include the importance of the proximity of families, the question of whether success in one location brings success in another, and the dubious assumption that a higher profit margin brings more profit. Flint should confirm these key facts before making his decision.

REMEMBER

The evaluators know that you're writing a rough draft. Your essays *can* have mistakes. They don't have to be perfect, but they need to be logical, well-organized, and clear.

Chapter **17**

Practicing Your Essays

nowing how to write the essays and actually writing them on the day of the test are two entirely different things. In this chapter, you can put into practice everything you discovered in Chapter 16 so you can write high-scoring essays.

Below are two essay prompts, one each for Analyze an Issue and Analyze an Argument, complete with directions similar to those you'll see on the actual GRE. Give yourself 30 minutes to write each essay. Following each essay question are two sample essays (one good and one sort of good) along with evaluator comments.

After writing your practice essay, read the 6-scoring essay and the evaluator's critique as a role model for what your essay should look like. Next, read and critique the 4-scoring essay. See if you can spot the flaws that prevent it from being a 6 — and then read the evaluator's comments to see what you may have missed.

TIP

Practicing the essays is crucial to writing well under pressure, avoiding writer's block, and finishing in the allotted time. It only takes a little practice — but you *have* to do it.

Setting the Stage for a Realistic Experience

To make your practice session more like what you'll experience on test day, set the stage by doing the following:

>> **Compose your essay on a computer rather than by hand.** Typing on a computer more effectively simulates the actual test-taking experience. You can write your *outline* on paper, but practice writing the essay itself on the computer.

>> **Turn off your word processor's spelling- and grammar-checking features.** Better yet — use Windows Notepad or Mac TextEdit with formatting turned off. The text box you type into on the actual test doesn't correct or highlight grammar and spelling errors or typos.

>> **Set your timer for 30 minutes per essay, but if time runs out, go ahead and finish the essay anyway.** You still have to practice writing the end of the essay, and the practice will help you write faster next time. Keep track of how much extra time you need so you know how much faster you need to work.

REMEMBER

Don't skip ahead and read the essays or evaluations before writing your own essay. The point is to practice composing an essay on the fly, with a timer. Read the directions followed by the issue or argument and then immediately write your essay.

Writing an Issue Essay: Some Samples

TIME: 30 minutes

Because society is always changing, laws should always change to reflect the times and be open to interpretation based on the facts of the individual circumstance.

DIRECTIONS: Write an essay in response to the preceding statement in which you discuss the extent to which you agree or disagree with the statement. Explain your reasoning in a clear, well-organized essay that supports your position. Consider both sides of the issue when developing your response.

Pause reading here and go type your practice essay. Then, check your notes and outline against the following information and insights. In this section, I present various ways to formulate and support a position in response to this Issue essay prompt.

Having trouble getting started? Begin by identifying some relevant examples

If you had trouble getting started, maybe you couldn't think of any examples to write about. This particular essay prompt is on laws that change and those that should be flexible (open to interpretation), so start by jotting down some examples of laws that meet those criteria.

Here are examples of laws that changed in response to the changing times:

>> New laws for new situations, such as cyberbullying laws today, DUI laws 50 years ago, and driver's license requirements 80 years ago

>> Evolving laws for evolving situations, such as the use of marijuana

>> Laws as a response to an event, such as terrorism or social media hacking

Examples of laws that may be flexible or open to interpretation include the following:

>> Outdated and irrelevant laws, such as no carrying goldfish in Philadelphia or no dancing on Sundays

>> Laws that justify killing, as in cases of self-defense or prevention of a tragedy

>> Laws that address censorship and free speech

And because the prompt specifically instructs you to consider both sides of the issue, you need to think about laws that perhaps shouldn't change over time or be open to interpretation, such as laws prohibiting:

>> Murder or assassination

>> Assault and battery

>> Burglary

>> Vandalism

>> Hate crimes

Don't worry if some listed items wouldn't fit the essay — this is just a brain dump, and you don't have time to write on all of them anyway. When writing your essay, just pick the best few.

WARNING

Don't use examples that are out of scope, including the enforcement of laws, punishment, and regional differences. Also, avoid any hard-line stand on a politically charged topic.

Sample essay — score 6 (outstanding)

Though laws should evolve and have some flexibility, I don't agree with the statement that laws should always change and be interpreted by each individual circumstance. Throughout history, laws have existed and evolved with society. Our laws today are based on a balance of rigidity and flexibility. There is always some adjustment and some interpretation, but to take away the foundation of the laws and leave them completely open to popularity and interpretation would lead us either to a libertine or totalitarian society, neither of which is healthy. In this essay, I will discuss laws that should evolve to keep pace with the new technology of an evolving society, especially regarding computers and cars. I will also discuss laws that should not be interpreted, such as premeditated murder, and finally laws that are no longer relevant and should possibly be scrubbed, such as how to carry goldfish. Though these are all valid topics for discussion, they do not suggest that all of our laws should be subject to interpretation and flexibility.

There are plenty of examples of laws that evolve with society out of necessity. Cyberbullying wasn't an issue 40 years ago, so there wouldn't be a law regarding this. Today, however, the framework for cyberbullying is in place, so the law exists out of necessity. When cars first came out, there were no laws requiring drivers' licenses or preventing drunk driving. The road was probably a very dangerous place! To keep up with a changing society, laws were introduced to regulate the road. Whether these laws are overreaching is another discussion, but overall the roads are safer with these laws than without them. In these cases — cyberbullying and roads — the laws are changing to reflect the times, and this is good.

However, these changes should be careful and deliberate. Other laws, such as prohibiting premeditated murder, cannot simply be flexible or interpreted based on circumstance. Around 1995, the Israeli prime minister Yitzchak Rabin was assassinated days before signing a peace treaty with Yasser Arafat, the leader of the PLO. The assassin was not a criminal before this, but he felt that the provision of the treaty would have placed the Israeli people in danger, and this was his motive for murder. His rationale was to kill one person to save many. Whether he was right is a topic for debate, but for the purpose of this essay, let's suppose that yes: the treaty would have led to the deaths of many Israelis. Was his act justified? This is the danger of leaving laws to interpretation. If you say that yes, in this case, it was justified, then it basically opens the door to quite a lawless society. The law against murder becomes null, because there's always a circumstance and interpretation making it OK. Our CEO is leading the company to bankruptcy. Kill her! My neighbor parties all night and keeps me up, so I may lose my job. Kill him! This is absolutely NOT the direction that things should go. Laws like this, prohibiting premeditated murder and certain other crimes, should not be open to flexibility and interpretation, and Rabin's assassin was rightly prosecuted in spite of his lofty motive.

There are also laws that have faded to irrelevancy and are no longer enforced, but this is not the same as interpretation or circumstantial allowance. For example, "It's illegal to walk on the sidewalks of Philadelphia carrying goldfish," or "It is a crime to sing to your horses in the hearing of others" are examples of laws that are no longer relevant. I have always wondered what would happen if one of these obscure laws were suddenly enforced again. Can you imagine walking out of a pet store on a Sunday afternoon with a goldfish and getting busted? Legally, law enforcement could do this — it's the law. Fortunately, they don't, but it brings up the point that as laws become irrelevant or obsolete, they may require some review. However, this is not the same as interpreting or making exceptions. These are laws that are obsolete because society has evolved away from them.

Laws should evolve and have some flexibility, but not too much. New technology, such as cars and computers, require new laws. Some old, obsolete laws probably have no place anymore in our modern society. However, certain laws cannot be flexible, such as killing one person to save many.

Evaluator comments on the score 6 essay

This essay presents an excellent answer to the question. The writer uses powerful, relevant examples to support his point and makes the clear case that though some flexibility and interpretation is warranted, it has to be controlled.

The writer's opinion is clear from the start and is supported by well-reasoned and thoroughly developed examples. Though the thesis is not blatantly declared, the author's position is clearly stated in the first paragraph and reinforced by the following paragraphs. The three examples are separated, yet they flow together well via the use of good transitions. The ending sums things up nicely and leaves no doubt as to the author's opinion.

TIP

Your examples are more powerful if they're relevant to real life. Also, the evaluators know that you're not able to do research while taking the GRE, so it's okay if you're not sure of a detail, such as the year something happened or who exactly said a certain quote. The evaluators are simply interested in whether you can make a point and support it well.

Sample essay — score 4 (adequate)

Laws must change when Society changes. This is true for all types of laws, the major laws and the minor laws. This is true for all types of Societies, the so-called First World and lesser developed countries. This is true for all types of situations, from the serious to the silly to the macabre.

An example of when a law must change is the death penalty. Many years ago, condemned prisoners were executed routinely. Such executions became major events, almost parties, with the public making an excursion to watch the hanging. The irony, of course, is that the huge crowds at the execution attracted additional criminals who then committed more crimes (theft, pickpocketing, assault) and perpetated the cycle. Today, while there are less executions, they have become media events. We don't attend the executions in person, but we live through them vicariously, watching them on tv. When Timothy McVeigh, the Oklahoma City bomber, was given a lethal injection, the tv stations carried a minute-by-minute report. The amount of money and time and energy that was put into this could have been better spent elsewhere.

A second reason laws must be flexible is in time of war or social upheaval. Take, for example, the 1960's. The United States had a sea of change during that decade. Many more things were acceptable socially then than had ever been before, and the laws had to change to reflect that fact. The possession of certain drugs became much less serious than it had been before. People weren't sentenced to twenty years for *using* drugs, just for *pushing* them. Today, people can use certain drugs legally, either recreationally or for medicinal purposes depending on the state where they live.

Traffic laws are a less serious, but still good, example of when laws should change. The speed limit in downtown New York must obviously be less than that in the outskirts of Podunk, Idaho (my apologies to the Podunkians!). Many people in Wyoming and other sparsely-populated Western states fought against having a federally-mandated speed limit of 55 on the freeways, rguing that in their areas, 65 or even 75 would be more logical. This is an example of the need for a change to meet the needs of a local community or Society. The same is true for the age at which youngsters can get a license, as they are more mature earlier now than before.

In conclusion, laws are not static because people are not static. We change from decade to decade, and from locale to locale. While it is important to adhere to the Declaration of Independence's statement that "all [people] are created equal," and thus should have equal rights, not all times are created equal, and thus should not have equal laws.

Evaluator comments on the score 4 essay

This is a generally acceptable response. The writer presents an unequivocal answer to the question and uses some good vocabulary ("macabre," "vicariously"). In addition, the length is good, with three well-organized examples.

However, the examples are out of scope. The money, time, and energy spent watching McVeigh's execution isn't relevant to changing laws. It's not clear why wars and social upheavals mandate a change in laws, or during which times the laws or the enforcement changed. And the speed limit differences in differently populated areas aren't shown to have changed; they are shown to be different.

The essay has additional weaknesses that prevent it from receiving a higher score, such as instances of inappropriate humor ("my apologies to the Podunkians!"). Although minor grammatical flaws are acceptable, "less executions" should be "fewer executions" and therefore isn't acceptable. Though an occasional typo and spelling or capitalization error is acceptable, this essay has far too many, such as *perpetated* instead of *perpetuated*, *tv* instead of *TV* or *television*, *rguing* instead of *arguing*, and *Society* instead of *society*.

Writing an Argument Essay: Some Samples

TIME: 30 minutes

The following appeared in an in-house memo sent from a marketing director to the editorial department of a television news station.

Our research shows that when the managing editor comes on screen at the end of the newscast to present his perspective on an issue, many viewers switch stations or turn off the television entirely. Besides losing viewers, which reduces our ability to charge top dollar for advertising spots, we lose the opportunity to show more ads. In addition, viewers have complained that they feel editorials are best read in the newspaper, not heard on television. Therefore, to increase ad revenue and stop losing viewers, we recommend stopping the editorial at the end of the newscast.

DIRECTIONS: Write a response to the preceding argument that analyzes its stated or implied assumptions, reveals how the argument's position depends on the assumptions, and explains the effect of any flawed assumptions on the argument's validity.

Pause reading here and type a practice essay. Then, check your notes and outline against the following information and insights. In this section, I present some of the faulty assumptions included in the argument.

Having trouble getting started? Begin by finding the faulty assumptions

This particular essay instruction tells you to analyze the argument's stated or implied assumptions. The essay you wrote is a product of whatever you identified as stated or implied assumptions. Start your essay by finding the faulty assumptions, like these:

>> The marketing director, who sent the memo, assumes that viewers leave because of the managing editor or the editorial, but viewers could leave for some other reason, such as another program starting on another channel. You need to know why the viewers leave.

>> The marketing director assumes that the ability to charge top dollar for the concluding ads is lost because viewers leave, but this ad space could be devalued for some other reason — maybe the last ads of any program have reduced value. You need to know why the value of the concluding ads has gone down.

>> The marketing director assumes that additional ads at the end can also be charged top dollar and implies that this will lead to more revenue, but more ads may dilute the value of the ad spots. You need to know the number of ads that can run at the end of a program and still hold value.

>> The marketing director assumes that because some viewers have stated that editorials are better in newspapers, they aren't welcome on TV, but plenty of TV viewers may also enjoy the editorials on TV. You need to know whether viewers appreciate or resent the TV editorials.

>> The marketing director assumes that "complaints from viewers" are reliable feedback, but complaints alone don't reflect the overall opinion. You need to know what the viewers as a whole would say.

Of course, you don't have time to write on *all* these faulty assumptions, though you can mention them in your intro. Use your limited time to explore the best two or three.

Sample essay — score 6 (outstanding)

The marketing director suggests that the news station should stop airing editorials because viewership decreases when a perspective is presented at the end of the newscast. The memo argues that the editorial drives viewers away, and that when people don't watch the end of the newscast, the station loses advertising revenue. More information is needed to support these assumptions, such as the reasons why viewers leave at the end of the program, what the viewers would stay to watch at the end of the newscast, and the reliability of the feedback on the editorial content.

First, the marketing director recommends that the station stop the editorials at the end of newscasts because people are turning off what is currently offered. However, it is not known why viewers leave or change the channel. They could be flipping to watch a show on another channel, or they could be turning the TV off to put their kids to bed, so regardless of whether the news station runs an editorial, that viewership is lost. Furthermore, halting the editorials may alienate the viewers who like the editorial and continue watching. It could be that the viewers who continue watching through the editorial will stop watching the news program altogether if this change is made. Before changing the content of the news program, it would be wise for the marketing director to find out why some viewers leave and whether the remaining viewers enjoy the editorial.

Second, the marketing director claims that the time devoted to the current editorial could be sold to advertisers. The director assumes, then, that people who turn off the television or switch stations when the editorial comes on will not do so when more ads come on instead. However, this is not a reliable assumption. If viewers stop watching the station when they know the news is over, they will probably still stop watching when they know only commercials are on. Furthermore, when advertisers find out that people are not watching their commercials, they may cancel their contracts. The marketing director would be well advised to find out what compels viewers to keep watching, before replacing the editorial segment with an ad segment.

Finally, the marketing director notes that "viewers have complained" that editorials are best read in the newspaper, not seen on television. Do these complaining viewers speak for the others? The marketing director assumes that these complaining viewers are representative of all the station's viewers. It could be that other viewers, who don't complain, stay and watch the editorials. The marketing director also fails to mention how numerous these complaints are and does not include information about viewers who have expressed the opposite opinion. Viewer feedback should be taken seriously, but first the marketing director needs to find out whether this feedback is shared by the general viewing population.

Therefore, to improve the argument, the marketing director needs to find answers to the questions raised above, including whether viewers would turn off any kind of editorial at the end of a newscast. The director needs to demonstrate that viewers would continue to watch advertisements after the presentation of news, and the director should also investigate whether the complaints are representative of the viewing audience. It is not recommended that the TV station take any action before finding these answers.

Evaluator comments on the score 6 essay

This very strong response presents a coherent, well-organized, direct analysis that introduces and fully develops the various points. The essay writer identifies three central gaps in knowledge that weaken or even undermine the argument, and explores them sufficiently to remove any doubt that valid questions still need to be answered. Finally, the writer summarizes these key points in a brief but complete conclusion. The language, grammar, spelling, and general writing skills also contribute to the excellence of this essay.

Sample essay — score 4 (adequate)

The argument presented in this memo is relatively well-reasoned, although flawed in some aspects. The primary weakness, in my opinion, is found at the beginning, where the memo states, "Our research has shown . . . ." without specifying what that research is. Did someone poll viewers who regularly watched the show? Did someone send out a questionnaire which was returned only by a small percentage of people, some of whom did not regularly watch the news? How were the questions phrased by the researcher (as we all know, a question can easily beg a desired answer, be skewed so as to direct the response in the direction the questioner wants it to go). A good argument will state the basis for the conclusions it makes.

The argument lacks specifics. Nowhere does the memo say why the viewers switch stations. Maybe they don't like that particular managing editor. The station can experiment by having the editorials read by others on the staff, by reporters, or even by the public at large. There are some stations where I live that do that, have local people at the end of the newscasts tell their opinions. Many of my friends, at least, tune in to watch what their peers have to say.

Is the purpose of the last few minutes of a newscast to sell ads? Maybe, if there were no editorial, there would be an extra two minutes of news reporting, not of advertisements. There are already so many ads in a newscast as it is; more would possibly alienate the viewers even more than the editorial does. Also, I believe there is an FCC mandate as to how many minutes per hour or half hour can be commercials, at least in prime time. If the station didn't have the editorial, but ran commercials, they may exceed this limit.

Evaluator comments on the score 4 essay

This response is adequate. The instructions are to analyze the assumptions, by which the writer poses questions to be answered. The organization is acceptable, although it would be improved by the use of transitional phrases. The writer comes close to nailing the points but doesn't quite do so. The start of the second paragraph reads, "Nowhere does the memo say why the viewers switch stations." That the research, not the memo, indicates viewers switch stations notwithstanding, I was expecting the writer to hit the nail on the head with "We don't know why viewers switch stations, so we can't attribute it to the editorial." Instead, the author speculates as to why viewers switch, proposes an evaluation of the managing editor and editorial, and then follows up with a digression about the writer's own local news stations.

The essay digresses again from its main focus by discussing the FCC mandate, which is out of scope. The purpose of the essay is to evaluate the assumptions, not discuss the laws of broadcasting. While the FCC mandate and the author's own local news stations might be relevant in an editorial meeting, they are off topic and distract from the purpose of this Analysis of an Argument. Finally, the lack of a coherent conclusion makes this paper a weak 4.

TIP

Looking for more practice? Good idea. Visit the online compendium of actual GRE essay topics provided, at the time of this writing, courtesy of ETS. Analysis of an Issue topics can be found at https://www.ets.org/content/dam/ets-org/pdfs/gre/issue-pool.pdf, while Analysis of an Argument topics are waiting for you at https://www.ets.org/content/dam/ets-org/pdfs/gre/argument-pool.pdf. You can also just search online for "GRE issue essay pool" or "GRE argument essay pool" to find these topics. Be sure to include the word "pool" in your search to find actual GRE topics.

You don't have to write essays for these online topics — just pick one and think of examples or faulty assumptions; then pick another, and so on, so that you have practice exploring ideas on test day. Just be sure to use these *actual* GRE essay topics for a true feel of what they ask.

5

Full-Length Practice Exams: Show Time

Chapter **18**

Practice Exam 1

You're now ready to take a practice GRE. Like the actual, computer-based GRE, the following exam consists of two 30-minute essays, two 30-minute Verbal Reasoning sections (20 questions each), and two 35-minute Quantitative Reasoning sections (20 questions each). The actual GRE typically includes an extra Verbal or Quantitative Reasoning section, which doesn't count toward your score, but this one has nothing like that.

Take this practice test under normal exam conditions and approach it as you would the real GRE.

TIP

>> **Work when you won't be interrupted.** Pick a quiet time of day when there are fewer opportunities for distraction.

>> **Use scratch paper that's free of any prepared notes.** On the actual GRE, you receive blank scratch paper before your test begins.

>> **Answer as many questions as time allows.** Consider answering all the easier questions within each section first and then going back to answer the harder questions. Because you're not penalized for guessing, go ahead and guess on the remaining questions before time expires.

>> **Set a timer for each section.** If you have time left at the end, you may go back and review answers (within the section), continue and finish your test early, or pause and catch your mental breath before moving on to the next section.

>> **Don't leave your desk while the clock is running on any section.** Though technically you're allowed to do this, it's not conducive to an effective time-management strategy.

>> **Take breaks between sections.** Take a one-minute break after each section and the optional ten-minute break after the first Verbal section.

>> **Type the essays.** Because you type the essays on the actual GRE, typing them now is good practice. Don't use software that checks spelling and grammar, such as Microsoft Word. Instead, use a simple text editor, such as Notepad. The GRE essay-writing space features undo, redo, copy, and paste functionality — but nothing else.

After completing this practice test, go to Chapter 19 to check your answers. Be sure to review the explanations for *all* the questions, not just the ones you missed. The answer explanations provide insight and a review of everything you went over in the previous chapters. This way, you also review the explanations for questions you weren't sure of.

REMEMBER

If you're taking the computerized GRE, the answer choices aren't marked with A, B, C, D, E, and F. Instead, they have clickable ovals and check boxes, boxes where you type in numeric answers, and click-a-sentence options (for some Reading Comprehension questions). Here, the questions and answer choices are formatted to challenge you in the same way and build the same skills that you'll use on test day.

Answer Sheet for Practice Exam 1

Section 1:
Verbal Reasoning

1. Ⓐ Ⓑ Ⓒ Ⓓ Ⓔ
2. Ⓐ Ⓑ Ⓒ Ⓓ Ⓔ
3. Ⓐ Ⓑ Ⓒ Ⓓ Ⓔ Ⓕ
4. Ⓐ Ⓑ Ⓒ Ⓓ Ⓔ Ⓕ
5. Ⓐ Ⓑ Ⓒ Ⓓ Ⓔ Ⓕ Ⓖ Ⓗ Ⓘ
6. Ⓐ Ⓑ Ⓒ Ⓓ Ⓔ Ⓕ Ⓖ Ⓗ Ⓘ
7. Ⓐ Ⓑ Ⓒ Ⓓ Ⓔ
8. Ａ Ｂ Ｃ Ｄ Ｅ
9. Ａ Ｂ Ｃ
10. Ａ Ｂ Ｃ
11. Ⓐ Ⓑ Ⓒ Ⓓ Ⓔ
12. Ａ Ｂ Ｃ
13. Ⓐ Ⓑ Ⓒ Ⓓ Ⓔ
14. Ⓐ Ⓑ Ⓒ Ⓓ Ⓔ
15. Ⓐ Ⓑ Ⓒ Ⓓ Ⓔ
16. Ⓐ Ⓑ Ⓒ Ⓓ Ⓔ
17. Ａ Ｂ Ｃ Ｄ Ｅ Ｆ
18. Ａ Ｂ Ｃ Ｄ Ｅ Ｆ
19. Ａ Ｂ Ｃ Ｄ Ｅ Ｆ
20. Ａ Ｂ Ｃ Ｄ Ｅ Ｆ

Section 2:
Quantitative Reasoning

1. Ⓐ Ⓑ Ⓒ Ⓓ Ⓔ
2. Ⓐ Ⓑ Ⓒ Ⓓ Ⓔ
3. ▭
4. ▭
5. Ⓐ Ⓑ Ⓒ Ⓓ
6. Ⓐ Ⓑ Ⓒ Ⓓ
7. Ⓐ Ⓑ Ⓒ Ⓓ
8. Ⓐ Ⓑ Ⓒ Ⓓ
9. Ⓐ Ⓑ Ⓒ Ⓓ
10. Ⓐ Ⓑ Ⓒ Ⓓ
11. Ⓐ Ⓑ Ⓒ Ⓓ
12. ▭
13. Ⓐ Ⓑ Ⓒ Ⓓ Ⓔ
14. Ⓐ Ⓑ Ⓒ Ⓓ Ⓔ
15. ▭
16. Ⓐ Ⓑ Ⓒ Ⓓ Ⓔ
17. Ⓐ Ⓑ Ⓒ Ⓓ Ⓔ
18. Ⓐ Ⓑ Ⓒ Ⓓ Ⓔ
19. Ⓐ Ⓑ Ⓒ Ⓓ Ⓔ
20. Ａ Ｂ Ｃ Ｄ Ｅ Ｆ

Section 3:
Verbal Reasoning

1. Ⓐ Ⓑ Ⓒ Ⓓ Ⓔ
2. Ⓐ Ⓑ Ⓒ Ⓓ Ⓔ
3. Ⓐ Ⓑ Ⓒ Ⓓ Ⓔ Ⓕ
4. Ⓐ Ⓑ Ⓒ Ⓓ Ⓔ Ⓕ
5. Ⓐ Ⓑ Ⓒ Ⓓ Ⓔ Ⓕ
6. Ⓐ Ⓑ Ⓒ Ⓓ Ⓔ Ⓕ Ⓖ Ⓗ Ⓘ
7. Ⓐ Ⓑ Ⓒ Ⓓ Ⓔ Ⓕ Ⓖ Ⓗ Ⓘ
8. Ⓐ Ⓑ Ⓒ Ⓓ Ⓔ
9. Ａ Ｂ Ｃ
10. Ⓐ Ⓑ Ⓒ Ⓓ Ⓔ
11. Ⓐ Ⓑ Ⓒ Ⓓ Ⓔ
12. Ⓐ Ⓑ Ⓒ Ⓓ Ⓔ
13. Ａ Ｂ Ｃ
14. Ⓐ Ⓑ Ⓒ Ⓓ Ⓔ
15. Ⓐ Ⓑ Ⓒ Ⓓ Ⓔ
16. Ⓐ Ⓑ Ⓒ Ⓓ Ⓔ
17. Ａ Ｂ Ｃ Ｄ Ｅ Ｆ
18. Ａ Ｂ Ｃ Ｄ Ｅ Ｆ
19. Ａ Ｂ Ｃ Ｄ Ｅ Ｆ
20. Ⓐ Ⓑ Ⓒ Ⓓ Ⓔ

Section 4:
Quantitative Reasoning

1. Ⓐ Ⓑ Ⓒ Ⓓ Ⓔ
2. Ⓐ Ⓑ Ⓒ Ⓓ Ⓔ
3. Ａ Ｂ Ｃ Ｄ Ｅ
4. Ⓐ Ⓑ Ⓒ Ⓓ
5. Ⓐ Ⓑ Ⓒ Ⓓ
6. Ⓐ Ⓑ Ⓒ Ⓓ
7. Ⓐ Ⓑ Ⓒ Ⓓ
8. Ⓐ Ⓑ Ⓒ Ⓓ
9. Ⓐ Ⓑ Ⓒ Ⓓ
10. Ⓐ Ⓑ Ⓒ Ⓓ
11. Ⓐ Ⓑ Ⓒ Ⓓ Ⓔ
12. Ⓐ Ⓑ Ⓒ Ⓓ Ⓔ
13. Ⓐ Ⓑ Ⓒ Ⓓ Ⓔ
14. Ａ Ｂ Ｃ
15. ▭
16. ▭
17. Ａ Ｂ Ｃ Ｄ Ｅ Ｆ
18. Ⓐ Ⓑ Ⓒ Ⓓ Ⓔ
19. ▭
20. Ａ Ｂ Ｃ Ｄ Ｅ Ｆ

Analytical Writing 1: Analyze an Issue

TIME: 30 minutes

Oversight of media and personal expression is an important part of any mature society.

DIRECTIONS: Write a response in which you express the extent to which you agree or disagree with the preceding statement and explain the reasoning behind your position. In support of your position, think of ways in which the statement may or may not be true and how these considerations influence your position.

DO NOT TURN THE PAGE UNTIL TOLD TO DO SO **STOP** **DO NOT RETURN TO A PREVIOUS TEST**

Analytical Writing 2: Analyze an Argument

TIME: 30 minutes

The following appeared in a letter to the editor of the *Arlington Town Times*.

> To serve the housing needs of our community, the Arlington council should encourage land developers to build many new houses, condominiums, and apartments. Arlington's population is growing and, based on current trends, will double over the next 40 years, thus making the existing housing inadequate. Furthermore, the average home price has risen in recent years, probably due to a shortage of supply. This initiative could further serve to grow the town, as attractive new homes could make prospective residents more likely to move to Arlington.

DIRECTIONS: Write a response in which you discuss the merits of the preceding argument. Discuss the evidence that would strengthen or weaken it.

DO NOT TURN THE PAGE UNTIL TOLD TO DO SO **STOP** DO NOT RETURN TO A PREVIOUS TEST

Section 1
Verbal Reasoning

TIME: 30 minutes for 20 questions

DIRECTIONS: Choose the best answer to each question. Blacken the corresponding ovals or boxes on the answer sheet.

Directions: For Questions 1–7, choose the one entry best suited for each blank from its corresponding column of choices.

1. Corporate leaders often try to _____ their intentions, as disclosing the motives that drive decisions may put the company's strategic advantage at risk.

Ⓐ occlude
Ⓑ stipulate
Ⓒ obfuscate
Ⓓ preclude
Ⓔ abjure

2. Refusing to consider criticism, however valid, may lead an individual in a position of power to suffer from one's own _____, leading to decisions that ultimately produce catastrophic results.

Ⓐ miscalculations
Ⓑ ambivalence
Ⓒ perfidy
Ⓓ ineptitude
Ⓔ hubris

3. Many observers of the trial believed that the judge's (i) _____ of the prosecutor for misconduct, after which the prosecutor appeared despondent, ultimately led to the defendant's (ii) _____.

Blank (i)	Blank (ii)
Ⓐ adjudication	Ⓓ conviction
Ⓑ excoriation	Ⓔ deposition
Ⓒ exoneration	Ⓕ exoneration

4. The report, (i) _____ from the company's own internal documents, revealed that its network was in fact not (ii) _____.

Blank (i)	Blank (ii)
Ⓐ coerced	Ⓓ vulnerable
Ⓑ gleaned	Ⓔ implacable
Ⓒ redacted	Ⓕ impregnable

GO ON TO NEXT PAGE

5. A (i) _____ democracy must be built on certain (ii) _____ in order to survive. Giving the populace the right to vote without establishing the rule of law makes a young democracy (iii) _____ to devolving into a dictatorship.

Blank (i)	Blank (ii)	Blank (iii)
ⓐ well-established	ⓓ precepts	ⓖ dedicated
ⓑ nascent	ⓔ criteria	ⓗ resolute
ⓒ representative	ⓕ precedents	ⓘ prone

6. A curved mirror produces an optical (i) _____ — a (ii) _____ in the appearance of the object it reflects. While looking in such a mirror may amuse some, others may find it (iii) _____.

Blank (i)	Blank (ii)	Blank (iii)
ⓐ vacillation	ⓓ distortion	ⓖ debilitating
ⓑ aberration	ⓔ divergence	ⓗ humorous
ⓒ translucence	ⓕ detraction	ⓘ discomfiting

Directions: Each of the following passages is followed by questions pertaining to the passage. Read the passage and answer the questions based on information stated or implied in that passage. For each question, select one answer choice unless instructed otherwise.

The following passage is an excerpt from The Role of the Father in Childhood Development, *5th Edition, by Michael E. Lamb, editor (Wiley).*

Whether and how much time fathers spend with their children are questions at the heart of much research conducted over the past three decades. In the mid-1970s a number of investigators sought to describe — often by detailed observation and sometimes also through detailed maternal and paternal reports — the extent of paternal interactions with children (Pleck & Masciadrelli, this volume; Lamb & Lewis, this volume). Many of these researchers have framed their research around the three types of paternal involvement (engagement, accessibility, responsibility) described by Lamb, Pleck, Charnov, and Levine (1987). As Pleck and Masciadrelli note, researchers have consistently shown that fathers spend much less time with their children than do mothers. In two-parent families in which mothers are unemployed, fathers spend about one-fourth as much time as mothers in direct interaction or engagement with their children, and about a third as much time being accessible to their children. Many fathers assume essentially no responsibility (as defined by participation in key decisions, availability at short notice, involvement in the care of sick children, management and selection of alternative child care, etc.) for their children's care or rearing, however, and the small subgroup of fathers who assume high degrees of responsibility has not been studied extensively. Average levels of paternal responsibility have increased over time, albeit slowly, and there appear to be small but continuing increases over time in average levels of all types of parental involvement.

7. Which sentence most clearly summarizes the research supporting the primary conclusion stated in this article?

   Ⓐ Whether and how much time fathers spend with their children are questions at the heart of much research conducted over the past three decades.

   Ⓑ Many of these researchers have framed their research around the three types of paternal involvement (engagement, accessibility, responsibility) described by Lamb, Pleck, Charnov, and Levine (1987).

Ⓒ As Pleck and Masciadrelli note, researchers have consistently shown that fathers spend much less time with their children than do mothers.

Ⓓ In two-parent families in which mothers are unemployed, fathers spend about one-fourth as much time as mothers in direct interaction or engagement with their children, and about a third as much time being accessible to their children.

Ⓔ Average levels of paternal responsibility have increased over time, albeit slowly, and there appear to be small but continuing increases over time in average levels of all types of parental involvement.

For Questions 8, 9, and 10, consider each answer choice separately and select all answer choices that are correct.

8. As defined in the paragraph, which of the following would not constitute "paternal responsibility"?

   Ⓐ Taking care of a child who is ill

   Ⓑ Reading to a child

   Ⓒ Choosing a childcare provider

   Ⓓ Providing food, clothing, and housing for a child

   Ⓔ Playing a game with a child

9. Data from which of the following were not included in the research?

   Ⓐ Single-parent families

   Ⓑ Two-parent families in which the fathers are unemployed

   Ⓒ Two-parent families in which the mothers are unemployed

10. Which of the following did researchers use as a measure of paternal involvement or responsibility?

   Ⓐ Engagement, accessibility, and the care of sick children

   Ⓑ Accessibility, responsibility, and financial support

   Ⓒ Engagement and availability at short notice

GO ON TO NEXT PAGE ➤

The following passage is an excerpt from World Literature in Theory *by David Damrosch, editor (Wiley-Blackwell).*

What are we to make of world literature today? The cultural and political realignments of the past two decades have opened the field of world literature to an unprecedented, even <u>vertiginous</u> variety of authors and countries. At once exhilarating and unsettling, the range and variety of literatures now in view raise serious questions of scale, of translation and comprehension, and of persisting imbalances of economic and cultural power. At the same time, the shifting landscape of world literature offers new opportunities for readers to encounter writers located well beyond the select few western European countries whose works long dominated worldwide attention. Whereas in past eras works usually spread from imperial centers to peripheral regions (from China to Vietnam, from London to Australia and Kenya, from Paris to almost everywhere), an increasingly multipolar literary landscape allows writers from smaller countries to achieve rapid worldwide fame. While still in his fifties, Orhan Pamuk became the second-youngest recipient of the Nobel Prize for Literature and was translated into 56 languages, Vietnamese included; he has many more readers abroad than in his native Turkey. Increasingly complex patterns of travel, emigration, and publication make "national" languages and literatures more and more international in character. The winner of the Nobel Prize in 2000, Gao Xingjian, has long lived in France and has become a French citizen, yet he continues to write in Chinese. Cultural hybridity is also found within the borders of China itself, as in the stories of the Sino-Tibetan writer Tashi Dawa, who has blended elements drawn from Tibetan folklore and international magical realism for his writings in Chinese; in a very real sense, his works were participating in world literature even before they began to be translated and read abroad.

11. In the context in which it appears, "vertiginous" most nearly means

   Ⓐ Conceivable

   Ⓑ Plausible

   Ⓒ Dizzying

   Ⓓ Enlightening

   Ⓔ Edifying

For Question 12, consider each answer choice separately and select all answer choices that are correct.

12. Which of the following is/are given as example(s) of cross-cultural influence in literature?

   Ⓐ Distributing literary works from London to Kenya

   Ⓑ A French citizen writing in Chinese

   Ⓒ Blending magical realism with Tibetan folklore

The following passage is an excerpt from Sensory Evaluation: A Practical Handbook *by Susan Kemp, Tracey Hollowood, and Joanne Hort (Wiley-Blackwell).*

<u>Volatile</u> molecules are sensed by olfactory receptors on the millions of hair-like cilia that cover the nasal epithelium (located in the roof of the nasal cavity). Consequently, for something to have an odour or aroma, volatile molecules must be transported in air to the nose. Volatile molecules enter the nose orthonasally during breathing/sniffing, or retronasally via the back of the throat during eating. There are around 17,000 different volatile compounds. A particular odour may be made up of several volatile compounds, but sometimes particular volatiles (character-impact compounds) can be associated with a particular smell, e.g., iso-amyl acetate and banana/pear drops. Individuals may perceive and/or describe single compounds differently, e.g., hexenol can be described as grass, green, unripe. Similarly, an odour quality may be perceived and/or described in different compounds, e.g., minty is used to describe both menthol and carvone.

13. Which of the following is not mentioned as a reason that associating an odor with a specific volatile compound may be difficult?

   Ⓐ Several volatiles may contribute to producing a specific odor.

   Ⓑ People may perceive the odor of compounds differently.

   Ⓒ A character-impact compound can be associated with a particular smell.

   Ⓓ The odors of different compounds may be perceived or described as having the same quality.

   Ⓔ People may describe the odor of compounds differently.

14. In the context in which it appears, "volatile" most nearly means

Ⓐ Explosive

Ⓑ Evaporating rapidly

Ⓒ Fleeting; transient

Ⓓ Fluctuating rapidly

Ⓔ Changeable

Typical silt loam soil is comprised of approximately 50 percent soil particles, 25 percent water, and 25 percent air. **Heavy farm equipment compacts the soil, significantly reducing the amount of air and water it can store and inhibiting the movement of air and water through the soil.** Soil compaction reduces crop yields in several ways. It impedes root penetration, reduces the amount of beneficial bacteria and fungi in the soil, increases the potential for runoff and soil erosion, reduces nutrient uptake, and stunts plant growth. To reduce soil compaction, **farmers are advised to avoid trafficking on wet soil, avoid using oversized equipment, reduce axle loads, limit tilling, and increase the soil's organic matter content.**

15. In this passage, the bolded portions play which of the following roles?

Ⓐ The first states a conclusion; the second provides evidence to support that conclusion.

Ⓑ The first states a problem, the effects of which are detailed in the second.

Ⓒ The first states a conclusion that the second provides evidence to oppose.

Ⓓ The first serves as an intermediate conclusion that supports a further conclusion stated in the second.

Ⓔ The first offers a supposition that is countered by the guidance in the second.

Since 1985, California's lottery has contributed more than $24 billion to public schools, including some $19 billion for K–12 schools. In this way, state lotteries increase revenue for education.

16. Which of the following, if true, most seriously undermines the argument?

Ⓐ In states without lotteries, citizens often cross the state line to play the lottery in a neighboring state.

Ⓑ The California Lottery is required to provide at least 34 percent of its revenues to public education.

Ⓒ The South Dakota Lottery has provided more than $1.7 billion to the Property Tax Reduction Fund.

Ⓓ Lottery revenue represents less than 5 percent of the total education budget in states that use lottery revenue for education.

Ⓔ Many states divert lottery dollars from their K–12 education programs to their general funds to make up for shortfalls.

Directions: Each of the following sentences has a blank indicating that a word or phrase is omitted. Choose the two answers that best complete the sentence and result in two sentences most alike in meaning.

17. Though exhausted, the victor remained _____ during his speech.

A vivacious

B lugubrious

C ebullient

D laconic

E mendacious

F disingenuous

GO ON TO NEXT PAGE

18. Con artists have been known to file _____ quitclaim deeds, which transfer ownership of the house from the victim to the perpetrator.

[A] extenuated

[B] inadvertent

[C] counterfeit

[D] exculpated

[E] pilfered

[F] spurious

19. In the United States, to protect young viewers, the Federal Communications Commission (FCC) enforces laws that prohibit the broadcast of certain images and language during certain hours, but it has had no success in restricting content that glorifies _____.

[A] truculence

[B] turpitude

[C] asperity

[D] infidelity

[E] depravity

[F] impertinence

20. The keynote speaker was incredibly _____, exceeding her allotted time by more than 45 minutes.

[A] eloquent

[B] loquacious

[C] voluble

[D] vivacious

[E] voluminous

[F] articulate

Section 2

Quantitative Reasoning

1. Simplify $\left(\sqrt{16}\right)^{\frac{1}{2}}$.

   Ⓐ 1
   Ⓑ 2
   Ⓒ 8
   Ⓓ 16
   Ⓔ 32

   [handwritten: $4^{\frac{1}{2}} = \sqrt{4} = 2$]

2. One bowl contains five hard candies, three of which are grape flavored. Another bowl contains three hard candies, two of which are grape flavored. If the candies all look the same and a child takes one candy from each bowl, what is the probability that the two selected candies are both grape flavored?

   Ⓐ $\frac{1}{5}$
   Ⓑ $\frac{2}{15}$
   Ⓒ $\frac{2}{5}$
   Ⓓ $\frac{4}{15}$
   Ⓔ $\frac{1}{3}$

   [handwritten: $\frac{2}{5} \times \frac{2}{3} = \frac{4}{15}$]

3. If n is the units digit of 5^{50}, what is the value of n?

   [answer box: 5]

   [handwritten: 5^{50} $5 \times 5 = 25$ IDK I vibedit]

4. $\dfrac{\sqrt{27} \times \sqrt{3}}{\sqrt{9}} =$

   [answer box: 3]

   [handwritten: $\frac{\sqrt{27} \times \sqrt{3}}{\sqrt{9}}$ $\frac{\sqrt{3 \cdot 3 \cdot 3} \times \sqrt{3}}{\sqrt{3 \cdot 3}} = \frac{\sqrt{3 \cdot 3 \cdot 3 \cdot 3}}{\sqrt{3 \cdot 3}}$ $\sqrt{3 \cdot 3}$]

Directions: For Questions 5–11, choose from the following answers:

Ⓐ Quantity A is greater.

Ⓑ Quantity B is greater.

Ⓒ The two quantities are equal.

Ⓓ The relationship cannot be determined from the information given.

5. A cart carries five parcels weighing 3 pounds each and ten parcels weighing 9 pounds each.

Quantity A	**Quantity B**
The average parcel weight	8 pounds

   [handwritten: $(3 \times 5) + (10 \times 9)$ 15]

6.

Quantity A	**Quantity B**
$\dfrac{9.99^{10}}{9.99^{-9}}$	0.1

   [handwritten: FRACTION; $\frac{1}{999}$; $9.99^{-1} = 0.1001001$; $\frac{1}{10}$]

7.

Quantity A	**Quantity B**
$\dfrac{1,000!}{997!}$	999^3

   [handwritten: $1000 \times 999 \times 998$]

8.

Quantity A	Quantity B
$\sqrt{27}$	6

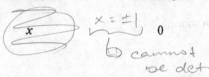

9. $(x-1)(x+1)=0$

Quantity A	Quantity B
x	0

$x = \pm 1$

cannot be det.

10.

© John Wiley & Sons, Inc.

The circle shown has a radius of 5. Angle CAB originates at the center of the circle and measures 36°.

Quantity A	Quantity B
The length of minor arc BC	π

sames

$36 = \frac{1}{10}$ circle

circum = 10π

11.

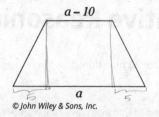

© John Wiley & Sons, Inc.

The trapezoid shown has an area of $(a-5)^2$.

Quantity A	Quantity B
The height of the trapezoid	$a-5$

$(a-10)h + 5h$
$=$
$(a-5)^2$

$(a-10)h + 5h$

$h((a-10)+5)$

$(a-5)$

$h = (a-5)$

$\Rightarrow$ same

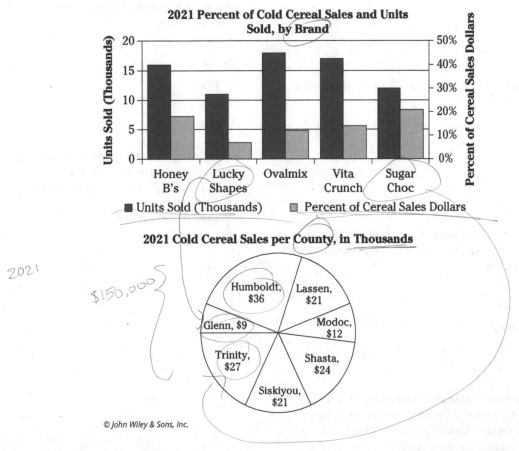

2021 Percent of Cold Cereal Sales and Units Sold, by Brand

2021 Cold Cereal Sales per County, in Thousands

© *John Wiley & Sons, Inc.*

[handwritten: 2021]

[handwritten: $150,000]

12. If the total 2021 cold cereal sales for the seven counties assessed is $150,000, what percent of these sales were purchased by Humboldt County? Disregard the percent symbol when entering your answer.

[handwritten: 36/150]

24	%

13. Which brand of cereal has the highest average selling price per box?

Ⓐ Honey B's

Ⓑ Lucky Shapes

Ⓒ Ovalmix

Ⓓ Vita Crunch

Ⓔ Sugar Choc *(circled)*

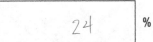

[handwritten: biggest dif. between dark & light bars lots $$ less units]

[handwritten: selling price]

14. If Lucky Shapes are sold primarily in Glenn County, while Sugar Choc is sold primarily in Trinity County, and residents of these counties tend to not purchase other brands, what is the approximate ratio of the price of Lucky Shapes to the price of Sugar Choc?

Ⓐ 5:1

Ⓑ 3:1

Ⓒ 1:1

Ⓓ 1:3 *(circled)*

Ⓔ 1:7

[handwritten: 12k sold $27k tot   11k sold $9k]

GO ON TO NEXT PAGE

15. $\dfrac{2^{17}}{16^4} =$

Handwritten: $16 = 2 \times 2$, (2^4)

$$\boxed{2}$$

16. The sum of $3x$ and $4y$ is 50. If $y = 5$, what is the value of x?

Ⓐ 5

Ⓑ 10 *(circled)*

Ⓒ 12

Ⓓ 15

Ⓔ 18

Handwritten: $3x + 4y = 50$, 20

17. If n is a positive integer, which of the following represents the product of n and the integer following n?

Ⓐ $n^2 + 1$

Ⓑ $n^2 + 2$

Ⓒ $(n+1)^2$

Ⓓ $n^2 + n$ *(circled)*

Ⓔ $2n^2$

Handwritten: $n > 0$, $n(n+1) = n^2 + n$

18. If a boy on a snow sled travels downhill at a constant rate of 25 kilometers per hour, how many meters does he travel in 18 seconds? (1 kilometer = 1,000 meters)

Ⓐ 5

Ⓑ 18

Ⓒ 25

Ⓓ 75

Ⓔ 125 *(circled)*

Handwritten: 25 km/h
$\dfrac{25 \text{ km}}{1 \text{ hr}} \cdot \dfrac{1000 \text{ m}}{\text{km}} \cdot \left(\dfrac{1 \text{ hr}}{60 \text{ m}} \cdot \dfrac{1 \text{ m}}{60 \text{ s}} \right) \dots \left(\dfrac{60 \text{ m}}{1 \text{ hr}} \cdot \dfrac{60 \text{ s}}{1 \text{ min}} \right) \times 18$
faster?

19. If 10 liters of a 6 percent saline solution are mixed with 5 liters of a 9 percent saline solution, what is the resulting percent of saline concentration?

Ⓐ 3%

Ⓑ 5%

Ⓒ 7% *(circled)*

Ⓓ 12% *(scribbled out)*

Ⓔ 15% *(scribbled out)*

Handwritten: 10 L 6% s, 5 L 9% s
$\dfrac{0.06}{10} \times \dfrac{0.09}{5}$, $\dfrac{.3}{50} + \dfrac{.9}{50} = $
15 tot, $\dfrac{0.6}{10} + \dfrac{0.45}{5}$, $\dfrac{3}{50} + \dfrac{4.5}{50} = \dfrac{7.5}{50}$

20. For all integers a and b, where $b > a > 0$, if $a \odot b = (ab)^2$ and $a \odot b < 100$, then which of the following could be the value of a?

Indicate all such values.

Ⓐ 1 *(circled)*

Ⓑ 2

Ⓒ 3

Ⓓ 4

Ⓔ 5

Ⓕ 6

Handwritten: $b > a > 0$, $a \odot b = (ab)^2$, < 100

Section 3

Verbal Reasoning

TIME: 30 minutes for 20 questions

DIRECTIONS: Choose the best answer to each question. Blacken the corresponding ovals or boxes on the answer sheet.

Directions: For Questions 1–7, choose the one entry best suited for each blank from its corresponding column of choices.

1. With many new models and falling prices, the electric car is likely to replace the hybrid vehicle as the _____ model of choice for conservation-minded commuters.

   Ⓐ inaccessible

   Ⓑ indispensable

   Ⓒ ubiquitous

   Ⓓ scarce

   Ⓔ salubrious

2. Following the presentation, the _____ lecturer left the room without asking whether anyone had questions.

   Ⓐ taciturn

   Ⓑ effusive

   Ⓒ indignant

   Ⓓ despondent

   Ⓔ malevolent

3. To some degree, epigenetics (i) _____ the Darwinian notion that gene mutations and natural selection alone drive evolution, as research shows that an organism's genes are affected by environmental factors and not (ii) _____ as Darwin claimed.

Blank (i)	Blank (ii)
Ⓐ obviates	Ⓓ imperturbable
Ⓑ expatiates	Ⓔ immutable
Ⓒ repudiates	Ⓕ inimitable

4. Accountants and other financial experts are known to be (i) _____, except when it comes to investing, when these individuals are often (ii) _____.

Blank (i)	Blank (ii)
Ⓐ dissident	Ⓓ audacious
Ⓑ prudent	Ⓔ pusillanimous
Ⓒ confident	Ⓕ aloof

GO ON TO NEXT PAGE

5. Given the (i) _____ of livestock and the (ii) _____ of corn, the farmers decided to market their corn for biofuel production instead of using it as feed.

Blank (i)	Blank (ii)
Ⓐ plethora	Ⓓ dearth
Ⓑ paucity	Ⓔ scarcity
Ⓒ overabundance	Ⓕ surfeit

6. The (i) _____ nature of the situation required that the CEO consult her most (ii) _____ advisors. After considering their advice, the CEO was able to make (iii) _____ decisions that greatly improved her company's market share.

Blank (i)	Blank (ii)	Blank (iii)
Ⓐ delicate	Ⓓ conscientious	Ⓖ sagacious
Ⓑ sensitive	Ⓔ confidential	Ⓗ salacious
Ⓒ involute	Ⓕ trenchant	Ⓘ sententious

7. Some teachers (i) _____ charter schools, claiming that the schools have an unfair advantage. (ii) _____ by Department of Education policies and state laws that govern education, charter schools can set very selective admissions standards and (iii) _____ their own policies, while traditional public schools cannot.

Blank (i)	Blank (ii)	Blank (iii)
Ⓐ extoll	Ⓓ Unencumbered	Ⓖ disallow
Ⓑ advocate	Ⓔ Hampered	Ⓗ forge
Ⓒ deprecate	Ⓕ Constrained	Ⓘ correlate

The following passage is an excerpt from Electricity from Wave and Tide: An Introduction, *by Paul A. Lynn (Wiley).*

In his famous book *Small Is Beautiful,* first published in 1973, E. F. Schumacher poured scorn on the idea that the problems of production in the industrialised world had been solved. Modern society, he claimed, does not experience itself as part of nature, but as an outside force seeking to dominate and conquer it. And it is the illusion of unlimited powers deriving from the undoubted successes of much of modern technology that is the root cause of our present difficulties, in particular because we are failing to distinguish between capital and income components of the earth's resources. We use up capital, including coal, oil, and gas reserves, as if they were steady and sustainable income, but they are actually once-and-only capital. Schumacher's heartfelt plea encouraged us to start basing industrial and energy policy on what we now call sustainability, recognising the distinction between capital and income and the paramount need to respect the planet's finite ability to absorb the polluting products of industrial processes — including electricity production.

Schumacher's message, once ignored or derided by the majority, is now seen as mainstream. For the good of Planet Earth and future generations, we have started to distinguish between capital and income and to invest heavily in renewable technologies that produce electricity free of carbon emissions.

8. Which of the following energy sources would Schumacher likely classify as income?

Ⓐ Heating oil

Ⓑ Hydroelectricity

Ⓒ Natural gas

Ⓓ Uranium

Ⓔ Coal

For Question 9, consider each answer choice separately and select all answer choices that are correct.

9. Which of the following notions are mentioned in this passage as being disparaged?

A Schumacher's message

B Modern society's attempt to dominate and conquer nature

C The assumption that production problems in the industrial world had been solved

10. Select the sentence that indicates the specific human activity described in the article.

Ⓐ In his famous book *Small Is Beautiful,* first published in 1973, E. F. Schumacher poured scorn on the idea that the problems of production in the industrialised world had been solved.

Ⓑ Modern society, he claimed, does not experience itself as part of nature, but as an outside force seeking to dominate and conquer it.

Ⓒ We use up capital, including coal, oil, and gas reserves, as if they were steady and sustainable income, but they are actually once-and-only capital.

Ⓓ Schumacher's heartfelt plea encouraged us to start basing industrial and energy policy on what we now call sustainability, recognising the distinction between capital and income and the paramount need to respect the planet's finite ability to absorb the polluting products of industrial processes — including electricity production.

Ⓔ For the good of Planet Earth and future generations, we have started to distinguish between capital and income and to invest heavily in renewable technologies that produce electricity free of carbon emissions.

GO ON TO NEXT PAGE ➡

The following passage is an excerpt from Leverage: How Cheap Money Will Destroy the World, *by Karl Denninger (Wiley).*

The economic crisis that gripped the nation in 2007 was not an accident, and the people responsible not only saw it coming but also knew the crisis would occur. It was inevitable and created by unsound policies at all levels of government and finance. The latest economic upheaval is nothing more than another in a long series of economic catastrophes that stem from fundamental failures to recognize and act on the mathematical realities of finance and rein in abuses of leverage promulgated by the rich and powerful in our society.

None of these issues has been addressed. Dodd-Frank, the recent financial reform law, does not force price transparency on derivatives and contains enough loopholes to drive a Mack truck through. The 2008 emergency bill, EESA/TARP, passed in no small part due to threats of financial Armageddon by both Ben Bernanke of the Federal Reserve and Hank Paulson of Treasury, in fact contained a Trojan horse provision that removed the legal requirement for all bank reserves, allowing banks to create infinite leverage. We have failed to force recognition of losses by the banking industry and have protected various firms from the consequences of their bad lending decisions. By failing to force banks to lend only in a safe and sound manner and to back up their unsecured lending with actual capital, we continue to perpetuate the myth that we can forevermore say "Charge it" and never pay off the debt we accumulate.

All of these acts have served to hold systemic debt at unsustainable levels rather than allow it to default. As a consequence, our economy remains moribund and employment anemic, despite claimed improvement.

11. Which of the following statements most accurately summarizes the main point of this passage?

   Ⓐ Accumulated debt must eventually be paid off.

   Ⓑ Establishing and enforcing sound financial policies is essential for a strong economy.

   Ⓒ Economic crises are caused by rich and powerful people who abuse their financial leverage.

   Ⓓ Legislation designed to rein in abuses in the financial markets is full of loopholes.

   Ⓔ Corrupt politicians protect banks from making bad lending decisions.

12. In the context in which it appears, "moribund" most nearly means

   Ⓐ robust

   Ⓑ extinct

   Ⓒ stout

   Ⓓ stagnant

   Ⓔ dead

For Question 13, consider each answer choice separately and select all answer choices that are correct.

13. According to the passage, which of the following issues that contributed to the economic crisis of 2007 has/have not been addressed?

   Ａ Banks forced to back up unsecured loans with capital

   Ｂ Price transparency on derivatives

   Ｃ Moribund economy and anemic employment

The following passage is an excerpt from The Prosperity Agenda: What the World Wants from America — and What We Need in Return, *by Nancy Soderberg (Wiley).*

A crucial reason fewer people in the world trust the United States is that countries do not see America helping them with their interests and addressing common threats. In 2007, citizens around the globe cited crime, political corruption, drugs, infectious disease, and pollution as their top national concerns. Terrorism, the poor quality of drinking water, and conflict were also high on the list. Unless America is seen to be helping with these issues, the world will not help America.

American leaders tend to center U.S. foreign policy entirely on "hard power" security issues such as nuclear proliferation and terrorism (and, in all honesty, oil). This is an incomplete approach because much good can be done to benefit our own interests while helping other countries with a global campaign against crime, infectious diseases, and dirty water. The world will not follow the United States unless it is seen to be helping the world address its challenges.

In today's dangerous world, the United States must again become the world's great persuader, not only the enforcer. To do so, America must act in a way that regains the world's trust. The good news is that if it does so, America can quickly regain the political support it has lost around the world.

When America does the right thing, the world notices. For instance, favorable opinions of America in southeast Asia reached record lows during the first year after the United States started the Iraq War. Yet that image began to rebound when America used its military and economic power to help the victims of the 2004 tsunami, which set off tidal waves that wiped out communities across the coastal areas of Indonesia, Thailand, Sri Lanka, India, Malaysia, and parts of Africa. America took the lead in providing military and logistical support, including $350 million in immediate humanitarian relief assistance. (For comparison, the United States spends twice that much money every day in Iraq.)

14. Which of the following statements most accurately summarizes this passage?

Ⓐ Humanitarian aid is more effective than military might in helping foreign countries.

Ⓑ The United States must use its military and economic power for good, not evil.

Ⓒ Foreign countries do not see America helping them address common threats.

Ⓓ U.S. foreign policy should focus on stopping nuclear proliferation and terrorism.

Ⓔ The United States can expand its influence in the world by building trust.

15. Which of these statements, if true, describes an event that was overlooked and does not factor into global citizens' unfavorable view of the United States?

Ⓐ The President's Malaria Initiative (PMI) works in 19 countries in sub-Saharan Africa and the Greater Mekong Subregion in Asia to fight malaria.

Ⓑ The U.S. launched the Global Health Initiative in 2009 to address global health challenges that threaten lives at home and abroad.

Ⓒ In the Iraq War, the U.S. removed from power Saddam Hussein, the president of Iraq who skimmed billions of dollars from the United Nation's oil-for-food program.

Ⓓ Secret documents prove that the U.S. National Security Agency has spied on its own allies, including Israel, France, and Germany.

Ⓔ USAid spent more than $270 million on projects in Haiti in 2013, but half that amount went to U.S. companies, and a third went to American nonprofits.

What are the costs to society of treating mental illness? Perhaps the better question is: What are the costs to society of *not* treating mental illness? Failure to treat mental illness often leads to job loss, homelessness, and sometimes even incarceration. Prisoners with mental illness cost the nation on average nearly $9 billion annually. By diagnosing and treating people with mental illness, state, federal, and local governments can actually save money while helping to preserve the dignity of the person with mental illness.

16. Select the sentence that offers evidence to support an answer to a question in the passage.

Ⓐ What are the costs to society of treating mental illness?

Ⓑ Perhaps the better question is what are the costs to society of *not* treating mental illness?

Ⓒ Failure to treat mental illness often leads to job loss, homelessness, and sometimes even incarceration.

Ⓓ Prisoners with mental illness cost the nation on average nearly $9 billion annually.

Ⓔ By diagnosing and treating people with mental illness, state, federal, and local governments can actually save money while helping to preserve the dignity of the person with mental illness.

Directions: Each of the following sentences has a blank indicating that a word or phrase is omitted. Choose the two answers that best complete the sentence and result in two sentences most alike in meaning.

17. Members of both parties encouraged their constituents to _____ violence on the grounds that it would be counterproductive.

Ⓐ embrace

Ⓑ avoid

Ⓒ appropriate

Ⓓ incite

Ⓔ eschew

Ⓕ denounce

GO ON TO NEXT PAGE ➡

18. One of Nikola Tesla's many _____ is that he calculated the cubic volume of each meal before eating it.

- [A] endowments
- [B] passions
- [C] quirks
- [D] idiosyncrasies
- [E] assimilations
- [F] obsessions

19. Choosing a career is _____ to a course of study, as medicine requires a basis of science and math, while law requires one of the humanities.

- [A] inconsequential
- [B] paramount
- [C] trivial
- [D] marginal
- [E] pivotal
- [F] urgent

Read the passage and answer the question based on information stated or implied in the passage.

The following passage is an excerpt from The Human Impact on the Natural Environment: Past, Present, and Future, *by Andrew S. Goudie (Wiley-Blackwell).*

A distinction can be drawn between cultivation and domestication. Whereas cultivation involves deliberate sowing or other management, and entails plants which do not necessarily differ genetically from wild populations of the same species, domestication results in genetic change brought about through conscious or unconscious human selection. This creates plants that differ morphologically from their wild relatives and which may be dependent on humans for their survival. Domesticated plants are thus necessarily cultivated plants, but cultivated plants may or may not be domesticated. For example, the first plantations of *Hevea* rubber and quinine in the Far East were established from seed which had been collected from the wild in South America. Thus at this stage in their history these crops were cultivated but not yet domesticated.

20. Based on the definition of "domestication" given in this passage, which of the following is not an example of domestication?

- Ⓐ Genetically modified corn
- Ⓑ Farm-raised catfish
- Ⓒ Hybrid crops
- Ⓓ Purebred dogs
- Ⓔ Seedless watermelon

DO NOT TURN THE PAGE UNTIL TOLD TO DO SO **STOP** DO NOT RETURN TO A PREVIOUS TEST

Section 4

Quantitative Reasoning

TIME: 35 minutes for 20 questions

NOTES:

- All numbers used in this exam are real numbers.
- All figures lie in a plane.
- Angle measures are positive; points and angles are in the position shown.

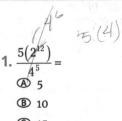

1. $\dfrac{5(2^{12})}{4^5} =$

   (A) 5

   (B) 10

   (C) 15

   (D) 20

   (E) 25

2. If y is an integer and $\sqrt{48y}$ is an integer, which of the following is the lowest possible value of y?

   (A) 1

   (B) 2

   (C) 3

   (D) 4

   (E) 6

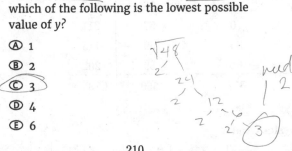

3. If n is an integer and $\dfrac{210}{n}$ is an integer, which of the following could be the value of n?

   Indicate all such values.

   ☑ A 6

   ☐ B 12

   ☑ C 14

   ☑ D 35

   ☑ E 42

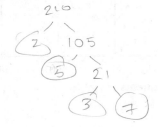

Directions: For Questions 4–10, choose from the following answers:

(A) *Quantity A is greater.*

(B) *Quantity B is greater.*

(C) *The two quantities are equal.*

(D) *The relationship cannot be determined from the information given.*

4. Fifteen candies are to be divided up among six children so that each child receives at least two candies.

Quantity A	*Quantity B*
The probability that any child receives six candies	0

5. Davis travels at a constant speed of 40 miles per hour for two hours and then at a constant speed of 60 miles per hour for one hour.

Quantity A	*Quantity B*
Davis's average speed for the entire trip	45 miles per hour

6.

Quantity A	*Quantity B*
900	$\sqrt{(30)(30)(30)(30)}$

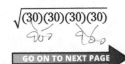

7. $f(x) = x^2 + 2x - 2$

Quantity A	Quantity B
The value of x when $f(x) = 13$	3

Unknown?

3 or 5 →

$13 = x^2 + 2x - 2$
$\Rightarrow 0 = x^2 + 2x - 15$

8.

Quantity A	Quantity B
$(0.99)^{99}$	1

9.

Quantity A	Quantity B
$5!$	$\dfrac{6!}{3!}$

$1 \times 2 \times 3 \times 4 \times 5$ $4 \times 5 \times 6$
6

10. A right circular cylinder has a volume of 36π.

Quantity A	Quantity B
The sum of the radius and height of the cylinder if the radius and height are both integers greater than 1	12

$r + h = ?$

36π
$\pi r^2 h$

Questions 11–13 are based on the following graphs.

Physics Grades and Enrollments of Middle School Students in the Fraser School District Enrollment

Subdistrict	6th Grade	7th Grade	8th Grade	Totals
Aguilar	83	99	89	271
Bayfield	107	103	96	306
Creede	74	70	67	211
De Beque	40	36	39	115
Eaton	69	64	69	202
Totals	373	372	360	1,105

$\dfrac{450}{1105}$

211 earn As
of 894,
~450 earn bs
~50%

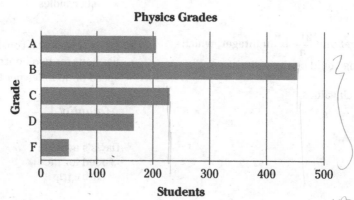

Physics Grades

© John Wiley & Sons, Inc.

$225, 450$
$2\frac{1}{4}$ $4\frac{2}{4}$
$\frac{9}{4}$ $\frac{18}{4}$

11. What is the approximate ratio of students earning a C to those earning a B?

(A) 1:2

(B) 2:1

(C) 3:2

(D) 4:3

(E) 1:1

12. If all the students from Creede, and only those students, are earning A's and the rest of the grades are evenly distributed among students in the other subdistricts, approximately how many students from Bayfield are earning B's?

(A) 50

(B) 75

(C) 150

(D) 225

(E) 306

13. If all the grades are evenly distributed throughout all districts and classes, approximately how many students in De Beque are *not* earning a B?

(A) 20

(B) 40

(C) 70

(D) 100

(E) 115

~2/3 not

Bs

14. If the range of set S is 9 and $S = \{2, 4, 5, 7, 8, 9, x\}$, which of the following *could* be the median of set S?

Indicate all possible answers.

[A] 5 ← x could be 0

google

[B] 6

[C] 7

15. $\left(\dfrac{1}{8} - \dfrac{3}{10}\right) + \left(\dfrac{1}{4} - \dfrac{1}{5}\right) + \left(\dfrac{5}{8} - \dfrac{1}{2}\right) =$

16. $\sqrt{9(36) + 12(36) + 15(36)} =$

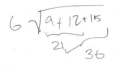

36

17. Given the inequality $x^2 < 25$, which of the following *could* be the value of x?

Indicate *all* such values.

$x < \pm 51$

[A] −6

[B] −5

[C] −3

[D] 0

[E] 3

[F] 5

18.

© John Wiley & Sons, Inc.

$r = 1$

area $= \pi$

$\pi - 2$

The square is inscribed within the circle and has a side length of $\sqrt{2}$. What is the area of the shaded portion of the drawing?

(A) $2 - \pi$

(B) $\pi - 2$

(C) $\pi - \sqrt{2}$

(D) $\pi - 4$

(E) $4 - \pi$

GO ON TO NEXT PAGE

19.

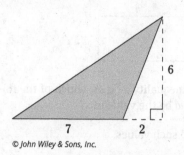

© John Wiley & Sons, Inc.

The area of the shaded triangle is

21

$\frac{1}{2}(9*6)$

54

27

21 } MINUS 6

20. If Clarissa's monthly mortgage payment is less than $\frac{1}{3}$ but more than $\frac{1}{4}$ of her monthly income, and if the monthly mortgage payment is $600, which of the following could not be her ⟨annual⟩ income?

Indicate all such values.

- A. $12,200
- B. $17,400
- C. $21,000
- D. $24,200
- E. $29,000
- F. $31,300

$\frac{1}{4} < \$600 < \frac{1}{3}$

$4 * 600 = 2400 \rightarrow 28800$

$3 * 600 = 1800 \rightarrow 21600$

Chapter 19

Practice Exam 1: Answers and Explanations

After taking Practice Exam 1 in Chapter 18, use this chapter to check your answers and see how you did. Carefully review the explanations because doing so can help you understand why you missed the questions you did and also give you a better understanding of the thought process that helped you select the correct answers. If you're in a hurry, flip to the end of the chapter for an abbreviated answer key.

Analytical Writing Sections

Have a friend or tutor read your essays: Refer that helpful person to Chapters 16 and 17 for scoring guidelines, and if the essays are clear, persuasive, and grammatically sound, you probably got it.

Section 1: Verbal Reasoning

1. **C.** Corporate leaders would try to *obfuscate* (conceal) their intentions in order to maintain a competitive advantage. *Occlude* makes a good runner-up, but it carries a meaning more along the lines of blocking off access to something. None of the other three choices is close: *Stipulate* means to demand something specific, *preclude* means to prevent or prohibit, and *abjure* means to avoid or reject.

2. **E.** *Hubris* is excessive pride or self-confidence, which is often characterized by a refusal to consider any criticism, as expressed in the opening phrase of the sentence. If it weren't for that qualifier, any of the other answer choices would work: *Miscalculations* can undermine a leader's plans, *ambivalence* is uncertainty or indecisiveness, *perfidy* is treachery, and *ineptitude* is incompetence.

3. **B, F.** The judge must have *excoriated* (severely criticized) the prosecutor in order for the prosecutor to be despondent, and that despondency likely led to the defendant's *exoneration* (acquittal) because the despondent prosecutor would be less effective. Otherwise, you could make a case for *exoneration* for the first blank and *conviction* for the second. *Adjudication* (a court order) is a legal term, but a judge doesn't adjudicate a person, and a *deposition* is done by a witness, not a defendant.

4. **B, F.** The report would have been *gleaned* (gathered) from internal documents, not *coerced* (gotten by force) or *redacted* (put into a suitable literary form). A company network is typically secure; the transition *in fact* tells you that's not the case here. Therefore, the network wasn't *impregnable* (able to withstand attack). *Vulnerable* would imply that security was stronger than IT thought. *Implacable* means unable to be satisfied or appeased.

5. **B, D, I.** The second sentence references a democracy in early development, so it must be a *nascent* (emerging) democracy that would need to be built on certain *precepts* (principles or guidelines) in order to be strong. Otherwise, the government would be *prone* (disposed to) to devolving into a dictatorship.

   For the first blank, you can rule out *well-established,* which is the opposite of *nascent,* and *representative,* which is just a type of democracy (direct or representative). For the second blank, both *criteria* and *precedents* would be good second choices, but because the second sentence mentions the right to vote and the rule of law, *precepts* is more accurate. *Criteria* also refers to qualifications, which doesn't fit. For the third blank, you can rule out *dedicated* because no democracy dedicates itself to becoming a dictatorship. You can rule out *resolute* (determined) for much the same reason.

6. **B, D, I.** The reflection in a curved mirror would be an *aberration* (an abnormality), not a *vacillation* (wavering) or *translucence* (semi-transparency), so the reflection in the mirror would be a *distortion* (misrepresentation). For the second blank, *divergence* (deviation or departure) would be a good second choice, but *distortion* is more precise. *Detraction* (disparagement or denigration) doesn't work. Some people find such a distorted reflection of themselves *discomfiting* (unsettling). *Debilitating* (incapacitating) is too strong a word, and *humorous* doesn't work because the last sentence is structured in a way that the missing word must be nearly the opposite of *amusing.*

7. **C.** You may be tempted to select the last sentence because it presents a summary of the data, but the main conclusion in this passage is that fathers spend considerably less time with their children than do mothers.

8. **B, D, E.** The paragraph defines paternal responsibility as "participation in key decisions, availability at short notice, involvement in the care of sick children, management and selection of alternative child care." Choice (D), food, clothing, and housing, may be considered "key decisions" as a stretch; Choice (B), reading, and Choice (E), playing a game, may be considered involvement, but the other choices clearly fall under the paragraph's definition of paternal responsibility.

9. **A, B.** The passage focuses on two-parent families in which mothers are unemployed and only mentions "the small subgroup of fathers who assume high degrees of responsibility." It doesn't provide data related to single-parent families or two-parent families in which the father stays home with the children.

10. **A, C.** Researchers did not include financial support as a measure of parental responsibility, so you can rule out answer Choice (B). Engagement, accessibility, availability at short notice, and the care of sick children are all mentioned as measures of parental responsibility.

11. **C.** *Vertiginous* means spinning, whirling — movement that would cause someone to become dizzy. Because this passage describes the variety of literature as overwhelming, in both positive and negative ways, the variety of authors and countries is considered vertiginous. You can immediately rule out the first two options, which both mean something along the lines of believable. Although literature may be *enlightening* (informative) and *edifying* (intellectually enriching), the *variety* of authors and countries would probably not be considered enlightening or edifying in this context.

12. **B, C.** Gao Xingjian is mentioned as a French citizen who continues to write in Chinese, while Tashi Dawa blends elements drawn from Tibetan folklore and international magical realism for his writings in Chinese. This question is a little tricky because cultural hybridity isn't mentioned until the second example of it is presented. Choice (A) is wrong because in this passage, *cultural hybridity* refers to the blending of cultures within a literary work, not the exchange of literary works between countries or cultures, although such exchanges no doubt promote cultural hybridity in literature.

13. **C.** The fact that a character-impact compound can be associated with a particular smell would help, not hinder, the ability to associate an odor with a specific volatile compound.

14. **B.** All the answer choices are definitions of *volatile*, but because the passage discusses molecules being distributed through the air, *evaporating rapidly* is the most accurate meaning.

15. **D.** The first bolded portion states the conclusion that heavy farm equipment compacts the soil, and the second bolded portion concludes that farmers must employ various strategies to reduce soil compaction. You can rule out Choice (A) because although the first states a conclusion, the second doesn't provide supporting evidence. Rule out Choice (B) because although the first states a problem, the second describes a possible solution to the problem, not the effects of that problem. Rule out Choices (C) and (E) because the second bolded portion doesn't oppose or counter the first.

16. **E.** This argument assumes that other states operate the same way as California. Choice (E) says, however, that other states divert monies from schools, which means that the lottery money doesn't actually increase revenue for education: Any money coming in from the lottery would be diverted away from education. Choices (A) and (C) are out of scope, while Choice (B) supports the argument, and (D) simply asserts that lottery funding represents a small portion of the total education budget in a state.

17. **A, C.** The victor was exhausted, but the transition *though* tells you that he behaved the opposite during his speech: *vivacious* (energetic) and *ebullient* (enthusiastic). You can easily rule out *lugubrious,* which means sad or gloomy; *laconic,* which means terse or concise; and *mendacious* and *disingenuous,* both meaning dishonest.

18. **C, F.** The deeds described here would be fake — *counterfeit* or *spurious. Extenuated* means severe and explained, as in *extenuating circumstance, inadvertent* means unintentional, and *exculpated* means freed from blame. *Pilfered* means stolen, but there is no other answer choice with a similar meaning, and anyway, filing a stolen deed wouldn't help the con artist transfer ownership of the property — it would have the true owner's name on it.

19. **B, E.** Think of something broadcast that can be harmful to young viewers but cannot be easily regulated. Because *turpitude* and *depravity* both mean immorality, and the passage focuses on indecent programming, these two choices are best. *Truculence* and *impertinence* both imply disrespectful behavior, but in a way that's not particularly harmful to youth. *Asperity,* which means harshness or sternness, has no choice comparable in meaning. Choice (D), *infidelity,* is tempting, but it doesn't have a match in the answer choices.

20. B, C. If the speaker exceeded her allotted time, she must have been *loquacious* or *voluble*, which both imply long-winded. She may have also been *eloquent* and *articulate* (well-spoken), but that wouldn't necessarily cause her to exceed her allotted speaking time. *Vivacious* means lively or energetic, and *voluminous* means large, neither of which has a comparable word in the list of answer choices and neither of which would necessarily cause the keynote speaker to run past her allotted time.

Section 2: Quantitative Reasoning

1. B. Take it step by step. $\sqrt{16}$ becomes 4, and the one-half power is a square root, so $(4)^{\frac{1}{2}} = \sqrt{4} = 2$

2. C. You find the probability of an event (selecting one grape candy from the first bowl) by putting the number of possibilities (three grape candies) over the total number of outcomes (five candies total). Thus, the probability of selecting a grape candy from the first bowl is $\frac{3}{5}$, and the probability of selecting a grape candy from the second bowl is $\frac{2}{3}$. These are independent events, so multiply the probabilities for the probability of *both* happening:

$$\frac{3}{5} \times \frac{2}{3} = \frac{2}{5}$$

3. 5. The *units digit* is the digit in the ones place, just before where the decimal point would be. For example, in the number 123, the units digit is 3. When you're multiplying two whole numbers, the units digits of the multipliers produce the units digit of the product. So when you multiply 12×13, for example, the 2 in 12 times the 3 in 13 produces the 6 in the product, 156.

For this question, 5 times itself any number of times results in a product with a units digit of 5:

$$5 \times 5 = 25$$
$$5 \times 5 \times 5 = 125$$

and so on.

4. 3. First, determine the value at the top of the fraction (the *numerator*): Multiply the $\sqrt{27}$ by the $\sqrt{3}$ for the $\sqrt{81}$, which equals 9. Determining the value at the bottom of the fraction (the *denominator*) is easy, because the square root of 9 is 3. Divide the numerator by the denominator for the correct answer:

$$\frac{9}{\sqrt{9}} = \frac{9}{3} = 3$$

5. B. To determine Quantity A, calculate the average parcel weight by totaling the weight of the parcels and then dividing the total weight by the number of parcels. You can use the following equation for weighted average:

$$\text{Weighted average} = \frac{(5 \times 3) + (10 \times 9)}{5 + 10}$$
$$= \frac{15 + 90}{15}$$
$$= \frac{105}{15}$$
$$= 7$$

Quantity A is 7 pounds, which is 1 pound less than Quantity B's 8 pounds, so Quantity B is greater.

6. **A.** To determine Quantity A, simplify the exponents and the fraction. To simplify each negative exponent, place a 1 on top:

$$\dfrac{\dfrac{1}{9.99^{10}}}{\dfrac{1}{9.99^{9}}}$$

To divide the fractions, flip the bottom fraction and multiply it by the top fraction:

$$\dfrac{1}{9.99^{10}} \times \dfrac{9.99^{9}}{1} = \dfrac{9.99^{9}}{9.99^{10}}$$

Now reduce the exponents. In the same way that $\dfrac{x^9}{x^{10}} = \dfrac{1}{x}$, reduce $\dfrac{9.99^9}{9.99^{10}} = \dfrac{1}{9.99}$.

Simplify the resulting fraction with the on-screen calculator. $\dfrac{1}{9.99}$ is slightly greater than 0.1, so Quantity A is greater.

7. **B.** Simplify the quantities so that Quantity A reads

$1,000 \times 999 \times 998$

and Quantity B reads

$999 \times 999 \times 999$

These products are still too big for the on-screen calculator. To resolve this, eliminate one 999 from each quantity so that Quantity A reads

$1,000 \times 998$

and Quantity B reads

999×999

Using the on-screen calculator, find the respective values as 998,000 and 998,001. You see that Quantity B is greater.

8. **B.** $\sqrt{36}$ equals 6, so $\sqrt{27}$ is less than 6.

9. **D.** Given $(x-1)(x+1)=0$, x equals either 1 or −1. You don't know which one, so you can't determine which quantity is greater based on the information given.

10. **C.** If the angle *CAB* measures 36°, minor arc *BC* also measures 36°, making it one-tenth of the circle:

$$\dfrac{36°}{360°} = \dfrac{1}{10}$$

A circle with a radius of 5 has a circumference of $2\pi r = 2 \times \pi \times 5 = 10\pi$. Multiply this circumference by the fraction of the circle, giving you a minor arc length of $10\pi \times \dfrac{1}{10} = \pi$. Therefore, the two values are equal.

11. **C.** You can find the area of a trapezoid with the formula

$$\left(\frac{b_1 + b_2}{2}\right)h$$

where b_1 represents one base, b_2 represents the other base, and h represents the height. To find the height, set the formula equal to the area and simplify it:

$$\text{Area} = \left(\frac{b_1 + b_2}{2}\right)h$$

$$(a-5)^2 = \left(\frac{a-10+a}{2}\right)h$$

$$(a-5)^2 = \left(\frac{2a-10}{2}\right)h$$

$$(a-5)^2 = (a-5)h$$

$$a-5 = h$$

Therefore, the two quantities are equal.

12. **24.** If total sales are $150,000 and Humboldt County spent $36,000, you can find the percent by placing the Humboldt County sales over the total sales:

$$\frac{36,000}{150,000} = \frac{24}{100} = 24\%$$

You can't type the percent symbol into the answer box. Because the percent symbol is already in place and the question asks for the percent, the correct answer is 24, not 0.24.

13. **E.** You can compare the box prices of each brand by estimating the ratio of sales dollars to units sold. The higher the ratio, the higher the brand's average selling price. Sugar Choc has the highest ratio of dollar sales to units sold, making it the highest-priced brand of cereal.

14. **D.** Though actual numbers aren't provided, you can use the bar graph to approximate the ratios. Because the question asks for an "approximate" answer and the answer choices are far apart, you can eyeball your numbers from the graphs.

Lucky Shapes and Sugar Choc show similar numbers of units sold, but the Lucky Shapes sales number in Glenn County, at $9,000, is about one-third that of Sugar Choc in Trinity County, at $27,000. This means, box for box, the price of Lucky Shapes is approximately one-third that of Sugar Choc, for a ratio of 1:3.

15. **2.** First, convert 16^4 to 2^{16} so the exponents match:

$$16^4 = (16)^4 = (2 \times 2 \times 2 \times 2)^4 = (2^4)^4 = 2^{16}$$

Now that the exponents match, reduce the fraction by subtracting the exponents:

$$\frac{2^{17}}{2^{16}} = 2^1 = 2$$

16. **B.** Set up the equation and substitute 5 for y:

$$3x + 4y = 50$$

$$3x + 4(5) = 50$$

$$3x + 20 = 50$$

$$3x = 30$$

$$x = 10$$

17. **D.** Suppose $n = 9$. You're looking for 9×10, which is the same as $(9 \times 9) + (9 \times 1)$, or $(9 \times 9) + 9$. Substitute n for 9, and you have $(n \times n) + n$, or $n^2 + n$.

18. **E.** You're given the number of kilometers per hour, and you need to determine the number of meters per second, so focus on the units of measurement: 25 kilometers is 25,000 meters, and 1 hour is 60 minutes times 60 seconds, or 3,600 seconds. You know that the sled is traveling 25,000 meters per 3,600 seconds for 18 seconds. Once you set it up, the fractions cancel nicely:

$$\frac{25,000}{3,600} \times 18 = \frac{250}{36} \times 18 = \frac{250}{2} = 125$$

19. **C.** First, identify the unknown. You know that you end up with 15 liters of a solution, but you don't know what its saline concentration is, so you have 15 liters of x.

Ten liters of 6 percent solution plus 5 liters of 9 percent solution gives you 15 liters of x, so set up the equation and simplify:

$$(10)(0.06) + (5)(0.09) = (15)(x)$$
$$0.6 + 0.45 = 15x$$
$$1.05 = 15x$$
$$0.07 = x$$
$$7\% = x$$

20. **A, B.** Don't let the circle with the dot confound you. The question indicates that its value is $(ab)^2$. However, because $b > a > 0$ and they're both integers, a is always at least 1 less than b. If b is 4, a can't be more than 3, and so forth. So try the possibilities, and the highest a and b can be is 2 and 3, because $(ab)^2 = (2 \times 3)^2 = 6^2 = 36$. Also, a and b can be 1 and 2, making $(ab)^2 = (1 \times 2)^2 = 2^2 = 4$. However, 3 and 4 don't work, because $(3 \times 4)^2 = 12^2 = 144$. Therefore, a can only be 1 or 2, but not 3 or higher.

Section 3: Verbal Reasoning

1. **C.** *Ubiquitous* means existing everywhere, which among conservation-minded commuters is what the electric car is likely to become. *Inaccessible* and *scarce* convey nearly the opposite meaning. Electric cars can't really be considered *indispensable* because commuters have been just fine without them. *Salubrious* doesn't fit because it means conducive to good health.

2. **A.** *Taciturn* means aloof or uncommunicative, which describes the lecturer who leaves without checking with the audience for questions. *Effusive* means outwardly enthusiastic, so you can immediately rule out Choice (B). *Indignant* means outraged or annoyed, but there's no mention of this. *Despondent* means depressed or dejected, which could work, but the passage contains nothing to indicate that the lecturer was depressed. And *malevolent* would indicate that the lecturer was dangerous, which also isn't mentioned in the text.

3. **C, E.** Epigenetics is the study of changes in gene activity that can be passed down to future generations. To some degree, it *repudiates* (rejects) Darwin's theory of evolution because a gene's expression can change; genes are not *immutable* (unchangeable). For the first blank, *obviates* (takes steps to render something unnecessary) doesn't work, nor does *expatiates*, which would imply that epigenetics elaborates on Darwin's theory of evolution. For the second blank, *imperturbable* would be a good second choice, but it means something more along the lines of being calm, cool, and collected. *Inimitable* (incomparable) just doesn't fit.

4. B, D. Financial experts are often depicted as being *prudent* (fiscally cautious), but when it comes to investing, they become the opposite: *audacious* (bold, daring). You can rule out *dissident* (rebellious) and *confident* based on the meaning of the second sentence — the word *however* indicates that the quality mentioned in the first sentence will be opposite of the quality in the second sentence. The opposite of *prudent* makes these individuals *audacious* (aggressive) when investing, not *pusillanimous* (timid) or *aloof* (standoffish).

5. B, F. With a *paucity* (too little) of livestock and a *surfeit* (too much) of corn, farmers would be more likely to market their corn for use in biofuel production instead of using it as feed. For the first blank, the other choices — *plethora* and *overabundance* — mean the opposite of *paucity.* For the second blank, the other choices — *dearth* and *scarcity* — are the opposite of *surfeit.*

6. C, F, G. The nature of the situation must have been *involute* (complex) to require input from *trenchant* (clever) advisors so that the CEO could make *sagacious* (shrewd) decisions. By starting at the end of the passage, you know that the decisions needed to be wise and not *salacious* (obscene) or *sententious* (self-righteous). *Conscientious* or *confidential* advisors wouldn't be best qualified to advise the CEO on making wise decisions; they'd be better in situations that were *delicate* or *sensitive* in nature, and that probably wouldn't lead to greatly improving the company's market share.

7. C, D, H. If teachers are claiming that charter schools have an unfair advantage, they must be critical of charter schools, so they would *deprecate* (express disapproval of) them, not *extoll* (praise) or *advocate* (speak or write in favor of) them. For the second blank, if charter schools have the power to set very selective admissions standards, they must be *unencumbered* (free of) Department of Education policies, not *hampered* or *constrained,* which both mean constricted or limited by. And, given that they're unencumbered by Department of Education policies, they must be free to *forge* their own policies. *Disallow* means prohibited, which is opposite of the meaning this blank calls for, and *correlate* means to arrange in some orderly fashion, which doesn't quite fit.

8. B. Schumacher classifies energy sources in two categories: capital, which is available in limited quantities, and income, which is clean and renewable. *Hydroelectricity* is the only answer choice that represents a renewable energy source. All the other energy sources (heating oil, natural gas, uranium, and coal) are nonrenewable.

9. A, C. In the first sentence of the passage, Schumacher scorns the idea that problems in the industrialized world had been solved. Near the end of the passage, the author mentions that Schumacher's message was derided by the majority of people. *Derided* and *scorned* are synonymous.

10. C. The only specific human activity that's described is the use of coal, oil, and gas. You may be tempted to choose (E), which mentions "we have started to distinguish . . . and to invest," but that phrase isn't as specific as the use of natural resources.

11. B. This passage is primarily about the need to establish and enforce sound financial policies for a strong economy, meaning no financial crisis. You can rule out Choice (A) because the passage doesn't mention the need to pay off debt; in fact, it mentions the possibility of defaulting on debt. Choice (C) is out because though the policies were flawed, per the passage they were the result of inaction, not necessarily corruption or greed. Choices (D) and (E) are each specific problems that occur when sound financial policies are not in place or not enforced; they serve as evidence to support the author's main point in the passage, but they are not the main point.

12. **D.** *Moribund* means declining or not progressing, *stagnant*. *Robust* and *stout* carry the opposite meaning and would be used to describe a healthy economy. The economy described in the passage is still a working economy, so it can't be *extinct* (nonexistent) or *dead* (kaput).

13. **A, B.** The passage states that the 2008 EESA/TARP bill failed to cure bad lending decisions by banks, Choice (A), and that Dodd-Frank failed to force transparency on derivatives, Choice (B). The states of the economy and employment are results, not contributors, of the economic crisis.

14. **E.** The main point of this passage is that the United States can expand its influence in the world by building trust. The passage does imply that humanitarian aid is more effective than military might in improving how the world views the United States (Choice [A]), but this is only one example of how to build trust — it's supporting evidence, not the main point. You can rule out Choice (B) because the passage doesn't mention the United States using its military and economic power for anything evil. You can also rule out Choice (D) because it's not mentioned in the passage. Choice (C) represents an assumption on which the main point of the article is based, but it's not the main point.

15. **C.** Global citizens didn't like it when the United States started the Iraq War, but they overlooked the benefit of removing Saddam Hussein from power, as indicated in Choice (C). Choices (A) and (B) are examples of U.S. initiatives developed to help other countries pursue their interests. The passage doesn't state that the United States doesn't have such programs in place, so these choices don't suggest that something was overlooked. Choice (D) is irrelevant. Choice (E) is a further example of the United States helping other countries, even though much of the funds went to U.S. organizations.

16. **D.** Choice (A) is an unanswered question. Choice (B) is the question that is answered and then supported. Choice (C) is the answer, but it doesn't offer evidence — specific data or an example — to support the answer. Choice (D) provides this support, which is what you're looking for. Choice (E) is a proposed solution, but not supporting evidence.

17. **B, E.** If violence would be counterproductive, then politicians from both parties would encourage their constituents to *avoid* or *eschew* violence, which carry nearly the same meaning. *Embrace, appropriate,* and *incite* would actually promote violence, which isn't something politicians would encourage if it was counterproductive. *Denounce* means to condemn, which sort of works in the sentence, but none of the other answer choices conveys a similar meaning.

18. **C, D.** Calculating the cubic volume of a meal before partaking in it would be a *quirk* or *idiosyncrasy. Passions* and *obsessions* make a fairly good pairing, but the behavior being described isn't ordinary, so these two choices aren't the best. Likewise, calculating the cubic volume of a meal may be considered an *endowment* (talent), but *idiosyncrasies* and *quirks* are more fitting choices; besides, none of the other answer choices is similar in meaning to *endowment. Assimilation* means the acquisition of something, such as a cultural trait; again, this isn't the best choice, and it has no synonym in the answer choices.

19. **B, E.** The second and third sentences express the *pivotal* nature of the career choice — you can envision an arrow turning around a pivot point depending on which career choice is made. The closest match to *pivotal* is *paramount,* which means "of great importance." Choices (A), (C), and (D) would make good pairings but mean the opposite of *pivotal* and *paramount.* The meaning of *urgent,* Choice (F), is more in line with *pivotal* and *paramount* but conveys more of a sense of requiring immediate action.

20. B. The definition of *domestication* in this passage is activity that "results in genetic change brought about through conscious or unconscious human selection," meaning certain specimens are selected and bred for their characteristics. Farm-raised catfish is an example of cultivation, but the individual catfish are not selected for their characteristics.

Section 4: Quantitative Reasoning

1. D. First, convert the 4^5 into $\left(2^2\right)^5$, which becomes 2^{10}. Then simplify the fraction by subtracting the exponents:

$$\frac{5\left(2^{12}\right)}{4^5} = \frac{5\left(2^{12}\right)}{2^{10}} = 5\left(2^2\right) = 5(4) = 20$$

2. C. Factor the $\sqrt{48y}$ into $\sqrt{4 \times 4 \times 3 \times y}$. The lowest possible value of y is 3, because in order for the square root of 48y to be an integer, the factors inside the square root must form numbers squared. You have 4×4, and you need another 3 to match the existing 3 for 3×3 inside the radical.

You could also try the answer choices, starting with the lowest value and working your way up: $\sqrt{48 \times 1} = \sqrt{48}$, which isn't an integer. $\sqrt{48 \times 2} = \sqrt{96}$, which isn't an integer. $\sqrt{48 \times 3} = \sqrt{144} = 12$, which is an integer. Factoring is faster, though.

3. A, C, D, E. $210 = 2 \times 3 \times 5 \times 7$, so n could be any product of 2, 3, 5, and 7, as long as each factor is used only once. 12 is wrong because it uses the factor 2 twice.

You could also solve this one by trying answer choices, but that's a lot of math.

4. C. Regardless of the distribution, no child will receive six candies. After you give each child two candies, three candies are left over. If these are given to one child, the child will have a total of five.

5. A. You can find the average speed by placing the entire distance over the entire time. If Davis travels at 40 miles per hour for two hours, he travels 80 miles during that time. Combine this with 60 miles for one hour for a total of 140 miles in three hours:

$$\frac{140 \text{ miles}}{3 \text{ hours}} = \frac{47 \text{ miles}}{1 \text{ hour}}$$

6. C. Simplify the radical:

$$\sqrt{(30)(30)(30)(30)} = (30)(30) = 900$$

7. D. Given that $f(x) = x^2 + 2x - 2$ and $f(x) = 13$, set up and simplify the equation with 13 as $f(x)$:

$$
\begin{aligned}
f(x) &= x^2 + 2x - 2 \\
13 &= x^2 + 2x - 2 \\
0 &= x^2 + 2x - 15 \\
0 &= (x-3)(x+5)
\end{aligned}
$$

Therefore, $x = 3$ or -5, but you don't know which one, so Quantity A could be either equal to or less than Quantity B. Because you don't know, go with Choice (D).

8. **B.** Any number between 0 and 1 becomes smaller when multiplied by itself. For example:

$$\left(\frac{1}{2}\right)^2 = \frac{1}{4}$$

Each time you multiply 0.99 by itself, the quantity becomes smaller and remains less than 1.

9. **C.** Simplify the factorial expressions:

$$5! \quad = 5 \times 4 \times 3 \times 2 = 120$$

$$\frac{6!}{3!} \quad = \frac{6 \times 5 \times 4 \times 3 \times 2}{3 \times 2} = 120$$

10. **B.** You can find the volume of a right circular cylinder with $\pi r^2 h$, where r is the radius and h is the height. If r and h are integers, the only way the volume can be 36π is if r is 3 and h is 4, with a sum of 7, or r is 2 and h is 9, with a sum of 11. Either way, the sum is less than 12.

11. **A.** The question asks for an "approximate" ratio, so eyeball the graph and compare the bars. The C bar is half the B bar, making the ratio 1:2.

12. **C.** If the 211 Creede students are earning A's, the remaining 894 students are earning all the other grades. Looking at the bar chart, the B bar is the length of the C, D, and F bars put together. This means that about half the remaining students are earning B's. Bayfield has 306 students, so approximately half that is 150.

13. **C.** From the bar chart, you can see that about $\frac{2}{5}$ of the grades are B grades, so about $\frac{3}{5}$ are the other grades. De Beque has 115 students, and the only answer choice that's about $\frac{3}{5}$ of that is 70.

    An estimate is usually good enough for these questions. The answer 70 isn't really close to the other answers, so if you eyeball the graph differently, you'll still get the right answer.

14. **A, C.** The range is the difference between the lowest and highest numbers. If the range of set S is 9 and none of the given numbers are 9 apart, x has to be either 0 or 11.

    The median is the middle number of the set. If x is 0, the median is 5; if x is 11, the median is 7.

15. **0.** The trap here is doing a lot of extra math work. Drop the parentheses to avoid this trap:

$$\frac{1}{8} - \frac{3}{10} + \frac{1}{4} - \frac{1}{5} + \frac{5}{8} - \frac{1}{2}$$

Now give the fractions common denominators of either 8 or 10:

$$\frac{1}{8} - \frac{3}{10} + \frac{2}{8} - \frac{2}{10} + \frac{5}{8} - \frac{5}{10}$$

The $\frac{1}{8}$, $\frac{2}{8}$, and $\frac{5}{8}$ add up to 1, and the $-\frac{3}{10}$, $-\frac{2}{10}$, and $-\frac{5}{10}$ add up to -1. The sum, therefore, equals 0.

Note that there are other ways to simplify the fractions. On the GRE, especially with fractions, you're looking for ways to cancel and simplify.

16. **36.** Combine $\sqrt{9(36)+12(36)+15(36)}$ = into $\sqrt{36(36)}$, which equals 36.

17. **C, D, E.** If $x^2 < 25$, x is both less than 5 and greater than -5, which you can write as

$$-5 < x < 5$$

The value of x cannot be equal to 5 or -5. It's greater than -5 and less than 5, so from the list of answer choices, x could be equal to -3, 0, or 3.

18. **B.** First, find the area of the square:

$$s^2 = \left(\sqrt{2}\right)^2 = 2$$

For the area of the circle, you need its radius. Cut the square in half, corner to corner, to form two 45-45-90 triangles, where each hypotenuse is the diameter of the circle. If the side of this triangle is $\sqrt{2}$, the hypotenuse is 2, because in a right triangle, the square of the hypotenuse is the sum of the squares of the other two sides:

$$\begin{aligned} c^2 &= a^2 + b^2 \\ &= \sqrt{2}^2 + \sqrt{2}^2 \\ &= 2 + 2 \\ &= 4 \end{aligned}$$

$c^2 = 4$, so $c = \sqrt{4} = 2$ is the diameter of the circle, and the radius of the circle is half the diameter, or 1. Now for the area of the circle:

$$\pi r^2 = \pi (1)^2 = \pi$$

Subtract the area of the square from the area of the circle for your answer:

$$\pi - 2$$

19. **21.** For the area of a triangle, multiply the base by the height and divide by 2. The base of this triangle is 7 and the height is 6, for an area of 21. The 2 in the drawing has no bearing.

20. **A, B, C, E, F.** $600 is $\frac{1}{3}$ of $1,800 and $\frac{1}{4}$ of $2,400. This means that Clarissa's monthly income is greater than $1,800 and less than $2,400. Multiply these values by 12 for an annual income greater than $21,600 and less than $28,800. Note that her income can't equal these amounts: It's greater than the lower number and less than the higher number. Common trap: missing the word "not" in the question.

Answer Key for Practice Exam 1

Section 1: Verbal Reasoning

1.	C	6.	B, D, I	11.	C	16.	E
2.	E	7.	C	12.	B, C	17.	A, C
3.	B, F	8.	B, D, E	13.	C	18.	C, F
4.	B, F	9.	A, B	14.	B	19.	B, E
5.	B, D, I	10.	A, C	15.	D	20.	B, C

Section 2: Quantitative Reasoning

1.	B	6.	A	11.	C	16.	B
2.	C	7.	B	12.	24	17.	D
3.	5	8.	B	13.	E	18.	E
4.	3	9.	D	14.	D	19.	C
5.	B	10.	C	15.	2	20.	A, B

Section 3: Verbal Reasoning

1.	C	6.	C, F, G	11.	B	16.	D
2.	A	7.	C, D, H	12.	D	17.	B, E
3.	C, E	8.	B	13.	A, B	18.	C, D
4.	B, D	9.	A, C	14.	E	19.	B, E
5.	B, F	10.	C	15.	C	20.	B

Section 4: Quantitative Reasoning

1.	D	6.	C	11.	A	16.	36
2.	C	7.	D	12.	C	17.	C, D, E
3.	A, C, D, E	8.	B	13.	C	18.	B
4.	C	9.	C	14.	A, C	19.	21
5.	A	10.	B	15.	0	20.	A, B, C, E, F

Chapter 20
Practice Exam 2

One practice GRE down, five to go (counting the three online and assuming you've taken Practice Exam 1 in Chapter 18)! Hopefully, you reviewed your wrong answers from the last exam, noted your trouble topics, and revisited those topics in Chapters 4 through 15.

This practice exam is like the last one: It mimics the actual, computer-based GRE with two 30-minute essays, two 30-minute Verbal Reasoning sections (20 questions each), and two 35-minute Quantitative Reasoning sections (20 questions each). Remember that the actual GRE may also include an extra Verbal or Quantitative Reasoning section that doesn't count toward your score but does make the overall experience more grueling.

Be sure to take this practice exam under normal exam conditions as you would the real GRE.

>> Work when you won't be interrupted.

>> Leave your phone and water in the other room.

>> Use blank scratch paper and a simple calculator.

>> Answer as many questions as you can and guess on the remaining questions.

>> Set a timer for each section.

>> Don't get up while the timer is running.

>> Take breaks between sections.

>> Type the essays using a simple text editor, such as Notepad.

After completing this practice exam, check your answers in Chapter 21 — along with explanations for *all* the questions, or at least any you marked for review or had trouble with, even if you got it right. Even if you answered the question correctly, there may be a faster and simpler way to find the answer.

Answer Sheet for Practice Exam 2

Section 1:
Verbal Reasoning

1. Ⓐ Ⓑ Ⓒ Ⓓ Ⓔ
2. Ⓐ Ⓑ Ⓒ Ⓓ Ⓔ
3. Ⓐ Ⓑ Ⓒ Ⓓ Ⓔ Ⓕ
4. Ⓐ Ⓑ Ⓒ Ⓓ Ⓔ Ⓕ
5. Ⓐ Ⓑ Ⓒ Ⓓ Ⓔ Ⓕ
6. Ⓐ Ⓑ Ⓒ Ⓓ Ⓔ Ⓕ Ⓖ Ⓗ Ⓘ
7. Ⓐ Ⓑ Ⓒ Ⓓ Ⓔ Ⓕ Ⓖ Ⓗ Ⓘ
8. Ⓐ Ⓑ Ⓒ Ⓓ Ⓔ
9. Ⓐ Ⓑ Ⓒ Ⓓ Ⓔ
10. Ⓐ Ⓑ Ⓒ
11. Ⓐ Ⓑ Ⓒ Ⓓ Ⓔ
12. Ⓐ Ⓑ Ⓒ Ⓓ Ⓔ
13. Ⓐ Ⓑ Ⓒ Ⓓ Ⓔ
14. Ⓐ Ⓑ Ⓒ Ⓓ Ⓔ
15. Ⓐ Ⓑ Ⓒ Ⓓ Ⓔ Ⓕ
16. Ⓐ Ⓑ Ⓒ Ⓓ Ⓔ Ⓕ
17. Ⓐ Ⓑ Ⓒ Ⓓ Ⓔ Ⓕ
18. Ⓐ Ⓑ Ⓒ Ⓓ Ⓔ Ⓕ
19. Ⓐ Ⓑ Ⓒ Ⓓ Ⓔ Ⓕ
20. Ⓐ Ⓑ Ⓒ Ⓓ Ⓔ

Section 2:
Quantitative Reasoning

1. Ⓐ Ⓑ Ⓒ Ⓓ
2. Ⓐ Ⓑ Ⓒ Ⓓ
3. Ⓐ Ⓑ Ⓒ Ⓓ
4. Ⓐ Ⓑ Ⓒ Ⓓ
5. Ⓐ Ⓑ Ⓒ Ⓓ
6. Ⓐ Ⓑ Ⓒ Ⓓ
7. Ⓐ Ⓑ Ⓒ Ⓓ
8. Ⓐ Ⓑ Ⓒ Ⓓ
9. Ⓐ Ⓑ Ⓒ Ⓓ Ⓔ
10. Ⓐ Ⓑ Ⓒ Ⓓ Ⓔ
11. Ⓐ Ⓑ Ⓒ Ⓓ Ⓔ Ⓕ
12. [_____]
13. [_____]
14. Ⓐ Ⓑ Ⓒ Ⓓ Ⓔ
15. Ⓐ Ⓑ Ⓒ Ⓓ Ⓔ
16. Ⓐ Ⓑ Ⓒ Ⓓ Ⓔ
17. Ⓐ Ⓑ Ⓒ Ⓓ Ⓔ
18. Ⓐ Ⓑ Ⓒ Ⓓ Ⓔ
19. Ⓐ Ⓑ Ⓒ Ⓓ Ⓔ
20. [_____]

Section 3:
Verbal Reasoning

1. Ⓐ Ⓑ Ⓒ Ⓓ Ⓔ
2. Ⓐ Ⓑ Ⓒ Ⓓ Ⓔ
3. Ⓐ Ⓑ Ⓒ Ⓓ Ⓔ Ⓕ
4. Ⓐ Ⓑ Ⓒ Ⓓ Ⓔ Ⓕ
5. Ⓐ Ⓑ Ⓒ Ⓓ Ⓔ Ⓕ
6. Ⓐ Ⓑ Ⓒ Ⓓ Ⓔ Ⓕ Ⓖ Ⓗ Ⓘ
7. Ⓐ Ⓑ Ⓒ Ⓓ Ⓔ Ⓕ Ⓖ Ⓗ Ⓘ
8. Ⓐ Ⓑ Ⓒ
9. Ⓐ Ⓑ Ⓒ Ⓓ Ⓔ
10. Ⓐ Ⓑ Ⓒ Ⓓ Ⓔ
11. Ⓐ Ⓑ Ⓒ Ⓓ Ⓔ
12. Ⓐ Ⓑ Ⓒ Ⓓ Ⓔ
13. Ⓐ Ⓑ Ⓒ Ⓓ Ⓔ
14. Ⓐ Ⓑ Ⓒ
15. Ⓐ Ⓑ Ⓒ Ⓓ Ⓔ Ⓕ
16. Ⓐ Ⓑ Ⓒ Ⓓ Ⓔ Ⓕ
17. Ⓐ Ⓑ Ⓒ Ⓓ Ⓔ Ⓕ
18. Ⓐ Ⓑ Ⓒ Ⓓ Ⓔ Ⓕ
19. Ⓐ Ⓑ Ⓒ Ⓓ Ⓔ Ⓕ
20. Ⓐ Ⓑ Ⓒ Ⓓ Ⓔ

Section 4:
Quantitative Reasoning

1. Ⓐ Ⓑ Ⓒ Ⓓ
2. Ⓐ Ⓑ Ⓒ Ⓓ
3. Ⓐ Ⓑ Ⓒ Ⓓ
4. Ⓐ Ⓑ Ⓒ Ⓓ
5. Ⓐ Ⓑ Ⓒ Ⓓ
6. Ⓐ Ⓑ Ⓒ Ⓓ
7. Ⓐ Ⓑ Ⓒ Ⓓ
8. Ⓐ Ⓑ Ⓒ Ⓓ Ⓔ
9. Ⓐ Ⓑ Ⓒ Ⓓ Ⓔ Ⓕ
10. Ⓐ Ⓑ Ⓒ Ⓓ Ⓔ
11. [_____]
12. [_____]
13. Ⓐ Ⓑ Ⓒ Ⓓ Ⓔ
14. Ⓐ Ⓑ Ⓒ Ⓓ Ⓔ
15. Ⓐ Ⓑ Ⓒ Ⓓ Ⓔ
16. Ⓐ Ⓑ Ⓒ Ⓓ Ⓔ
17. Ⓐ Ⓑ Ⓒ Ⓓ Ⓔ
18. Ⓐ Ⓑ Ⓒ Ⓓ Ⓔ Ⓕ
19. Ⓐ Ⓑ Ⓒ Ⓓ Ⓔ
20. Ⓐ Ⓑ Ⓒ Ⓓ Ⓔ

Analytical Writing 1: Analyze an Issue

TIME: 30 minutes

Equal opportunity means parity in pay. Everyone should not earn the same amount of money, but it's ridiculous to see an athlete earning tens of millions of dollars in a single year while the average household income is right around $60,000.

DIRECTIONS: Write a response in which you express the extent to which you agree or disagree with the preceding statement and explain the reasoning behind your position. In support of your position, think of ways in which the statement may or may not be true and how these considerations influence your position.

Analytical Writing 2: Analyze an Argument

TIME: 30 minutes

More and more cities and towns are installing speed limit enforcement cameras on freeways to catch speeders in the act. In one year alone, speeding accounted for 7,620 fatal crashes in the United States and 137,000 injuries. A study conducted by the Federal Highway Administration noted a 25 percent reduction in speed-related accidents at sections of freeways having these cameras. Because people fail to voluntarily honor the law, these speed limit enforcement cameras are essential to enforcing the law and ensuring public safety.

DIRECTIONS: Write a response in which you discuss the merits of the preceding argument. Discuss the evidence that would strengthen or weaken it.

Section 1

Verbal Reasoning

TIME: 30 minutes for 20 questions

DIRECTIONS: Choose the best answer to each question. Blacken the corresponding ovals or boxes on the answer sheet.

Directions: For Questions 1–7, select the one entry best suited for each blank from its corresponding column of choices.

1. The Republic of India currently ranks ninth in military _____ among nations, leading it to have the third-largest standing army in the world.

Ⓐ prowess
Ⓑ innovation
Ⓒ legacy
Ⓓ expenditure
Ⓔ allegiance

2. The creators of *Sesame Street* were the first to use _____ to shape a TV show's content and achieve educational goals.

Ⓐ innovation
Ⓑ a curriculum
Ⓒ adroitness
Ⓓ a timetable
Ⓔ a character lineup

3. Although the (i) _____ system typically can detect only five different tastes, individuals with a more (ii) _____ palate are capable of distinguishing subtle differences in even the most similar foods.

Blank (i)	Blank (ii)
Ⓐ gustatory	Ⓓ discrete
Ⓑ lymphatic	Ⓔ discerning
Ⓒ digestive	Ⓕ distended

4. The tsunami (i) _____ the small seaside resort and served as a (ii) _____ for a much-needed renovation.

Blank (i)	Blank (ii)
Ⓐ inundated	Ⓓ symbol
Ⓑ dissembled	Ⓔ mendicant
Ⓒ drowned	Ⓕ catalyst

5. After several attempts to broach the (i) _____ castle walls, the enemy's vigor began to (ii) _____.

Blank (i)	Blank (ii)
Ⓐ amenable	Ⓓ flag
Ⓑ impeccable	Ⓔ regroup
Ⓒ impervious	Ⓕ fight

GO ON TO NEXT PAGE ▶

6. To address the (i) _____ national debt, Congress passed legislation to impose a strict (ii) _____ program to (iii) _____ spending.

Blank (i)	Blank (ii)	Blank (iii)
Ⓐ pervasive	Ⓓ austerity	Ⓖ curtail
Ⓑ shrinking	Ⓔ spending	Ⓗ attenuate
Ⓒ burgeoning	Ⓕ defense	Ⓘ desiccate

7. The (i) _____ between the records and the testimony, along with the (ii) _____ evidence, led the prosecutor to reevaluate his approach for trying the (iii) _____ case against the alleged perpetrator.

Blank (i)	Blank (ii)	Blank (iii)
Ⓐ correlation	Ⓓ corroborated	Ⓖ compelling
Ⓑ discrepancy	Ⓔ vetted	Ⓗ tenuous
Ⓒ relationship	Ⓕ unsubstantiated	Ⓘ conclusive

Directions: Each of the following passages is followed by questions pertaining to the passage. Read the passage and answer the questions based on information stated or implied in that passage. For each question, select one answer choice unless instructed otherwise.

In a poll conducted by Washington Post-ABC News, 70 percent of Americans support the use of passenger profiling to determine which passengers are most closely scrutinized at airports. They believe that the cost savings and added convenience for a large majority of passengers is worth the questionable practice of singling out specific passengers for closer scrutiny. In addition, passengers feel that pat-downs and full body scans are highly invasive.

When most Americans discuss profiling, they are referring to profiling based on race, nationality, religion, and gender, which many people consider a civil rights violation. Most experts agree that profiling in this way is inefficient and ineffective. They recommend profiling by behavior and intelligence, using no-fly and watch lists, personal data, travel histories, and so forth to identify potential threats.

Civil liberty organizations claim that this solution is no better and perhaps worse in terms of violating civil liberties, because it gives government agencies license to collect sensitive information on any and all citizens. They believe that the only fair solution is to inspect all or randomly selected passengers and luggage.

When it comes to airport security, ultimately we face a choice. Either we protect civil liberties and accept the cost and inconvenience of inspecting all passengers and luggage, or we relinquish our civil liberties or the civil liberties of certain groups or individuals to increase effectiveness, reduce costs, and streamline baggage and checkpoint inspections.

8. According to experts, which of the following is most effective in ensuring airline security?

   Ⓐ Profiling passengers based on race, nationality, religion, and gender

   Ⓑ Inspecting all passengers and their luggage

   Ⓒ Profiling by behavior and intelligence

   Ⓓ Interviewing all passengers before boarding

   Ⓔ Streamlining baggage and checkpoint inspections

9. Which of the following, if true, most effectively undermines the argument that the only choice we have is between security and civil liberties?

   Ⓐ Bomb-sniffing dogs are more effective and less intrusive at detecting explosives than human inspectors or electronic security devices.

   Ⓑ A combination of profiling and targeted interviews has proven most effective and efficient.

   Ⓒ Precertification as a safe flyer significantly improves efficiency at checkpoints.

   Ⓓ Checked baggage is more likely than carry-on luggage to contain explosives.

   Ⓔ No security measure is 100 percent effective.

The following passage is an excerpt from Causes of War *by Jack S. Levy and William R. Thompson (Wiley-Blackwell).*

It is hard to imagine what life would have been like in the late twentieth century in the absence of World War I and World War II, which had such profound effects on the global system and on domestic societies. The same can be said for the Cold War. For nearly a half century it shaped both international and domestic politics and cultures, not only in the United States and the Soviet Union but also in Western Europe and the Third World (Weart, 1989). The development of new states in the contemporary era continues to be influenced by warfare and preparations for war. With the proliferation of nuclear weapons, and with the threat of the acquisition of nuclear weapons by terrorist groups and "rogue states," new threats to the security of even the most powerful states in the system have emerged. The proliferation of civil wars and conflicts involving "non-state" actors has changed life throughout the developing world. A better understanding of the causes of war is a necessary first step if we are to have any hope of reducing the occurrence of war and perhaps mitigating its severity and consequences.

GO ON TO NEXT PAGE ➡

10. According to the passage, which of the following are effects of war and preparations for war?

[A] Reshaping of international and domestic politics and cultures

[B] The proliferation of civil wars and conflicts

[C] Development of new states

11. One could reasonably infer from this passage that the greatest security threat is which of the following?

Ⓐ Proliferation of civil wars

Ⓑ Terrorists

Ⓒ Rogue states

Ⓓ The Cold War

Ⓔ Proliferation of nuclear weapons

The following passage is an excerpt from UnMarketing: Stop Marketing. Start Engaging *by Scott Stratten (Wiley).*

To successfully UnMarket your business, your goal should be to get to the point where you are a recognized expert in your field. You can choose to be recognized for a certain discipline, whether it is time management or sales or marketing in general. You can also aim to be recognized as an expert to a specific industry. What you have to realize is that there is an important difference between somebody who is selling something and somebody who is an expert. This is one of the problems when you use advertising or direct mail for your marketing — if your potential customer does not have an immediate need for your product or service, then you are potentially turning them off and losing them for the future. When you position yourself as an expert with useful information for people, your marketplace will always have a need for that information. You have successfully pulled people into your funnel, you have their attention, and now you need to do something great for them.

12. Select the sentence which most clearly describes the means to the goal of UnMarketing.

Ⓐ Sentence 2: "You can choose . . . in general."

Ⓑ Sentence 4: "What you have to . . . an expert."

Ⓒ Sentence 5: "This is . . . the future."

Ⓓ Sentence 6: "When you position . . . that information."

Ⓔ Sentence 7: "You have success-fully . . . for them."

13. Which of the following is the most important difference between marketing and UnMarket-ing as explained in the passage?

Ⓐ Advertising versus direct mail

Ⓑ Salesperson versus expert

Ⓒ Time management versus marketing

Ⓓ Expert in a field versus expert in a discipline

Ⓔ Getting people's attention versus doing something great for them

With the passage of a universal healthcare bill, the government not only has the right but also the responsibility to regulate what people eat. Face it: the fact that the United States spends 50 percent more per capita for healthcare than most European countries is because people in the United States consume far more junk food. If taxpayers are footing the bill for healthcare, then the government is responsible for controlling healthcare costs, and the most effective way to do that is to crack down on the junk food industry.

14. Which of the following, if true, most effec-tively challenges the argument that poor die-tary habits, such as junk food, lead to higher healthcare costs?

Ⓐ Countries in Europe do not impose such regulations on their food producers.

Ⓑ Labeling foods enables people to regulate their own consumption.

Ⓒ Healthcare service prices are on average 50 percent higher in the United States than in most European countries.

Ⓓ The healthcare bill does not mandate dietary restrictions.

Ⓔ Some food items considered junk food actually contain healthy ingredients.

15. With nothing to lose and the coach's _____ approval, the teammates decided to abandon the game plan and just have some fun.

   A ambiguous

   B tacit

   C cautious

   D implicit

   E enthusiastic

   F salubrious

16. Few could believe that the champion competitive eater could be so _____.

   A hedonistic

   B self-indulgent

   C epicurean

   D courteous

   E abstemious

   F ascetic

17. Though the event was not out of the ordinary, it was described with a(n) _____ that captivated the audience.

   A sarcasm

   B allegory

   C embellishment

   D hyperbole

   E ennui

   F overemphasis

18. The child was _____, while the siblings had gentler dispositions.

   A pugnacious

   B lackadaisical

   C quiescent

   D truculent

   E irascible

   F soporific

19. In this business, the divide between statement and action suggests a(n) _____ among parties.

   A sincerity

   B disingenuousness

   C duplicitousness

   D unpretentiousness

   E hypocrisy

   F authenticity

To reduce the number of factory accidents, managers at Smith Inc. are implementing a workplace training program for all of the company's factory workers. The program places emphasis on preventing, recognizing, and avoiding safety and health hazards while providing information on workers' rights, employer responsibilities, and filing complaints.

20. Which of the following, if true, suggests that the managers' plan to reduce factory accidents through training will not succeed?

   Ⓐ Many workers are from the Wilson factory, where such training programs are in place and workers attend regularly.

   Ⓑ The factory accidents from both this year and last year were from delivery drivers unable to navigate the sharp turn to the loading dock.

   Ⓒ The Smith factory has already implemented advanced safety measures and has fewer factory accidents than the industry standard.

   Ⓓ While potentially damaging to equipment and products, most factory accidents are not actually dangerous to workers.

   Ⓔ The same workplace training program did not reduce the number of accidents at the Olson factory, which, like the Smith factory, produces machine shop supplies.

Section 2
Quantitative Reasoning

TIME: 35 minutes for 20 questions

NOTES:

- All numbers used in this exam are real numbers.

- All figures lie in a plane.

- Angle measures are positive; points and angles are in the position shown.

Directions: For Questions 1–8, choose from the following answers:

Ⓐ *Quantity A is greater.*

Ⓑ *Quantity B is greater.*

Ⓒ *The two quantities are equal.*

Ⓓ *The relationship cannot be determined from the information given.*

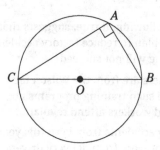

© John Wiley & Sons, Inc.

1. Diameter $BC = 2$ and $AB = 1$.

Quantity A	*Quantity B*
The area of triangle ABC	$\dfrac{\sqrt{3}}{2}$

2. The average (arithmetic mean) of ten test scores is 120, and the average of 20 additional test scores is 90.

Quantity A	*Quantity B*
The weighted average of these scores	105

3. $10 < n < 15$ and $d = 20$

Quantity A	*Quantity B*
$\dfrac{n}{d}$	0.72

4. A certain recipe requires $\dfrac{4}{3}$ cups of lentils and makes six servings.

Quantity A	*Quantity B*
The amount of lentils required for the same recipe to make 15 servings	3 cups

5.

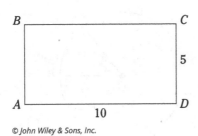

© John Wiley & Sons, Inc.

Quantity A	*Quantity B*
The area of rectangle *ABCD*	The area of trapezoid *EFGH*

6.

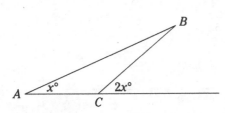

© John Wiley & Sons, Inc.

Note: Drawing not to scale

Quantity A	*Quantity B*
The length of line segment *AC*	The length of line segment *BC*

7. $x^2 - x - 6 = 0$

Quantity A	*Quantity B*
The sum of the roots of the equation	-1

8. The average of the numbers 8, 8, 11, 18, and *x* is 2*x*.

Quantity A	*Quantity B*
Twice the average of the numbers	11

9. What is the units digit of $219,473 \times 162,597$?

Ⓐ 1
Ⓑ 2
Ⓒ 3
Ⓓ 4
Ⓔ 5

10. In the *xy* plane, what is the slope of the line whose equation is $2x + 3y = 5$?

Ⓐ 1
Ⓑ $\frac{3}{2}$
Ⓒ $-\frac{3}{2}$
Ⓓ $\frac{2}{3}$
Ⓔ $-\frac{2}{3}$

11. Bill is budgeting the expenditure of a new car based on his gross income from last year. If his gross income from last year was $50,000 and Bill wants to spend between 15 percent and 30 percent on a new car, which of the following could be the cost of the new car?

Indicate **all** possible costs of the new car.

Ⓐ $8,000
Ⓑ $10,000
Ⓒ $12,000
Ⓓ $14,000
Ⓔ $16,000
Ⓕ $18,000

GO ON TO NEXT PAGE ➡

12. If the sporting center has two baseballs for every nine baseball gloves and three baseball bats for every five baseballs, what is the lowest number of sporting items that could be in the sporting center?

13. If the average of x, y, and z is 5, what is the average of $4x + y, 2y - x$, and $3z + 27$?

14.

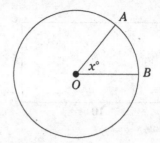

The circle shown has the center O and a radius of 8. If $x = 45$, what is the length of minor arc AB?

Ⓐ $\dfrac{\pi}{2}$

Ⓑ π

Ⓒ $\dfrac{3\pi}{2}$

Ⓓ 2π

Ⓔ $\dfrac{5\pi}{2}$

Questions 15–17 are based on the following data.

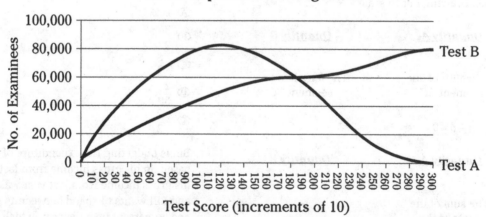

Score Distribution of 1,412,393 Examinees from Sept. 2018 to Aug. 2021

Note: Chart is drawn to scale.

Percentile Ranking Based on Score

Score	Test A Percentile	Test B Percentile
0	0	0
10	0	1
20	1	1
30	2	2
40	4	3
50	7	4
60	12	6
70	17	7
80	22	9
90	27	11
100	33	13
110	38	16
120	44	18
130	50	21
140	55	24
150	61	28
160	66	32
170	71	35
180	77	40
190	81	44
200	85	48
210	89	53
220	91	58
230	94	63
240	96	67
250	97	72
260	98	76
270	99	81
280	99	86
290	99	90
300	99	94

15. Approximately what ratio of examinees taking Test B scored a perfect 300?

Ⓐ 1 out of 100

Ⓑ 1 out of 90

Ⓒ 1 out of 50

Ⓓ 1 out of 20

Ⓔ 1 out of 10

16. If a Test A examinee is among a group of 40,000 examinees with the same score, which *could* be the examinee's score?

Ⓐ 20

Ⓑ 40

Ⓒ 90

Ⓓ 180

Ⓔ 210

17. A Test A examinee improving his score from 100 to 120 surpasses approximately how many other examinees?

Ⓐ 40,000

Ⓑ 80,000

Ⓒ 150,000

Ⓓ 240,000

Ⓔ 300,000

18. If the radius r of a circle increases by 50 percent, what is the area of the new circle in terms of r?

Ⓐ $\dfrac{3\pi r^2}{2}$

Ⓑ $2\pi r^2$

Ⓒ $\dfrac{4\pi r^2}{3}$

Ⓓ $3\pi r^2$

Ⓔ $\dfrac{9\pi r^2}{4}$

19. The circle is inscribed within the square of area 36. What fraction of the square is occupied by the circle?

Ⓐ $\dfrac{\pi}{2}$

Ⓑ $\dfrac{\pi}{3}$

Ⓒ $\dfrac{\pi}{4}$

Ⓓ $\dfrac{1}{3}$

Ⓔ $\dfrac{1}{6}$

20. What is the radius of a right circular cylinder with a volume of 50π and a height of 2?

DO NOT TURN THE PAGE UNTIL TOLD TO DO SO **STOP** DO NOT RETURN TO A PREVIOUS TEST

Section 3
Verbal Reasoning

TIME: 30 minutes for 20 questions

DIRECTIONS: Choose the best answer to each question. Blacken the corresponding ovals or boxes on the answer sheet.

Directions: For Questions 1–7, select the one entry best suited for each blank from its corresponding column of choices.

1. Linguists and etymologists use a technique known as the *comparative method* to compare related languages and make inferences about the shared language structure and _____.

Ⓐ culture
Ⓑ grammar
Ⓒ vocabulary
Ⓓ politics
Ⓔ decorum

2. Driven by the rotation of Earth, the wind flow around an atmospheric high-pressure area can go in a clockwise or counterclockwise direction, depending on the _____.

Ⓐ hemisphere
Ⓑ stratosphere
Ⓒ moon's orbit
Ⓓ solar winds
Ⓔ wind circulation

3. A streamlined e-commerce experience mitigates the online shopper's (i) _____ behavior and the (ii) _____ for failing to complete the transaction.

Blank (i)	Blank (ii)
Ⓐ capricious	Ⓓ inkling
Ⓑ predictable	Ⓔ penchant
Ⓒ fatuous	Ⓕ passion

4. Because the compensation was (i) _____ with the time and effort required for the project, the contractor did not (ii) _____ over the deadlines.

Blank (i)	Blank (ii)
Ⓐ discordant	Ⓓ quibble
Ⓑ pursuant	Ⓔ acquiesce
Ⓒ commensurate	Ⓕ concede

5. Attempts to control the (i) _____ situation only served to (ii) _____ the tension.

Blank (i)	Blank (ii)
Ⓐ intractable	Ⓓ precipitate
Ⓑ imperturbable	Ⓔ exonerate
Ⓒ indolent	Ⓕ augment

6. The (i) _____ caused the mixture to become (ii) _____. Student safety (iii) _____ all other concerns, so the teacher ushered her students out of the lab.

Blank (i)	Blank (ii)	Blank (iii)
Ⓐ neutralizer	Ⓓ volatile	Ⓖ superseded
Ⓑ buffer	Ⓔ acidic	Ⓗ preceded
Ⓒ catalyst	Ⓕ piquant	Ⓘ negated

7. When asked whether the antique vase was in (i) _____ condition, its owner (ii) _____ that it certainly was. When the buyer received it, however, she discovered that she had been (iii) _____.

Blank (i)	Blank (ii)	Blank (iii)
Ⓐ pristine	Ⓓ corroborated	Ⓖ sidetracked
Ⓑ primordial	Ⓔ proved	Ⓗ duped
Ⓒ rudimentary	Ⓕ averred	Ⓘ ostracized

GO ON TO NEXT PAGE

The following passage is an excerpt from Carnegie *by Peter Krass (Wiley).*

Great Britain had taken an early lead in the Industrial Revolution. The isles, with rich coal-fields to provide fuel for steam engines, many natural waterways for cheap transportation, and a booming international trade with its colonies, was ideally suited for a transformation from an agricultural-based economy to a manufacturing-based economy, from a handicraft system to a factory system. As country folk, in search of steady jobs, migrated to the cities in increasing numbers, the transition proved painful because already poor living conditions in urban centers were exacerbated by a population explosion. Contributing to this unprecedented growth were the Irish, who, seeking work, arrived in waves. Thus, employers had such a large labor pool to select from that they were able to dictate low wages and long hours, further suppressing the working poor. Disillusioned and embittered, the working class formed both trade and political unions to exert pressure, and activism increased dramatically.

For Question 8, consider each answer choice separately and select all answer choices that are correct.

8. Which of the following is specifically cited as contributing to Great Britain's ability to take an early lead in the Industrial Revolution?

   A Trade unions

   B International trade

   C Abundance of coal

9. Select the sentence that states the reasons why wages were so low.

   Ⓐ "The isles . . . factory system."

   Ⓑ "As country folk . . . population explosion."

   Ⓒ "Contributing . . . arrived in waves."

   Ⓓ "Thus, employers . . . working poor."

   Ⓔ "Disillusioned and embittered . . . increased dramatically."

10. Which of the following would make the most accurate title for this passage?

    Ⓐ Great Britain's Industrial Revolution: From Boom to Bust

    Ⓑ Exploitation of the Poor during Great Britain's Industrial Revolution

    Ⓒ The Birth of Unions in the Industrial Revolution

    Ⓓ Britain's Industrial Revolution from the Eyes of the Poor

    Ⓔ Great Britain's Industrial Revolution: Natural Resources, Migration, and Unions

The current trend of holding teachers accountable for the failures of school systems and students is only a blame game that makes teachers the scapegoats. Even with the passage of No Child Left Behind, intended to make schools and teachers more accountable, students in the U.S. continue to underperform students in other countries in math and science. If we are to get serious about education in the United States, we need to hold everyone accountable, not only schools and teachers but also students, parents, and society at large. As long as sports, celebrity worship, television, video games, and consumerism are higher on our list of priorities than education, academic performance will continue to decline.

11. Which of the following, if true, most effectively undermines the argument that holding teachers accountable is not a solution to improving student academic performance?

    Ⓐ A study conducted at one school found that students of certain teachers showed significant improvement, while students of other teachers did not.

    Ⓑ Socioeconomic differences among students contribute significantly to student performance.

    Ⓒ Studies show a direct link between school funding and student performance.

    Ⓓ With the passage of No Child Left Behind, students of teachers who teach to the test perform significantly better on standardized tests.

    Ⓔ From 1975 to 1990, more high-school students have taken the SAT, while scores have declined.

The thylacine, also known as the Tasmanian tiger, hunted in small packs and mainly at night. Evidence found on the island of Tasmania shows that though the thylacine preyed on birds, rodents, and sheep, its main staple was wombats and other small marsupials. Clearly this animal showed a preference for marsupials as its prey.

12. Which of the following, if true, most weakens the claim that the thylacine primarily sought marsupials for prey?

Ⓐ The thylacine on Tasmania has been extinct since the 1930s, while the number of marsupials on that island has only risen slightly.

Ⓑ Some farm records show losses of sheep and chickens to thylacine attacks.

Ⓒ Most animals of prey on Tasmania that were not domesticated were marsupials.

Ⓓ Marsupials are also prey to other predators, including foxes, eagles, and certain lizards.

Ⓔ Scratches and bite marks found on some thylacine bones are presumed to be defensive scars from certain marsupials.

This passage is an excerpt from Film Theory: An Introduction by Robert Stam (Wiley-Blackwell).

There are many possible ways to describe the history of film theory. It can be a triumphant parade of "great men and women": Munsterberg, Eisenstein, Arnheim, Dulac, Bazin, Mulvey. It can be a history of orienting metaphors: "cine-eye," "film language," "window on the world," "camera-pen," "film mirror," "film dream." It can be a story of the impact of philosophy on theory: Kant and Munsterberg, Mounier and Bazin, Bergson and Deleuze. It can be a history of cinema's *rapprochement* with (or rejection of) other arts: film as painting, film as music, film as theater (or anti-theater). It can be a sequence of paradigmatic shifts in theoretical/interpretive grids and discursive styles — formalism, semiology, psychoanalysis, feminism, cognitivism, queer theory, postcolonial theory — each with its talismanic keywords, tacit assumptions, and characteristic jargon.

13. In the context of this passage, which of the following is the best synonym for the word *rapprochement?*

Ⓐ relationship

Ⓑ reconciliation

Ⓒ disapproval

Ⓓ agreement

Ⓔ harmony

For Question 14, consider each answer choice separately and select all answer choices that are correct.

14. Which of the following does the author list as possible ways to describe the history of film theory?

Ⓐ History of psychoanalysis

Ⓑ History of film language

Ⓒ Triumphant parade of great men and women

Directions: Each of the following sentences has a blank indicating that a word or phrase is omitted. Choose the two answers that best complete the sentence and result in two sentences most alike in meaning.

15. Antics making one the life of the party in one context may be _____ in another.

Ⓐ courteous

Ⓑ loutish

Ⓒ decorous

Ⓓ capricious

Ⓔ boorish

Ⓕ contentious

16. The plans were so _____ that nobody on staff could figure out exactly what was supposed to be done.

Ⓐ diffident

Ⓑ desultory

Ⓒ methodical

Ⓓ convoluted

Ⓔ proscribed

Ⓕ tortuous

GO ON TO NEXT PAGE ➤

17. While citizens demanded strong leadership, _____ candidates pandered to the polls.

- [A] pusillanimous
- [B] impudent
- [C] audacious
- [D] sanctimonious
- [E] craven
- [F] intransigent

18. Although parents are often reluctant to _____ their children, they know it is their duty to do so.

- [A] sanction
- [B] admonish
- [C] vilify
- [D] disparage
- [E] reprimand
- [F] congratulate

19. The department of transportation offered to pay well above the market value of the home, but the _____ couple refused to move out of the house where the children had grown up.

- [A] obdurate
- [B] recalcitrant
- [C] obstinate
- [D] assiduous
- [E] subversive
- [F] fundamentalist

A recent study shows that a certain food preservative causes drowsiness and irritability in some dog breeds. This preservative is used primarily in the ABD brand dog treats, which is the only source of the dogs' exposure to it. Therefore, the dogs' disposition should improve rapidly if the preservative is no longer used.

20. Which of the following, if true, most strengthens the argument?

- Ⓐ The preservative is harmless to dogs if the treats are exposed to air for 30 minutes before being eaten.
- Ⓑ Dogs rid their bodies of the preservative quickly once they stop eating it.
- Ⓒ House cats have also eaten the ABD treats with no adverse effect on their disposition.
- Ⓓ In high concentrations, the preservative is toxic to other animal species.
- Ⓔ The preservative in the dog treats is less concentrated today than it was two years ago.

DO NOT TURN THE PAGE UNTIL TOLD TO DO SO STOP **DO NOT RETURN TO A PREVIOUS TEST**

Section 4

Quantitative Reasoning

TIME: 35 minutes for 20 questions

NOTES:

- All numbers used in this exam are real numbers.

- All figures lie in a plane.

- Angle measures are positive; points and angles are in the position shown.

Directions: For Questions 1–7, choose from the following answers:

Ⓐ *Quantity A is greater.*

Ⓑ *Quantity B is greater.*

Ⓒ *The two quantities are equal.*

Ⓓ *The relationship cannot be determined from the information given.*

1. A furniture dealer sold two sofas for $400 each, for a 25 percent profit on one and a 20 percent loss on the other.

Quantity A	**Quantity B**
The amount of profit on the first sofa	The amount of loss on the second sofa

2. n is a positive integer between 200 and 500.

Quantity A	**Quantity B**
The number of possible values of n with a units digit of 5	31

3. $ab < 0$

Quantity A	**Quantity B**
$|a+b|$	$|a|+|b|$

4. $\dfrac{x}{y} = \dfrac{2}{3}$

Quantity A	**Quantity B**
x	y

Questions 5 and 6 are based on the following information.

Square $ABCD$ is in the xy-coordinate plane, and each side of the square is parallel to either the x-axis or the y-axis. Points A and C have coordinates $(-2, -1)$ and $(3, 4)$, respectively.

5.

Quantity A	**Quantity B**
The area of square $ABCD$	24

6.

Quantity A	**Quantity B**
The distance between points A and C	$5\sqrt{2}$

GO ON TO NEXT PAGE

7. $n > 0$

Quantity A	*Quantity B*
n	$\dfrac{1}{n}$

8. A car travels at a constant rate of 20 meters per second. How many kilometers does it travel in 10 minutes? (1 kilometer = 1,000 meters)

Ⓐ 5

Ⓑ 12

Ⓒ 15

Ⓓ 20

Ⓔ 25

9. If $(x-5)^2 = 900$, what are the two possible values of x?

Indicate <u>two</u> such numbers.

A 10

B −10

C −25

D 30

E 35

F 40

10. A circular pool of radius r feet is surrounded by a circular sidewalk of width $\dfrac{r}{2}$ feet. In terms of r, what is the area of the sidewalk?

Ⓐ $2\pi r^2$

Ⓑ $\dfrac{5\pi r^2}{4}$

Ⓒ $\dfrac{9\pi r^2}{4}$

Ⓓ πr^2

Ⓔ $\dfrac{\pi r^2}{2}$

11.

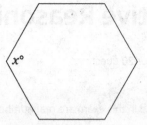

The preceding figure shows a regular hexagon. What is the value of x?

12. If n divided by 35 has a remainder of 3, what is the remainder when n is divided by 7?

13. If the length of a rectangle were increased by 20 percent and the width were decreased by 20 percent, what is the ratio of the original area to the new area?

Ⓐ 4:3

Ⓑ 5:4

Ⓒ 10:9

Ⓓ 15:13

Ⓔ 25:24

Questions 14–16 are based on the following data.

Education pays

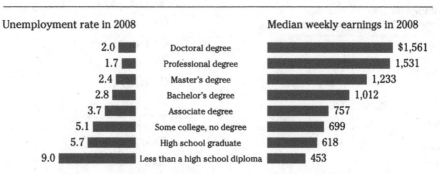

Unemployment rate in 2008

2.0	Doctoral degree
1.7	Professional degree
2.4	Master's degree
2.8	Bachelor's degree
3.7	Associate degree
5.1	Some college, no degree
5.7	High school graduate
9.0	Less than a high school diploma

Median weekly earnings in 2008

Doctoral degree	$1,561
Professional degree	1,531
Master's degree	1,233
Bachelor's degree	1,012
Associate degree	757
Some college, no degree	699
High school graduate	618
Less than a high school diploma	453

Source: Bureau of Labor Statistics. Current Population Survey

© John Wiley & Sons, Inc.

14. Approximately what were the median monthly earnings of someone with a bachelor's degree in 2008?

- (A) $1,012
- (B) $1,233
- (C) $4,050
- (D) $4,400
- (E) $4,750

15. In 2008, if there were 10,000 doctoral-degree holders and 200,000 master's-degree holders, what was the ratio of unemployed doctoral-degree holders to unemployed master's-degree holders?

- (A) 1:20
- (B) 1:24
- (C) 1:48
- (D) 1:50
- (E) 1:200

16. If an associate-degree holder earning 20 percent less than the median for that degree went on to get a bachelor's degree and earn 25 percent more than the median for that degree, which of the following is closest to the change in the degree holder's annual income?

- (A) $28,200
- (B) $30,500
- (C) $31,500
- (D) $34,300
- (E) $49,500

17. What is the area of an equilateral triangle with a base of 6?

- (A) $6\sqrt{3}$
- (B) $9\sqrt{3}$
- (C) $12\sqrt{3}$
- (D) $15\sqrt{3}$
- (E) $18\sqrt{3}$

GO ON TO NEXT PAGE

18.

House Values of a Neighborhood in Town X

Value Range (In Thousands of Dollars)	Number of Houses
Under $100	6
$100–$149	14
$150–$199	12
$200–$250	10
Over $250	7

For the 49 houses from the neighborhood in Town X, which of the following could be the median value, in thousands of dollars?

Indicate all such values.

- [A] $148
- [B] $162
- [C] $170
- [D] $195
- [E] $210
- [F] $225

19. Two lines represented by the equations $y = x + 1$ and $y = 2x + 3$ intersect at point P. What are the coordinates of P?

- Ⓐ $(-2, -1)$
- Ⓑ $(-1, 2)$
- Ⓒ $(1, -2)$
- Ⓓ $(2, -1)$
- Ⓔ $(1, 2)$

20. $\dfrac{5^{10} - 5^8}{5^9 - 5^7} =$

- Ⓐ 0
- Ⓑ 1
- Ⓒ 5
- Ⓓ 25
- Ⓔ 125

DO NOT TURN THE PAGE UNTIL TOLD TO DO SO **STOP** **DO NOT RETURN TO A PREVIOUS TEST**

Chapter 21

Practice Exam 2: Answers and Explanations

After taking Practice Exam 2 in Chapter 20, use this chapter to check your answers and see how you did. Carefully review the explanations because doing so can help you understand why you missed the questions you did and also give you a better understanding of the thought process that helped you select the correct answers. If you're in a hurry, flip to the end of the chapter for an abbreviated answer key.

Analytical Writing Sections

Have a friend or tutor read your essays: Refer that helpful person to Chapters 16 and 17 for scoring guidelines, and if the essays are clear, persuasive, and grammatically sound, you probably got it.

Section 1: Verbal Reasoning

1. **D.** Military *expenditure*, which is the money spent on the military, leads to the military's size. Even though the other qualities may be true, only expenditure directly *leads* to the size of the military.

2. **B.** Though the other qualities may be true, *a curriculum* leads to educational goals. *Adroitness* is the quality of being clever and appropriate, but it isn't specific enough to reach educational goals.

3. **A, E.** The *gustatory* system is responsible for the sense of taste, and a more *discerning* (perceptive) palate is able to distinguish subtle differences. The *lymphatic* system fights infection, while the *digestive* system breaks down food. For the second blank, *discrete* (distinct) doesn't work, and *distended* (swollen) isn't even in the ballpark.

4. **A, F.** A *tsunami* is a wave that would *inundate* (flood) the resort, causing property damage that would act as a *catalyst* (stimulus) for any renovation. Choice (C), *drowned*, fits the meaning, but the resort isn't a living thing, so it can't drown. *Dissembled* (concealed) isn't even close. Although a tsunami could be a *symbol* for something, it's hardly a symbol for the much-needed renovation. Flooding could result in a *mendicant* (vagrant), but it would not serve as one.

5. **C, D.** Castle walls that are *impervious* cannot be penetrated, and after several attempts to *broach* (break through) them, an enemy's *vigor* (strength) would begin to *flag* (weaken). Walls cannot be *amenable* (agreeable). They may be *impeccable* (flawless), but because they frustrated the enemy's attempts to penetrate, *impervious* is a better choice. As for the other choices for the second blank, the enemy's vigor wouldn't *regroup* (reorganize) or *fight*, although the enemy certainly would.

6. **C, D, G.** Aware of the *burgeoning* (growing) debt, Congress would impose an *austerity* (disciplined) program to *curtail* (reduce) spending. For the first blank, *pervasive* (widespread) would be a good second choice, but *shrinking* is the opposite of what's needed here. For the second blank, *spending* would be a decent second choice, but it's not quite strong enough and it's a little redundant because it appears at the end of the sentence. *Defense* definitely doesn't fit. For the third blank, *attenuate* may be okay, but it means something more like to decrease in strength. *Desiccate* (dehydrate) doesn't make the cut, either.

7. **B, F, H.** If the prosecutor will reevaluate his approach, then he has problems with the case. A *discrepancy* (difference) between the records and the testimony would be a problem, while a *correlation* or *relationship*, both meaning connection, would not. The words *along with* suggest that the evidence is also a problem and therefore would be *unsubstantiated* (without support), not *corroborated* (confirmed) or *vetted* (examined closely). This means the prosecutor's case would be *tenuous* (shaky), not *compelling* (convincing) or *conclusive* (certain).

8. **C.** The second paragraph, third sentence states that experts recommend profiling by behavior and intelligence.

9. **A.** If true, Choice (A) describes a solution that improves security without compromising civil liberties. Choices (B) and (C) may be effective for security, but per the passage, are violations of civil liberties. Choices (D) and (E) are observations that do not address the question.

10. **A, C.** The third sentence states that the Cold War shaped international and domestic politics and cultures, and the fourth sentence states that war has influenced the development of new states. Choice (B) is wrong, because the next-to-last sentence presents civil wars and conflicts as causes of change, not effects of war.

11. **E.** Terrorists and rogue states are mentioned only in respect to the possibility that they'll acquire nuclear weapons, while nuclear proliferation — which includes the acquisition of nuclear weapons by rogue states — is singled out as a threat unto itself. According to the passage, the Cold War has ended and the proliferation of civil wars is mentioned not as a threat but only as an agent of change in the developing world.

12. **D.** The sixth sentence describes the means to the goal stated in the first sentence — to position yourself as a recognized expert with useful information so the marketplace will always need what you have to offer. Choice (D), which describes getting people's attention, is the result of achieving that goal.

13. **B.** The fourth sentence answers this question in saying that "there is an important difference between somebody who is selling something and somebody who is an expert." Most of the choices are differences mentioned in the passage but are not *the* difference between marketing and UnMarketing.

14. **C.** If service prices are on average 50 percent higher in the United States, then this accounts for the fact that the United States spends 50 percent more per capita on healthcare than most European countries, undermining the argument that poor diet leads to poor health and is thus responsible for the difference.

15. **B, D.** *Tacit* and *implicit* both indicate that the coach approved without having to say so. Perhaps during practice the coach had expressed a desire that the team play with more heart and throw caution to the wind. Choices (C), *cautious,* and (E), *enthusiastic,* are both fitting words to describe approval, but neither has a suitable match in the list. *Ambiguous* (unclear) and *salubrious* (healthy) obviously don't fit.

16. **E, F.** A champion competitive eater would need a hearty appetite, so few would believe that such a person is *abstemious* (moderate) or *ascetic* (prone to self-denial). Choice (D), *courteous,* neither contradicts a hearty appetite nor has a match, and the other three choices all mean the opposite of moderate.

17. **C, D.** *Embellishment* is an addition or ornament, such as details added to a story, and *hyperbole* is an exaggeration; both words carry the positive connotation of improving something or making it more interesting. Choice (F), *overemphasis* is an overstated importance placed on something, which doesn't change the nature of what's being overstated. None of the remaining choices come close: *sarcasm* (irony), *allegory* (parable), and *ennui* (boredom).

18. **A, D.** The transition word *while* tells you that the child had the opposite of a gentle disposition. *Pugnacious* and *truculent* mean confrontational and aggressive, which fit. *Irascible* (irritable) is close but doesn't mean the opposite of gentle, nor does it have a match. Choices (B) and (C), *lackadaisical* (easygoing) and *quiescent* (calm), are nearly identical in meaning but aren't the opposite of gentle. Choice (F), *soporific* (sleep-inducing), also doesn't fit.

19. **B, C.** A divide between statement and action, meaning what you say isn't what you do, suggests the parties are lying, which as a noun is *disingenuousness* (think *genuine* with a *dis-* in front of it) or *duplicitousness* (think of *dupli* as two or two-faced). Choices (A), *sincerity,* and (F), *authenticity,* are nearly the opposite of what's needed here, both meaning genuine or real. *Hypocrisy* is close but has more to do with pretending to hold a certain belief.

20. **B.** If accidents are caused by delivery drivers, then training factory workers won't change anything. There are trap answers, however. In Choice (A), if some workers are already trained, then others (who cause accidents) may still need training. In Choice (C), though the Smith factory already has a good safety record, it could still improve. In Choice (D), the result of the accident isn't part of prevention. Choice (E) is a trap, making you think the training program isn't effective. However, the program could be effective, but the Olson factory could be accident-prone for other reasons, such as a poor setup.

Section 2: Quantitative Reasoning

1. **C.** To get the area of triangle ABC, you need the base and the height. Because sides $BC = 2$ and $AB = 1$, this is a 30-60-90 triangle with a side-length ratio of $1 : 2 : \sqrt{3}$: The base is 1 and the height is $\sqrt{3}$. The area of the triangle is thus $\frac{1}{2}$ base × height $= \frac{\text{base} \times \text{height}}{2}$, making Quantity A equal to Quantity B.

2. **B.** The weighted average is always closer to the average of the larger group, which in this case is 90. 105 is the simple average of 120 and 90, so the weighted average is closer to 90 and less than 105.

   You can also do the math. To get the weighted average, add the product of 10 and 120 to the product of 20 and 90: $1,200 + 1,800 = 3,000$. Divide by the total number of test scores (30), and the weighted average is 100, less than 105.

3. **D.** If you assumed the highest possible value of n is 14, making $\frac{n}{d} = \frac{14}{20} = 0.7$, then you fell for the trap and picked Choice (B). However, because n isn't necessarily an integer, it could be equal to 14.999, which is greater than 0.72 when placed over 20. Because n could also be 11, $\frac{n}{d}$ could be either less than or greater than 0.72.

4. **A.** If you start with six servings, multiply this by $\frac{5}{2}$ for 15 servings, as $\frac{5}{2} \times 6 = \frac{30}{2} = 15$. You need $\frac{4}{3}$ cups of lentils for six servings, so use $\frac{5}{2} \times \frac{4}{3} = \frac{20}{6} = \frac{10}{3}$ cups for 15 servings. Because $\frac{10}{3}$ is more than 3, Choice **(A)** is the correct answer.

5. **C.** Remember how to find the area of a trapezoid? Average the two bases and multiply by the height. Because the bases are 9 and 11, the average is 10. Multiplying by the height gives you 50, which is the same as the area of the rectangle.

6. **C.** Call the interior angles of the triangle A, B, and C, according to the labels on the drawing. Because the angle supplementary to angle C is $2x$, angle C equals $180 - 2x$. The three angles of any triangle total 180, making angle B equal to 180 minus the other two angles, or $180 - x - (180 - 2x)$, which you can rewrite as $180 - x - 180 + 2x$. The 180s cancel, and $-x + 2x$ becomes x. Now you know two of the angles are equal, making the triangle isosceles and segments AC and BC equal.

7. **A.** The equation $x^2 - x - 6 = 0$ becomes $(x - 3)(x + 2) = 0$, making the roots of the equation 3 and −2. (The roots are the two values for x, either of which makes the statement true.) The sum of these two numbers is 1, making Quantity A greater than Quantity B. If you thought the roots were −3 and 2 and picked Choice (C), then you fell for the trap by thinking that −3 and +2 in the factored equation are the roots.

8. **A.** First set up the equation with x as the number and $2x$ as the average:

$$\frac{8 + 8 + 11 + 18 + x}{5} = 2x$$

$$\frac{45 + x}{5} = 2x$$

Now place the 2x over 1 and cross multiply:

$$\frac{45+x}{5} = \frac{2x}{1}$$
$$45 + x = 10x$$
$$45 = 9x$$
$$5 = x$$

x is 5, so the average of the numbers is 10. Twice the average is 20, making Choice (A) greater than Choice (B).

9. **A.** The units digit of any product depends on the units digits of the two numbers being multiplied. To find the units digit of $219,473 \times 162,597$, just use the units digits of the two numbers: 3 and 7. Then $3 \times 7 = 21$, so the units digit of $219,473 \times 162,597$ is 1.

10. **E.** To find the slope of the line, convert the equation to slope-intercept form, which is $y = mx + b$. Solve for y, and m is the slope.

$$2x + 3y = 5$$
$$3y = -2x + 5$$
$$y = \frac{-2}{3}x + \frac{5}{3}$$

11. **A, B, C,** and **D.** These four answer choices are correct because 15 to 30 percent of $50,000 is $7,500 to $15,000. In this type of question, you select *all* correct answer choices.

12. **61.** Set the ratios up as baseballs : gloves = 2 : 9 and baseballs : bats = 5 : 3. Because baseballs are in both ratios, once as 2 and once as 5, the actual number of baseballs has to be a multiple of both 2 and 5. The question asks for the *lowest* number, and the lowest common multiple of 2 and 5 is 10. If the ratio of baseballs to gloves is 2 : 9 and there are 10 baseballs, there must be 45 gloves (multiply both sides of the ratio by 5). Also, if the ratio of baseballs to bats is 5 : 3 and there are 10 baseballs, there must be 6 bats (multiply both sides of the ratio by 2). Add these up for the number of sporting items:
10 baseballs + 45 gloves + 6 bats = 61 items.

13. **24.** If the average of x, y, and z is 5, then $x + y + z = 15$. To find the average of the expressions $4x + y$, $2y - x$, and $3z + 27$, add them up and divide by 3. The equations $4x + y$, $2y - x$, and $3z + 27$ simplify to $3x + 3y + 3z + 27$. Because $x + y + z = 15$, $3x + 3y + 3z = 3(15) = 45$. Add the 27 for a total of 72. Finally, $72 \div 3$ is 24.

14. **D.** If the central angle is 45 degrees, then the resulting arc is also 45 degrees, which is $\frac{45°}{360°} = \frac{1}{8}$ of the circle. If the radius of the circle is 8, then the circumference is 16π. And $\frac{1}{8}$ of 16π is 2π.

15. **D.** The table shows that on Test B, a score of 300 placed the examinee in the 94th percentile ranking. This means that the examinee scored higher than 94 percent of the other examinees. Therefore, 5 percent of the examinees, or 1 out of every 20 examinees, scored 300. You can use the graph for a similar result: Of 1,412,393 test-takers, 80,000 scored 300 on Test B.

$$\frac{80,000}{1,412,393} = .057 \approx 5\%, \text{ for 1 out of 20.}$$

Note the question says "approximately," and the other answers are not even close.

16. **E.** In the first graph, the line for Test A examinees crosses the 40,000 line at two points: 30 and 210. However, 30 isn't an answer choice, so if you selected Choice (A) or (B), you fell for the trap of not looking far enough on the chart. This examinee could also have a score of 210, which *is* an answer choice and the correct answer. Choice (C), 90, is the group of 40,000 similar scorers on Test B, another trap. Choice (D), 180, is the score at which the two testing trend lines cross.

17. **C.** Using the line chart, you see that approximately 70,000 examinees scored 100 and 80,000 scored 110. By jumping from 100 to 120, the examinee surpasses about $70,000 + 80,000 = 150,000$ examinees. Note that the graph label says that the test scores are in "increments of 10," so you know that no one scored, say, 105 or 109. You only need to account for students with scores of 100 and 110.

18. **E.** The area of any circle is πr^2. Because the radius of the original circle increased by 50 percent, the new radius is $\frac{3r}{2}$. Plug the new radius into the area formula with $\frac{3r}{2}$ as r:

$$\pi\left(\frac{3r}{2}\right)^2 = \pi\left(\frac{3r}{2}\right)\left(\frac{3r}{2}\right) = \frac{9\pi r^2}{4}$$

19. **C.** If the circle is inscribed within the square, then the diameter of the circle is equal to one side of the square, which is 6. This makes the radius of the circle 3 and the area $\pi(3)^2 = 9\pi$. The circle occupies $\frac{9\pi}{36}$ of the square, which reduces to $\frac{\pi}{4}$.

20. **5.** You can find the volume of a cylinder with $\pi r^2 h$ (the base area times the height). You're given the volume and height, so back-solve to find the radius. Begin with $50\pi = \pi r^2 2$ (because the height is 2). Eliminate the π and 2 from both sides for $25 = r^2$, making the radius 5.

Section 3: Verbal Reasoning

1. **C.** A language is composed of structure and *vocabulary*, and an *etymologist* studies the history of language. Though *grammar* is also relevant, it's redundant to structure, which is already in the sentence. The other choices, *culture, politics,* and *decorum* (proper behavior), are not directly related to languages or language structure.

2. **A.** The wind flow is driven by the rotation of Earth, so look for an answer choice related to that — especially one with a clockwise or counterclockwise orientation. Only *hemisphere* is related to the rotation of Earth, which would appear to go clockwise in one hemisphere and counterclockwise in the other. You don't need geographical knowledge to answer this question — just eliminate answer choices that aren't related to the rotation of Earth.

3. **A, E.** A *capricious* (fickle) shopper changes heart easily and has a *penchant* (tendency) to abandon the transaction before completing it. For the first blank, *predictable* doesn't work because it's the opposite of capricious, and *fatuous* means silly or inane. For the second blank, neither *inkling* (hunch) nor *passion* (desire) makes sense in this context.

4. **C, D.** Because the compensation was *commensurate* (proportional), the contractor wouldn't *quibble* (argue) over the deadlines. For the first blank, *discordant* (conflicting) means nearly the opposite of *commensurate,* and *pursuant* means in agreement with (as in the terms of a contract). *Acquiesce* and *concede* both mean to go along with, neither of which fits the connotation of this sentence.

5. **A, F.** Attempts to control didn't work, so the situation was more likely *intractable* (difficult to control) than *imperturbable* (calm and cool) or *indolent* (lazy). If the attempts made things worse, they *augmented* (increased) the tension, rather than *precipitated* (triggered) or *exonerated* (forgave) it.

6. **C, D, G.** Reading the sentence from the end, you know that the teacher was concerned about student safety, so safety issues would have *superseded* (taken precedence over) all other concerns and not *preceded* (come earlier) or *negated* (canceled) them. If safety became a concern, the mixture must have become *volatile* (changing rapidly, which could be dangerous), definitely not *piquant* (spicy), but perhaps *acidic,* although that wouldn't necessarily require an evacuation. Something helped change the nature of the mixture, so that would be a *catalyst* (an agent of change), not just any old *chemical,* and certainly not a *neutralizer,* which would have made the mixture less dangerous.

7. **A, F, H.** *Pristine* means perfect. *Primordial* is more along the lines of prehistoric, and *rudimentary* means basic. If the owner said that the vase *certainly was,* he *averred* (confirmed) that the vase was in pristine condition. *Corroborated* would have required someone else saying it before he did, and if he *proved* it, the vase really would have been in pristine condition. For the last blank, *however* is the key word; knowing that the owner claimed the vase was in pristine condition, *however* clues you in that it really wasn't, in which case the buyer was *duped* (fooled), not *sidetracked* (diverted) or *ostracized* (excluded).

8. **B, C.** The second sentence names three factors that contributed to Great Britain's ability to take an early lead in the Industrial Revolution: coal, waterways, and international trade. Choice (A), trade unions, is mentioned near the end but only as a reaction by the working class to the low pay and poor working conditions.

9. **D.** "Thus, employers had such a large labor pool to select from that they were able to dictate low wages and long hours, further suppressing the working poor." The sentence clearly states that the wages were so low because "employers had such a large labor pool to select from."

10. **E.** "Great Britain's Industrial Revolution: Natural Resources, Migration, and Unions." The passage covers these three topics but isn't entirely based on any one. Choice (A) is wrong because the passage never says Great Britain went bust. Choice (B) is wrong because it describes only half the passage. Choice (C) is wrong because unions are mentioned only in the final sentence and the passage doesn't say that unions originated in Great Britain. Choice (D) is wrong because the passage's perspective is that of the historian, not the exploited poor.

11. **A.** If some teachers have a better track record than others in educating students at the same school, the difference in teacher expertise is probably the reason why. Choices (B), (C), and (E) would help point toward some other cause, while Choice (D) is off topic.

12. **C.** You know that thylacines mainly ate marsupials; the question is why. The passage suggests that thylacines had a preference. Choice (C) offers a different reason: Marsupials were the easiest to get to. Choice (A) is out of scope: There may not have been enough thylacines to affect the marsupial population. Choice (B) affirms that thylacines ate other animals, but they may still have preferred marsupials. Choice (D) is out of scope: The point is what thylacines ate, not other animals of prey. And Choice (E) only says that the marsupials fought back.

13. **B.** Even if you don't know the meaning of *rapprochement,* the following parenthetical *rejection of* provides a clue that it means the opposite of rejection of, so it means something like acceptance of. *Reconciliation* is the closest in meaning to acceptance of.

14. **C.** The second sentence mentions the only answer choice that's correct: "It can be a triumphant parade of 'great men and women.'" Choice (A) is wrong because although the passage mentions psychoanalysis, it does so only as one of a sequence of paradigmatic shifts. Choice (B) is wrong because although the passage mentions film language, it does so only as an example of an orienting metaphor.

15. **B, E.** Antics that go great at a party may not go so well outside the party. This behavior would appear *loutish* or *boorish,* both of which mean rude. *Courteous* and *decorous* both mean polite, *capricious* means fickle, and *contentious* means quarrelsome, none of which fits in this context.

16. **D, F.** *Convoluted* and *tortuous* both mean complex, full of twists and turns, which would make the plans difficult to follow and execute. *Desultory* means aimless or unfocused, making it a good word to describe the plans, but it doesn't have a match in the answer choices. If the plans were *methodical* (systematic), they'd be easy to follow, and if they were *proscribed* (prohibited), nobody on staff would be allowed to carry them out. *Diffident* means not confident, which doesn't fit.

17. **A, E.** If the candidates weren't strong and were pandering, they must have been *pusillanimous* or *craven* (cowardly). They certainly would not be *impudent* (bold, in a disrespectful way), *audacious* (daring), *sanctimonious* (self-righteous), or *intransigent* (stubborn).

18. **B, E.** Parents are reluctant but expected to *admonish* (scold) or *reprimand* (punish) children but not *vilify* (slander) or *disparage* (ridicule). Parents may *sanction* (approve of) or *congratulate* children, but they would not be reluctant to do so.

19. **A, C.** *Obdurate* and *obstinate* both convey a sense of stubbornness. *Recalcitrant* and *subversive* convey a sense of rebellion, which isn't the case: It's sentimentality. *Assiduous* means hardworking, which the couple may have been, but that wouldn't necessarily make them reluctant to move. *Fundamentalist* (die-hard or unyielding) also misses the sentimental point.

20. **B.** If the dogs rid their bodies of the preservative quickly once they stop eating it, then they should be fine. The opposite is if the preservative lingers for a long time, which means they'll continue feeling lousy. Choice (A) is out, because most dogs don't wait before gobbling the treats. Choices (C) and (D) are out of scope, because the passage is about dogs, not cats or other species. Choice (E) is out, because what the treats were two years ago isn't pertinent to today.

Section 4: Quantitative Reasoning

1. **B.** The profit and loss percents are based on the dealer's purchase price, not the dealer's selling price. If he sold a sofa for \$400 at a 25 percent profit, then he sold it for 125 percent, or $\frac{5}{4}$, of what he paid for it, which is x, so

$$\frac{5}{4}x = 400$$

$$x = {}^{80}\!\!\not{400} \cdot \frac{4}{1\not{5}}$$

$$x = 320$$

The net gain was $400 - 320 = 80$.

The dealer sold the other sofa for \$400 at a 20 percent loss, or for $100\% - 20\% = 80\%$, or $\frac{8}{10} = \frac{4}{5}$ of what he paid for it (call it y). Therefore, the dealer purchased it for

$$\frac{4}{5}y = 400$$

$$y = {}^{100}\!\!\not{400} \cdot \frac{5}{1\not{4}}$$

$$y = 500$$

The net loss was $500 - 400 = 100$, so Quantity B is larger. If you picked Choice (A), then you calculated the profit and loss on the dealer's *sale* prices of \$400, not the dealer's *purchase* prices.

2. **B.** The number of integers between 200 and 500 with a units digit of 5, starting with 205 and ending with 495, is 30. Just look at the 20 from 205 and the 49 from 495. 20 to 49, inclusive, is 30.

3. **B.** If $ab < 0$, then either a or b (but not both) is negative, and neither equals 0. Making them both positive, as in Quantity B, and then adding them produces a higher number than adding them first (with one as a negative) and then making the result positive.

4. **D.** If you opted for Choice (B), then you fell for the trap. Just because $\frac{x}{y} = \frac{2}{3}$ doesn't mean that $x = 2$ or $y = 3$. They could be 20 and 30, for example. Or x and y could both be negative, such as -2 and -3.

5. **A.** Draw the xy-coordinate plane and place the points A and C as directed. These are two points of the square, and you know they're the opposite corners because the question tells you the sides of the square are parallel to the axes. Measure the width and height and multiply for an area of 25. (Or measure the width *or* the height and then square that for the answer.)

6. **C.** Drawing a line from point A to point C splits the square into two 45-45-90 triangles. The side ratio of this triangle is $x : x : x\sqrt{2}$, so if two of the sides are 5, then the hypotenuse is $5\sqrt{2}$.

7. **D.** If n equals 2, then Quantity A is greater; if n equals $\frac{1}{2}$, then Quantity B is greater. All you know is that n is positive, not whether it's an integer or a fraction less than 1.

8. B. Set up the conversions as fractions and do the math:

$$\left(\frac{2\cancel{0}\ \cancel{\text{meters}}}{1\ \cancel{\text{sec}}}\right)\left(\frac{1\ \text{km}}{1,\cancel{000}\ \cancel{\text{meters}}}\right)\left(\frac{6\cancel{0}\ \cancel{\text{sec}}}{1\ \cancel{\text{min}}}\right)\left(\frac{1\cancel{0}\ \cancel{\text{min}}}{1}\right)=12\ \text{km}$$

Note that the three zeros in the numerators cancel the three zeros in the denominator of the second fraction.

9. C, E. If $(x-5)^2=900$, then take the square root of both sides to get $x-5=30$ and $x-5=-30$. Add 5s all around, and x equals either 35 or −25.

10. B. If the radius of the pool is r and the width of the sidewalk is $\frac{r}{2}$, then the radius from the center of the pool to the outer circumference of the sidewalk is $r+\frac{r}{2}=\frac{3r}{2}$. First, calculate the area of the pool and sidewalk by substituting $\frac{3r}{2}$ for r in the equation for the area of a circle:

$$A=\pi r^2$$
$$=\pi\left(\frac{3r}{2}\right)^2$$
$$=\pi\left(\frac{3r}{2}\right)\left(\frac{3r}{2}\right)$$
$$=\frac{9\pi r^2}{4}$$

Next, calculate the area of the pool alone, which is more straightforward: $A=\pi r^2$. Finally, subtract the area of the pool from the total area of the pool plus the sidewalk, with a common denominator to subtract:

$$\frac{9\pi r^2}{4}-\pi r^2=\frac{9\pi r^2}{4}-\frac{4\pi r^2}{4}=\frac{5\pi r^2}{4}$$

11. 120. The sum of angles for any polygon can be found with the formula $(n-2)(180°)$, making the sum of the hexagon's angles 720 degrees. The hexagon is a regular hexagon, meaning all sides and angles are the same, so divide the total of 720 by 6 for 120 degrees per angle.

12. 3. Pick a number that has a remainder of 3 when divided by 35, such as 38 or 73. Divide this number by 7, and it has the same remainder. This is because 7 divides perfectly into 35.

13. E. Pick simple numbers (which easily adjust by 20 percent, so multiples of 5) for the length and width of the rectangle, such as 10 and 5, for an area of 50. Increase one by 20 percent and decrease the other by 20 percent for a new length and width of 12 and 4 and a new area of 48. Now, reduce the ratio of 50:48 to 25:24. Regardless of the numbers you pick, the ratio of the area of the original rectangle to the area of the new rectangle is 25:24. Who knew?

14. D. If you multiplied the bachelor's-degree holder's median weekly earnings of $1,012 by 4 and picked Choice (C), you fell for the trap. An average month is $4\frac{1}{3}$ weeks long:

$$\frac{52\ \text{weeks}}{12\ \text{months}}=4\frac{4}{12}=4\frac{1}{3}\ \text{weeks/month}$$

Now multiply the median weekly earnings of $1,012 by the number of weeks per month: $1,012\times4\frac{1}{3}=\$4,385.33$, which is closest to Choice (D), $4,400.

15. B. To count the unemployed doctoral-degree holders, take 2 percent of 10,000, which is 200. To count the unemployed master's-degree holders, take 2.4 percent of 200,000, which is 4,800. Reduce the ratio of 200 : 4,800 to 1 : 24.

16. D. Good thing you get a calculator. To find the annual earnings of the associate-degree holder earning 20 percent less than the median, multiply the median amount of $757 by 0.8 and by 52, for an annual salary of $31,491. To find the annual earnings of the bachelor's-degree holder earning 25 percent above the median, multiply the median amount of $1,012 by 1.25 and by 52, for an annual salary of $65,780. The difference is $34,290, making the closest answer choice $34,300.

17. B. You can find the area of an equilateral triangle by using the formula $\dfrac{s^2\sqrt{3}}{4}$, where s is a side length. You can also consider the equilateral triangle to be two 30-60-90 triangles, giving the triangle a height of $3\sqrt{3}$, and use the $A = \dfrac{1}{2}\text{base} \times \text{height}$ formula.

18. B, C, D. Of the 49 houses, the median value will be of house number 25, in order of value. This places the median house in the third group, valued in thousands from $150 to $199. This median value can be any value in that range.

19. A. With the two equations, subtract one from the other to eliminate y:

$$\begin{array}{r} y = x + 1 \\ -(y = 2x + 3) \\ \hline 0 = -x - 2 \\ x = -2 \end{array}$$

Since x is -2, substitute x in either original equation, for the value of y as -1.

20. C. The idea is to simplify this fraction as quickly and easily as possible. Factor the $\dfrac{5^{10} - 5^8}{5^9 - 5^7}$ into $\dfrac{5^8\left(5^2 - 1\right)}{5^7\left(5^2 - 1\right)}$. Cancel the $\left(5^2 - 1\right)$ from the top and bottom, and reduce the $\dfrac{5^8}{5^7}$ to 5.

Answer Key for Practice Exam 2

Section 1: Verbal Reasoning

1.	D	6.	C, D, G	11.	E	16.	E, F
2.	B	7.	B, F, H	12.	D	17.	C, D
3.	A, E	8.	C	13.	B	18.	A, D
4.	A, F	9.	A	14.	C	19.	B, C
5.	C, D	10.	A, C	15.	B, D	20.	B

Section 2: Quantitative Reasoning

1.	C	6.	C	11.	A, B, C, D	16.	E
2.	B	7.	A	12.	61	17.	C
3.	D	8.	A	13.	24	18.	E
4.	A	9.	A	14.	D	19.	C
5.	C	10.	E	15.	D	20.	5

Section 3: Verbal Reasoning

1.	C	6.	C, D, G	11.	A	16.	D, F
2.	A	7.	A, F, H	12.	C	17.	A, E
3.	A, E	8.	B, C	13.	B	18.	B, E
4.	C, D	9.	D	14.	C	19.	A, C
5.	A, F	10.	E	15.	B, E	20.	B

Section 4: Quantitative Reasoning

1.	B	6.	C	11.	120	16.	D
2.	B	7.	D	12.	3	17.	B
3.	B	8.	B	13.	E	18.	B, C, D
4.	D	9.	C, E	14.	D	19.	A
5.	A	10.	B	15.	B	20.	C

Chapter 22

Practice Exam 3

Y ou're doing great — now for another. The idea is that on exam day, there's nothing you're not expecting, and that comes from practice. Remember to revisit any rough topics in Chapters 4 through 15.

Like the others in this book, this exam consists of two 30-minute essays, two 30-minute Verbal Reasoning sections (20 questions each), and two 35-minute Quantitative Reasoning sections (20 questions each).

Remember the rules: Take this practice test under normal exam conditions and approach it as you would the real GRE.

>> Work when you won't be interrupted.

>> Use scratch paper that's free of any prepared notes.

>> Answer as many questions as time allows and guess on the remaining questions.

>> Set a timer for each section.

>> Don't leave your desk while the clock is running on any section.

>> Take a one-minute break after each section and the optional ten-minute break after the first Verbal section.

>> Type the essays using a simple text editor, such as Notepad.

Then go to Chapter 23 to check your answers and review the explanations for *all* the questions, not just the ones you miss.

Answer Sheet for Practice Exam 3

Section 1:
Verbal Reasoning

1. Ⓐ Ⓑ Ⓒ Ⓓ Ⓔ
2. Ⓐ Ⓑ Ⓒ Ⓓ Ⓔ
3. Ⓐ Ⓑ Ⓒ Ⓓ Ⓔ Ⓕ
4. Ⓐ Ⓑ Ⓒ Ⓓ Ⓔ Ⓕ
5. Ⓐ Ⓑ Ⓒ Ⓓ Ⓔ Ⓕ
6. Ⓐ Ⓑ Ⓒ Ⓓ Ⓔ Ⓕ Ⓖ Ⓗ Ⓘ
7. Ⓐ Ⓑ Ⓒ Ⓓ Ⓔ Ⓕ Ⓖ Ⓗ Ⓘ
8. Ⓐ Ⓑ Ⓒ
9. Ⓐ Ⓑ Ⓒ Ⓓ Ⓔ
10. Ⓐ Ⓑ Ⓒ Ⓓ Ⓔ
11. Ⓐ Ⓑ Ⓒ
12. Ⓐ Ⓑ Ⓒ Ⓓ Ⓔ
13. Ⓐ Ⓑ Ⓒ Ⓓ Ⓔ
14. Ⓐ Ⓑ Ⓒ Ⓓ Ⓔ
15. Ⓐ Ⓑ Ⓒ Ⓓ Ⓔ Ⓕ
16. Ⓐ Ⓑ Ⓒ Ⓓ Ⓔ Ⓕ
17. Ⓐ Ⓑ Ⓒ Ⓓ Ⓔ Ⓕ
18. Ⓐ Ⓑ Ⓒ Ⓓ Ⓔ Ⓕ
19. Ⓐ Ⓑ Ⓒ Ⓓ Ⓔ Ⓕ
20. Ⓐ Ⓑ Ⓒ Ⓓ Ⓔ

Section 2:
Quantitative Reasoning

1. Ⓐ Ⓑ Ⓒ Ⓓ
2. Ⓐ Ⓑ Ⓒ Ⓓ
3. Ⓐ Ⓑ Ⓒ Ⓓ
4. Ⓐ Ⓑ Ⓒ Ⓓ
5. Ⓐ Ⓑ Ⓒ Ⓓ
6. Ⓐ Ⓑ Ⓒ Ⓓ
7. Ⓐ Ⓑ Ⓒ Ⓓ
8. Ⓐ Ⓑ Ⓒ Ⓓ
9. Ⓐ Ⓑ Ⓒ Ⓓ Ⓔ
10. Ⓐ Ⓑ Ⓒ Ⓓ Ⓔ
11. Ⓐ Ⓑ Ⓒ Ⓓ Ⓔ
12. Ⓐ Ⓑ Ⓒ Ⓓ Ⓔ
13. Ⓐ Ⓑ Ⓒ Ⓓ Ⓔ
14. Ⓐ Ⓑ Ⓒ
15. [_____]
16. [_____]
17. [_____]
18. Ⓐ Ⓑ Ⓒ Ⓓ Ⓔ Ⓕ
19. Ⓐ Ⓑ Ⓒ Ⓓ Ⓔ Ⓕ
20. Ⓐ Ⓑ Ⓒ

Section 3:
Verbal Reasoning

1. Ⓐ Ⓑ Ⓒ Ⓓ Ⓔ
2. Ⓐ Ⓑ Ⓒ Ⓓ Ⓔ
3. Ⓐ Ⓑ Ⓒ Ⓓ Ⓔ Ⓕ
4. Ⓐ Ⓑ Ⓒ Ⓓ Ⓔ Ⓕ
5. Ⓐ Ⓑ Ⓒ Ⓓ Ⓔ Ⓕ
6. Ⓐ Ⓑ Ⓒ Ⓓ Ⓔ Ⓕ Ⓖ Ⓗ Ⓘ
7. Ⓐ Ⓑ Ⓒ Ⓓ Ⓔ Ⓕ Ⓖ Ⓗ Ⓘ
8. Ⓐ Ⓑ Ⓒ Ⓓ Ⓔ
9. Ⓐ Ⓑ Ⓒ Ⓓ Ⓔ
10. Ⓐ Ⓑ Ⓒ
11. Ⓐ Ⓑ Ⓒ
12. Ⓐ Ⓑ Ⓒ Ⓓ Ⓔ
13. Ⓐ Ⓑ Ⓒ Ⓓ Ⓔ
14. Ⓐ Ⓑ Ⓒ Ⓓ Ⓔ
15. Ⓐ Ⓑ Ⓒ Ⓓ Ⓔ
16. Ⓐ Ⓑ Ⓒ Ⓓ Ⓔ Ⓕ
17. Ⓐ Ⓑ Ⓒ Ⓓ Ⓔ Ⓕ
18. Ⓐ Ⓑ Ⓒ Ⓓ Ⓔ Ⓕ
19. Ⓐ Ⓑ Ⓒ Ⓓ Ⓔ Ⓕ
20. Ⓐ Ⓑ Ⓒ Ⓓ Ⓔ Ⓕ

Section 4:
Quantitative Reasoning

1. Ⓐ Ⓑ Ⓒ Ⓓ
2. Ⓐ Ⓑ Ⓒ Ⓓ
3. Ⓐ Ⓑ Ⓒ Ⓓ
4. Ⓐ Ⓑ Ⓒ Ⓓ
5. Ⓐ Ⓑ Ⓒ Ⓓ
6. Ⓐ Ⓑ Ⓒ Ⓓ
7. Ⓐ Ⓑ Ⓒ Ⓓ
8. Ⓐ Ⓑ Ⓒ Ⓓ
9. Ⓐ Ⓑ Ⓒ Ⓓ Ⓔ
10. Ⓐ Ⓑ Ⓒ Ⓓ Ⓔ
11. Ⓐ Ⓑ Ⓒ Ⓓ Ⓔ
12. Ⓐ Ⓑ Ⓒ Ⓓ Ⓔ
13. Ⓐ Ⓑ Ⓒ Ⓓ Ⓔ
14. Ⓐ Ⓑ Ⓒ
15. [_____]
16. [_____]
17. [_____]
18. Ⓐ Ⓑ Ⓒ Ⓓ Ⓔ Ⓕ
19. Ⓐ Ⓑ Ⓒ
20. Ⓐ Ⓑ Ⓒ

Analytical Writing 1: Analyze an Issue

TIME: 30 minutes

Consumerism has contributed significantly to alleviating human suffering.

DIRECTIONS: Write a response in which you express the extent to which you agree or disagree with the preceding statement and explain the reasoning behind your position. In support of your position, think of ways in which the statement may or may not be true and how these considerations influence your position.

Analytical Writing 2: Analyze an Argument

TIME: 30 minutes

Though touted as the key to building a strong economy, microlending (making small loans to entrepreneurs in impoverished countries) can actually do more harm than good. In the small country of Bogata, for instance, microlending was introduced in key regions, and the gross domestic product (total value of all goods and services produced) declined by 20 percent. During the same time, the neighboring country of Byrn did not introduce microlending practices, and its gross domestic product increased 25 percent. The practice of microlending therefore should be discouraged from any economy.

DIRECTIONS: Write a response in which you discuss the merits of the preceding argument. Discuss the evidence that would strengthen or weaken it.

Section 1
Verbal Reasoning

TIME: 30 minutes for 20 questions

DIRECTIONS: Choose the best answer to each question. Blacken the corresponding ovals or boxes on the answer sheet.

Directions: For Questions 1–7, pick the one entry best suited for each blank from its corresponding column of choices.

1. In Shakespeare's *Julius Caesar*, Brutus and Cassius make a(n) _____ reference to a mechanical clock, though in the time of the story it had not yet been invented.

Ⓐ ambiguous
Ⓑ anachronistic
Ⓒ ancient
Ⓓ archaic
Ⓔ euphemistic

2. An unbiased journalist is responsible to the public and the profession for the _____ of the story.

Ⓐ veracity
Ⓑ plausibility
Ⓒ tenacity
Ⓓ originality
Ⓔ righteousness

3. Galileo was not the first astronomer to question the (i) _____ view of Earth as being at the center of the universe, but he was the most vocal, so his ideas were (ii) _____ by the Catholic Church.

Blank (i)	Blank (ii)
Ⓐ heliocentric	Ⓓ authorized
Ⓑ Eurocentric	Ⓔ proscribed
Ⓒ geocentric	Ⓕ legitimized

4. There is the debate of whether the (i) _____ used in dental fillings poses a health risk; though it contains mercury and other metals, experts question the (ii) _____ that the toxic mercury is dangerous, as its level of exposure is too low to pose a serious threat.

Blank (i)	Blank (ii)
Ⓐ element	Ⓓ supposition
Ⓑ metal	Ⓔ accusation
Ⓒ amalgam	Ⓕ allegation

GO ON TO NEXT PAGE

5. Law students often have (i) _____ to study the letter of the law over the spirit of the law, so that they become so consumed in (ii) _____ legal language and technicalities that they completely miss the point.

Blank (i)	Blank (ii)
Ⓐ an aptitude	Ⓓ sophisticated
Ⓑ the propensity	Ⓔ recondite
Ⓒ a desire	Ⓕ erudite

6. Teachers who are (i) _____ typically perform better and last longer than those who are choleric. In junior high especially, classroom management can become quite (ii) _____, which over time, only increases one's (iii) _____ to students and the profession.

Blank (i)	Blank (ii)	Blank (iii)
Ⓐ equanimous	Ⓓ truculent	Ⓖ antipathy
Ⓑ sanguine	Ⓔ elementary	Ⓗ opposition
Ⓒ melancholic	Ⓕ onerous	Ⓘ hostility

7. Some say that increasing oil production will be insufficient to meet (i) _____ demand. Others (ii) _____ that oil powers the economy and brings technological innovation, which (iii) _____ dependence on oil.

Blank (i)	Blank (ii)	Blank (iii)
Ⓐ escalating	Ⓓ allude	Ⓖ extenuates
Ⓑ nascent	Ⓔ imply	Ⓗ mitigates
Ⓒ proliferating	Ⓕ maintain	Ⓘ propagates

This passage is an excerpt from Psychology *by Robin M. Kowalski, PhD, and Drew Westen (Wiley).*

Since its origins in the nineteenth century, one of the major issues in behavioral neuroscience has been **localization of function.** In 1836, a physician named Marc Dax presented a paper suggesting that lesions on the left side of the brain were associated with *aphasia,* or language disorders. The notion that language was localized to the left side of the brain (the left hemisphere) developed momentum with new discoveries linking specific language functions to specific regions of the left hemisphere. Paul Broca (1824–1880) discovered that brain-injured people with lesions in the front section of the left hemisphere were often unable to speak fluently but could comprehend language. Carl Wernicke (1848–1904) showed that damage to an area a few centimeters behind the section Broca had discovered could lead to another kind of aphasia: These individuals can speak fluently and follow rules of grammar, but they cannot understand language, and their words make little sense to others (e.g., "I saw the bats and cuticles as the dog lifted the hoof, the pauser").

For the following question, consider each of the choices separately and choose all that apply.

8. Which of the following, if true, supports the notion of localization of function?

   A A person suffering from a lesion in part of the frontal lobe of the left hemisphere of the brain can no longer recall certain words.

   B The region of the brain known as the *fusiform gyrus* is more active than other regions of the brain when the subject is engaged in facial recognition.

   C Unconsciousness occurs when almost the entire cortex has been compromised or invaded by convulsive activity.

9. Which of the following statements, if true, would most effectively challenge the notion that complex thoughts or emotions happen exclusively in a single localized part of the brain?

   Ⓐ While nearly 95 percent of right-handed people are left-hemisphere dominated for language, only 18 percent of left-handed people are right-hemisphere dominated for language.

   Ⓑ While the back edge of the frontal lobes controls voluntary motor movement, the occipital lobe controls one's visual ability.

   Ⓒ A woman with lesions in the top part of the temporal lobe suffers hearing loss, but her vision improves.

   Ⓓ Due to a lesion in one area of his brain, a man cannot consciously recognize his wife's face, but his heart rate increases upon seeing her face.

   Ⓔ Convulsions may be accompanied by a loss of consciousness.

10. The discoveries of Broca and Wernicke contribute to Dax's findings by showing that

   Ⓐ language functions are not as localized as Dax had suspected.

   Ⓑ language comprehension is not localized to the left hemisphere of the brain.

   Ⓒ language functions are even more localized than Dax had suspected.

   Ⓓ language acquisition and grammar are localized in different areas of the brain.

   Ⓔ aphasia encompasses more than simply language disorders.

GO ON TO NEXT PAGE

This passage is taken from The Egyptians (Peoples of Africa) *by Barbara Watterson (Wiley-Blackwell).*

The Egyptian section of the Nile — the 1,250 kilometers from the First Cataract to the Mediterranean — was, in its formative stage, much wider than it is today, and bordered by marshland and swamps. Gradually, the river bed cut deeper and the Nile narrowed, flowing through terrain that was rocky and barren. The land sloped very gently to the north, and large quantities of the gravel, sand and silt carried by the river were deposited at its mouth to form the delta, later to become one of the most fertile areas of Egypt. In addition, large amounts of detritus sank to the bottom of the river so that, over the millennia, it aggraded: the different levels of the river are still visible, in the form of cliffs and terraces on the east and west sides of the Nile Valley.

For the following question, consider each of the choices separately and choose all that apply.

11. According to the passage, compared to earlier times, parts of the Nile River are now
    - A Wider
    - B Deeper
    - C More fertile

12. Which of the following is the most accurate definition of the word *terraces* as used in the passage?
    - Ⓐ A strip of land having an abrupt descent
    - Ⓑ A raised platform faced with masonry or turf
    - Ⓒ The platform top of a structure
    - Ⓓ A flat roof
    - Ⓔ An outdoor living area, such as a deck

This passage is taken from The Idea of Culture (Blackwell Manifestos) *by Terry Eagleton (Wiley-Blackwell).*

'Culture' is said to be one of the two or three most complex words in the English language, and the term which is sometimes considered to be its opposite — nature — is commonly awarded the accolade of being the most complex of all. Yet though it is fashionable these days to see nature as a derivative of culture, culture, etymologically speaking, is a concept derived from nature. One of its original meanings is 'husbandry' or the tending of natural growth. The same is true of our words for law and justice, as well as of terms like 'capital', 'stock', 'pecuniary' and 'sterling'. The word 'coulter', which is a cognate of 'culture', means the blade of a ploughshare. We derive our word for the finest of human activities from labour and agriculture, crops and cultivation. Francis Bacon writes of 'the culture and manurance of mines', in a suggestive hesitancy between dung and mental distinction. 'Culture' here means an activity, and it was a long time before the word came to denote an entity. Even then, it was probably not until Matthew Arnold that the word dropped such adjectives as 'moral' and 'intellectual' and came to be just 'culture', an abstraction of itself.

13. Select the sentence in the passage that most accurately expresses the main idea of the passage.
    - Ⓐ First sentence: "'Culture' is said to be . . . the most complex of all."
    - Ⓑ Second sentence: "Yet though it is fashionable . . . a concept derived from nature."
    - Ⓒ Third sentence: "One of its original meanings . . . of natural growth."
    - Ⓓ Fourth sentence: "The same is true of our words . . . 'pecuniary' and 'sterling'."
    - Ⓔ Sixth sentence: "We derive our word for . . . crops and cultivation."

14. Which of the following words does the author of the passage not cite as being a concept derived from nature?

    Ⓐ Capital

    Ⓑ Culture

    Ⓒ Stock

    Ⓓ Pecuniary

    Ⓔ Manurance

Directions: Each of the following sentences has a blank indicating that a word or phrase is omitted. Choose the two answers that best complete the sentence and result in two sentences most alike in meaning.

15. To most Western listeners, traditional Japanese music may sound _____, aimless, and even monotonous, but this is only because Westerners lack the foundation for appreciating it.

    A dissonant

    B symphonic

    C disparate

    D raucous

    E cacophonous

    F mellifluous

16. Filmmakers tend to stereotype scientists and depict them as either _____ humanitarians or passionately mad people.

    A sentient

    B stygian

    C impassive

    D zealous

    E profound

    F stolid

17. Diabetics are prone to simple yet _____ wounds requiring long-term treatment.

    A refractory

    B recalcitrant

    C acute

    D severe

    E perspicacious

    F excruciating

18. Although communities must deal with this locally, _____ is a global issue and not always the result of laziness.

    A malnutrition

    B illiteracy

    C indigence

    D famine

    E penury

    F squalor

19. By focusing almost exclusively on the contentious dialogue between the countries' leaders, the media brings misconceptions that lead to irrational enmity between the people of the two countries; instead, the media should _____ this potential antagonism.

    A mitigate

    B augment

    C assuage

    D incite

    E repress

    F subjugate

GO ON TO NEXT PAGE

This passage is taken from Healing Gardens: Therapeutic Benefits and Design Recommendations *by Clare Cooper Marcus and Marni Barnes (Wiley).*

The idea of a healing garden is both ancient and modern. Long after humans had begun to erect dwellings, local healing places were nearly always found in nature — a healing spring, a sacred grove, a special rock or cave. The earliest hospitals in the Western world were infirmaries in monastic communities where herbs and prayer were the focus of healing and a cloistered garden was an essential part of the environment.

Over the centuries, the connection between healing and nature was gradually superseded by increasingly technical approaches — surgery, medicines, drugs, X-rays. A separation occurred between attention to body and spirit and increasingly, different parts of the body (eyes, heart, digestive tract, etc.) and different afflictions (cancer, arthritis, etc.) were treated by specialists. The idea that access to nature could assist in healing was all but lost.

20. One could reasonably infer from this passage that the author believes which of the following?

Ⓐ Specialization enhances modern medicine.

Ⓑ Modern hospitals should be located in natural settings.

Ⓒ Nature can improve the healing process.

Ⓓ The earliest hospitals are superior to their modern counterparts.

Ⓔ Every hospital should have a decorative courtyard.

Section 2

Quantitative Reasoning

TIME: 35 minutes for 20 questions

NOTES:

- All numbers used in this exam are real numbers.
- All figures lie in a plane.
- Angle measures are positive; points and angles are in the position shown.

Directions: For Questions 1–8, choose from the following answers:

Ⓐ *Quantity A is greater.*

Ⓑ *Quantity B is greater.*

Ⓒ *The two quantities are equal.*

Ⓓ *The relationship cannot be determined from the information given.*

1.

Quantity A	**Quantity B**
$\dfrac{\sqrt{25} \times \sqrt{4}}{\sqrt{10}}$	3.5

2.

Quantity A	**Quantity B**
The sum of all integers from 99 to 198, inclusive	The sum of all integers from 101 to 199, inclusive

3. $9 < x < 10$

Quantity A	**Quantity B**
x^2	99

4. For all integers a and b, $a \Delta b = ab + 2(a+b)$.

Quantity A	**Quantity B**
$\dfrac{1}{1\Delta 2}$	$(0\Delta 1)^{-3}$

5. The perimeter of a certain right triangle with the two other angles measuring 30° and 60° is $3 + \sqrt{3}$.

Quantity A	**Quantity B**
The hypotenuse of the right triangle	2

6. From a group of ten students, three are attending a meeting.

Quantity A	**Quantity B**
The number of different groups that could attend from the 10 students	720

7. A standard six-sided die is thrown.

Quantity A	**Quantity B**
The probability that the die will show either an odd number or a 2	$\dfrac{2}{3}$

GO ON TO NEXT PAGE

8. Tom invested part of $8,000 at 3 percent and the rest at 5 percent annual interest for a total return of $340.

Quantity A	_Quantity B_
The amount invested at 3%	The amount invested at 5%

9. If *n* is a positive even integer, which of the following represents the product of *n* and the consecutive even integer following *n*?

Ⓐ $n^2 + 2$

Ⓑ $(n+2)^2$

Ⓒ $n^2 + 2n$

Ⓓ $2n^2$

Ⓔ It cannot be represented.

10. If a circular garden with a radius of 3 feet is surrounded by a circular sidewalk 2 feet wide, then the area of the sidewalk is

Ⓐ 4π

Ⓑ 9π

Ⓒ 12π

Ⓓ 15π

Ⓔ 16π

11. Bobby has eight more toy cars than Jackie. If Bobby gives two of his cars to Jackie, Bobby will have twice the cars that Jackie has. How many toy cars does Bobby currently have?

Ⓐ 18

Ⓑ 16

Ⓒ 14

Ⓓ 12

Ⓔ 10

Use the following graphs to answer Questions 12–14.

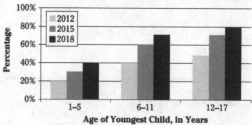

Percentage of Mothers in the Workforce in Country *X* by Age of Youngest Child (2012, 2015, and 2018)

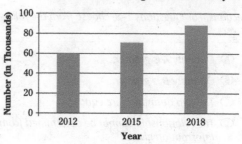

Approximate Number of Mothers with Children under the Age of 18 in Country *X*

Note: Graphs drawn to scale.

© John Wiley & Sons, Inc.

12. If the number of mothers with children under the age of 18 increased by 10 percent from 2018 to 2019 and the percentage of mothers in the workforce stayed about the same during that time, what was the approximate number of mothers with youngest children ages 12 to 17 in the workforce in 2019?

Ⓐ 75,000

Ⓑ 80,000

Ⓒ 85,000

Ⓓ 90,000

Ⓔ 95,000

13. What is the approximate ratio of the percentage of mothers in the workforce in 2012 with youngest children ages 1 to 5 to the percentage of mothers in the workforce in 2015 with youngest children ages 12 to 17?

Ⓐ 2 to 7

Ⓑ 4 to 7

Ⓒ 1 to 3

Ⓓ 5 to 9

Ⓔ 6 to 11

For the following question, choose all that apply.

14. Which of the following can be inferred from the data in the graphs?

    A The population of Country *X* is steadily increasing.

    B The percentage of single mothers is steadily increasing.

    C The demand for daycare in Country *X* is steadily increasing.

15. In the given sequence a_1, a_2, a_3, a_4, a_5, ... a_n, where $a_1 = 38$ and $a_{n+1} = \dfrac{a_n + 2}{2}$, what is the lowest value of *n* for which a_n is not an integer?

    [   ]

16. $\sqrt{(6)(7)(18)(21)} =$

    [   ]

17. What is the smallest prime factor of 1,532,475?

    [   ]

For the following question, choose all that apply.

18. A certain manufacturer produces an engine lift with three pulleys and seven levers. If each box contains eight pulleys and the manufacturer is starting with unopened boxes and does not want to have a partial box of pulleys remaining, which of the following could *not* be the number of levers used in the manufacturing job?

    A 56

    B 84

    C 112

    D 168

    E 196

    F 224

For the following question, choose all that apply.

19. If *n* is an integer and $\dfrac{396}{n}$ is an integer, which of the following could be the value of *n*?

    A 11

    B 12

    C 18

    D 24

    E 27

    F 66

For the following question, choose exactly two answers.

20. If *n* is a positive integer, for which of the following would the units digit always be equal to the units digit of *n*?

    A n^5

    B n^{10}

    C n^{25}

Section 3
Verbal Reasoning

TIME: 30 minutes for 20 questions

DIRECTIONS: Choose the best answer to each question. Blacken the corresponding ovals and boxes on the answer sheet.

Directions: For Questions 1–7, select the one entry best suited for each blank from its corresponding column of choices.

1. Many Shakespeare plays contain scenes and discussions seemingly _____ but central to the theme.

Ⓐ essential
Ⓑ incisive
Ⓒ tangential
Ⓓ concurrent
Ⓔ predominant

2. The speaker supported his case in such a way that he _____ the need for further clarification.

Ⓐ precluded
Ⓑ anticipated
Ⓒ adjourned
Ⓓ prohibited
Ⓔ obviated

3. A(n) (i) _____ existence typically leads to a loss of self-discipline followed by self-loathing, where a seemingly hedonistic paradise becomes a (ii) _____ asylum.

Blank (i)	Blank (ii)
Ⓐ ascetic	Ⓓ stygian
Ⓑ libertine	Ⓔ quixotic
Ⓒ Spartan	Ⓕ utopian

4. In Ayn Rand's *For the New Intellectual*, Galt questions the overriding belief at the time in the (i) _____ of body and soul. According to Galt, proponents of this belief have (ii) _____ the individual into two elements, both symbols of death: a corpse (a body without a soul) and a ghost (a soul without a body).

Blank (i)	Blank (ii)
Ⓐ paradox	Ⓓ dissected
Ⓑ irony	Ⓔ bifurcated
Ⓒ dichotomy	Ⓕ bisected

5. In diplomacy, if talks fail to move forward, one party may accuse the other of (i) _____, which may (ii) _____ conflict.

Blank (i)	Blank (ii)
Ⓐ tractability	Ⓓ expedite
Ⓑ indolence	Ⓔ precipitate
Ⓒ intransigence	Ⓕ motivate

6. Over the years, interrogators have discovered that overly aggressive interrogations often (i) _____ bad information. Rather than engage or give in, suspects often (ii) _____ to "give the interrogator what is wanted." This calls into question not only the ethics of overly aggressive tactics but also their (iii) _____.

Blank (i)	Blank (ii)	Blank (iii)
Ⓐ dissemble	Ⓓ prevaricate	Ⓖ efficiency
Ⓑ elicit	Ⓔ prognosticate	Ⓗ alacrity
Ⓒ disseminate	Ⓕ adjudicate	Ⓘ efficacy

7. With no land masses to (i) _____ them, high winds and large waves are (i) _____ to the Southern Ocean. Plankton gather in relatively (iii) _____ pools, where they attract additional wildlife.

Blank (i)	Blank (ii)	Blank (iii)
Ⓐ debilitate	Ⓓ endemic	Ⓖ quiescent
Ⓑ impede	Ⓔ pandemic	Ⓗ dormant
Ⓒ disperce	Ⓕ intrinsic	Ⓘ truculent

Directions: Each of the following passages is followed by questions pertaining to the passage. Read the passage and answer the questions based on information stated or implied in that passage. For each question, select one answer choice unless instructed otherwise.

This passage is taken from Better Living through Reality TV: Television and Post-Welfare Citizenship *by Laurie Ouellette and James Hay (Wiley-Blackwell).*

To understand the political rationality of reality-based charity TV, a brief detour through the conceptual history of welfare will be helpful. We take our bearings partly from political theorist Nikolas Rose, who situates the changing "mentali-ties" of government leading up to welfare reform within the stages of liberalism. According to Rose's account, the liberal state was called upon to become more directly involved in the care of citizens in the late nineteenth and early twentieth centuries, a period of time that happens to correspond with the development and progression of industrial capitalism. As relations among elites and workers became increasingly antagonistic, rulers were "urged to accept the obligation to tame and govern the undesirable consequences of industrial life, wage labor and urban existence in the name of society." What Rose calls a "state of welfare" emerged to provide basic forms of social insurance, child welfare, health, mental hygiene, universal education, and similar services that both "civilized" the working class and joined citizens to the State and to each other through formalized "solidarities and dependencies." Through this new "social contract" between the State and the population, Rose contends, the autonomous political subject of liberal rule was reconstituted as a "citizen with rights to social protection and social education in return for duties of social obligation and social responsibility."

GO ON TO NEXT PAGE ▶

8. Select the sentence in the passage that explains the purpose of welfare, according to Nikolas Rose, in greatest detail.

   Ⓐ First sentence: "To understand the political rationality . . . will be helpful."

   Ⓑ Second sentence: "We take our bearings partly from . . . the stages of liberalism."

   Ⓒ Third sentence: "According to Rose's account . . . progression of industrial capitalism."

   Ⓓ Fourth sentence: "As relations among elites and workers . . . in the name of society.'"

   Ⓔ Fifth sentence: "What Rose calls a 'state of welfare' . . . through formalized 'solidarities and dependencies.'"

This passage is taken from GMAT For Dummies, *5th Edition, by Scott Hatch, JD, and Lisa Hatch, MA (Wiley).*

It is hard for us to imagine today how utterly different the world of night used to be from the daylight world. Of course, we can still re-create something of that lost mystique. When we sit around a campfire and tell ghost stories, our goose bumps (and our children's) remind us of the terrors that night used to hold. But it is all too easy for us to pile in the car at the end of our camping trip and return to the comfort of our incandescent, fluorescent, floodlit modern world. Two thousand, or even two hundred, years ago there was no such escape from the darkness. It was a physical presence that gripped the world from sunset until the cock's crow.

"As different as night and day," we say today. But in centuries past, night and day really were different. In a time when every scrap of light after sunset was desperately appreciated, when travelers would mark the road by piling up light stones or by stripping the bark off of trees to expose the lighter wood underneath, the Moon was the traveler's greatest friend. It was known in folklore as "the parish lantern." It was steady, portable, and — unlike a torch — entailed no risk of fire. It would never blow out, although it could, of course, hide behind a cloud.

Nowadays we don't need the moon to divide the light from the darkness because electric lights do it for us. Many of us never even see a truly dark sky. According to a recent survey on light pollution, 97 percent of the U.S. population lives under a night sky at least as bright as it was on a half-moon night in ancient times. Many city-dwellers live their entire lives under the equivalent of a full moon.

9. The primary purpose of this passage is to

   Ⓐ Compare and contrast nighttime in the modern world with the dark nights of centuries past.

   Ⓑ Explain why the invention of the electric light was essential to increasing productivity.

   Ⓒ Lament the loss of the dark nights and the danger and excitement that moonless nights would bring.

   Ⓓ Describe the limited brightness of the moon and the subsequent need for more electric lights.

   Ⓔ Argue for regulation of light pollution.

For the following question, consider each of the choices separately and choose all that apply.

10. The passage mentions which of the following as possible ways for travelers to find the path at night?

   Ⓐ Piles of light-colored stones or bark-stripped trees

   Ⓑ The moon or a torch

   Ⓒ Railings made of light wood

This passage is taken from Bad Medicine: Misconceptions and Misuses Revealed, from Distance Healing to Vitamin O *by Christopher Wanjek (Wiley).*

How can we be certain that we don't use only 10 percent of the brain? As Beyerstein succinctly says, "The armamentarium of modern neuroscience decisively repudiates this notion." CAT, PET and MRI scans, along with a battery of other tests, show that there are no inactive regions of the brain, even during sleep. Neuroscientists regularly hook up patients to these devices and ask them to do math problems, listen to music, paint, or do whatever they please. Certain regions of the brain fire up with activity depending on what task is performed. The scans catch all this activity; the entire brain has been mapped this way.

Further debunking of the myth is the fact that the brain, like any other body part, must be used to remain healthy. If your leg remains in a cast for a month, it wilts. A 90-percent brain inactivity rate would result in 90 percent of the brain rapidly deteriorating. Unused neurons (brain cells) would shrivel and die. Clearly, this doesn't happen in healthy individuals. In Alzheimer's disease, there is a diffuse 10 percent to 20 percent loss of neurons. This has a devastating effect on memory and consciousness. A person would be comatose if 90 percent of the brain — any 90 percent — were inactive.

For the following question, consider each of the choices separately and choose all that apply.

11. Which of the following does the passage provide as scientific evidence to disprove the myth that humans use only 10 percent of their brains?

   A Brain scans show activity in all regions of the brain, even during sleep.

   B Brain cells shrivel and die when not in use.

   C A loss of 10 to 20 percent of the brain results in Alzheimer's disease.

This passage is taken from The Daily Show and Philosophy: Moments of Zen in the Art of Fake News *by Jason Holt (Wiley-Blackwell).*

The fact that television provides entertainment isn't, in and of itself, a problem for Postman. He warns, however, that dire consequences can befall a culture in which the most important public discourse, conducted via television, becomes little more than irrational, irrelevant, and incoherent entertainment. Again, we shall see that this is a point often suggested by *The Daily Show*'s biting satire. In a healthy democracy, the open discussion of important issues must be serious, rational, and coherent. But such discussion is often time-consuming and unpleasant, and thus incompatible with television's drive to entertain. So, it's hardly surprising to see television serving up important news analyses in sound bites surrounded by irrelevant graphics and video footage, or substituting half-minute ad spots for substantial political debates. On television, thoughtful conversations about serious issues are reserved for only the lowest-rated niche programs. Just as ventriloquism and mime don't play well on radio, "thinking does not play well on television." Instead, television serves as the sort of "gut"-based discourse celebrated by Stephen Colbert.

12. Which of the following most accurately expresses the main point of this passage?

   A Television can entertain, but it cannot inform.

   B Television inherently is a poor medium for discussion of important issues.

   C Conversations about serious issues play better on radio than on TV.

   D Television's drive to entertain is incompatible with serious discussion of complex issues.

   E Public discourse presented on TV is irrational, irrelevant, incoherent entertainment.

GO ON TO NEXT PAGE

This passage is taken from GMAT For Dummies, 5th Edition, by Scott Hatch, JD, and Lisa Hatch, MA (Wiley).

Snakes exist on every continent except for Antarctica, which is inhospitable to all cold-blooded animals. The continent of Australia is home to many of the deadliest snakes in the world. However, the nearby island nation of New Zealand has no snakes at all. Scientists estimate that snakes originated about 100 million years ago when the continents were joined and the snakes stayed on the main land masses of the continents when they split apart. Snakes are absent from New Zealand because they are unable to swim and therefore could not make the journey.

13. Which of the following, if true, would most weaken the premise that certain species of snakes are absent from New Zealand because they are unable to swim?

    Ⓐ Snakes are found in South America at latitudes farther south than New Zealand.

    Ⓑ Islands like Hawaii and New Zealand are very aggressive about preventing an accidental introduction of snakes.

    Ⓒ The monitor lizard swims but lives only in Australia.

    Ⓓ The Tasman Sea, separating Australia from New Zealand, is home to sharks that prey on snakes.

    Ⓔ Snakes are found on many other islands of the Pacific Ocean.

Although many people in the United States complain about the tax burden, some of the countries with the highest taxes are ranked happiest in the world. One notable example is Denmark, where these happy people pay some of the highest taxes — between 50 and 70 percent of their total income.

How can that be? The reason is Denmark's healthcare and education services. In exchange for handing over sizeable portions of their income, Danes receive good universal healthcare coverage and free, quality education. While in school, students receive a stipend to cover living expenses and free daycare if they have children. The government also spends more per capita on caring for

children and the elderly than any country in the world. Without having to worry so much about paying doctor bills and sending their kids to college, no wonder the Danes are so happy.

14. Which of the following, if true, most effectively challenges the connection between social services and happiness?

    Ⓐ The United States pays more per capita on healthcare.

    Ⓑ Denmark is a relatively small country with a population of approximately 5.5 million people.

    Ⓒ Between 2004 and 2008, Denmark's per capita GDP grew at an average annual rate of 1.5 percent — one of the lowest in the world.

    Ⓓ Several countries that provide universal healthcare and free education rank much lower in happiness than Denmark.

    Ⓔ Denmark is ranked first in entrepreneurship and opportunity.

15. Which of the following is the main idea of this passage?

    Ⓐ Stipends and daycare help students meet their needs.

    Ⓑ Social programs are a key to happiness.

    Ⓒ High taxes are a means to an end.

    Ⓓ Citizens need only good healthcare and education.

    Ⓔ Denmark is a great place to live.

Directions: Each of the following sentences has a blank indicating that a word or phrase is omitted. Choose the two answers that best complete the sentence and result in two sentences most alike in meaning.

16. Communications experts recommend taking a time-out from a heated debate for a more _____ attitude.

    Ａ complaisant
    Ｂ incendiary
    Ｃ apprehensive
    Ｄ conciliatory
    Ｅ beguiling
    Ｆ complacent

17. To foster bipartisanship and encourage coop-eration, the speaker delivered a speech crafted to avoid allowing extemporaneous discourse to lapse into an impassioned _____.

    A supplication

    B vernacular

    C malapropism

    D invective

    E hyperbole

    F diatribe

18. Although most employers want team players, _____ individuals are more prone to cheer from the sidelines than get into the game.

    A fawning

    B assertive

    C timorous

    D obsequious

    E indignant

    F aggressive

19. Though delivered from a genuine desire to help, the presentation seemed exaggerated and came across as _____.

    A erroneous

    B duplicitous

    C loquacious

    D disingenuous

    E sagacious

    F equanimous

20. Two hours playing sports is definitely more _____ than two hours on the couch.

    A salacious

    B specious

    C salubrious

    D pernicious

    E wholesome

    F propitious

Section 4
Quantitative Reasoning

Directions: For Questions 1–8, choose from the following answers:

Ⓐ *Quantity A is greater.*

Ⓑ *Quantity B is greater.*

Ⓒ *The two quantities are equal.*

Ⓓ *The relationship cannot be determined from the information given.*

1.

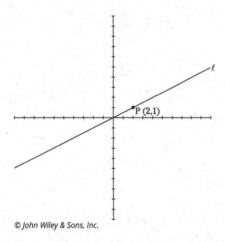

© John Wiley & Sons, Inc.

In the *xy*-coordinate plane shown above, line ℓ passes through the origin, point *P* lies on line ℓ, and the (*x, y*) coordinates of point *P* are (2, 1).

Quantity A	*Quantity B*
The slope of line ℓ	The slope of any line perpendicular to line ℓ

2.

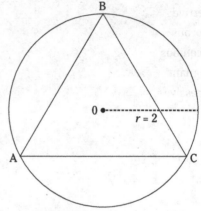

© John Wiley & Sons, Inc.

The equilateral triangle shown above is inscribed within the circle of radius 2.

Quantity A	*Quantity B*
The length of minor arc *AC*	π

3.

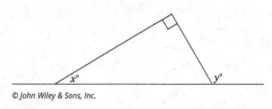

© John Wiley & Sons, Inc.

Quantity A	*Quantity B*
x	*y* − 90

4.

Quantity A	Quantity B
$\dfrac{2^{20}}{3^{15}}$	$\dfrac{16^5}{27^5}$

5. A car dealer purchased a used car, marked it up to make a 20 percent profit, and then sold it at a 20 percent discount from the sticker price.

Quantity A	Quantity B
The amount that the dealer paid for the car, before taxes and fees	The amount for which the dealer sold the car, before taxes and fees

6.

Quantity A	Quantity B
$\dfrac{100!}{98!}$	99^2

7.

Quantity A	Quantity B
The sum of all the integers from 1 to 20	210

8.

Quantity A	Quantity B
$\sqrt{4 \times 9 \times 25 \times 49 \times 121}$	$\sqrt{2,310 \times 2,310}$

9. If a jogger runs 10 kilometers per hour, how many meters does she run in 30 seconds? (1 kilometer = 1,000 meters)

  Ⓐ $\dfrac{5}{54}$

  Ⓑ $\dfrac{25}{18}$

  Ⓒ $\dfrac{250}{3}$

  Ⓓ $\dfrac{250}{9}$

  Ⓔ $\dfrac{125}{18}$

10. If a chalkboard eraser measuring 1 inch by 2 inches by 6 inches is placed inside a tennis ball can with a radius of 1.5 inches and a height of 10 inches, what is the volume of the unoccupied space in the tennis ball can?

  Ⓐ $3\pi - 12$

  Ⓑ $22.5\pi - 12$

  Ⓒ $30\pi - 12$

  Ⓓ $225\pi - 12$

  Ⓔ $300\pi - 12$

11. Given the equation $\left|x^2 - 2\right| > 1$, which of the following could *not* be a value of *x*?

  Ⓐ -1

  Ⓑ -2

  Ⓒ -3

  Ⓓ -4

  Ⓔ -5

GO ON TO NEXT PAGE

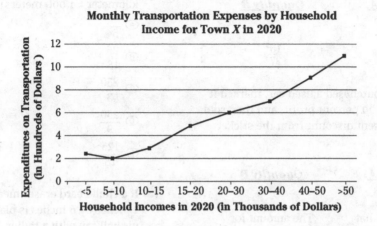

Monthly Transportation Expenses by Household Income for Town *X* in 2020

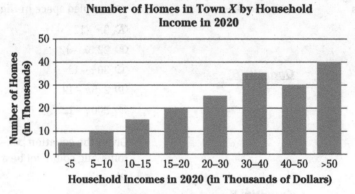

Number of Homes in Town *X* by Household Income in 2020

Note: Graphs drawn to scale.

© John Wiley & Sons, Inc.

12. For the homes with household incomes of $20,000 to $30,000, what was the approximate total expenditure for Town *X* on transportation in 2020?

Ⓐ $1,500,000

Ⓑ $15,000,000

Ⓒ $18,000,000

Ⓓ $150,000,000

Ⓔ $180,000,000

13. What is the approximate ratio of homes with household incomes between $5,000 and $10,000 to homes with household incomes between $30,000 and $40,000?

Ⓐ 2 to 7

Ⓑ 4 to 7

Ⓒ 1 to 3

Ⓓ 5 to 9

Ⓔ 6 to 11

For the following question, choose all that apply.

14. Which of the following *cannot* be inferred from the data in the graphs?

   A There are more homes with household incomes between \$50,000 and \$60,000 than homes with household incomes between \$30,000 and \$40,000.

   B There are more homes being built for the \$30,000 to \$40,000 income demographic than for any other demographic.

   C The median household income in Town *X* is between \$30,000 and \$40,000.

15.

The drawing above shows a heptagon, which is a seven-sided polygon. What is the sum of its angles?

16. At a certain dinner party, there are three drinking glasses for every four utensils and six utensils for every seven plates. If there are 27 drinking glasses total, how many plates are there?

17. If the average of $x, y,$ and z is 1, what is the average of $8x + 2z$, $z - 2x + 3y$, $y - x + z$, and $4 - x$?

For the following question, choose all that apply.

18. For which of the following values of n would the units digit of n be equal to the units digit of n^3?

   A 3

   B 4

   C 5

   D 6

   E 7

   F 8

For the following question, choose exactly two answers.

19. If y is an integer and $\sqrt{60y}$ is an integer, which of the following could be the value of y?

   A 15

   B 30

   C 60

For the following question, choose one or two answers.

20. If $x^2 - 4x = 0$, which could be the value of x?

   A 0

   B 2

   C 4

Chapter **23**

Practice Exam 3: Answers and Explanations

After taking Practice Exam 3 in Chapter 22, use this chapter to check your answers and see how you did. Carefully review the explanations because doing so can help you understand why you missed the questions you did and also give you a better understanding of the thought processes that helped you select the correct answers. If you're in a hurry, flip to the end of the chapter for an abbreviated answer key.

Analytical Writing Sections

Give your essays to someone to read and evaluate for you. Refer that helpful person to Chapters 16 and 17 for scoring guidelines.

Section 1: Verbal Reasoning

1. **B.** *Anachronistic* is a reference to something that couldn't have existed in the time it's referenced, like Brutus and Cassius's discussion of a mechanical clock. *Archaic* (outdated) also refers to time, but it doesn't work as well as *anachronistic* in this context. *Ancient* refers to something really old, which the reference itself may be, but otherwise doesn't fit. *Ambiguous* refers to something that isn't clear, but the reference is perfectly clear. And *euphemistic* refers to a mild form of an expression that may be offensive or not politically correct.

2. **A.** *Veracity* means truth or accuracy, which is an essential quality of any story a journalist may report. *Plausibility* doesn't mean the story is true, only that it's believable. None of the remaining choices (*tenacity,* meaning persistence, *originality,* and *righteousness*) work here.

3. **C, E.** *Geocentric* means, as the phrase after it explains, that Earth is at the center of the universe. If Galileo was labeled a heretic for questioning a belief, his ideas would be *proscribed* (prohibited).

4. **C, D.** *Amalgam* is a metal alloy (mixture) commonly used in dental fillings. Although amalgam is *metal*, it contains several metals, including mercury, so *amalgam* is the better choice. Experts would question the *supposition* (speculation) because people who believe amalgam fillings pose a health risk are not only making an *accusation* or *allegation* but also basing their hypothesis on the reasoning that because the fillings contain mercury, the mercury must leach out in levels high enough to pose a threat.

5. **B, E.** *Propensity* means inclination. Law students may also have an *aptitude* (skill) and *desire*, but *propensity* conveys a sense that they're more likely than not to do something. As a result, law students would become consumed in *recondite* (obscure) language, not *sophisticated* (refined) or *erudite* (learned) language.

6. **A, F, G.** *Equanimous* (even-tempered) teachers would be the opposite of *choleric* (irritable) and would perform better and last longer in junior high school, where classroom management can become *onerous* (burdensome), certainly not *elementary* and not necessarily *truculent* (aggressive, hostile), although the students may be. *Sanguine* (confident, optimistic) could work for the first blank, but because the rest of the passage talks about oppositional students, *equanimous* is a better choice. *Melancholic* (sad) teachers would certainly not perform as well under such conditions. Over time, a choleric temperament would increase *antipathy* (aversion or dislike), not *opposition* (resistance) and usually not *hostility* (aggression), which is too strong a word.

7. **A, F, H.** For the first blank, *escalating* fits because it means increasing, while *nascent* means emerging, as in being born, which doesn't work because the demand already exists, and *proliferating* refers to growing in number. The second blank, *maintain* (contend), indicates that these contenders are holding their ground, whereas *allude* and *imply* are more gentle than arguing. The third blank, *mitigates* (reduces the effect), is what technological innovation does to dependence on oil, while *extenuates* (provides a reasonable context) doesn't fit, nor does *propagates* (spreads and promotes).

8. **A, B.** Choices (A) and (B) are correct because they demonstrate specific regions of the brain controlling specific functions — that is, *localization*. The third choice is wrong because it describes a case in which a large portion of the brain must be affected for something to occur.

9. **D.** Choice (D) is correct because it shows that facial recognition isn't linked solely to the damaged area of the man's brain. The conscious recognition occurs in one region, while the involuntary heartbeat response occurs in another.

10. **C.** The big clue here is the sentence that transitions from Dax's to Broca's research: "The notion that language was localized to the left side of the brain (the left hemisphere) developed momentum with new discoveries linking specific language functions to specific regions of the left hemisphere."

11. **B, C.** The passage states that the river bed cut deeper and the Nile *narrowed* (the opposite of becoming wider). Also, it states that the delta, which is part of the river, became more fertile over time.

12. **A.** The terraces in this passage are features carved by the Nile River. The four other answer choices refer to features of man-made structures.

13. **B.** The second sentence explains that the word *culture* is derived from nature. The rest of the passage supports and expands on that statement.

14. **E.** *Manurance* (cultivation) appears in the passage but only as part of one of the examples showing that the word *culture* was first used to describe an activity. All the other words in the answer choices are specifically cited as being derived from nature.

15. **A, E.** *Dissonant* (harsh sounding) and *cacophonous* (grating) are the two correct answers. *Symphonic* and *mellifluous* both mean harmonious, which is the opposite of what's needed here. *Disparate* means dissimilar, and *raucous* means something more like loud and unruly, which could work but doesn't have a matching word in the answer choices.

16. **C, F.** *Impassive* and *stolid* both mean unemotional, which would be the opposite of passionately mad. *Sentient* means conscious of or aware, which doesn't fit the meaning of the sentence or have a suitable match among the answer choices. *Stygian* means hellish, which doesn't generally apply to scientists. *Zealous* (passionate, enthusiastic) doesn't work because it doesn't contrast with the idea of a passionately mad scientist. Finally, although most scientists have *profound* thoughts, you wouldn't describe a person as profound.

17. **A, B.** *Refractory* and *recalcitrant* mean resistant to treatment in this context. An *acute* wound would probably not require long-term treatment, and although the wounds may be *severe* or *excruciating*, neither of those qualities would necessarily make the wounds resistant to treatment. *Perspicacious* means wise, which definitely doesn't work here.

18. **C, E.** *Indigence* and *penury* both mean poverty. They're the only two words in the list that match. *Malnutrition* and *famine* are related but not very close in meaning, and neither is commonly attributed to laziness. *Illiteracy* has no match, and *squalor* means something more like filth or uncleanliness, which may accompany poverty but isn't necessarily a global issue.

19. **A, C.** *Mitigate* and *assuage* both mean to lessen or alleviate. *Augment* (amplify) and *incite* (provoke) obviously don't work, and *repress* and *subjugate*, both of which mean to put down by force, are too strong.

20. **C.** "Nature can improve the healing process" is the best answer, supported by the second paragraph: "The idea that access to nature could assist in healing was all but lost." All the other choices go too far and lack support in the passage. Choices (A) and (D) are wrong because the passage only states that changes and specialization have occurred, not that they are better or worse. Choice (B) is out because the passage discusses the function, not the location, of modern hospitals, and Choice (E) doesn't work because a decorative courtyard doesn't assist with healing.

Section 2: Quantitative Reasoning

1. **B.** Combine the $\sqrt{25} \times \sqrt{4}$ to equal $\sqrt{100}$, and reduce $\dfrac{\sqrt{100}}{\sqrt{10}}$ to $\sqrt{10}$. Because $\sqrt{10}$ is closer to $\sqrt{9}$ than to $\sqrt{16}$, its value is closer to 3 than to 4.

2. **C.** For each quantity, count only the numbers that aren't in the other quantity. Both quantities have the numbers 101 to 198, so those numbers won't affect which is greater. Only Quantity A has 99 and 100 (which total 199), and only Quantity B has 199.

3. **D.** Because x is between 9 and 10, it could be equal to 9.001 or 9.999. Don't square those — square the 9 and the 10 instead, for 81 and 100.

4. **C.** To use the equation $a\Delta b = ab + 2(a+b)$, substitute the numbers before and after the triangle for a and b, respectively, in the equation. For Quantity A, $\frac{1}{1\Delta 2}$ becomes $\frac{1}{(1\times 2)+2(1+2)} = \frac{1}{8}$. For Quantity B, $0\Delta 1$ becomes $(0\times 1)+2(0+1) = 2$. To the power of -3, the answer becomes $\frac{1}{8}$, the same as Quantity A.

5. **C.** The side ratio of the 30-60-90 triangle is $x : x\sqrt{3} : 2x$, with $2x$ being the hypotenuse. The only way that the perimeter could be $3+\sqrt{3}$ is if x were 1, making the hypotenuse 2.

6. **B.** The formula for combinations is $C_r^n = \dfrac{n!}{r!(n-r)!}$, with C being the number of possibilities, n being the group of students, and r being the students attending the meeting. And $\dfrac{10!}{3!7!}$ reduces to 120 as follows: $\dfrac{10!}{3!7!} = \dfrac{10 \times \cancel{9}^{3} \times \cancel{8}^{4} \times \cancel{7!}}{\cancel{3} \times \cancel{2} \times 1 \times \cancel{7!}} = 120$.

7. **C.** The formula for probability is $\text{Probability} = \dfrac{\text{Number of possible desired outcomes}}{\text{Number of total possible outcomes}}$. The number of possible desired outcomes is four (1, 2, 3, and 5), and the number of total possible outcomes is six. So $\frac{4}{6}$ reduces to $\frac{2}{3}$.

8. **B.** Let x represent the amount invested at 3 percent and set the equation up like this:

$$(x)(0.03) + (8{,}000 - x)(0.05) = 340$$

Solve for x, and Tom invested \$3,000 at 3 percent and \$5,000 at 5 percent.

9. **C.** Pick two consecutive even integers, such as 8 and 10, giving you a product of 80. Only one formula returns 80 if you plug in 8 for n.

10. **E.** This is basically a large circle around a small circle, and your task is to find the difference between the two. The large circle has a radius of 5 (the 3-foot-radius garden plus the 2-foot-wide sidewalk), giving it an area of 25π. Subtract from that the area of the small circle (the garden), 9π, for a difference of 16π.

11. **E.** Set this up as two different equations: $b - 8 = j$ and $b - 2 = 2(j + 2)$. Solve for b by substituting $(b - 8)$ for j in the second equation: $b - 2 = 2(b - 8 + 2)$. Solve for b, which equals 10.

12. **B.** The number of mothers with children under the age of 18 in 2018 was about 90,000. A 10 percent increase in 2019 brings the number to about 100,000. The percentage of mothers in the workforce with youngest children ages 12 to 17 in 2018 was 80 percent. The percentage stays about the same in 2019, and 80 percent of 100,000 is 80,000.

13. **A.** The first number is 20 percent, and the second number is 70 percent. This produces a ratio of 2 to 7.

14. **A, C.** Choice (A) is correct because more mothers are having children, so the population is increasing. Choice (B) is wrong because mothers in the workforce aren't necessarily single. Choice (C) is correct because with more mothers working and more babies, some fathers will stay at home, but others won't, and the demand for daycare increases.

15. 4. To solve for a_2, substitute a_1 for a_n and a_2 for a_{n+1} in the equation provided. Because a_1 equals 38, a_2 equals 20. Now use the equation to solve for a_3 by substituting 20 for a_2 and a_3 for a_{n+1}. Thus, a_3 equals 11. Do this again for a_4, which equals 6.5 and is the first non-integer value of a_n, so 4 is the lowest value for n.

16. 126. Factor the numbers under the radical: $\sqrt{(6)(7)(18)(21)}$ becomes $\sqrt{(2\times3)(7)(2\times3\times3)(7\times3)}$. Find number pairs to remove from the radical: Two 7s means a 7 comes out, two 2s means a 2 comes out, four 3s means two 3s come out, and nothing is left under the radical. Multiply all the numbers that came out: $7\times3\times3\times2=126$.

17. 3. Add up the digits of $1,532,475$: $1+5+3+2+4+7+5=27$. Because 27 is divisible by 3, the number $1,532,475$ is also divisible by 3. If you chose 5 because the number ends with 5, that was a good try.

18. B, E. Each engine lift uses three pulleys, and each box contains eight pulleys. To avoid having any pulleys left over, the number of pulleys used has to be a multiple of 24. The ratio of pulleys to levers is $3:7$, so the ratio used in the manufacturing job has to be a multiple of $24:56$. Any number of levers that isn't a multiple of 56 can't be the number used in the manufacturing job.

19. A, B, C, F. Because $396 = 2\times2\times3\times3\times11$, any answer choice that cancels completely with those primes produces an integer. The remaining answer choices don't work because 24 has too many 2s and 27 has too many 3s.

20. A, C. The units digit of any product depends on the units digit of the numbers multiplied. For example, any number with a units digit of 7 times any number with a units digit of 3 produces a number ending with a units digit of 1 because $7\times3=21$. The units digit of any number to the fifth power is the same as the units digit of the original number. For example, $2^5 = 32$, $3^5 = 243$, and $4^5 = 1,024$, making n^5 one of the answers. And $n^{10} = \left(n^5\right)^2$, so if n is 2, $n^5 = 32$, but 32 squared has a units digit of 4. However, $n^{25} = \left(n^5\right)^5$, preserving the n^5 rule and making n^{25} the other answer.

TIP

The GRE doesn't expect you to just *know* all these things. The point isn't the mathematical principles. It's that you're resourceful and can solve problems on the fly. By trying out simple numbers (such as 2^5 and 3^5) to see how the math works, you use your creativity to solve the problem.

Section 3: Verbal Reasoning

1. C. The transition word *but* tells you that the scenes and discussions don't appear central to the theme. *Tangential* conveys this, while *essential* (necessary) and *predominant* (main, principal) convey the opposite. *Incisive* (perceptive) may be true but doesn't fit the context. Scenes could be *concurrent* (happening at the same time), but this doesn't convey the sense that the scenes are of less importance.

2. E. You know that the speaker made the need for further clarification either necessary or unnecessary; the note that he "supported" the case tells you that his speech was sound and that clarification was unnecessary. *Obviated* means something along the lines of "made unnecessary." *Precluded* (prevented) and *prohibited* (banned) are too strong, and although the speaker *anticipated* questions by addressing them, that would not anticipate the need for clarification. *Adjourned* doesn't work because you adjourn a meeting, not a need.

3. **B, D.** A *libertine* (morally unrestrained) existence could conceivably lead to a loss of self-discipline, but a *Spartan* (simple) or *ascetic* (puritan) lifestyle would tend to make someone more disciplined. Following this logic, for the second blank, a *hedonistic* (pleasurable) paradise wouldn't be so divine, so the opposite makes *stygian* (hellish) the only choice. *Quixotic* means idealistic, and *utopian* means perfect (in a good way).

4. **C, F.** This passage is all about twos — the body and soul — so filling the first blank is relatively easy: *Dichotomy* is a separation into two. A *paradox* is an apparent contradiction that may be true, and *irony* is the use of words to express the opposite of what the words mean. Finding the right match for the second blank is more challenging because all the words have *two* or *separation* in their meaning. *Bisected* (divided in two) is the best choice. *Bifurcated* is divided but more like a fork in a road, and *dissected* is more along the lines of dividing into several parts.

5. **C, E.** *Intransigence* is inflexibility, and *precipitate* means to bring about. *Tractability* (compliance) is the opposite of what's needed for the first blank, and *indolence* means laziness. For the second blank, *expedite* (hasten) would make a decent second choice, but *precipitate* is more fitting. *Motivate* (provide with a motive) doesn't work because you may motivate individuals but not actions (such as conflict).

6. **B, D, I.** An interrogator wants to *elicit* (extract) information, not *dissemble* (mislead) or *disseminate* (spread) it. To stop interrogations without giving in, suspects may *prevaricate* (mislead, lie), not *prognosticate* (predict) or *adjudicate* (mediate). The prevaricating would call into question the *efficacy* (effectiveness) of such methods, not their *efficiency* (ability to accomplish something with minimal effort) or *alacrity* (speed).

7. **B, D, G.** High winds and large waves would occur if nothing was in their way to *impede* (slow) them, not *debilitate* (incapacitate) them. *Disperse* (scatter) would make a good second choice. These high winds and large waves would be *endemic* (characteristic of) rather than *pandemic* (epidemic) or *intrinsic* (fundamental). Plankton would gather in pools, which tend to be more *quiescent* (calm) than a wavy ocean, not *dormant* (sleeping) and definitely not *truculent* (hostile).

8. **E.** The correct answer is the fifth sentence, with the details "social insurance, child welfare, health, mental hygiene, universal education, and similar services." Several other sentences explain the origin and purpose of welfare, but only this sentence gives specific detail.

9. **A.** *Compare and contrast, explain,* and *describe* reflect the author's purpose, but *lament* and *argue* imply more emotion on the part of the author than is displayed in the passage, so eliminate Choices (C) and (E). Productivity has nothing to do with showing how our ancestors perceived night differently, so you can eliminate Choice (B). Choice (D) is simply wrong: The author doesn't suggest that the need for lighting is from the limited moonlight, just that it's outshone by electric lights.

10. **A, B.** The second paragraph mentions Choice (A), light-colored stones or trees with bark stripped off, and Choice (B), the moon or a torch. Railings aren't mentioned anywhere in the passage.

11. **A.** Choice (A) is correct because the passage describes brain scans, which are scientific evidence. Choice (B) is wrong because although the passage implies that brain cells shrivel and die when not in use, it provides no scientific evidence to support this claim. Choice (C) is wrong because cause and effect are flipped: Although a 10 to 20 percent loss of neurons may occur in Alzheimer's, the passage doesn't state that a 10 to 20 percent loss of neurons causes Alzheimer's.

12. **D.** "Television's drive to entertain is incompatible with serious discussion of complex issues." The other choices go too far, saying that TV *cannot* instead of that it *does not*. The passage doesn't criticize television itself but how it's used.

13. **D.** Choice (D) suggests that maybe the snakes *can* swim, but they get eaten by sharks before reaching New Zealand. Choices (A) and (E) are out of scope: Snakes could have reached South America or the Pacific Islands any number of ways. Choice (B) has to do with island governance, not the snakes themselves. Finally, Choice (C) is out because the passage is about snakes, not monitor lizards.

14. **D.** "Several countries that provide universal healthcare and free education rank much lower in happiness than Denmark." If other countries provide the same social services as Denmark but rank lower in happiness, then something *other* than social services is boosting Denmark to the number one position.

15. **B.** "Social programs are a key to happiness." The passage focuses on how Denmark uses tax-funded social programs to provide for the needs of its citizens. Choice (A) may be true, but it's not the main idea. Choices (C) and (E) are reasonable candidates, but the phrases *means to an end* and *great place to live* extend beyond the scope of the passage. Choice (D) is wrong because citizens may need more than healthcare and education.

16. **A, D.** Taking a break from a heated debate means the parties return more willing to please. *Complaisant* and *conciliatory* mean this, while *incendiary* (provocative) means the opposite, and *beguiling* means deceiving with trickery. *Apprehensive* means anxious, and *complacent*, included to trip you up with its similarity to *complaisant*, means satisfied or content.

17. **D, F.** *Invective* and *diatribe* refer to bitter, abusive language, something you'd want to avoid to foster bipartisanship and cooperation. None of the other choices match: *supplication* (plea), *vernacular* (dialect), *malapropism* (confusion of words that sound similar), and *hyperbole* (exaggeration).

18. **A, D.** *Fawning* and *obsequious* refer to agreeably showing favor, which would incline people to act as cheerleaders instead of players. *Assertive* and *aggressive* players would probably get into the game. *Timorous* means shy, which would make a good second choice, but it has no match. *Indignant* is more along the lines of being annoyed.

19. **B, D.** *Duplicitous* and *disingenuous* mean deceitful, or lying. *Erroneous* means false. *Loquacious* is more along the lines of talking a lot, which fits with *exaggerated*, but doesn't have a match in the answer choices. *Sagacious* means wise, and *equanimous* means even-tempered.

20. **C, E.** *Salubrious* and *wholesome* are both good for you. *Salacious* (scandalous), *specious* (unsupported), and *pernicious* (malicious) aren't. *Propitious* (favorable) could be good for you but doesn't express the meaning of being healthy, which is what's needed here.

Section 4: Quantitative Reasoning

1. **A.** You could calculate the slope of line ℓ with the good ol' formula Slope $= \dfrac{\text{rise}}{\text{run}} = \dfrac{(y_2 - y_1)}{(x_2 - x_1)}$. But you actually don't need to. Going left to right, line ℓ goes up, giving it a positive slope, and its perpendicular goes down, giving it a negative slope.

2. **A.** Minor arc AC originates from the angle of the equilateral triangle and is 60 degrees and one-third of the circle. Because the circle has a radius of 2, its circumference is 4π. One-third of that is $\dfrac{4\pi}{3}$, which is greater than π.

3. **C.** The angle supplementary to y, inside the triangle, can be represented as $(180 - y)°$. Because the triangle's angles total 180 degrees, add up the angles and set them equal to 180:

   $$x + 90 + 180 - y = 180$$

   Solve for x, which equals $y - 90$.

4. **C.** The two numerators are equal: $2^{20} = \left(2^4\right)^5 = 16^5$. The two denominators are also equal: $3^{15} = \left(3^3\right)^5 = 27^5$. Therefore, the two quantities are equal.

5. **A.** Because no price is given, pick \$100 as the starting point for the value of the car, which is Quantity A. So \$100 marked up 20 percent is \$120, and the 20 percent discount from \$120 brings the price to \$96, Quantity B.

6. **A.** From Quantity A, $\dfrac{100!}{98!}$ becomes $\dfrac{100 \times 99 \times 98!}{98!}$, which reduces to 100×99 and is greater than 99^2, which is 99×99.

7. **C.** You can find the sum of all integers from 1 to 20 using the formula $\dfrac{n(n+1)}{2}$, where n represents the 20:

   $$\frac{20(21)}{2} = 210$$

8. **C.** Don't fall for the trap of multiplying all these numbers and looking for the square roots. Instead, solve for Quantity A by finding and multiplying the square roots of each of the numbers under the radical: $\sqrt{4 \times 9 \times 25 \times 49 \times 121} = 2 \times 3 \times 5 \times 7 \times 11 = 2{,}310$. To compare this to Quantity B, consider that $2{,}310 = \sqrt{2{,}310 \times 2{,}310}$.

9. **C.** Set up the conversion steps as a series of fractions with *unit* as the 30-second interval, which happens twice per minute:

   $$\left(\frac{10 \text{ km}}{1 \text{ hour}}\right)\left(\frac{1{,}000 \text{ meters}}{1 \text{ km}}\right)\left(\frac{1 \text{ hour}}{60 \text{ mins}}\right)\left(\frac{1 \text{ min}}{2 \text{ units}}\right)$$

   First, cancel the labels:

   $$\left(\frac{10}{1}\right)\left(\frac{1{,}000 \text{ meters}}{1}\right)\left(\frac{1}{60}\right)\left(\frac{1}{2 \text{ units}}\right)$$

Next, cancel the numbers:

$$\left(\frac{1}{1}\right)\left(\frac{250 \text{ meters}}{1}\right)\left(\frac{1}{3}\right)\left(\frac{1}{1 \text{ unit}}\right)=\frac{250}{3}\text{ meters/unit}$$

The *unit* represents the 30-second interval the question asks for. Avoid putting *30 secs* as the unit, which will lead to a math mistake.

10. **B.** To find the volume of the remaining space, subtract the volume of the eraser, which is $1\times2\times6=12$, from the volume of the tennis ball can, which is $\pi r^2 h = \pi(1.5)^2(10)=22.5\pi$.

11. **A.** Place each answer choice for x and see what works. The only number that doesn't work is -1: $\left|(-1)^2-2\right|>1$ becomes $|1-2|>1$ and then $1>1$, which isn't true.

12. **E.** Check both graphs at the 20–30 points. The first graph shows $600 per month. The second graph shows 25,000 homes. Multiply these together, for a monthly expenditure of $15,000,000, which is the trap answer, Choice (B). For the correct answer, multiply this by 12, for an annual expenditure of $180,000,000.

13. **A.** The graph shows approximately 10,000 homes with household incomes between $5,000 and $10,000 and approximately 35,000 homes with household incomes between $30,000 and $40,000. The ratio of 10,000 to 35,000 reduces to 2 to 7.

14. **A, B.** This question asks you to choose the answers that *cannot* be inferred. For Choice (A), you only know how many homes have incomes over $50,000, not the number between $50,000 and $60,000. For Choice (B), you don't know how many homes are being built and for which demographic. Finally, for Choice (C), 75,000 homes have incomes lower than $30,000 to $40,000, and 70,000 homes have higher incomes. Because 35,000 homes are within the $30,000 to $40,000 bracket, the median income is also in that bracket.

15. **900.** The formula for calculating the sum of angles of any polygon is $(n-2)180$, where n represents the number of angles. Therefore, $(7-2)180$, or 5×180, is 900.

16. **42.** Combine the ratios so that $3:4$ glasses to utensils combined with $6:7$ utensils to plates produces a combined ratio of glasses to utensils to plates of $9:12:14$. To get 27 drinking glasses total, multiply the entire ratio by 3, for a proportion of $27:36:42$.

17. **4.** Because the average of x, y, and z is 1, write out the equation as an averages formula: $\frac{x+y+z}{3}=1$, which tells you that $x+y+z=3$. From the question, simplify $8x+2z$, $z-2x+3y$, $y-x+3$, and $4-x$ by adding them together, giving you $4x+4y+4z+4$. Divide this sum by 4, for an average of $x+y+z+1$. Because $x+y+z=3$, the answer is 4.

18. **B, C, D.** The *units* digit is the farthest-right digit. Try each answer choice to see whether its unit digit matches the starting number: $3^3=27$ doesn't work; $4^3=64$ works; $5^3=125$ works; $6^3=216$ works; $7^3=343$ doesn't work; and $8^3=512$ also doesn't work.

19. **A, C.** For any square root to be an integer, each factor under the radical has to be in a pair. For example, $\sqrt{4}$ is an integer because it equals $\sqrt{2\times2}$ and the 2s are in a pair. For $\sqrt{60y}$ to be an integer, all the factors of 60 have to be in pairs: $\sqrt{60y}=\sqrt{2\times2\times3\times5\times y}$. The 2s are in a pair, but the y has to complete both the 3 pair and the 5 pair to make an integer. So y has to contain both 3 and 5, making 15 one possible value. However, y could also be 15 times any other perfect square, such as 4. $15\times4=60$, which is the other possible value of y in this list.

20. **A, C.** Factor $x^2-4x=0$ into $x(x-4)=0$, making both 0 and 4 possible answers for x.

Answer Key for Practice Exam 3

Section 1: Verbal Reasoning

1.	B	6.	A, F, G	11.	B, C	16.	C, F
2.	A	7.	A, F, H	12.	A	17.	A, B
3.	C, E	8.	A, B	13.	B	18.	C, E
4.	C, D	9.	D	14.	E	19.	A, C
5.	B, E	10.	A, E	15.	A, E	20.	C

Section 2: Quantitative Reasoning

1.	B	6.	B	11.	E	16.	126
2.	C	7.	C	12.	B	17.	3
3.	D	8.	B	13.	A	18.	B, E
4.	C	9.	C	14.	A, C	19.	A, B, C, F
5.	C	10.	E	15.	4	20.	A, C

Section 3: Verbal Reasoning

1.	C	6.	B, D, I	11.	A	16.	A, D
2.	E	7.	B, D, G	12.	D	17.	D, F
3.	B, D	8.	E	13.	D	18.	A, D
4.	C, F	9.	A	14.	D	19.	B, D
5.	C, E	10.	A, B	15.	B	20.	C, E

Section 4: Quantitative Reasoning

1.	A	6.	A	11.	A	16.	42
2.	A	7.	C	12.	E	17.	4
3.	C	8.	C	13.	A	18.	B, C, D
4.	C	9.	C	14.	A, B	19.	A, C
5.	A	10.	B	15.	900	20.	A, C

6

The Part of Tens

IN THIS PART . . .

Review ten important points about the GRE that can move your score.

Learn ten mistakes that others have made but now you won't.

Refresh ten ways to make the most of the practice exams.

Chapter 24

Ten Key Facts about the GRE

Y ou've probably heard stories from your friends about the GRE. Rumors abound, growing wilder with each telling: "You have to know calculus!" (Absolutely not true.) "It's an open-book test this year!" (You wish!) "You can take it at home!" (Actually, this one is true.)

As a GRE-prep instructor, I field questions all the time from students looking for a sense of what to expect on the test. This chapter revisits several key facts that you need to know when prepping for the exam and heading into the testing center.

You May Return to Previous Questions in the Same Section

The GRE allows you to return to previous questions in any given math or verbal section as long as you haven't moved on to the next section. One strategy is to flip through the questions, answer all the easy ones first, and then go back to handle the challenging questions.

WARNING

The worst thing that can happen is getting stuck on a question. Even if you get the right answer, if it takes you five minutes, the question still won and you still lost — because you'll run out of time and miss the last few questions! Fortunately, you can make sure this doesn't happen.

TIP

Flag any question that you want to return to by clicking the Mark for Review button at the top of the screen. You can then visit a review screen at any time during the section by clicking the Review button (also at the top of the screen). This review screen shows you which questions are marked for review along with which are still unanswered. From there, you can jump directly to any question. Practice navigating the questions and review screen with the free online practice exam provided by ETS at www.ets.org/gre/revised_general/prepare/powerprep/ so you're familiar with this feature on test day. Use the POWERPREP Online option.

If you don't want to use the Mark for Review button, you don't have to. Write down the question number on the corner of your scratch paper. When you're ready to go back, use the Back and Next buttons to navigate to the question. Either way, remember the Golden Rule (my version anyway): *If you can't answer the question in one minute, take a guess and come back to it afterward.*

The GRE Doesn't Penalize for Guessing

A question answered incorrectly affects your score exactly the same way as a question left unanswered, so you're better off guessing than skipping. Yet another reason it's okay to guess on a question you can't answer! If you do this, though, be sure to flag the question or write down the number so you can return to it with any remaining time.

The GRE Uses a Percentile-Based Scoring System

The purpose of the GRE, besides ruining your weekend, is to see how well you perform against other candidates for the school you're applying to. Immediately after you complete the test, you receive an estimated percentile ranking based on exam scores from the previous year.

The number of GRE test-takers worldwide increases each year. More test-takers means more graduate-school applicants, which makes admissions more competitive. This also means that scoring as well as you can on the GRE is more important than ever.

TIP

Find out what the acceptable GRE score is for admission to your target school. When they give you a number, be sure to ask whether that's the *minimum* or the *average* score. Then ask what score is needed for a scholarship. You could be in reach!

Practice Makes All the Difference

Although you may not be able to dress-rehearse the entire test-taking experience, using the practice tests makes the actual test-taking experience more familiar and reduces the element of surprise. Take advantage of the practice tests included in this book. Also, the free practice exam software ETS provides has the exact feel of the actual GRE, so make it something you know well. Write the practice essays, too, so the entire experience is as familiar as a day at the office. (Go back to Part 4 for more on essay writing.)

Review your practice tests afterwards to discover a lot of silly mistakes that can lead to wrong answers. Making these mistakes *in practice* is good — it's why you practice. Knowing you're prone to certain mistakes decreases your chances of making the same types of mistakes on the actual test.

REMEMBER

A good sense of familiarity and knowing what to expect truly boosts your confidence on test day. I require a three-practice-test minimum from my students, and it's like pulling teeth. But I also track their progress and see a marked improvement from one practice test to the next. At what point on the improvement curve do you want to be when you take the actual GRE?

You Must Prepare for the GRE

Though stories of folks taking the exam unprepared yet scoring dramatically high are out there, incidents of these unprepared folks bombing and having to retake the GRE are far more common — and not as well told. (But those folks call me.) It's like stories of people who survived a car crash *because* they didn't wear their seat belt. Stories of people who *died* because they didn't wear a seat belt aren't as well told.

I'd put my money on an average Joe or Jolene who's well-prepared over a budding Einstein going in unprepared, every time. So prepare for the exam. This book is your best resource and includes all the study materials you need.

The GRE Is Different from the SAT and ACT

Maybe you didn't study much for the SAT, figuring that you could always get into *some* college, somewhere, somehow, regardless of your score. You were probably right. But getting into a good graduate school is more competitive, and the college-level GRE is more challenging than the high-school-level SAT and ACT.

The GRE Also Measures Your Stamina and Performance under Pressure

The GRE measures a number of things besides your skills in math, verbal reasoning, and writing. It measures your ability to prepare, your stamina, and your performance under pressure. Many people are quite capable of solving math problems with plenty of time and room for mistakes, but only those who have honed their skills through practice can come up with the right answers when the timer is ticking and the pressure is on. The good news: You can build these skills too!

The General GRE Is Not Program-Specific

The GRE is accepted for entrance into almost any graduate program. I'll have in one class candidates for construction management, physician assistant, master of social work, and PhD programs. Even law and MBA programs accept the GRE. Regardless of the field of your graduate program, if it's at a good school, the GRE is probably part of the admissions process.

You Can Practice the GRE on Your Own Computer

The only way to experience the real GRE is to take it. However, you can simulate the test-taking experience at home and get as close to a real-life experience as possible. After you've studied and acquainted yourself with the different question types, practice on your own computer. Visit www. dummies.com/go/getaccess to access the practice questions online and get comfortable with answering questions on the computer.

TIP

Try to simulate, as closely as possible, the actual test-taking experience. Set aside several hours to take the equivalent of a practice test (two sets of 20 Verbal Reasoning questions and two sets of 20 Quantitative Reasoning questions plus two essays). If you live alone or have a quiet room in your house or apartment, that's perfect. Otherwise, consider taking the practice test in a library, an office, or some other quiet place.

Besides the online exams you get with this book, use the free online practice exams from ETS. Go to `www.ets.org/gre/revised_general/prepare/powerprep/`, select the POWERPREP Online option, and take one of the practice tests.

You Can't Bring Anything into the Testing Center

I once saw a photo of a confiscated plastic water bottle with math formulas written on the inside of the label. Though you probably wouldn't go to such lengths, the testing center staff wants to ensure zero opportunities to cheat on the GRE. Because of this, you can't take anything with you — not even a wristwatch. You can store food and water in a locker, but be prepared to empty your pockets and be fingerprinted upon entering the actual testing area.

WARNING

Don't bring your GRE books, even if you intend to leave them in the locker. If the proctors think you checked your books during your breaks, you may not be allowed to finish the exam. This actually happened to one of my students, who pleaded with the proctor and was finally allowed to finish his exam. I asked him why he brought his books; he said it was a habit.

If you take the GRE at home, of course, these rules are different. To prevent you from cheating, ETS has quite the stringent set of guidelines, which cover what you can have in the room, what can be on your computer, and even how you do your scratch work for math. For the full rundown, check out the fully detailed At Home Testing page at `www.ets.org`.

Chapter 25

Ten Mistakes You Won't Make (While Others Will)

Throughout this book, you discover techniques for doing your best on the GRE. I'm sorry to say, however, that you may still encounter pitfalls for messing up big-time on the test. The good news is that I've seen others hit those pitfalls so I can guide you on how to dodge them. Take a few minutes to read through mistakes that others have made while taking the exam. By becoming aware of these catastrophes, you can prevent them from happening to you.

You Won't Cheat

Cheating on the GRE simply doesn't work, so don't even consider it. They're on to you. When you get to the testing center, and before you begin your test, the proctors separate you from anything that you can possibly use to cheat, including your phone, wristwatch, water bottle, jacket, and hat. On top of that, you're monitored by a camera while taking the test. Any semblance of privacy goes right out the window. How would you cheat anyway? You can't copy all those vocabulary words or write all the math formulas on anything accessible during the test. Besides, the GRE tests your critical-reasoning and problem-solving skills more than your memorization skills.

Even if you test at home, the GRE has controls in place to keep you honest. ETS monitors everything from the software on your computer to the electronics in your room. Be careful, and make sure you follow the rules — even a misunderstanding could cost you your score. Refer to the full set of rules on the At Home Testing page at www.ets.org.

WARNING

Someone caught cheating can be banned from taking the test for up to ten years! In the world of college education, that's nearly a lifetime.

You Won't Run Out of Steam

The GRE tests your stamina as much as anything else. Most people aren't able to maintain high levels of concentration for four straight hours, so they end up fizzing out. Through preparation and practice, you can gain a definite edge over the other test-takers.

TIP

Like training for a marathon, preparing for the GRE means slowly building yourself up. Practice for a few hours at a time and stop when you get too tired. Repeat this exercise, and eventually you'll be able to go the full distance without fail. Don't push yourself too hard, though, because you'll burn yourself out: Building your stamina up should be a gradual process.

You Won't Neglect Your Breaks

Some people don't take advantage of the breaks offered during the GRE. Be sure not to miss the opportunity to take a breather. You're allowed short breaks (in one- or ten-minute increments) between sections. If you don't take these breaks, you'll be sitting still for hours. Though your stamina may be good (because you practiced), you still want to stay hydrated, eat a good snack, and stretch every now and then to keep your mind clear. Don't plan on studying during your breaks, though — the review of any GRE-prep materials during breaks can be considered cheating.

TIP

Pack some water bottles and healthy snacks to keep in a locker for your breaks, because you won't have time to go grab something. Don't drink too much water, though — you can't pause the exam to run to the restroom.

You Won't Dwell on Questions from Previous Sections

When guessing on a question and marking it for review, let it go until the end of the section so you can focus on the other questions at hand. When you reach the end of the section (but before moving on to the next section or before the time expires), you may return to the questions you skipped or marked and check or change your answers.

When you move on to the next section, however, that's it: You can't go back to a previous section. You have no choice but to move forward, so don't add to your anxiety by focusing on past questions that you can do nothing about.

You Won't Panic Over the Time Limit

Some test-takers fret over the clock. The key to success is to be aware of the clock while remaining calm. Practice working with a timer, so you're used to the timer on the GRE exam screen. As you become more accustomed to working with the clock during practice, you'll eventually settle into a comfortable pace and be used to the timer on test day.

If you have practiced and are prepared, the clock won't matter as much. Knowing what to do means you'll work through questions faster and you won't get stuck on as many.

The mistakes you make while relaxed are different from the mistakes you make while under pressure from the clock. Practice with a timer to get used to the pressure and become aware of the mistakes you'll make — and fix them *before* the test.

You Won't Rush Through the Questions

Some test-takers think that they need to rush to answer all the questions in the time limit. This is true, if you want to get most of them wrong by missing key details and making careless mistakes.

I'd rather you get half the questions right and run out of time than rush through the questions and miss them all. But it shouldn't come to that anyway: The amount of time the GRE gives you is more than enough to properly, correctly, and calmly answer all the questions — *if you don't get stuck.*

Remember the Other Golden Rule: *The secret to working fast and getting it right isn't rushing — it's knowing what to do.* The way you know what to do is by learning what's on the exam and practicing it. Most of my students tell me that timing isn't an issue — but only after weeks of preparation.

You Definitely Won't Choke on the Essays

Choking, by definition (on the GRE), means getting stuck on something and becoming so flustered that you can't focus on anything after that. This can happen at any point on the test, but because you can flag the multiple-choice questions and go back to them at the end of the section, you're less likely to choke on those.

Essays, however, are another story. On the GRE, you have to write two essays in 60 minutes. What's worse, they're at the beginning of the test, so if you choke on one, you're toast for the entire exam. Of course, this won't happen to *you*, because you reviewed Chapters 16 and 17, where I guide you through writing two perfect essays, step by step. This makes writer's block — and choking — something that happens to others, but not you.

Practice the essays! Like any skill, essay-writing takes practice, and you don't want to be at the start of the learning curve on test day.

You Won't Fret Over the Hard Questions

The GRE contains some seemingly difficult questions, and most test-takers don't get perfect scores. Do the best you can, score in the high percentiles, and get accepted to graduate school! No one expects a perfect score, so you shouldn't either.

REMEMBER

The GRE is only one of many parts of the application process. Your GPA, work experience, admissions essays, and any other relevant character-building experience (such as sports participation, military service, volunteer work, or leadership training) also count toward your chances of admission. Turn to Chapter 1 for more on how your score fits within the application process.

You Won't Take the Exam with a Friend

You and your buddy may be able to schedule your tests for the same time. Big mistake. Two of my students from the same class took the exam at the same time, side by side, and both told me afterward that rather than providing support, taking the GRE together was distracting. Fortunately, they both scored well, but I wonder how different their results would have been had they tested separately. It's good to *study* with a friend (and celebrate after), but don't buddy up for the actual test.

You Won't Change Your Morning Routine

The GRE is stressful enough. The last thing you need to do is add more anxiety to the whole experience by changing your morning routine.

If you normally have one cup of coffee, should you have an extra cup for more energy or only half a cup to reduce anxiety? Should you have an omelet for more protein or just toast to avoid the blood sugar crash later? Here's a thought: *Do what you normally do.* It works every other day, and it'll work just as well on the day of the test. Don't change your routine.

WARNING

If you're tempted to try an energy drink or something unusual for an enhanced test-taking experience, try it first on a practice test! Make sure your new concoction doesn't upset your stomach or give you a headache. You don't need that distraction.

Chapter 26

Ten Ways to Build Your Skills with the Online Practice Exams

Sure, you can answer the GRE questions. You've mastered the analysis of an argument, the manipulation of a decimal, and the elimination of the wrong vocab word. This, however, does you no good if you can't handle the pressure from the actual test. Besides your ability to answer the questions, the GRE challenges your ability to take the exam. Most students focus on the former while ignoring the latter, but being able to answer the questions is only half of what you need. The other half requires that you hone your test-taking skills, and the best way to do this is to take the online GRE practice exams. Here are ten suggestions on how to build your skills with the online experience. (See Chapter 2 for details on ETS's Powerprep software, which simulates a real-life GRE.)

Build Your Stamina by Taking a Practice Exam in One Sitting

How well you can answer the questions doesn't matter if you can't maintain your energy for the length of the exam. Your brain accounts for up to 20 percent of your body's total energy consumption, and when you're taking a challenging exam like the GRE, your brain is in overdrive. It needs to get used to working intensely for four hours at a stretch so you can go the distance on exam day.

TIP

For extra practice credit, at the end of the practice exam, take a short break and then work two more sections of another practice exam. If you're used to working at the GRE level for close to five hours, then the actual exam at four hours will be easy. (Imagine that. "GRE" and "easy" in the same sentence.) For one thing, the real GRE has that unscored extra section, so the actual exam is longer anyway. Also, on test day, you're likely to be amped up and burn out faster, so any extra stamina under your belt can only do you good.

Recognize the Mistakes You Make under Pressure

Did you get stuck on an early question and not reach the second half of a section? Did you leave a bunch of questions unanswered, intending to return to them, but forget? Did you get lost in the software, unable to find the questions you wanted to return to? That's okay, it happens to everyone, but make sure it happens during practice, not on the real thing. Fortunately, you can work out the bugs on the practice exam.

Only by falling into a trap do you fully learn how to avoid it. Make these mistakes at home, where it doesn't matter, instead of on the actual exam, where it's life or death (or a scholarship).

Get Used to Others Being in the Room

Nothing is more distracting during your GRE than hearing someone typing, sighing, cursing, or (if they used *GRE Prep 2024 For Dummies*) chuckling confidently while working the test. Get used to distractions by taking your practice exams in a roomful of people, perhaps along with a friend or two who are also taking practice exams. The sounds as they work and sigh and groan and perhaps pat themselves on the back (because they also got *GRE Prep 2024 For Dummies*) become less of a distraction as you get used to the noise and the pressure.

Some testing centers offer earplugs to block out the other test-takers. If your plan is to use earplugs, try them out on a full-length practice test *before* test day. Some people can't stand earplugs for ten seconds, let alone four hours. You, however, might be okay with them. Maybe not. Either way, try them out first.

Make It a Dress Rehearsal

Play by the rules of the testing center. No phone, hat, drink, snack, neck pillow, or anything that provides a modicum of comfort is allowed within reach in the exam room. Your breaks are short, and your scratch paper is rationed. If this isn't something you're used to, it will be distracting, so make sure you're used to it, and it won't bother you on exam day.

Do you get thirsty? Hungry? Uncomfortable? What do you wish you had: water, a sandwich, an energy bar, coffee, aspirin? Keep that in mind and plan accordingly on test day. You have access to your personal belongings during the breaks, so bring these things in a bag and grab a quick refreshment during your break.

Get a Competitive Edge

The practice test doesn't matter, so why try hard? In the third hour of the exam, you're exhausted, and you just want to get through it. One student told me that halfway through a practice, she ran out of steam and just went with Choice (C) because it's right in the middle. Naturally, this isn't an effective approach.

On the real exam, finding yourself flagging is fatal, but on the practice test, it's okay, right? Wrong. If you've never worked at full capacity for the duration of a practice exam, you won't do it easily on the real exam. You may intend to, but fading after 90 minutes is a hard habit to break. Instead, practice at full throttle for the entire practice. Then, staying focused and competitive for the entire actual experience becomes that much easier.

One way to get around the mid-practice lull is to record your scores and try to beat your last performance. Another way is to try to beat a friend's score. It's like running on a track by yourself versus racing against someone else: You try harder when others are in the game. Make it real and competitive, and you'll bring that edge to the actual exam.

Practice Your Test-Taking Strategies

As you study and practice, also develop your strategies for taking the exam. Maybe you work all the easy math questions first and then go back to the tougher questions. Maybe you answer all the Reading Comprehension questions first, or the Text Completions, or you just go through the section backwards. (Why not?) These strategies give you control over the exam, and different strategies work for different test-takers. What works for you? What doesn't? You should know this before you take the exam.

As you take the GRE practice exams, try out your strategies. You'll realize what works and what doesn't, along with ways to improve on an effective strategy. This is a very important part of your prep process: Find and hone strategies that work, but do it *before* test day.

Go through a practice exam that you've already worked so the questions are familiar to you. Since you've seen the questions, you can focus more on the actual strategies.

Know the Exam Software

If you placed Ernest Hemingway in front of Microsoft Word, would he be able to write anything? Probably not, even though he's one of the most noted authors of our time. For him, the problem wouldn't be the writing; it would be the software. The same applies to you: You can answer the questions, but the software is another story. How do you mark questions to return to? How do you call up the calculator? How do you check the clock? Where is the back button? Does that button end the section? The software is easy to learn, but you have enough on your mind during the exam. Master the software *before* the exam.

Take the ETS GRE practice tests at www.ets.org/gre/revised_general/prepare/powerprep/. It's free and looks and feels exactly like the real thing, providing you with a more genuine simulation.

Get Used to Starting with the Essays

The essays can wear you out, especially if you're not used to writing them. Focusing on 100 math and verbal questions is even more challenging *after* an hour of essays (two essays at 30 minutes each). Make sure this isn't a stretch by actually writing the essays on the practice exams. Don't just skip the essays in practice, as non-Dummies-prepared test-takers do. Are *they* in for a surprise.

Find Your Areas of Focus

Do you miss more Reading Comprehension or Text Completion questions? Do you handle triangles better than you do exponents? Do you lose steam (causing your performance to drop) halfway through the exam? Do you run out of time? With the online practice exams, you can get a sense of how you work and where you need to focus. *You cannot fix your gaps unless you find them first.* That's from an actual fortune cookie.

TIP

Raise your skill level in your weakest areas. The more you improve, the more you'll start to enjoy — or not mind as much — tackling those challenging question types, and in turn, you'll improve even more.

Review the Answers and Explanations

After taking a four-hour practice test, the last thing you probably want to do is spend more time reviewing it, so take a well-deserved break and then come back to the answers and explanations. When you're rested, take the following steps to review:

>> Have your English teacher or a friend who's skilled at writing review your essays.

>> Identify which math and verbal questions you answered correctly and incorrectly.

>> Read the answer explanation for each question you answered incorrectly and review any relevant material so you're prepared for a similar question next time.

>> Also read the answer explanation for any question you may have guessed on correctly.

>> Best yet: Get a pizza and review the practice exam with your friend or friends who took the same practice exam. You can help with each others' wrong answers and research questions that you all missed.

TIP

If you're not inclined to check the answer explanations for all the questions, then while you're taking the exam, mark any questions you're not sure of, and at least read the explanations for those answers. That way, if you guessed correctly or took too long with the question, you'll get a better understanding of how to answer a similar question next time.

Index

About the Author

Ron Woldoff completed his dual master's degrees at Arizona State University and San Diego State University, where he studied the culmination of business and technology. After working as a corporate consultant, Ron opened his own company, National Test Prep, to help students reach their goals on college entrance exams. He created the programs and curricula for these tests from scratch, using his own observations of the tests and feedback from students.

Ron has instructed his own GMAT and GRE programs at both Northern Arizona University and the internationally acclaimed Thunderbird School of Global Management. Ron has also assisted at various high schools, where he led student groups and coached student instructors to help others prepare for the SAT, ACT, and PSAT. Ron lives in Phoenix, Arizona, with his lovely wife, Leisah, and their three amazing boys, Zachary, Jadon, and Adam. You can find Ron on the web at testprepaz.com.

Dedication

This book is humbly dedicated to all those whom I've helped reach their goals. I've learned as much from you as you have from me.

— Ron Woldoff, Phoenix, Arizona

Author's Acknowledgments

I would like to thank my friends Ken Krueger, Lionel Hummel, and Jaime Abromovitz, who helped get things started when I had this crazy idea of helping people prepare for standardized exams. I would absolutely like to thank my wife, Leisah, for her continuing support and always being there for me.

For the team behind this book, I would like to thank agent Bill Gladstone of Waterside Productions in Cardiff, California, for bringing me this opportunity. Also thanks to Christopher Morris for his patience and help in bringing the manuscript through editing and production. Also, thanks to technical editor David Lynch, who reviewed my work and kept me honest and on track — not always easy to do. Big thumbs up to Lindsay Lefevere and Elizabeth Stilwell, our acquisitions editors, who were ultimately responsible for trusting me and Chris to revise this edition and for handling all the little things to keep it going.

For previous contributors, I would like to acknowledge Suzee Vlk, who broke ground on the *GRE For Dummies* series, along with Michelle Rose Gilman and Veronica Saydak, who eventually took the reins from Suzee. Finally, a shout-out to Joe Kraynak, my co-author in crime, for providing such valuable guidance on previous *GRE For Dummies* editions and my very first *For Dummies* project. This book reflects all of your voices and talent.